MAGAZINE

WRITING

2012

THE BEST AMERICAN MAGAZINE WRITING

2012

Compiled by the American Society of Magazine Editors

Columbia University Press   New York

Columbia University Press
Publishers Since 1893
New York   Chichester, West Sussex
cup.columbia.edu
Copyright © 2012 Columbia University Press

Library of Congress Cataloging-in-Publication Data
ISSN 1541-0978
ISBN 978-0231-16223-4 (pbk.)

Columbia University Press books are printed on permanent and durable
acid-free paper.
This book is printed on paper with recycled content.
Printed in the United States of America
p 10 9 8 7 6 5 4 3 2 1

Cover Design: Catherine Casalino

Contents

Terry McDonell

Introduction

"Any point of view was welcome as long as the writer was sufficiently skillful to carry it off."
—Harold Hayes, *Smiling Through the Apocalypse:
Esquire's History of the Sixties*

When he was editing *Esquire* with the élan of a cultural sorcerer back in the 1960s, the singular Harold Hayes liked to say that a magazine was a promise, "sometimes fulfilled, sometimes not." The "fulfilled" part can come from the strong reporting, the fine writing. The "sometimes not" is always the editor's fault.

Every contributor to Wikipedia is called an "editor," but they are not who I mean. The editors honored here by the inclusion of pieces from their magazines are a lot more trouble. They instigate; they decide; they fool around. Magazine writing has become more and more specialized as publishing platforms have expanded and multiplied. Ditto magazine editing. The editors of these magazines all have different charges and portfolios, but all share eclectic views of their jobs. Most are entrepreneurial. Audacity is a good thing.

In early May, I gave a speech to perhaps a hundred editors at an ASME lunch meeting the day before the pieces in this volume were to be honored at the National Magazine Awards Dinner.

The assignment was to talk about editing, and I began by telling them about Bob Sherrill, an editor who had more or less defined for me what editors did then (in the late 1970s) and still do. I recalled very specifically the afternoon he was riding shotgun with a Mexican beer between his knees as we motored down the Pacific Coast Highway toward Manhattan Beach. Bob was wearing his white high-top Chuck Taylors with the florescent red laces (untied) and his baggy blue and white seersucker suit with a black T-shirt and his green and pink silk bandana tied around his neck and his Black Watch beret over his shaggy strawberry-blond hair. Plus Ray-Bans (of course).

Bob was colorful, like a kind of flipped-out ice cream man, but handsome, too, and women liked him, and I worked for him as a reporter at a startup weekly called *LA* that we were saying was like, you know, "the *Village Voice* but for Los Angeles." Bob had come West on a kind of "editorial whim" (his phrase) after some turbulent years at *Esquire* under *the* Harold Hayes (see above), where he had been a sly packager and "midwifed" (Bob's phrase too) any number of journalistic innovations, from "Dubious Achievements" to that string of genre-cracking pieces that came to be known as New Journalism. Tom Wolfe, Gay Talese, Mailer, you know the list …

I was flattered when he said that he *thought* that I *thought* like an editor and should think about that. Think about becoming an editor. Think about editing. "Think about monkeys jumping out of boxes" is what he said. I had not heard that one. "Plus," he said, finally, taking another pull from his Tecate, "really good editors never have to drive."

He was offering not just a new job but a new way of looking at things, and I was an editor from then on, or at least that's how I thought of myself. As I got to edit more and more, I began to say that the definition of a good editor was a person with no friends. I was talking about dealing with writers, you know, editing them with a firm hand and terrifying simplicity. I quoted Mark Twain:

"When you catch an adjective, kill it." That was all macho posturing because the truth is a good editor needs lots of friends, or at least people who like you enough that you can talk them into doing what you want them to do.

That was a lot of the job for me in the beginning. What I found was that you only irritate people if you try to flatter them into working for you. I had this problem with a lot of writers because I loved their work so much, especially, say, Joan Didion, who is not a big fan of ass kissing. The point is that the relationship between editors and writers has to live on the intelligence and standards of the best journalism. And the self-defining commonality of the editors represented in this volume is that they are all journalists, and they will tell you that. They will also tell you that it is a tricky business, editing.

There can be failures of nerve, as well as conceptual flops, but in theory if the editor simply makes the right assignments, matching writer to subject, all he or she ever has to do is hook paragraphs. It happens. Christopher Hitchens's work for *Vanity Fair* won the magazine National Magazine Awards for Columns and Commentary in 2007, 2011, and, posthumously, in 2012. "He was one of the bravest men I have ever known," Graydon Carter, *Vanity Fair's* editor, said while accepting the ASME award. Carter went on to say that Hitchens "wrote with speed and accuracy" until the very end and was the kind of writer who didn't really need an editor. This is where things begin to come together.

As always, Carter was smart, sharply moving in the personal details that opened for the audience the great friendship he and Hitchens must have shared. And, of course, Hitchens's essays are all *upsettingly brilliant* (a Hitchens phrase), but most upsettingly so is "Unspoken Truths"—an audacious meditation on the loss of his voice that accompanied the cancer that killed him even as he wrote for *Vanity Fair*: "To my writing classes I used to open by saying that anybody who could talk could also write. Having cheered them up with this easy-to-grasp ladder, I then replaced it with a huge and loathsome snake: 'How many people in this class, would you say, can talk? I mean really talk?' That had its duly woeful effect. I told them to read every composition aloud, preferably to a trusted friend. The rules are much the same: Avoid stock expressions (like the plague, as William Safire used to say) and repetitions. Don't say that as a boy your grandmother used to read to you, unless at that stage of her life she really *was* a boy, in which case you have probably thrown away a better intro. If something is worth hearing or listening to, it's very probably worth reading. So, this above all: Find your own voice."

I read that passage over and over for both its nuance and its precision. Voice is more than the heart of writing; it is, well, the *voice* of the magazine as well as its writers. This is the way magazine editors should think, and clearly it informs every word in Carter's *Vanity Fair*, which he has edited for twenty years, relentlessly fulfilling Hayes's promise.

·   ·   ·

For all top editors there are many private and sublime thrills that no one else can borrow, such as opening a new piece by a favorite writer. You crack the file and you know, just reading the lede, that it will absolutely make your mix and give your entire issue a subtext that will echo how smart you want the magazine to be. I first heard this articulated by Robert Silvers of the *New York Review of Books* when he was explaining the joys of editing Zadie Smith. Graydon Carter no doubt felt the same way opening a piece from Hitchens. For me it has become a long list, especially where I work now at *Sports Illustrated*, which received a nomination for *SI* senior writer Chris Ballard's profile of Dewayne Dedmon, a naturally gifted basketball player on his way to being seven feet tall.

Like every piece in this collection, "Dewayne Dedmon's Leap of Faith" has a publishing story behind it. This is where to look for additional understanding of the author of a particular story and also the workings of the magazine. The idea for the Dedmon piece came, like many do, from the margins of the news. Ballard read an item, maybe one hundred words or so, noting that a seventeen-year-old from Antelope Valley, northeast of L.A., had signed to play basketball at USC but that he hadn't played at all in high school "because of religious reasons." Bingo.

A little digging turned up that Dedmon was a Jehovah's Witness and that it was his mother who had forbidden him from playing. That's where the stories ended and where Ballard's began. When he pitched the story to his editors in New York, there were questions about where the narrative would go and if Dedmon would be a high profile enough player. Editors were skeptical until Ballard, who lives in Berkeley, flew to L.A. to meet Dedmon, talking to him and, more importantly, listening. "I began to understand that the story had its own soul," Ballard says. "Dedmon was a likable protagonist, sure, but more important, he remained conflicted—torn between what he wanted and his love for his mother."

From there, Ballard took the long road, laying down his story brick by brick, meticulously tracking Dedmon's growth from guileless boy to budding superstar. When, at eighteen, Dedmon defied his mother, his became a story of faith—in both God and personal transformation. "As a father myself," Ballard says, "I was fascinated by the questions that came up about religion, authority, family bonds and following one's passion."

The piece was an investment over eighteen months and underlines the importance of enterprise on the part of the writer and patience on the part of the editors. The same is true for many other pieces represented here. Consider the winner in the extremely competitive Reporting category: *The New Yorker* for "The Apostate," by Lawrence Wright. It charts the history of the Church of Scientology as it tells the story of the screenwriter and director Paul Haggis, who left the church when leaders announced their opposition to gay marriage. Most surprisingly in this story of surprises, it is a window into the editorial practices of the magazine, including a description of the eight-hour meeting between *New Yorker* editors and Scientology representatives at which they debated the reporting of the story. The reader learns that in response to nearly a thousand queries, the Scientology contingent traveled to New York and "handed over forty-eight binders of supporting material, stretching nearly seven linear feet."

The ferocity of the reporting and the courage to stand by the truth of that reporting are inspiring in a most old-fashioned way. They also light up the role of magazine journalism—especially the long form—within American culture.

The truth is the truth, and all of the pieces in this anthology have that going for them. Based on more than a year of reporting, *The New Yorker*'s winner in Public Interest, "The Invisible Army," by Sarah Stillman, uncovers a festering system of labor supply for our military bases in Iraq and Afghanistan that amounts to indentured servitude for tens of thousands of foreign workers. *Men's Health*'s contributing editor Bob Drury wrote with fierce detail about genital damage caused by improvised explosive devices in Iraq and Afghanistan. His piece led to significant changes in military policy. *Glamour*'s Personal Service winner "The Secret That Kills Four Women a Day," by Liz Brody, documents how more than 1,400 women will be murdered this year by someone they once loved. Susan Ince's "Fractured," from *Good Housekeeping*, demonstrates what's wrong with traditional treatments of osteoporosis—a disease that is routinely misdiagnosed and mistreated. All of these are based on hard-core reporting. In its own way, even "The Hox River Window," the short story by Karen Russell that brought *Zoetrope: All-Story* a win in the Fiction category, is as true in allegory as any reported dispatch ever was about survival on the American frontier.

Read through the table of contents and you will see that although this book is called *The Best American Magazine Writing*, it is more than that because it is representative of the best in all categories of magazine journalism, from the most nuanced profile writing to investigative reporting to hard-core service pieces that bring clarity to the complications of our lives. For example, the comprehensive weight of *New York*'s winning Single-Topic Issue, "The Encyclopedia of 9/11," is defined by previously unimaginable detail ("a partially melted fire truck") and unbearable clarity ("Jumpers").

The categories in which National Magazine Awards are given are more eclectic than those represented in this collection, which includes nineteen winners or finalists in nine (out of thirty-two) categories, representing only sixteen titles. *New York* (edited by Adam Moss), *The New Yorker* (David Remnick), and *Rolling Stone* (Jann Wenner) are each represented twice. I mention this because the editors of all sixteen of these magazines would make a great run of names and they should all get pointed out and given credit. But I am not going to do that for the reason their names were not part of the byline when the stories originally ran. They are editors; their names appear on top of their mastheads, the way they like it. Except, of course, at the *New Yorker*, which does not run a masthead, and at *D Magazine*, where Tim Rogers, who won for Profile Writing with "He Is Anonymous," also edits the magazine.

Besides monkeys jumping out of boxes, Bob Sherrill used to talk about how editors should try to "play a well-known song in a different language." That was another one of his. Or maybe he stole it because editors steal. But it is my hunch that all editors believe something along the lines of culture being memory and that all of us in the culture know who we are by telling one another about the way we live. And that the stories we write down are the most important ones.

This book is a history of a complicated year, how we lived it, and how we thought about that, a run of pointed descriptions of who we were going in and who we became coming out. Finally, it is mostly concerned with the infinite variety of both shared memory and dissimilar experience, two complicated and conflicting ideas that all good editors keep in their heads at the same time. That's what editors do, helping all those monkeys sing well-known songs in different languages.

Sid Holt,
chief executive,
American Society of
Magazine Editors

Acknowledgments

This year marks the forty-sixth anniversary of the National Magazine Awards. When the American Society of Magazine Editors was organized in 1963, one of the central goals of the founders was the creation of an awards program for magazine journalism. The model, of course, was the Pulitzer Prizes, which had been established in 1917 to honor the work of newspaper journalists. And indeed, ASME partnered with the institution that administered the Pulitzer Prizes—the Columbia University Graduate School of Journalism—to launch the National Magazine Awards.

The first National Magazine Award was presented to *Look* in 1966 "for its skillful editing, imagination and editorial integrity," particularly for its treatment of the "racial issue." The same year Certificates of Special Recognition were given to *The New Yorker* for its publication of Truman Capote's *In Cold Blood* (the judges called it "a new art form"), *Scientific American* for its coverage of urbanization, and *Ebony* for its special issue headlined "The White Problem in America."

The National Magazine Awards have grown since then—this year there were more than thirty award winners, including, yes, *The New Yorker*, along with magazines ranging from *Inc.*, *IEEE Spectrum*, and *The Daily Beast* to *Vogue*, *Saveur*, and O, *The Oprah Magazine*—but the stories collected in this edition of *Best*

American Magazine Writing, all of them 2012 winners and finalists, represent only a small sample of the extraordinary journalism to be discovered at any hour in convenience stories and airport terminals, on websites and digital newsstands. And as if to prove it, there are now more magazine readers than ever before—in fact, nine out of every ten Americans read magazines.

The enthusiasm of magazine readers is shared by magazine editors—if, that is, editorial passion can be measured by the number of entries in the National Magazine Awards. In 2012, some 270 print and digital magazines participated in the awards, submitting a record-breaking 1,800 entries. From these, 160 finalists were chosen in 32 categories, including 11 digital media categories. A list of the categories, finalists, and winners is printed on pages 481 to 495, and a searchable database of past finalists and winners appears on the ASME website at magazine.org/asme.

The National Magazine Award finalists and winners are chosen by judges selected by ASME. In 2012 there were 360 judges, including distinguished writers, editors, art directors, photo editors, and journalism educators from around the country. The judges and judging leaders are listed on pages 497 to 508. They prepare for the judging by reading nearly a dozen stories or complete issues, then gather in sometimes cramped and always charmless conference rooms for three days of still more reading—days that always end with favorite stories or magazines going unnominated. Yet many editors consider the judging to be one of the highlights of their year. ASME is indebted to the judges for their dedication, which guarantees the integrity of the awards.

The awards process concludes with the presentation of the Ellies at two separate events, the Digital Ellies lunch in March and the National Magazine Awards Dinner in May. This year 300 editors and publishers attended the lunch, and nearly 600 magazine journalists and their publishing counterparts gathered for the dinner, which was hosted by Brian Williams, the anchor and managing editor of *NBC Nightly News* and *Rock Center*. For his efforts, Mr. Williams received a copy of every winning magazine and an ASME tote bag to carry them home in—plus the admiration, bordering on adulation, of his print colleagues.

The ASME Board of Directors oversees the administration of the National Magazine Awards. They are chiefly responsible for the success of the awards. A list of the board members appears on page 509. Special thanks are due to Larry Hackett, the managing editor of *People*, whose two-year term as president of ASME concluded with the presentation of the awards in May.

The Columbia University Graduate School of Journalism continues to sponsor the National Magazine Awards with ASME. I want to thank our colleagues at Columbia, the dean of the school and Henry R. Luce Professor, Nicholas Lemann, and the associate dean of programs and prizes, Arlene Notoro Morgan.

I am especially grateful to Terry McDonell, the editor of the Time Inc. Sports Group, for writing the introduction to this edition of *Best American Magazine Writing*. Mr. McDonell was elected to the Magazine Editors? Hall of Fame this year and was honored at the National Magazine Awards Dinner. Readers who want to know more about his achievements can watch the presentation of his Hall of Fame award on YouTube. As the chief editor of *Sports Illustrated*, Mr. McDonell was just a little busy this Olympic summer, so his work on this book is truly appreciated.

The members of ASME are thankful to our agent, David McCormick of McCormick & Williams, for his skillful representation of our interests. More than ever, I am thankful for the talent and enthusiasm of our editors at the Columbia University Press, Philip Leventhal and Michael Haskell.

On behalf of ASME, I want to thank our colleagues at MPA—the Association of Magazine Media, especially the chair of the board of directors, Michael Clinton of Hearst Magazines. I also want to thank Nina Link, the president and CEO of MPA, as well as Frank Costello, Howard Polskin, Cristina Dinozo, Sarah Hansen, and Caitlin Cheney.

I say it one way or another year after year, but Nina Fortuna makes the National Magazine Awards happen. A lifetime subscription to every ASME-member magazine is hers for the asking. I also want to acknowledge my predecessors at ASME, Marlene Kahan and the late Robert Kenyon, who shepherded the National Magazine Awards through their first four decades.

And finally, ASME thanks the writers, editors, and magazines that permitted their work to be published in *Best American Magazine Writing 2012*. Magazine publishing faces many challenges, but magazine journalism thrives as never before. For this we should all be thankful.

THE BEST
AMERICAN
MAGAZINE
WRITING

2012

Esquire

WINNER—FEATURE WRITING

"On May 22," wrote the editors of Esquire *when this piece was published in the October 2011 issue, "a three-quarter-mile-wide tornado carved a six-mile-long path through Joplin, Missouri, killing 160. Unable to escape, two dozen strangers sought shelter in a gas station's walk-in cooler while the funnel ripped apart every building, car, and living thing around. This is their story."* Luke Dittrich is a contributing editor at Esquire, *and "Joplin!"—cited by the National Magazine Award judges for its "brilliant and restrained evocation of desperation and bravery"—won the magazine its third award for Feature Writing in less than a decade.*

Luke Dittrich

Joplin!

Ruben

As he rushes from the rear to the front of the store, Ruben Carter leans on the half-moon cash-register island with his left hand, using the island as a sort of crutch and springboard to propel himself along. He could cover the distance without support, but his cerebral palsy, the damage to the parts of his brain that control his coordination and balance, would make him do so with his usual stiff plod, and there is no time for that. When he reaches the door, he unlocks it, then pushes forward. Since he doesn't have much authority over the muscles of his arms, he pushes this door like he pushes most doors, shoving with the weight and strength of his entire body. The accelerating wind shoves back, but Ruben wins out. A father and three children stagger through the opening, slipping and almost falling on the wet tiles. When Ruben stops leaning into the door, the wind slams it shut.

Except for the wan and skittery illumination of a few cell-phone screens and the intermittent flash of lightning, the inside of the store is very dark. The power went out several minutes ago, and though the sun should still be shining, the storm has blotted it out. Ruben orders the newcomers to join the others crouched against the back wall, using words that, in another context, could have been the lyrics to a disco song.

"Everybody back, back, back, way back!" he says. "Everybody get down, all on the ground!"

He's wearing clothes that conform to the Fastrip employee dress code: black shoes, khaki slacks, and a green polo shirt with a little name tag pinned onto it. The pants and shoes belong to him. The polo shirt belongs to Grace Energy, the parent company that owns the Fastrip chain. Every week, a $1.25 uniform fee is deducted from his paycheck. He once calculated that his immediate supervisor, who has been working at Fastrip for thirteen years, had spent more than $800 for the privilege of wearing her polo shirt. Ruben has been working at Fastrip for only seven months, but the uniform fee is among the many irritations that make him feel as though he's been here seven months too long.

Last year, he was living a thousand miles away, in Salt Lake City, had a solid job working for the state of Utah. Foster-care case management. He helped get kids back home to their parents, or, if their parents were incapable of parenting, he helped them find new ones. Ruben majored in psychology in college, has a half-completed master's degree in counseling, and though foster-care case management is hard, draining work and burns a lot of people out, he was good at it and had been doing it for six years. Then one morning he got a big speeding ticket, seventy-five in a twenty-five-mile-per-hour zone. No excuse, really: Sometimes he just likes to move fast. He couldn't scrape up the money to cover the $400 fine, so the DMV suspended his license, which resulted in an automatic dismissal from his job with the state. He'd been living paycheck to paycheck, and with his job gone, he didn't have enough money to cover rent. He left Utah last July, came back home to Missouri, where he was born. He's applied for dozens of new jobs since getting here, casting a wide net, hitting up everything from video stores to child protective services. Fastrip is still the only place that's called him back.

So he's thirty-five years old, living with his parents, working at a gas-station convenience store. He's usually not the self-pitying type, really, but it's pretty much a literal fact that he's way over-qualified for this gig. Sometimes he finds himself wondering just what the hell he's doing here. In his darker moments, the self-pity can turn into a sort of all-purpose irritability directed at humanity in general. Like when a customer complains that she can't pay at the pump and Ruben has to go out and demonstrate that you have to slide the credit card into the credit-card reader, not the receipt dispenser. Or, just about a quarter-hour ago, right after the tornado siren began to blare, when one of his regulars rushed in to stock up on Marlboro Special Blend Gold 100's. Ruben smokes, understands the craving, but still: There's a tornado warning, people! Like most folks who've spent any time in this town, he knows that almost all of these sirens are false alarms, and he expects that this one is as well, but he also knows that even a bad thunderstorm in Joplin can easily generate dangerous, glass-shattering winds. Everyone should know that. But just a couple minutes ago, when it was clearly getting really bad outside, Ruben still had to tell some members of the burgeoning crowd inside his store to move away from the big sheet-glass windows that look out onto the parking lot, where rain was falling nearly horizontally and the high-tensile-steel canopies over the gas pumps were beginning to flap vaguely up and down like giant wings.

What the hell is Ruben Carter doing here, renting a polo shirt, working this dead-end job, spewing common sense into a vacuum?

That's not the important question right now.

Ruben stands in the darkness, in front of two dozen people huddled together against a wall covered with little bags of cheap candy and nuts, a wall that he hopes is far enough away from the windows to provide them shelter from the storm. A strange sound, a sort of piercing roar, has been building in the background for a while, and now seems much louder, much closer.

"Is that the tornado?" a woman asks. "Is that what that roar is?"

Which isn't the important question, either, since its answer, in just a few moments, will become blindingly, terribly obvious.

The important question is what is Ruben Carter going to do next.

Rick and Jonah and Abby and Hannah

"Is pink bad?" Hannah Ward shoots off the text to her friend Cindy, who's a bit of a weather geek. It's late Sunday afternoon, and Hannah's dad, Rick, is in his easy chair, dozing off to televised golf, his favorite soporific. A tornado warning is scrolling across the bottom of the screen, and in the lower-left-hand corner there's a Doppler radar image of southwest Missouri. The radar shows an amorphous, multicolored blob moving slowly from west to east. The blob is mostly blue and green and red and orange. Occasionally, however, right in the middle of the blob, in the part that seems to be heading directly toward Joplin, Hannah has been noticing flashes of hot pink.

Her phone vibrates, and she looks down and reads Cindy's response.

"Yes," it says. "Pink is very bad."

Hannah is sixteen years old. She and her younger siblings, fifteen-year-old Jonah and nine-year-old Abby, arrived in Joplin on Thursday, three days ago. The plan is to stay here, at their dad's place, for a month-long visit, and then go back home to Wellington, Kansas, to their mom's place. For the first six years after the split, they did things the other way around, with their primary residence at their dad's. But their dad has started going back to school, studying drafting and design at Missouri Southern State University, and now they're trying a new arrangement: a full month in the summer here with him, then just one weekend a month during the school year. It's been a good visit so far, playing epic games of Settlers of Catan, watching all three hours and fifteen minutes of *The Green Mile* on DVD, trying to teach

Abby how to solve sudoku puzzles, gorging themselves on Rick's familiar goulash . . .

Hannah looks out the window of the second-floor apartment. It's sunny and cloudless, just like it's been all day. Jonah is in the next room with Abby, trying to get her down for a nap.

One of the things about kids who grow up shuttling between two different households, between two different authority figures, is sometimes they can become pretty self-sufficient, and a bit precocious about exercising their own authority and trusting their own instincts.

Hannah takes another look at the blob on the screen, with its coruscating flashes of pink.

"Dad," she says, loudly and firmly enough to rouse him from his golf-induced stupor. "We've got to go."

And so they go, piling into Rick's '98 Pontiac Grand Prix just as a light rain begins to fall, heading east out of the Hampshire Terrace apartment complex, down Twentieth Street, planning to drive to their uncle Dave's house, out of town. Uncle Dave has a basement.

Ten minutes later, after the storm overtakes them, after they decide they need to find immediate shelter somewhere, anywhere, after they pull into the parking lot of the Fastrip at the corner of Twentieth and Duquesne, after they bolt through the buffeting winds and pound on the glass door, after the terrible moments that elapse before Ruben Carter materializes out of the darkness on the other side of the glass and lets them in, after they rush inside onto the slippery tiles, after they crouch down with all the other refugees against the back wall—after all of that, Hannah, being the sixteen-year-old girl that she is, realizes with a sudden gut-roiling jolt of loss and disconnection that she doesn't know where her cell phone is. She wonders if it's back at her dad's apartment.

By the time this thought hits her, her dad's apartment has already ceased to exist.

Carl and Jennifer and Trace and Cory

The Fastrip is just down the street from their home, so that's a big part of its appeal, but what really hooked the Hennings on the place, what keeps them coming back two, three, four times a day, is the soda. The price of it. Cheapest in town. Seventy-five cents for a refill. And if you bring your own cup, even the first fill-up of the day is considered a refill. Doesn't matter the size of the cup. Carl uses a mammoth sixty-four-ounce insulated one he purchased years ago from Fastrip's biggest local competitor, Kum & Go, which charges $1.29 (!) for refills. His wife, Jennifer, has a similar Kum & Go cup, but only half the size. She drinks Coke and Carl drinks Mountain Dew. And the boys? Fifteen-year-old Cory's a Fanta man, and eleven-year-old Trace is currently on a Dr. Pepper kick.

They know all the employees, of course. Spacey, good-natured Jake, who works the morning shift, and Diane, the manager, energetic as a coiled spring, who usually works the same shift but spends a lot of time in the back office. They know Ruben best, have even become Facebook friends with him. He's a good listener, always seems interested in what's going on in their lives, which means, especially this time of year, that he spends a lot of time listening to them talk about Little League baseball. The boys are fanatical about it, and Carl and Jennifer are probably even more so. They're both members of the board of Joplin South Little League, which means they've always got lots of baseball-related business to attend to on top of the games themselves, which have recently been numbering ten or eleven a week. It's a lot of work, a lot of driving, a lot of cheering, a lot of laundry, a lot of fun.

Both boys played in tournaments earlier today. Trace's team, the Joplin Sliders, won one and lost one against the Lamar Tigers. Cory's team, the Joplin Miners, played only once, losing to the Black Sox. It was bright and clear but windy, and the wind made hitting and catching extra challenging. You could smack a ball straight up and it would trace a curve like the St. Louis Arch.

Not long after they got home from Trace's second game, the Hennings found themselves standing in their living room, staring at their television. The television was tuned to the local news on KSNF, channel 16, and KSNF was streaming a live feed from its tower cam. The feed showed something gray and dark approaching Joplin from the west. The image was a bit blurry and rain spattered. The thing moving toward the city looked almost a mile wide, and there were occasional bright flashes of light on its periphery. At first the news anchors were saying that the flashes might be lightning. Perhaps whatever they were looking at was just a huge thunderstorm. But then the flashes continued, one after another, a regular rhythm almost, and the anchors finally recognized what was causing them: power lines rupturing. They stopped sounding like anchors then. They began talking over one another in an emotional jumble, as though speaking directly to whatever friends or acquaintances or loved ones were within digital earshot of their voices.

"Take cover!" one said.

"Yes, please!" said the other.

"Right now!"

"Please do!"

"I'm telling you to take cover!"

"Take cover!"

"Right now!"

The Hennings live in an A-frame, lots of glass, no basement.

They've lived there together for six years, started dating four years before that, back when Jennifer was Carl's boss at a McDonald's in the local Walmart. She's thirty-six and Carl's twenty-seven. The boys are from her previous marriage. Though the Hennings no longer work together—Carl's now a forklift operator, Jennifer a medical assistant—sometimes, when they have to make a decision, their old boss-employee dynamic flares up. But standing in their living room, watching the monster approach, listening to the news anchors lose it, the decision they made was entirely mutual. Ruben had always told them that if something big was ever heading toward the neighborhood, they should come to the Fastrip, ride it out there. It's a sturdier building than their A-frame. Plus, he'd told them, if things ever got really bad, there was always the walk-in beer cooler.

The Fastrip was five blocks down the road. Their Mustang covered the distance in less than a minute. Jennifer drove.

And now here they are, huddled with the others against the rear wall, listening to the awful roar get closer. Trace is still wearing his sweat- and grass-stained baseball uniform. Suddenly the rear wall begins to move, swelling out and then sucking in and then swelling out again. There's a high-pitched chiming and crackling sound as glass bottles begin rattling and rupturing against one another.

"Ruben," Jennifer says, "stuff's breaking in the back!"

"Yeah, I know, I know," he says.

"Should we go in the cooler?"

"Ah," Ruben says, but before he can finish his thought he hears a sharp sound and looks over at the big windows at the front of the store, which are spidering with cracks.

Then the windows explode.

Donna Barnes

She believes in the Pentecost.

She believes that a bowl of Multi Grain Cheerios with low-fat milk is a good breakfast, and there's no reason not to have it every single day.

She believes that seven weeks after the Resurrection the Holy Spirit descended on the Apostles, and she believes that it happened just the way the Bible describes it in chapter 2 of the Book of Acts: *And suddenly there came a sound from heaven as of a mighty rushing wind, and it filled the house where they were sitting.*

She believes that a sliced banana is optional.

She believes that ever since the day of the Pentecost, people like her, who have been baptized into the Pentecostal Church, have the Holy Spirit inside them, literally.

She believes that the work she does, cleaning houses, is good for her degenerative spinal arthritis, because it keeps her moving, which keeps her vertebral column limber and lubricated.

She believes that sometimes, when the spirit overflows, people can speak in a language they themselves do not understand, the same language that angels speak.

She believes that the one-dollar boxes of Little Debbie cakes she buys most Sundays at this Fastrip are the best deal in town.

She believes that the Joplin Full Gospel Church, which departed the physical world approximately two minutes ago, is as much her home as her thirty-year-old Solitaire trailer.

She believes that the roar that fills the Fastrip as soon as the windows explode is one of the worst sounds she's heard in all of her sixty years.

She believes that the sound of the screams of the two little boys next to her is even worse.

She believes that Ruben, though she can't hear his shouts very well above the screaming and the roaring, is commanding them all to pass through a silver doorway by the potato-chip rack.

She believes that God has already chosen the time and place of your death before you are born.

Donna Barnes enters the cooler on her hands and knees.

Chris and Lacey and Nathan and Jarrett

Lacey Little was almost hit by a tornado once. She was in kindergarten, she thinks. The sirens went off and they all hid under their desks. She remembers seeing the sunlight outside turning murky and green. She remembers hearing the wind, and she remembers hearing the ambulances afterward. Her mom ran a daycare out of their home back then, and Lacey remembers worrying about the kids her mom was caring for and hoping they were all right.

That's the closest she's come. But she's been through tons of other warnings, tons of what people who don't live around here would call close calls. Sometimes she talks to people who don't live around here, and they ask her why she or anyone would raise a family on this wide plain, this alley that stretches through Kansas and Oklahoma and Missouri, this land where the monsters roam. She just asks them why anyone would live on the coast, with its hurricanes. Or in the north, with its blizzards.

There's always something.

She's a mobile phlebotomist. She works for a company called Boyce & Bynum Pathology Laboratories. She does most of her work in nursing homes. She goes and she takes blood and she leaves, and sometimes they make vampire jokes. She split up with Nathan and Jarrett's dad a few years ago, but he's still involved. He's a musician. He tours. Her boyfriend, Chris Carmer, is a solid guy with a steady job. He gets up at four A.M., works at Able Manufacturing, manages a crew of twenty industrial painters. This morning both Chris and her ex attended Nathan's baptism. Nathan's seven. His uncle, Lacey's brother, did the honors, just like he did for Jarrett a few years ago. Jarrett's eleven. Afterward Lacey and Chris and Jarrett and Nathan went to McDonald's for a celebratory lunch, and then they went and fooled around at the batting cages, and then they went to Petland to pick up some stuff for Chomper, their bullmastiff.

It was while they were driving back from Petland that they started hearing the warnings on the radio. They turned on Twentieth, thinking they'd ride it out in the Home Depot. Something made them decide against it. Just a feeling they had. They kept driving. By the time they got to the Fastrip, it felt like driving farther would be suicide.

Chris kind of settled into the role of Ruben's deputy as soon as they got inside. That's just like Chris. When Ruben went up to the front, to let in Rick Ward and his family, Chris was following right behind, using a flashlight app on his cell phone to help light the way.

He's a good man.

But while Chris is on the outside of the huddle, helping Ruben manage the crowd, Lacey has the kids to herself. They're both crying. They started crying even before they reached the Fastrip. They heard what the people were saying on the radio. There's nothing scarier to a kid than a scared grown-up. Nathan, freshly baptized Nathan, is the younger of the two, and so most of Lacey's attention is on him. As the back wall begins to breathe in and out and the roaring gets louder and you sort of know in your bones that it's coming, Nathan starts sobbing that he doesn't want to die, and you can't imagine what it feels like as a mother to hear your seven-year-old saying that. She's doing her best to hold herself together while she holds him, and she's grateful to the woman next to her, who's squeezing Jarrett's hand and telling him that everything is going to be okay, that it's just like tornado drills at school, that they just have to stay down low and cover their heads. The woman has a fancy camera with a long lens. Lacey wonders if she's a storm chaser.

The windows spider. The windows explode.

Lacey's boys start screaming.

It is a terrible sound.

Stacy and Aaron and Allie

What you do on a job like this is you make sure you get two good shots of each graduate. One just before they start walking across the stage toward the little podium where the principal stands, and the other when they're actually taking the diploma into their hands. GradImages, the company that hired Stacy LaBarge to shoot this graduation, also hired another photographer, and the two of them have split their duties. It's Stacy's responsibility to get the second shot, the last shot, when the graduate receives his or her diploma. She's set herself up just below the stage, about six feet from the podium. She's got a Nikon D3000 with an 18-to-105mm Nikkor lens.

When Stacy graduated from high school, nineteen years ago, she already knew she wanted to be a photographer. She imagined herself drifting through the grittiest parts of America, documenting the real lives of real people, taking pictures that revealed the rough beauty of the everyday. She loves the work of Dorothea Lange. She sometimes wishes, in a half-serious way, that she had been alive during the Great Depression, when the government would pay people like Lange to travel through hard-scrabble communities and just shoot and shoot and shoot. The photography Stacy does now, it's not like that. She makes a living. She shoots graduations, weddings, babies. She has three children. This is the fourth year in a row she's made the three-hour drive from Kansas City to shoot the Joplin High School graduation.

Stacy keeps her left eye on the viewfinder and her right eye closed. It's a long gig, 429 graduates, and after a while her subjects lose their individual contours altogether and become simply fleeting microchallenges—smiles are good, blinking eyelids are bad. These kids here this afternoon, balancing on their high heels or tugging at the too-tight neckties that their fathers helped cinch, are practically exploding with promise, though the precise nature of their promise is hidden from Stacy's lens. The beauty and the limitation of photography is that it can show only the present moment, without context. So when a graduate named Aaron Frost grins and gives the principal's hand a vigorous shake, Stacy's lens captures an image of a tall, blond, handsome boy but doesn't see the star quarterback of Joplin High, the one with NFL dreams, a football scholarship to Missouri Southern, and a beautiful girlfriend, Allie Pederson, who's sitting in the audience in a black strapless dress, clapping her heart out. Similarly, when another grad, Will Norton, receives his piece of paper, his ticket to the next stage of his life, the lens sees just a mop-topped cherub, not the burgeoning Internet celebrity known as Willdabeast, who has five thousand subscribers to his YouTube page, where he chronicles the ups and downs of teenagerhood in charming little fast-cut vignettes.

And Stacy's lens is, of course, as blind to where these kids are going as it is to where they've come from.

It doesn't show Will Norton beginning to drive home after the ceremony ends or the moment when the vortex overtakes him, shredding his seat belt and yanking him out through the sunroof into the maelstrom, where the flame of his promise is snuffed out in a terrible instant.

Nor does it show Aaron and his girlfriend, Allie, at about that same moment, scrambling to get inside the beer cooler of the disintegrating Fastrip, right behind Stacy herself. Like Stacy, Aaron and Allie will find shelter at the store, and then they will find that their shelter was no shelter at all.

Sandy and Matt and Michaela

Sandy Latimer has always been unusually terrified of thunderstorms. And not big ones, either. Just a little rain, a little lightning, a few claps and rumbles in the middle of the night, and she'll tumble out of bed and head straight to her living room and sit in the middle of it, on her carpet, which she realizes is probably no safer than staying in bed, but still feels safer for some reason. She's fifty-four years old, and this phobia has followed her around her entire life. Her mom thinks it may have been passed down to her like a virus, from a storm-phobic older cousin she played with a lot as a toddler, but to Sandy the fear seems like something innate, something integral to her being.

So the terror she experienced even before she pulled into the Fastrip, even before the lights went out, even before she huddled in the back with all the others, was raw and potent.

Then Sandy felt the wall behind her begin to move, in and out, as though it were breathing, as though she had taken shelter against the chest of some enormous creature and the creature was now waking up. The sensation kicked her terror up to another level.

When the windows explode, Sandy's mind is already incandescent with panic.

She can't make a sound, and when she tries to stand up, she finds she can't do that, either, but instead falls to the ground. She tries to crawl toward the opening, toward the door of the cooler that someone has just yanked open, the opening that all these people are now rushing toward. It's not working. It's like her body has abandoned her. It's like it won't do what she wants it to do, like the air, now full of flying glass, has become soupy, heavy, quicksandish, like the air in a nightmare. You hear about people falling and being trampled all the time for the stupidest reasons: Black Friday sales at Walmart, when all that's at stake is a discounted television. The stakes here are much higher, as high as they get, really. There are at least a dozen people behind Sandy, desperate to pass through the door. Sandy lies helpless before them, flopping on the wet tiles like a fish in a boat.

Michaela Sieler and Matt Doerr are right behind Sandy. They are both third-year college students at Missouri Southern, but have been a couple since sophomore year of high school. They came to Joplin from Yankton, South Dakota, by comparison with which Joplin is a metropolis. Matt is studying accounting and Michaela is studying early-childhood education. Michaela is holding her dog, a six-year-old dachshund named Tinkerbell. Matt is holding Michaela's purse. They have never seen Sandy before in their lives, and now she is blocking the way to the only hope they have of extending their lives another minute. It would be easy to step over her, step around her, step on her. Neither one of them wants to die.

Along with the howling of the wind and the roaring of what's approaching behind the wind, along with the screaming of the children and now the screaming of the adults, there is the sound of Ruben Carter's voice. He's repeating a phrase, over and over. It's a phrase that's both familiar and unfamiliar because it's a phrase that everyone hears all the time in movies and on television, but almost no one ever hears in real life.

"Women and children first!" he's saying. "Women and children first!"

And he's standing there, to the side of the door, and Matt and Michaela know he could have been the first one inside but instead he's out here with them, in this terrible blizzard of flying glass, shouting those words over and over, his voice insistent and strong and somehow calm.

Matt bends down and hoists Sandy up a bit, and Michaela bends and helps also, holding on to Sandy with one arm and Tinkerbell with the other, and the two of them, Matt and Michaela, half guide and half shove Sandy ahead of them, pushing her forward, into the chilled darkness of the cooler.

Isaac and Corey and Brennan

Isaac Duncan has a YouTube account, but it's kind of dead. Like everyone else in the world, he has a video camera on his phone, but so far the only thing he's shot that has been worth uploading is a short clip of a drunk girl outside a bar kicking the side-view mirror off a cop car. That was four months ago. Still, whenever anything halfway interesting is happening around him, he tries to make a habit of documenting it. So today, at a little after five-forty P.M., Isaac points his phone at the windshield of his buddy

Brennan Stebbins's Ford Taurus and starts recording, capturing the rain-smeary taillights of the vehicles ahead of them, stopped at a red light.

"Jesus, people, c'mon," Brennan says.

Isaac is in the front passenger seat, Brennan's driving, and their friend Corey Waterman is in the backseat. The three have been driving around all afternoon, sort of aimlessly, listening to baseball on the radio. It's the I-70 series this weekend, the St. Louis Cardinals against the Kansas City Royals. They all like baseball, but mostly this afternoon has just been about hanging out. They're in their early twenties, best friends, and this might be the last summer they spend together. Isaac's probably going to move away soon, to Austin, to kick his music career into higher gear. Brennan just graduated earlier this month from Missouri Southern, was the editor of the school paper, has started applying for journalism gigs all over the country. Corey's thinking of maybe enrolling in film school, but he's not sure where yet.

Around the fifth inning, severe weather warnings start cutting into the game. They don't pay much attention at first. It's summer in Tornado Alley. They know the drill. But the warnings keep coming, and eventually they switch over from the Kansas AM station carrying the game to a local FM news station, which for the last little while has been just one extended warning, growing more and more urgent. By the time Isaac starts shooting video, the radio reporters sound kind of helpless. The power has gone out at the station, and though an emergency backup generator is allowing them to broadcast, they no longer have access to radar or to their computers, so their storm-tracking capabilities have become extremely primitive.

"Right now at the KZRG twenty-four-hour storm center, it is impossible to see," one reporter says.

"It's cloudy," says the other. "You can't see anything out the windows."

"Let's get the fuck out of here!" Corey says.

The light turns green and they drive south down Duquesne Road, and just before they reach Twentieth, one of them notices something both beautiful and dreadful: a veil of wispy clouds just above the tree line, rotating and congealing like sugar strands in a slow-motion cotton-candy machine. They decide they need to get off the road right away. The Fastrip is just ahead, and they pull up near the front and sprint through the quickening rain to the door. Ruben lets them in. He leads them to the back wall, where they hunker down with the small group that has already gathered there. Isaac aims the camera lens of his phone back toward the front windows, out at the parking lot, which in a matter of seconds has transitioned from a dusky twilight gray into a midnight black. The canopy above the gas pumps has just begun to flap. Soon the final refugees, Rick Ward and his three children, will arrive and start pounding on the glass outside, and Ruben will rush forward and unlock the door and force it open against the wind, and by that time it will be so dark that the camera will hardly register the scene at all.

"Man," Isaac says to no one in particular. "Shit is getting real."

The phone will continue to record for the next five minutes and seven seconds, though by the two-minute-twenty-second mark, when Isaac is scrambling with everyone else to get inside the cooler, he is no longer trying to aim it at any particular thing and has, in fact, forgotten that it is recording at all.

Ruben

Once almost everyone has made it into the cooler, Ruben glances to his right, back toward the Fastrip's front entrance.

He sees inventory—newspapers and breath mints and chocolate bars and cheap sunglasses and twelve-packs of Coke—leaping through the open maw of the window frames and vanishing into the blackness. Then he sees the entire front of the store—not just the window frames and the door but the wall containing them—jerk forward, off its foundation, as though a monster truck with chains affixed to all four corners of the building had suddenly floored its accelerator.

Chris, who's been helping Ruben get everyone inside, is in front of him. Ruben can see debris beginning to pelt Chris's back. He places his hands on Chris and shoves forward, and once Chris is all the way inside, he steps in after him and turns and grabs the edge of the cooler door and gives it a yank. The door has no latch or handle on the inside, to prevent people from locking themselves in. He closes it as far as he can, and as he's turning away from it, he sees one more thing through the opening.

He sees the entire front of his store, now that it's been unmoored, suddenly shoot skyward, like a rocket.

Then something, the wind or a flying object, impacts the other side of the door and slams it the rest of the way shut.

·   ·   ·

The cooler is about twenty-five feet long and seven feet high, though a pair of suspended air conditioners makes the ceiling about two feet lower in places. It is approximately eight feet wide, but most of that width is taken up by heavy steel shelving, leaving only about three feet of space between them. The shelves support cases of Miller Lite and Budweiser and Keystone Light and Busch and Busch Light and Coors and Coors Light and Milwaukee's Best Premium. Of the eleven Fastrips that the Grace Energy company owns in the area, this one is the oldest, and it has the biggest beer cooler.

The roaring outside escalates, and there are other sounds, too, the sounds of metal tearing and wood cracking. The cooler begins to shake. Objects pummel its walls.

Some of the people in the cooler are screaming and some are crying and some are completely quiet. There isn't much room. It's cold, but nobody notices. Some are squatting, and some are on their hands and knees. Some are calling out in a panic to the people they came with, unsure if they made it in. Eleven-year-old Jarrett Little wonders if they are flying, if they have been picked up and are being transported somewhere new, like Dorothy's house was. Tinkerbell, the dachshund, whines and whimpers.

After a few seconds things quiet down. The roaring eases off. The cooler shakes less violently and the pummeling slows.

"Dude," Isaac says, and the relief in his voice is as thick and sweet as honey. "We're good. We're good. We're good!"

And then the tornado, and not just the storm preceding it, crests the hill and hits them with its full force.

·　　·　　·

When the roof collapses, it hits Chris Carmer in the head and he drops to the floor and he's on his knees and now the wall with the shelves full of beer is falling toward him and then the roof opens up above and behind him and it sounds like the devil is shrieking in his ear and he feels his legs being sucked up toward the hole and he knows that Rick Ward is squatting next to him and so he grabs Rick Ward's belt with one hand and the falling shelves with the other and he buries his face in Rick's soft back and he tells himself that although he is about to die he should just hold on for as long as he can because it is better to go down fighting.

·　　·　　·

Tinkerbell is squirming and twisting in Michaela's arms, trying to look up at the widening holes in the roof. The tornado, unlike the storm clouds that shrouded it and concealed its approach, is not entirely dense and black. Dim, green, aquatic light, like the light scuba divers see, brightens the cooler a bit even as the cooler is being torn apart.

The tornado stretches twenty thousand feet into the sky. It is three quarters of a mile wide. It is not empty.

It is carrying two-by-fours and drywall and automobiles.

It is carrying baseball cards, laptop computers, family photo albums.

It is carrying people, as naked as newborns, their clothes stripped away like tissue paper.

It is carrying fragments of the Walmart where Carl and Jennifer met, of the church where Donna worships, of three of the nursing homes where Lacey works.

It has traveled six miles through the city, and now it is carrying a great deal of the city within itself.

Michaela pushes Tinkerbell's head down, but she can feel her squirrelly little neck straining against her hand, wanting to look up, wanting to see.

• • •

She believes in the Pentecost.

She believes that it happened just as the Bible describes it in chapter 2 of the Book of Acts, and she believes in something else that is written in the same chapter, about the end of the world: *The sun shall be turned into darkness and the moon into blood, before the great and notable day of the Lord come: And it shall come to pass that whosoever shall call on the name of the Lord shall be saved.*

She doesn't know who is on top of her, and she doesn't know who she is on top of.

She knows that what was outside has come inside.

She hears the impossible wind, and she feels it trying to carry her away.

"Heavenly father," Donna shouts. "Jesus! Jesus! Jesus! Jesus! Jesus! Jesus! Jesus! Jesus! Jesus! Jesus! Jesus! Jesus! Jesus!"

•   •   •

Corey Waterman is sprawled across Jennifer Henning and her youngest son, Trace. Jennifer's husband, Carl, is on the other end of the cooler, too far away. Corey has never met Jennifer and Trace. To Jennifer it feels like Corey is intentionally shielding them with his body, protecting them. Corey himself isn't sure: He thinks maybe he just fell and landed this way when the cooler wall fell and knocked him over. A hole is tearing open in the roof above, and he feels pellets of debris beginning to hit his back and he knows that bigger and heavier debris will follow. The cooler has become a jumbled tangle of people, but within the tangle certain units remain intact. In the gray-green aquatic light of the vortex Corey sees Aaron Frost, the high school quarterback, embracing his girlfriend, Allie, a few feet away.

Corey wishes he had someone who loved him holding him during these last moments of his life.

But he does not. So he holds, instead, these strangers. The breach grows wider. He feels the wind. He knows this is it.

Isaac, Corey's oldest friend, has been thrown forward and is lying across the legs of someone next to Jennifer and Trace. Corey reaches out and places a hand on Isaac's shoulder and grips it tight.

Isaac looks at Corey. There is a piece of debris lodged in Isaac's throat and he chokes it up and spits it out.

"I love you," Isaac says.

"I love you, bro," Corey says.

"I know," Isaac says, and then he looks away and shouts into the wind.

"I love everyone. I love everyone, man."

.   .   .

It spreads.

The wind permits Isaac's words to travel only a few feet before it whips them into oblivion, but that is enough to reach the ears of several people here on this far end of the cooler, including those of Matt and Michaela, who are squeezed against the rest but still squatting together, Matt holding Michaela, Michaela holding Tinkerbell. They are praying silently, preparing themselves to die.

They look up.

"I love you all," shouts Matt.

"I love everyone," shouts Michaela.

And then the people around Matt and Michaela hear the words, and so on, and the words travel in this way down the length of the cooler, and even the people who don't repeat the words hear the words.

Finally, at the far end of the cooler, the words reach Ruben Carter. The roof just inside the door of the cooler has collapsed almost all the way to the ground and somehow instead of crushing him it has simply pushed him forward, like toothpaste at the bottom of a tube. He doesn't know who said the words. The wind has stripped them of even their sex, leaving behind only their sentiment.

Ruben raises his head.

"I love all of you!" he shouts back into the crowd.

Then he drops his head again and closes his eyes and waits for whatever comes next.

.   .   .

Trace, eleven-year-old Trace, with his buzz cut and his grass-stained baseball uniform, is looking up at Corey, smiling, showing him something cradled in the palm of his hand.

It is a hailstone the size of a golf ball.

The wind is still howling and the cooler is still shaking and Corey's back is still being pelted with debris and he wonders if the kid is in shock.

But Trace, who used to be kind of obsessed with tornadoes, who spent fifth grade exercising his library card to learn everything he could on the subject, who knows that hail is associated with their edges, and that therefore, if you are hit by a tornado, hail is a sign that the worst is over, continues to smile up at Corey, showing off his melting jewel.

More hail falls around them now, bouncing and pinging and ricocheting, making a joyful noise.

·　　·　　·

"Is everyone okay below me?"

"I'm okay!"

"I'm trying not to lay on someone."

"Somebody is on my back."

"Am I hurting anybody?"

"Who's under me?"

"Is anyone under me?"

"Everybody stay calm. It's over."

"Are you okay back there? Are you okay?"

"Oh, I'm sorry."

"Be careful, there's glass on your back!"

"Are you okay?"

"I'm great."

"I'm okay. I'm okay."

"I love you, Mama."

"I love you, too. I love you."

"Ma'am, are you okay?"

"I'm okay."

"Is that you right below me?"

"Yeah."

"That's not someone else?"

"No."

There is the rich smell of upturned earth, like the smell of a freshly plowed field. There is the yeasty smell of spilled beer and the thick smell of wet plaster and the sharp smell of split wood. There is the faint smell of something burning, and the strong smell of gas.

There are a number of holes in what remains of the cooler's roof, but the biggest is on the end farthest from where the door used to be. The wall there is tipped at a steep angle, and there is a ragged gash near the top, where it should join the ceiling. Corey, who likes to scramble around the cliffs south of Joplin, climbs up the slick aluminum slope and pulls himself up over the lip and looks out over the edge and takes in what he sees, but when he looks back down he doesn't tell anyone because there isn't really anything he can say, so he just tells them the most important thing.

"We can make it out."

•   •   •

Michaela gives Tinkerbell to someone to hold, and then she climbs up a pyramid of Miller Lite cases that Carl has built at the base of the tilted wall. She reaches up to Corey and Isaac, who are balancing together at the top of the wall, and then they pull her up.

She looks around.

The skies above are still cloudy, but it's no longer dark and she can see plenty far. About thirty feet away is what used to be a maple tree. Most of its bark has been stripped off, along with most of its branches, and so the tree looks sort of like a gnarled and lumber-colored telephone pole. High above the tree's base, wrapped around its trunk, is a crumpled mass of gray and black metal. This used to be a pickup truck or an SUV, but it is impossible to tell which. There are other vehicles and parts of vehicles scattered everywhere, including an upside-down maroon Hyundai sedan that lies on the rubble of the Fastrip, maybe three feet from the edge of the half-collapsed roof of the cooler. Beyond the stripped tree, Michaela can see a small field with cows in it. Pieces of wood and metal are sticking out of the sides of some of the cows and others don't have all of their legs and the ones that aren't already dead will be soon enough. Where houses should be, for as far as Michaela can see, there are just stone foundations, stubbly with splintered wood. Here and there, against the backdrop of white sky, pockets of fire and smoke rise.

For the past couple of weeks, there's been a lot of talk on the news about some preacher in California who'd been predicting that the end of the world, the Rapture, would happen on May 21. That was yesterday. Michaela hadn't paid much attention, because she believes what the Bible says, which is that even the angels don't know when the end will come. Now Michaela wonders if the preacher was only one day off.

She wonders if she has been left behind.

An empty lattice of wooden beams that must once have been part of a wall is wedged up against the other side of the cooler, and Michaela uses it to lower herself to the ground. She's wearing flip-flops, and she takes a few ginger steps forward, careful to avoid stepping on glass or nails or other sharp debris.

Then she turns and waits for Matt and Tinkerbell to join her.

•   •   •

Some small chunks of flying glass buried themselves deep in Ruben's right hand while he was helping everyone get inside the cooler, but during the long wait to get out, his hand doesn't hurt at all. His legs, though, are cramping up bad. He cramps easily. It's one of the symptoms of his cerebral palsy.

Symptoms doesn't seem like the right word, really, because it's not like it's a disease or sickness that comes and then goes away or a terminal condition that gets progressively worse. It's a static thing, with him since birth. It's possible it was caused by the manner of his birth, though nobody can say for sure. He was born wrong, feet-first, and it took the doctors and nurses a while to get him free and breathing on his own, and maybe that's when the damage happened. Regardless, he's never known anything else, any other way of life, of living. He has damage to parts of his brain, and because of this damage he has trouble controlling his muscles, and when his muscles are forced into an awkward position for an extended period of time, as happened when the roof collapsed and pressed him down into this sort of fetal squat, they cramp.

He watches while the others crawl and scramble and are pushed out the exit. Eventually Ruben and Chris are the only ones left inside. Ruben makes his way to the leaning wall at the back. He steps onto the little pyramid of Miller Lite boxes and he stretches up and he grips the top of the wall and starts pulling himself up toward the opening. The wall is slick with rain and some blood is leaking down it from the wound in his hand and he is sort of kicking against the wet aluminum and his feet are slipping and he isn't making progress and so Chris comes up behind him and takes a hold of his legs and pushes.

Ruben emerges headfirst, blinking in the brightening sun.

·   ·   ·

Ruben, Matt and Michaela, Rick and Hannah and Abby and Jonah, Stacy, Aaron and Allie, Donna, Jennifer and Carl and Trace and Cory, Lacey and Chris and Jarrett and Nathan, Sandy, Isaac and Corey and Brennan. They wait till they've all made it out, and then they pick their way through the debris to Twentieth Street, and they know that it is Twentieth Street because they can see the concrete roundabout at the corner, and it's still the same even if nothing else is.

They get their bearings. The orange and beige ruins on the left side of Twentieth, about three quarters of a mile from where they are, must be the Home Depot, which means downtown lies that way.

They begin to disperse, walking away from one another, alone or in small groups, every destination different.

The New Yorker

"The Apostate" tells the story of the screenwriter and director Paul Haggis, a member of the Church of Scientology who left the organization when leaders announced their opposition to gay marriage. But this is also a history of Scientology—and an account of the editorial practices of The New Yorker, including a description of the eight-hour meeting between New Yorker editors and Scientology representatives in which they debated the reporting of the story. The New Yorker won the National Magazine Award for Lawrence Wright's "Remembering Satan" in 1994, and his book The Looming Tower: Al Qaeda and the Road to 9/11 won the Pulitzer Prize in 2007.

Lawrence Wright

The Apostate

On August 19, 2009, Tommy Davis, the chief spokesperson for the Church of Scientology International, received a letter from the film director and screenwriter Paul Haggis. "For ten months now I have been writing to ask you to make a public statement denouncing the actions of the Church of Scientology of San Diego," Haggis wrote. Before the 2008 elections, a staff member at Scientology's San Diego church had signed its name to an online petition supporting Proposition 8, which asserted that the State of California should sanction marriage only "between a man and a woman." The proposition passed. As Haggis saw it, the San Diego church's "public sponsorship of Proposition 8, which succeeded in taking away the civil rights of gay and lesbian citizens of California—rights that were granted them by the Supreme Court of our state—is a stain on the integrity of our organization and a stain on us personally. Our public association with that hate-filled legislation shames us." Haggis wrote, "Silence is consent, Tommy. I refuse to consent." He concluded, "I hereby resign my membership in the Church of Scientology."

Haggis was prominent in both Scientology and Hollywood, two communities that often converge. Although he is less famous than certain other Scientologists, such as Tom Cruise and John Travolta, he had been in the organization for nearly thirty-five years. Haggis wrote the screenplay for *Million Dollar Baby*, which won the Oscar for Best Picture in 2004, and he wrote and directed *Crash*, which won Best Picture the next year—the only time in Academy history that that has happened.

Davis, too, is part of Hollywood society; his mother is Anne Archer, who starred in *Fatal Attraction* and *Patriot Games*, among other films. Before becoming Scientology's spokesperson, Davis was a senior vice president of the church's Celebrity Centre International network.

In previous correspondence with Davis, Haggis had demanded that the church publicly renounce Proposition 8. "I feel strongly about this for a number of reasons," he wrote. "You and I both know there has been a hidden anti-gay sentiment in the church for a long time. I have been shocked on too many occasions to hear Scientologists make derogatory remarks about gay people, and then quote L.R.H. in their defense." The initials stand for L. Ron Hubbard, the founder of Scientology, whose extensive writings and lectures form the church's scripture. Haggis related a story about Katy, the youngest of three daughters from his first marriage, who lost the friendship of a fellow Scientologist after revealing that she was gay. The friend began warning others, "Katy is '1.1.'" The number refers to a sliding Tone Scale of emotional states that Hubbard published in a 1951 book, *The Science of Survival*. A person classified "1.1" was, Hubbard said, "Covertly Hostile"—"the most dangerous and wicked level"—and he noted that people in this state engaged in such things as casual sex, sadism, and homosexual activity. Hubbard's Tone Scale, Haggis wrote, equated "homosexuality with being a pervert." (Such remarks don't appear in recent editions of the book.)

In his resignation letter, Haggis explained to Davis that, for the first time, he had explored outside perspectives on Scientology. He had read a recent exposé in a Florida newspaper, the *St. Petersburg Times*, which reported, among other things, that senior executives in the church had been subjecting other

Scientologists to physical violence. Haggis said that he felt "dumbstruck and horrified," adding, "Tommy, if only a fraction of these accusations are true, we are talking about serious, indefensible human and civil-rights violations."

Online, Haggis came across an appearance that Davis had made on CNN in May 2008. The anchor John Roberts asked Davis about the church's policy of "disconnection," in which members are encouraged to separate themselves from friends or family members who criticize Scientology. Davis responded, "There's no such thing as disconnection as you're characterizing it. And certainly we have to understand—"

"Well, what is disconnection?" Roberts interjected.

"Scientology is a new religion," Davis continued. "The majority of Scientologists in the world, they're first generation. So their family members aren't going to be Scientologists. . . . So, certainly, someone who is a Scientologist is going to respect their family members' beliefs—"

"Well, what is disconnection?" Roberts said again.

"—and we consider family to be a building block of any society, so anything that's characterized as disconnection or this kind of thing, it's just not true. There isn't any such policy."

In his resignation letter, Haggis said, "We all know this policy exists. I didn't have to search for verification—I didn't have to look any further than my own home." Haggis reminded Davis that, a few years earlier, his wife had been ordered to disconnect from her parents "because of something absolutely trivial they supposedly did twenty-five years ago when they resigned from the church. . . . Although it caused her terrible personal pain, my wife broke off all contact with them." Haggis continued, "To see you lie so easily, I am afraid I had to ask myself: what else are you lying about?"

Haggis forwarded his resignation to more than twenty Scientologist friends, including Anne Archer, John Travolta, and Sky Dayton, the founder of EarthLink. "I felt if I sent it to my friends they'd be as horrified as I was, and they'd ask questions as well," he says. "That turned out to be largely not the case. They were horrified that I'd send a letter like that."

Tommy Davis told me, "People started calling me, saying, 'What's this letter Paul sent you?'" The resignation letter had not circulated widely, but if it became public it would likely cause problems for the church. The *St. Petersburg Times* exposé had inspired a fresh series of hostile reports on Scientology, which has long been portrayed in the media as a cult. And, given that some well-known Scientologist actors were rumored to be closeted homosexuals, Haggis's letter raised awkward questions about the church's attitude toward homosexuality. Most important, Haggis wasn't an obscure dissident; he was a celebrity, and the church, from its inception, has depended on celebrities to lend it prestige. In the past, Haggis had defended the religion; in 1997, he wrote a letter of protest after a French court ruled that a Scientology official was culpable in the suicide of a man who fell into debt after paying for church courses. "If this decision carries it sets a terrible precedent, in which no priest or minister will ever feel comfortable offering help and advice to those whose souls are tortured," Haggis wrote. To Haggis's friends, his resignation from the Church of Scientology felt like a very public act of betrayal. They were surprised, angry, and confused. "'Destroy the letter, resign quietly'—that's what they all wanted," Haggis says.

• • •

Last March, I met Haggis in New York. He was in the editing phase of his latest movie, *The Next Three Days*, a thriller starring Russell Crowe, in an office in SoHo. He sat next to a window with drawn shades as his younger sister Jo Francis, the film's editor, showed him a round of cuts. Haggis wore jeans and a black T-shirt. He is bald, with a trim blond beard, pale-blue eyes, and a nose that was broken in a schoolyard fight. He always has several projects going at once, and there was a barely contained feeling of frenzy. He glanced repeatedly at his watch.

Haggis, who is fifty-seven, was preparing for two events later that week: a preview screening in New York and a trip to Haiti. He began doing charitable work in Haiti well before the 2010 earthquake, and he has raised millions of dollars for that country. He told me that he was planning to buy ten acres of land in Port-au-Prince for a new school, which he hoped to have open in the fall. (In fact, the school—the first to offer free secondary education to children from the city's slums—opened in October.) In Hollywood, he is renowned for his ability to solicit money. The actor Ben Stiller, who has accompanied Haggis to Haiti, recalls that Haggis once raised four and a half million dollars in two hours.

While watching the edits, Haggis fielded calls from a plastic surgeon who was planning to go on the trip and from a priest in Haiti, Father Rick Frechette, whose organization is the main beneficiary of Haggis's charity. "Father Rick is a lot like me—a cynical optimist," Haggis told me. He also said of himself, "I'm a deeply broken person, and broken institutions fascinate me."

Haggis's producing partner, Michael Nozik, says, "Paul likes to be contrarian. If everyone is moving left, he'll feel the need to move right." The actor Josh Brolin, who appeared in Haggis's film *In the Valley of Elah* (2007), told me that Haggis "does things in extremes." Haggis is an outspoken promoter of social justice, in the manner of Hollywood activists like Sean Penn and George Clooney. The actress Maria Bello describes him as self-deprecating and sarcastic but also deeply compassionate. She recalls being with him in Haiti shortly after the earthquake; he was standing in the bed of a pickup truck, "with a cigarette hanging out of his mouth and a big smile on his face, and absolutely no fear." Though Haggis is passionate about his work, he can be cool toward those who are closest to him. Lauren Haggis, the second daughter from his first marriage, said that he never connected with his children. "He's emotionally not there," she says. "That's funny, because his scripts are full of emotion."

In the editing room, Haggis felt the need for a cigarette, so we walked outside. He is ashamed of this habit, especially given that, in 2003, while directing *Crash*, he had a heart attack. After Haggis had emergency surgery, his doctor told him that it would be four or five months before he could work again: "It would be too much strain on your heart." He replied, "Let me ask you how much stress you think I might be under as I'm sitting at home while another director is *finishing my fucking film!*" The doctor relented but demanded that a nurse be on the set to monitor Haggis's vital signs. Since then, Haggis has tried repeatedly to quit smoking. He had stopped before shooting *The Next Three Days*, but Russell Crowe was smoking, and that did him in. "There's always a good excuse," he admitted. Before his heart attack, he said, "I thought I was invincible." He added, "I still do."

Haggis had not spoken publicly about his resignation from Scientology. As we stood in a chill wind on Sixth Avenue, he was obviously uncomfortable discussing it, but he is a storyteller, and he eventually launched into a narrative.

Haggis wasn't proud of his early years. "I was a bad kid," he said. "I didn't kill anybody. Not that I didn't try." He was born in 1953, and grew up in London, Ontario, a manufacturing town midway between Toronto and Detroit. His father, Ted, had a construction company there, which specialized in pouring concrete. His mother, Mary, a Catholic, sent Paul and his two younger sisters, Kathy and Jo, to Mass on Sundays—until she spotted their priest driving an expensive car. "God wants me to have a Cadillac," the priest explained. Mary responded, "Then God doesn't want us in your church anymore."

Haggis decided at an early age to be a writer, and he made his own comic books. But he was such a poor student that his parents sent him to a strict boarding school, where the students were assigned cadet drills. He preferred to sit in his room reading *Ramparts*, the radical magazine from America—the place he longed to be. He committed repeated infractions, but he learned to pick locks so that he could sneak into the prefect's office and eliminate his demerits.

After a year of this, his parents transferred him to a progressive boys' school in Bracebridge, Ontario, where there was very little system to subvert. Haggis grew his curly blond hair to his shoulders. He discovered a mentor in his art teacher, Max Allen, who was politically radical and gay. Flouting Ontario's strict censorship laws, Allen opened a theater in Toronto that showed banned films; Haggis volunteered at the box office.

Haggis got caught forging a check, and he soon left school. He was drifting, hanging out with hippies and drug dealers. Two friends died from overdoses. "I had a gun pointed in my face a couple of times," he recalls. He attended art school briefly, then quit; after taking some film classes at a community college, he dropped out of that as well. He began working in construction full time for his father. He also was the manager of a hundred-seat theater that his father had created in an abandoned church. On Saturday nights, he set up a movie screen onstage, introducing himself and other film buffs to the works of Bergman, Hitchcock, and the French New Wave. He was so affected by Michelangelo Antonioni's *Blow-Up* that in 1974 he decided to move to England in order to become a fashion photographer, like the hero of the movie. That lasted less than a year.

Back in London, Ontario, he fell in love with Diane Gettas, a nurse, and they began sharing a one-bedroom apartment. He was starting to get his life together, but he was haunted by something that his grandfather had said to him on his deathbed. "He was a janitor in a bowling alley," Haggis told me. "He had left England because of some scandal we don't know about. He died when I was twelve or thirteen. He looked terrible. He turned to me and said, 'I've wasted my life. Don't waste yours.'"

One day in 1975, when he was twenty-two, Haggis was walking to a record store. When he arrived at the corner of Dundas and Waterloo Streets, a young man pressed a book into his hands. "You have a mind," the man said. "This is the owner's manual." The man, whose name was Jim Logan, added, "Give me two dollars." The book was *Dianetics: The Modern Science of Mental Health*, by L. Ron Hubbard, which was published in 1950. By the time Haggis began reading it, *Dianetics* had sold about two and a half million copies. Today, according to the church, that figure has reached more than twenty-one million.

Haggis opened the book and saw a page stamped with the words "Church of Scientology."

"Take me there," Haggis said to Logan.

Haggis had heard about Scientology a couple of months earlier, from a friend who had called it a cult. The thought that he might be entering a cult didn't bother him. In fact, he said, "it drew my interest. I tend to run toward things I don't understand." When he arrived at the church's headquarters, he recalled, "it didn't look like a cult. Two guys in a small office above Woolworth's."

At the time, Haggis and Gettas were having arguments; the Scientologists told him that taking church courses would improve the relationship. "It was pitched to me as applied philosophy," Haggis says. He and Gettas took a course together and, shortly afterward, became Hubbard Qualified Scientologists, one of the first levels in what the church calls the Bridge to Total Freedom.

.   .   .

The Church of Scientology says that its purpose is to transform individual lives and the world. "A civilization without insanity, without criminals and without war, where the able can prosper and honest beings can have rights, and where man is free to rise to greater heights, are the aims of Scientology," Hubbard wrote. Scientology postulates that every person is a Thetan—an immortal spiritual being that lives through countless lifetimes. Scientologists believe that Hubbard discovered the fundamental truths of existence, and they revere him as "the source" of the religion. Hubbard's writings offer a "technology" of spiritual advancement and self-betterment that provides "the means to attain true spiritual freedom and immortality." A church publication declares, "Scientology works 100 percent of the time when it is properly applied to a person who sincerely desires to improve his life." Proof of this efficacy, the church says, can be measured by the accomplishments of its adherents. "As Scientologists in all walks of life will attest, they have enjoyed greater success in their relationships, family life, jobs and professions. They take an active, vital role in life and leading roles in their communities. And participation in Scientology brings to many a broader social consciousness, manifested through meaningful contribution to charitable and social reform activities."

In 1955, a year after the church's founding, an affiliated publication urged Scientologists to cultivate celebrities: "It is obvious what would happen to Scientology if prime communicators benefitting from it would mention it." At the end of the sixties, the church established its first Celebrity Centre, in Hollywood. (There are now satellites in Paris, Vienna, Düsseldorf, Munich, Florence, London, New York, Las Vegas, and Nashville.) Over the next decade, Scientology became a potent force in Hollywood. In many respects, Haggis was typical of the recruits from that era, at least among those in the entertainment business. Many of them were young and had quit school in order to follow their dreams, but they were also smart and ambitious. The actress Kirstie Alley, for example, left the University of Kansas in 1970, during her sophomore year, to get married. Scientology, she says, helped her lose her craving for cocaine. "Without Scientology, I would be dead," she has said.

In 1975, the year that Haggis became a Scientologist, John Travolta, a high-school dropout, was making his first movie, *The*

Devil's Rain, in Durango, Mexico, when an actress on the set gave him a copy of *Dianetics*. "My career immediately took off," he told a church publication. "Scientology put me into the big time." The testimonials of such celebrities have attracted many curious seekers. In *Variety*, Scientology has advertised courses promising to help aspiring actors "make it in the industry."

One of those actors, Josh Brolin, told me that, in a "moment of real desperation," he visited the Celebrity Centre and received "auditing"—spiritual counseling. He quickly decided that Scientology wasn't for him. But he still wonders what the religion does for celebrities like Cruise and Travolta: "Each has a good head on his shoulders, they make great business decisions, they seem to have wonderful families. Is that because they were helped by Scientology?" This is the question that makes celebrities so crucial to the religion. And, clearly, there must be something rewarding if such notable people lend their names to a belief system that is widely scorned.

Brolin says that he once witnessed John Travolta practicing Scientology. Brolin was at a dinner party in Los Angeles with Travolta and Marlon Brando. Brando arrived with a cut on his leg, and explained that he had injured himself while helping a stranded motorist on the Pacific Coast Highway. He was in pain. Travolta offered to help, saying that he had just reached a new level in Scientology. Travolta touched Brando's leg and Brando closed his eyes. "I watched this process going on—it was very physical," Brolin recalls. "I was thinking, This is really fucking bizarre! Then, after ten minutes, Brando opens his eyes and says, 'That really helped. I actually feel different!'" (Travolta, through a lawyer, called this account "pure fabrication.")

Many Hollywood actors were drawn into the church by a friend or by reading *Dianetics*; a surprising number of them, though, came through the Beverly Hills Playhouse. For decades, the resident acting coach there was Milton Katselas, and he taught hundreds of future stars, including Ted Danson, Michelle

Pfeiffer, and George Clooney. "Most of Hollywood went through that class," Anne Archer told me. In 1974, two years after her son Tommy Davis was born, she began studying with Katselas. She was a young mother in a dissolving marriage, coming off a television series (*Bob & Carol & Ted & Alice*) that had been cancelled after one season. Katselas had a transformative effect. She recalled discussions "about life, people, and behavior," and said that Katselas "said some things in class that were really smart." Some of the other students told her that Katselas was a Scientologist, so she began the Life Repair program at the Celebrity Centre. "I went two or three times a week, probably for a couple of weeks," she said. "I remember walking out of the building and walking down the street toward my car and I felt like my feet were not touching the ground. And I said to myself, 'My God, this is the happiest I've ever been in my entire life. I've finally found something that works.'" She added, "Life didn't seem so hard anymore. I was back in the driver's seat."

Jim Gordon, a veteran police officer in Los Angeles, and also an aspiring actor, spent ten years at the Playhouse, starting in 1990. He told me that Scientology "recruited a ton of kids out of that school." Like Scientology, the Playhouse presented a strict hierarchy of study; under Katselas's tutelage, students graduated from one level to the next. As Gordon advanced within the Playhouse, he began recognizing many students from the roles they were getting in Hollywood. "You see a lot of people you know from TV," Gordon says. He began feeling the pull of the church. "When you started off, they weren't really pushing it, but as you progressed through the Playhouse's levels Scientology became more of a focus," he told me. After a few years, he joined. Like the courses at the Playhouse, Scientology offered actors a method that they could apply to both their lives and their careers.

Not long after Gordon became a Scientologist, he was asked to serve as an "ethics officer" at the Playhouse, monitoring the progress of other students and counseling those who were having trouble. He was good at pinpointing students who were struggling. "It's almost like picking out the wounded chicks," he says. He sometimes urged a student to meet with the senior ethics officer at the Playhouse, a Scientologist who often recommended courses at the Celebrity Centre. "My job was to keep the students active and make sure they were not being suppressed," Gordon says. In the rhetoric of Scientology, "suppressive persons"—or S.P.s—block an individual's spiritual progress. Implicitly, the message to the students was that success awaited them if only they could sweep away the impediments to stardom, including S.P.s. Katselas received a 10 percent commission from the church on the money contributed by his students.

Katselas died in 2008, and Scientology no longer has a connection with the Beverly Hills Playhouse. Anne Archer told me that the reputation of Katselas's class as, in Gordon's words, a "Scientology clearinghouse" is overblown. "His classes averaged about fifty or sixty people, and there would be maybe seven to ten people in it who would be Scientologists," she says. But the list of Scientologists who have studied at the Playhouse is long— it includes Jenna Elfman, Giovanni Ribisi, and Jason Lee—and the many protégés Katselas left behind helped cement the relationship between Hollywood and the church.

·　　·　　·

Haggis and I travelled together to L.A., where he was presenting *The Next Three Days* to the studio. During the flight, I asked him how high he had gone in Scientology. "All the way to the top," he said. Since the early eighties, he had been an Operating Thetan VII, which was the highest level available when he became affiliated with the church. (In 1988, a new level, O.T. VIII, was introduced to members; it required study at sea, and Haggis declined to pursue it.) He had made his ascent by buying "intensives"—

bundled hours of auditing, at a discount rate. "It wasn't so expensive back then," he said.

David S. Touretzky, a computer-science professor at Carnegie Mellon University, has done extensive research on Scientology. (He is not a defector.) He estimates that the coursework alone now costs nearly three hundred thousand dollars, and, with the additional auditing and contributions expected of upper-level members, the cumulative cost of the coursework may exceed half a million dollars. (The church says that there are no fixed fees, adding, "Donations requested for 'courses' at Church of Scientology begin at $50 and could never possibly reach the amount suggested.")

I asked Haggis why he had aligned himself with a religion that so many have disparaged. "I identify with the underdog," he said. "I have a perverse pride in being a member of a group that people shun." For Haggis, who likes to see himself as a man of the people, his affiliation with Scientology felt like a way of standing with the marginalized and the oppressed. The church itself often hits this note, making frequent statements in support of human rights and religious freedom. Haggis's experience in Scientology, though, was hardly egalitarian: he accepted the privileges of the Celebrity Centre, which offers notables a private entrance, a V.I.P. lounge, separate facilities for auditing, and other perks. Indeed, much of the appeal of Scientology is the overt elitism that it promotes among its members, especially celebrities. Haggis was struck by another paradox: "Here I was in this very structured organization, but I always thought of myself as a freethinker and an iconoclast."

During our conversations, we spoke about some events that had stained the reputation of the church while he was a member. For example, there was the death of Lisa McPherson, a Scientologist who died after a mental breakdown, in 1995. She had rear-ended a car in Clearwater, Florida—where Scientology has its spiritual headquarters—and then stripped off her clothes and wandered naked down the street. She was taken to a hospital, but, in the company of several other Scientologists, she checked out, against doctors' advice. (The church considers psychiatry an evil profession.) McPherson spent the next seventeen days being subjected to church remedies, such as doses of vitamins and attempts to feed her with a turkey baster. She became comatose, and she died of a pulmonary embolism before church members finally brought her to the hospital. The medical examiner in the case, Joan Wood, initially ruled that the cause of death was undetermined, but she told a reporter, "This is the most severe case of dehydration I've ever seen." The State of Florida filed charges against the church. In February 2000, under withering questioning from experts hired by the church, Wood declared that the death was "accidental." The charges were dropped, and Wood resigned.

Haggis said that, at the time, he had chosen not to learn the details of McPherson's death. "I had such a lack of curiosity when I was inside," Haggis said. "It's stunning to me, because I'm such a curious person." He said that he had been "somewhere between uninterested in looking and afraid of looking." His life was comfortable, he liked his circle of friends, and he didn't want to upset the balance. It was also easy to dismiss people who quit the church. As he put it, "There's always disgruntled folks who say all sorts of things." He was now ashamed of this willed myopia, which, he noted, clashed with what he understood to be the ethic of Scientology: "Hubbard says that there is a relationship between knowledge, responsibility, and control, and as soon as you know something you have a responsibility to act. And, if you don't, shame on you."

Since resigning, Haggis had been wondering why it took him so long to leave. In an e-mail exchange, I noted that higher-level Scientologists are supposed to be free of neuroses and allergies and resistant to the common cold. *Dianetics* also promises heightened powers of intelligence and perception. Haggis had told me that he fell far short of this goal. "Did you feel it was your fault?" I asked. Haggis responded that, because the auditing took place over a number of years, it was easy to believe that he might actually be smarter and wiser because of it, just as that might be true after years of therapy. "It is all so subjective, how is one supposed to know?" he wrote. "How does it feel to be smarter today than you were two months ago? . . . But yes, I always felt false."

He noted that a Scientologist hearing this would feel, with some justification, that he had misled his auditors about his progress. But, after hundreds of hours of auditing sessions, he said, "I remember feeling I just wanted it over. I felt it wasn't working, and figured that could be my fault, but did not want the hours of 'repair auditing' that they would tell me I needed to fix it. So I just went along, to my shame. I did what was easy . . . without asking them, or myself, any hard questions."

.   .   .

When Haggis first turned to Scientology, he considered himself an atheist. Scientology seemed to him less a religion than a set of useful principles for living. He mentioned the ARC Triangle; "ARC" stands for "Affinity, Reality, and Communication." Affinity, in this formulation, means the emotional response that partners have toward each other; reality is the area of common agreement. Together, these contribute to the flow of communication. "The three parts together equal understanding," Haggis said. "If you're having a disagreement with someone, your affinity drops quickly. Your mutual reality is shattered. Your communication becomes more halted. You begin to talk over each other. There's less and less understanding. But all you need to do is to raise one part of the triangle and you increase the others as well. I still use that."

Some aspects of Scientology baffled him. He hadn't been able to get through *Dianetics*: "I read about thirty pages. I thought it was impenetrable." But much of the coursework gave him a feeling of accomplishment. He was soon commuting from London, Ontario, to Toronto to take more advanced courses, and, in 1976, he travelled to Los Angeles for the first time. He checked in at the old Chateau Élysée, on Franklin Avenue. Clark Gable and Katharine Hepburn had once stayed there, but when Haggis arrived it was a run-down church retreat called the Manor Hotel. (It has since been spectacularly renovated and turned into the flagship Celebrity Centre.) "I had a little apartment with a kitchen I could write in," he recalls. "There was a feeling of camaraderie that was something I'd never experienced—all these atheists looking for something to believe in, and all these loners looking for a club to join."

Recruits had a sense of boundless possibility. Mystical powers were forecast; out-of-body experiences were to be expected; fundamental secrets were to be revealed. Hubbard had boasted that Scientology had raised some people's IQ one point for every hour of auditing. "Our most spectacular feat was raising a boy from 83 I.Q. to 212," he told the *Saturday Evening Post*, in 1964.

At the Manor Hotel, Haggis went "Clear." The concept comes from *Dianetics*; it is where you start if you want to ascend to the upper peaks of Scientology. A person who becomes Clear is "adaptable to and able to change his environment," Hubbard writes. "His ethical and moral standards are high, his ability to seek and experience pleasure is great. His personality is heightened and he is creative and constructive." Someone who is Clear is less susceptible to disease and is free of neuroses, compulsions, repressions, and psychosomatic illnesses. "The dianetic *Clear* is to a current normal individual as the current normal is to the severely insane."

Going Clear "was not life-changing," Haggis says. "It wasn't, like, 'Oh, my God, I can fly!'" At every level of advancement, he was encouraged to write a "success story" saying how effective his training had been. He had read many such stories by other

Scientologists, and they felt "overly effusive, done in part to convince yourself, but also slanted toward giving somebody upstairs approval for you to go on to the next level."

In 1977, Haggis returned to Canada to continue working for his father, who could see that his son was struggling. Ted Haggis asked him what he wanted to do with his life. Haggis said that he wanted to be a writer. His father recalls, "I said, 'Well, there are only two places to do that, New York and Los Angeles. Pick one, and I'll keep you on the payroll for a year.' Paul said, 'I think I'll go to L.A., because it's warmer.'"

Soon after this conversation, Haggis and Diane Gettas got married. Two months later, they loaded up his brown Camaro and drove to Los Angeles, where he got a job moving furniture. He and Diane lived in an apartment with her brother, Gregg, and three other people. In 1978, Diane gave birth to their first child, Alissa. Haggis was spending much of his time and money taking advanced courses and being audited, which involved the use of an electropsychometer, or E-Meter. The device, often compared in the press to a polygraph, measures the bodily changes in electrical resistance that occur when a person answers questions posed by an auditor. ("Thoughts have a small amount of mass," the church contends in a statement. "These are the changes measured.") In 1952, Hubbard said of the E-Meter, "It gives Man his first keen look into the heads and hearts of his fellows." The Food and Drug Administration has compelled the church to declare that the instrument has no curative powers and is ineffective in diagnosing or treating disease.

During auditing, Haggis grasped a cylindrical electrode in each hand; when he first joined Scientology, the electrodes were empty soup cans. An imperceptible electrical charge ran from the meter through his body. The auditor asked systematic questions aimed at detecting sources of "spiritual distress." Whenever Haggis gave an answer that prompted the E-Meter's needle to jump, that subject became an area of concentration until the auditor was satisfied that Haggis was free of the emotional consequences of the troubling experience.

Haggis found the E-Meter surprisingly responsive. It seemed to gauge the kinds of thoughts he was having—whether they were angry or happy, or if he was hiding something. The auditor often probed for what Scientologists call "earlier similars." Haggis explained, "If you're having a fight with your girlfriend, the auditor will ask, 'Can you remember an earlier time when something like this happened?' And if you do then he'll ask, 'What about a time before that? And a time before that?'" Often, the process leads participants to recall past lives. The goal is to uncover and neutralize the emotional memories that are plaguing one's behavior.

Although Haggis never believed in reincarnation, he says, "I did experience gains. I would feel relief from arguments I'd had with my dad, things I'd done as a teenager that I didn't feel good about. I think I did, in some ways, become a better person. I did develop more empathy for others." Then again, he admitted, "I tried to find ways to be a better husband, but I never really did. I was still the selfish bastard I always was."

Haggis was moving furniture during the day and taking photographs for church yearbooks on the weekends. At night, he wrote scripts on spec. He met Skip Press, another young writer who was a Scientologist. Press had read one of Haggis's scripts— an episode of *Welcome Back, Kotter* that he was trying to get to the show's star, John Travolta. Haggis and Press started hanging out with other aspiring writers and directors who were involved with Scientology. "We would meet at a restaurant across from the Celebrity Centre called Two Dollar Bill's," Press recalls. Chick Corea and other musicians associated with the church played there. Haggis and a friend from this circle eventually got a job writing for cartoons, including *Scooby-Doo* and *Richie Rich*.

By now, Haggis had begun advancing through the upper levels of Scientology. The church defines an Operating Thetan as "one who can handle things without having to use a body or physical means." An editorial in a 1959 issue of the Scientology magazine *Ability* notes that "neither Lord Buddha nor Jesus Christ were O.T.s, according to the evidence. They were just a shade above Clear." According to several copies of church documents that have been leaked online, Hubbard's handwritten instructions for the first level list thirteen mental exercises that attune practitioners to their relationship with others, such as "Note several large and several small male bodies until you have a cognition. Note it down." In the second level, Scientologists engage in exercises and visualizations that explore oppositional forces:

> Laughter comes from the rear half and calm from the front half simultaneously. Then they reverse. It gives one a sensation of total disagreement. The trick is to conceive of both at the same time. This tends to knock one out.

Haggis didn't have a strong reaction to the material, but then he wasn't expecting anything too profound. Everyone knew that the big revelations resided in level O.T. III.

Hubbard called this level the Wall of Fire. He said, "The material involved in this sector is so vicious, that it is carefully arranged to kill anyone if he discovers the exact truth of it. . . . I am very sure that I was the first one that ever did live through any attempt to attain that material." The O.T. III candidate is expected to free himself from being overwhelmed by the disembodied, emotionally wounded spirits that have been implanted inside his body. Bruce Hines, a former high-level Scientology auditor who is now a research physicist at the University of Colorado, explained to me, "Most of the upper levels are involved in exorcising these spirits."

"The process of induction is so long and slow that you really do convince yourself of the truth of some of these things that don't make sense," Haggis told me. Although he refused to specify the contents of O.T. materials, on the ground that it offended

Scientologists, he said, "If they'd sprung this stuff on me when I first walked in the door, I just would have laughed and left right away." But by the time Haggis approached the O.T. III material he'd already been through several years of auditing. His wife was deeply involved in the church, as was his sister Kathy. Moreover, his first writing jobs had come through Scientology connections. He was now entrenched in the community. Success stories in the Scientology magazine *Advance!* added an aura of reality to the church's claims. Haggis admits, "I was looking forward to enhanced abilities." Moreover, he had invested a lot of money in the program. The incentive to believe was high.

In the late seventies, the O.T. material was still quite secret. There was no Google, and Scientology's confidential scriptures had not yet circulated, let alone been produced in court or parodied on *South Park*. "You were told that this information, if released, would cause serious damage to people," Haggis told me.

Carrying an empty, locked briefcase, Haggis went to the Advanced Organization building in Los Angeles, where the material was held. A supervisor then handed him a folder, which Haggis put in the briefcase. He entered a study room, where he finally got to examine the secret document—a couple of pages, in Hubbard's bold scrawl. After a few minutes, he returned to the supervisor.

"I don't understand," Haggis said.

"Do you know the words?" the supervisor asked.

"I know the words, I just don't understand."

"Go back and read it again," the supervisor suggested.

Haggis did so. In a moment, he returned. "Is this a metaphor?" he asked the supervisor.

"No," the supervisor responded. "It is what it is. Do the actions that are required."

Maybe it's an insanity test, Haggis thought—if you believe it, you're automatically kicked out. "I sat with that for a while," he says. But when he read it again he decided, "This is madness."

•　　　•　　　•

The many discrepancies between L. Ron Hubbard's legend and his life have overshadowed the fact that he was a fascinating man: an explorer, a best-selling author, and the founder of one of the few new religious movements of the twentieth century to have survived into the twenty-first. There are several unauthorized Hubbard biographies—most notably, Russell Miller's *Bare-Faced Messiah*, Jon Atack's *A Piece of Blue Sky*, and Bent Corydon's *L. Ron Hubbard: Messiah or Madman?* All rely on stolen materials and the accounts of defectors, and the church claims that they present a false and fabricated picture of Hubbard's life. For years, the church has had a contract with a biographer, Dan Sherman, to chronicle the founder's life, but there is still no authorized book, and the church refused to let me talk to Sherman. ("He's busy," Davis told me.) The tug-of-war between Scientologists and anti-Scientologists over Hubbard's legacy has created two swollen archetypes: the most important person who ever lived and the world's greatest con man. Hubbard was certainly grandiose, but to label him merely a fraud is to ignore the complexity of his character.

Hubbard was born in Tilden, Nebraska, in 1911. His father, a naval officer, was often away, and Hubbard spent part of his childhood on his grandparents' ranch in Montana. When his father got posted to Guam in 1927, Hubbard made two trips to see him. According to Hubbard, on the second trip he continued on to Asia, where he visited the Buddhist lamaseries in the Western Hills of China, "watching monks meditate for weeks on end."

In 1933, Hubbard married Margaret Grubb, whom he called Polly; their first child, Lafayette, was born the following year. He visited Hollywood, and began getting work as a screenwriter, very much as Paul Haggis did some forty years later. Hubbard worked on serials for Columbia Pictures, including one called *The Secret of Treasure Island*. But much of his energy was devoted to publishing stories, often under pseudonyms, in pulp magazines such as *Astounding Science Fiction.*

During the Second World War, Hubbard served in the U.S. Navy, and he later wrote that he was gravely injured in battle: "Blinded with injured optic nerves and lame with physical injuries to hip and back at the end of World War II, I faced an almost nonexistent future. I was abandoned by family and friends as a supposedly hopeless cripple." While languishing in a military hospital in Oakland, California, he said, he fully healed himself, using techniques that became the foundation of Scientology. "I had no one to help me; what I had to know I had to find out," he wrote in an essay titled "My Philosophy." "And it's quite a trick studying when you cannot see." In some editions of Hubbard's book *The Fundamentals of Thought*, published in 1956, a note on the author says, "It is a matter of medical record that he has twice been pronounced dead."

After the war, Hubbard's marriage dissolved, and he moved to Pasadena, where he became the housemate of Jack Parsons, a rocket scientist who belonged to an occult society called the Ordo Templi Orientis. An atmosphere of hedonism pervaded the house; Parsons hosted gatherings involving "sex magick" rituals.

In a 1946 letter, Parsons described Hubbard: "He is a gentleman, red hair, green eyes, honest and intelligent." Parsons then mentioned his wife's sister, Betty Northrup, with whom he had been having an affair. "Although Betty and I are still friendly, she has transferred her sexual affections to Ron." One day, Hubbard and Northrup ran off together. In the official Scientology literature, it is claimed that Hubbard was assigned by naval intelligence to infiltrate Parsons's occult group. "Hubbard broke up black magic in America," the church said in a statement.

Hubbard and Northrup ended up in Los Angeles. He continued writing for the pulps, but he had larger ambitions. He began codifying a system of self-betterment and set up an office near the corner of La Brea and Sunset, where he tested his techniques on the actors, directors, and writers he encountered. He named his system Dianetics.

The book *Dianetics* appeared in May 1950 and spent twenty-eight weeks on the *New York Times* best-seller list. Written in a bluff, quirky style and overrun with footnotes that do little to substantiate its findings, *Dianetics* purports to identify the source of self-destructive behavior—the "reactive mind," a kind of data bank that is filled with traumatic memories called "engrams" and that is the source of nightmares, insecurities, irrational fears, and psychosomatic illnesses. The object of Dianetics is to drain the engrams of their painful, damaging qualities and eliminate the reactive mind, leaving a person "Clear."

Dianetics, Hubbard said, was a "precision science." He offered his findings to the American Psychiatric Association and the American Medical Association but was spurned; he subsequently portrayed psychiatry and psychology as demonic competitors. He once wrote that if psychiatrists "had the power to torture and kill everyone they would do so."

Scientists dismissed Hubbard's book, but hundreds of Dianetics groups sprang up across the United States and abroad. The Church of Scientology was officially founded in Los Angeles in February 1954 by several devoted followers of Hubbard's work.

In 1966, Hubbard—who by then had met and married another woman, Mary Sue Whipp—set sail with a handful of Scientologists. The church says that being at sea provided a "distraction-free environment," allowing Hubbard "to continue his research into the upper levels of spiritual awareness." Within a year, he had acquired several oceangoing vessels. He staffed the ships with volunteers, many of them teenagers, who called themselves the Sea Organization. Hubbard and his followers cruised the Mediterranean searching for loot he had stored in previous lifetimes. (The church denies this.) The defector Janis Grady, a former Sea Org member, told me, "I was on the bridge with him, sailing past

Greek islands. There were crosses lining one island. He told me that under each cross is buried treasure."

The Sea Org became the church's equivalent of a religious order. The group now has six thousand members. They perform tasks such as counseling, maintaining the church's vast property holdings, and publishing its official literature. Sea Org initiates—some of whom are children—sign contracts for up to a billion years of service. They get a small weekly stipend and receive free auditing and coursework. Sea Org members can marry, but they must agree not to raise children while in the organization.

As Scientology grew, it was increasingly attacked. In 1963, the *Los Angeles Times* called it a "pseudo-scientific cult." The church attracted dozens of lawsuits, largely from ex-parishioners. In 1980, Hubbard disappeared from public view. Although there were rumors that he was dead, he was actually driving around the Pacific Northwest in a motor home. He returned to writing science fiction and produced a ten-volume work, *Mission Earth*, each volume of which was a best-seller. In 1983, he settled quietly on a horse farm in Creston, California.

Around that time, Paul Haggis received a message from the church about a film project. Hubbard had written a treatment for a script titled *Influencing the Planet* and, apparently, intended to direct it. The film was supposed to demonstrate the range of Hubbard's efforts to improve civilization. With another Scientologist, Haggis completed a script, which he called "quite dreadful." Hubbard sent him notes on the draft, but no film by that name was ever released.

In 1985, with Hubbard in seclusion, the church faced two of its most difficult court challenges. In Los Angeles, a former Sea Org member, Lawrence Wollersheim, sought twenty-five million dollars for "infliction of emotional injury." He claimed that he had been kept for eighteen hours a day in the hold of a ship docked in Long Beach and deprived of adequate sleep and food.

That October, the litigants filed O.T. III materials in court. Fifteen hundred Scientologists crowded into the courthouse, trying to block access to the documents. The church, which considers it sacrilegious for the uninitiated to read its confidential scriptures, got a restraining order, but the *Los Angeles Times* obtained a copy of the material and printed a summary. Suddenly, the secrets that had stunned Paul Haggis in a locked room were public knowledge.

"A major cause of mankind's problems began 75 million years ago," the *Times* wrote, when the planet Earth, then called Teegeeack, was part of a confederation of ninety planets under the leadership of a despotic ruler named Xenu. "Then, as now, the materials state, the chief problem was overpopulation." Xenu decided "to take radical measures." The documents explained that surplus beings were transported to volcanoes on Earth. "The documents state that H-bombs far more powerful than any in existence today were dropped on these volcanoes, destroying the people but freeing their spirits—called thetans—which attached themselves to one another in clusters." Those spirits were "trapped in a compound of frozen alcohol and glycol," then "implanted" with "the seed of aberrant behavior." The *Times* account concluded, "When people die, these clusters attach to other humans and keep perpetuating themselves."

The jury awarded Wollersheim thirty million dollars. (Eventually, an appellate court reduced the judgment to two and a half million.) The secret O.T. III documents remained sealed, but the *Times* report had already circulated widely, and the church was met with derision all over the world.

The other court challenge in 1985 involved Julie Christofferson-Titchbourne, a defector who argued that the church had falsely claimed that Scientology would improve her intelligence and even her eyesight. In a courtroom in Portland, she said that Hubbard had been portrayed to her as a nuclear physicist; in fact, he had failed to graduate from George Washington University. As for

Hubbard's claim that he had cured himself of grave injuries in the Second World War, the plaintiff's evidence indicated that he had never been wounded in battle. Witnesses for the plaintiff testified that, in one six-month period in 1982, the church had transferred millions of dollars to Hubbard through a Liberian corporation. The church denied this and said that Hubbard's income was generated by his book sales.

The jury sided with Christofferson-Titchbourne, awarding her thirty-nine million dollars. Scientologists streamed into Portland to protest. They carried banners advocating religious freedom and sang "We Shall Overcome." Scientology celebrities, including John Travolta, showed up; Chick Corea played a concert in a public park. Haggis, who was writing for the NBC series *The Facts of Life* at the time, came and was drafted to write speeches. "I wasn't a celebrity—I was a lowly sitcom writer," he says. He stayed for four days.

The judge declared a mistrial, saying that Christofferson-Titchbourne's lawyers had presented prejudicial arguments. It was one of the greatest triumphs in Scientology's history, and the church members who had gone to Portland felt an enduring sense of kinship. (A year and a half later, the church settled with Christofferson-Titchbourne for an undisclosed sum.)

In 1986, Hubbard died, of a stroke, in his motor home. He was seventy-four. Two weeks later, Scientologists gathered in the Hollywood Palladium for a special announcement. A young man, David Miscavige, stepped onto the stage. Short, trim, and muscular, with brown hair and sharp features, Miscavige announced to the assembled Scientologists that, for the past six years, Hubbard had been investigating new, higher O.T. levels. "He has now moved on to the next level," Miscavige said. "It's a level beyond anything any of us ever imagined. This level is, in fact, done in an exterior state. Meaning that it is done completely exterior from the body. Thus, at twenty-hundred hours, the twenty-fourth of January, A.D. 36"—that is, thirty-six years after the publication of *Dianetics*—"L. Ron Hubbard discarded the body he had used in this lifetime." Miscavige began clapping and led the crowd in an ovation, shouting, "Hip hip hooray!"

Miscavige was a Scientology prodigy from the Philadelphia area. He claimed that, growing up, he had been sickly and struggled with bad asthma; Dianetics counseling had dramatically alleviated the symptoms. As he puts it, he "experienced a miracle." He decided to devote his life to the religion. He had gone Clear by the age of fifteen, and the next year he dropped out of high school to join the Sea Org. He became an executive assistant to Hubbard, who gave him special tutoring in photography and cinematography. When Hubbard went into seclusion in 1980, Miscavige was one of the few people who maintained close contact with him. With Hubbard's death, the curtain rose on a man who was going to impose his personality on an organization facing its greatest test, the death of its charismatic founder. Miscavige was twenty-five years old.

•   •   •

In 1986, Haggis appeared on the cover of the Scientology magazine *Celebrity*. The accompanying article lauded his rising influence in Hollywood. He had escaped the cartoon ghetto after selling a script to *The Love Boat*. He had climbed the ladder of network television, writing movies of the week and children's shows before settling into sitcoms. He worked on *Diff'rent Strokes* and *One Day at a Time*, then became the executive producer of *The Facts of Life*. The magazine noted, "He is one of the few writers in Hollywood who has major credits in all genres: comedy, suspense, human drama, animation."

In the article, Haggis said of Scientology, "What excited me about the technology was that you could actually handle life, and your problems, and not have them handle you." He added, "I also liked the motto, 'Scientology makes the able more able.'"

He credited the church for improving his relationship with Gettas. "Instead of fighting (we did a lot of that before Scientology philosophy) we now talk things out, listen to each other and apply Scientology technology to our problems."

Haggis told *Celebrity* that he had recently gone through the Purification Rundown, a program intended to eliminate body toxins that form a "biochemical barrier to spiritual well-being." For an average of three weeks, participants undergo a lengthy daily regimen combining sauna visits, exercise, and huge doses of vitamins, especially niacin. According to a forthcoming book, *Inside Scientology*, by the journalist Janet Reitman, the sauna sessions can last up to five hours a day. In the interview, Haggis recalled being skeptical—"My idea of doing good for my body was smoking low-tar cigarettes"—but said that the Purification Rundown "was WONDERFUL." He went on, "I really did feel more alert and more aware and more at ease—I wasn't running in six directions to get something done, or bouncing off the walls when something went wrong." Haggis mentioned that he had taken drugs when he was young. "Getting rid of all those residual toxins and medicines and drugs really had an effect," he said. "After completing the rundown I drank a diet cola and suddenly could really taste it: every single chemical!" He recommended the Rundown to others, including his mother, who at the time was seriously ill. He also persuaded a young writer on his staff to take the course, in order to wean herself from various medications. "She could tell Scientology worked by the example I set," Haggis told the magazine. "That made me feel very good."

Privately, he told me, he remained troubled by the church's theology, which struck him as "intergalactic spirituality." He was grateful, however, to have an auditor who was "really smart, sweet, thoughtful. I could always go to talk to him." The confessionals were helpful. "It just felt better to get things off my chest." Even after his incredulous reaction to O.T. III, he continued to "move up" the Bridge. He saw so many intelligent people on the path, and expected that his concerns would be addressed in future levels. He told himself, "Maybe there *is* something, and I'm just missing it." He felt unsettled by the lack of irony among many fellow Scientologists—an inability to laugh at themselves, which seemed at odds with the character of Hubbard himself. When Haggis felt doubts about the religion, he recalled sixteen-mm films he had seen of Hubbard's lectures from the fifties and sixties. "He had this amazing buoyancy," Haggis says. "He had a deadpan humor and this sense of himself that seemed to say, 'Yes, I am fully aware that I might be mad, but I also might be on to something.'"

Haggis finally reached the top of the Operating Thetan pyramid. According to documents obtained by WikiLeaks, the activist group run by Julian Assange, the final exercise is: "Go out to a park, train station or other busy area. Practice placing an intention into individuals until you can successfully and easily place an intention into or on a Being and/or a body."

Haggis expected that, as an O.T. VII, he would feel a sense of accomplishment, but he remained confused and unsatisfied. He thought that Hubbard was "brilliant in so many ways" and that the failing must be his. At one point, he confided to a minister in the church that he didn't think he should be a Scientologist. She told him, "There are all sorts of Scientologists," just as there are all sorts of Jews and Christians, with varying levels of faith. The implication, Haggis said, was that he could "pick and choose" which tenets of Scientology to believe.

Haggis was a workaholic, and as his career took off he spent less and less time with his family. "He never got home till late at night or early in the morning," his oldest daughter, Alissa, said. "All the time I ever spent with him was on the set." Haggis frequently brought his daughters to work and assigned them odd jobs; Alissa earned her Directors Guild card when she was fifteen.

In 1987, Ed Zwick and Marshall Herskovitz, the creators of the new series *thirtysomething*, hired Haggis to write scripts.

When I talked to them recently, Herskovitz recalled, "Paul walked in the door and said, 'I love the fact that you guys are doing a show all about emotions. I don't like talking about my emotions.'" In the show's first season, one of Haggis's scripts won an Emmy. Since he rarely discussed his religion, his bosses were surprised to learn of his affiliation. Herskovitz told me, "The thing about Paul is his particular sense of humor, which is ironic, self-deprecating—"

"And raw!" Zwick interjected.

"It's not a sense of humor you often encounter among people who believe in Scientology," Herskovitz continued. "His way of looking at life didn't have that sort of straight-on, unambiguous, unambivalent view that so many Scientologists project."

Observing Zwick and Herskovitz at work got Haggis interested in directing, and when the church asked him to make a thirty-second ad about Dianetics he seized the chance. He was determined to avoid the usual claim that Dianetics offered a triumphal march toward enlightenment. He shot a group of Scientologists talking about the practical ways that they had used Dianetics. "It was very naturalistic," he recalls. Church authorities hated it. "They thought it looked like an AA meeting." The spot never aired.

In 1992, he helped out on the pilot for *Walker, Texas Ranger*, a new series starring Chuck Norris. It ran for eight seasons and was broadcast in a hundred countries. Haggis was credited as a cocreator. "It was the most successful thing I ever did," he says. "Two weeks of work. They never even used my script!"

With his growing accomplishments and wealth, Haggis became a bigger prize for the church. In 1988, Scientology sponsored a Dianetics car in the Indianapolis 500. David Miscavige was at the race. It was one of the few times that he and Haggis met. They sat near each other at a Scientology-sponsored dinner event before the race. "Paul takes no shit from anybody," the organizer of the event recalled. Several times when Miscavige made some comment during the dinner, the organizer said, "Paul challenged him in a lighthearted way." His tone was perceived as insufficiently deferential; afterward, Miscavige demanded to know why Haggis had been invited. (Miscavige declined requests to speak to me, and Tommy Davis says that Miscavige did not attend the event.) The organizer told me, "You have to understand: no one challenges David Miscavige."

.   .   .

Haggis's marriage had long been troubled, and he and his wife were entering a final state of estrangement. One day, Haggis flew to New York with a casting director who was also a Scientologist. They shared a kiss. Haggis felt bad about it and confessed to it during an "ethics" session. He was given instruction on how to fix the problem. It didn't work. He had a series of liaisons, each of which he confessed. Yet, perhaps because of his fame, he was not made to atone for what Scientologists call "out ethics" behavior.

Haggis and Gettas began a divorce battle that lasted nine years. Their three girls lived with Gettas, visiting Haggis occasionally. Gettas enrolled them in private schools that used Hubbard's educational system, which is called Study Tech. It is one of the more grounded systems that he developed. There are three central elements. One is the use of clay, or other materials, to help make difficult concepts less abstract. Alissa explains, "If I'm learning the idea of how an atom looks, I'd make an atom out of clay." A second concept is making sure that students don't face "too steep a gradient," in Hubbard's words. "The schools are set up so that you don't go on to the next level until you *completely* understand the material," Alissa says. The third element is the frequent use of a dictionary to eliminate misunderstandings. "It's really important to understand the words you're using."

Lauren, the middle sister, initially struggled in school. "I was illiterate until I was eleven," she told me. Somehow, that fact escaped her parents. "I assume it was because of the divorce," she says.

When the divorce became final in 1997, Haggis and Gettas were ordered by the court to undergo psychological evaluations—a procedure abhorred by Scientologists. The court then determined that Haggis should have full custody of the children.

His daughters were resentful. They had lived their entire lives with their mother. "I didn't even know why he wanted us," Lauren says. "I didn't really know him."

Haggis put his daughters in an ordinary private school, but that lasted only six months. The girls weren't entirely comfortable talking to people who weren't Scientologists, and basic things like multiple-choice tests were unfamiliar. At a regular school, they felt like outsiders. "The first thing I noticed that I did, that others didn't, is the Contact," Alissa told me, referring to a procedure the church calls Contact Assist. "If you hurt yourself, the first thing I and other Scientology kids do is go quiet." Scientology preaches that, if you touch the wound to the object that caused the injury and silently concentrate, the pain lessens and a sense of trauma fades.

The girls demanded to be sent to boarding school, so Haggis enrolled them at the Delphian School, in rural Oregon, which uses Hubbard's Study Tech methods. The school, Lauren says, is "on top of a hill in the middle of nowhere." She added, "I lived in a giant bubble. Everyone I knew was a Scientologist."

For one course, she decided to write a paper about discrimination against various religions, including Scientology. "I wanted to see what the opposition was saying, so I went online," she says. Another student turned her in to the school's ethics committee. Information that doesn't correspond to Scientology teachings is termed "entheta"—meaning confused or destructive thinking. Lauren agreed to stop doing research. "It was really easy not to look," she says. By the time she graduated from high school, at the age of twenty, she had scarcely ever heard anyone speak ill of Scientology.

Alissa was a top student at Delphian, but she found herself moving away from the church. She still believed in some ideas promoted by Scientology, such as reincarnation, and she liked Hubbard's educational techniques, but by the time she graduated she no longer defined herself as a Scientologist. Her reasoning was true to Hubbard's philosophy. "A core concept in Scientology is: 'Something isn't true unless you find it true in your own life,'" she told me.

After starting boarding school, Alissa did not speak to her father for a number of years. She was angry about the divorce. Haggis mined the experience for the script of *Million Dollar Baby*, in which the lead character, played by Clint Eastwood, is haunted by his estrangement from his daughter.

"I'm very proud of Alissa for not talking to me," Haggis told me, his eyes welling with tears. "Think what that *takes*." It was the only time, in our many conversations, that he displayed such emotion.

Haggis and Alissa slowly resumed communication. When Alissa was in her early twenties, she accepted the fact that, like her sister Katy, she was gay. She recalls, "When I finally got the courage to come out to my dad, he said, 'Oh, yeah, I knew that.'" Now, Alissa says, she and Haggis have a "working relationship." As she puts it, "We do see each other for Thanksgiving and some meals." Recently, Alissa, who is also a writer, has been collaborating on screenplays with her father. Haggis also gave her the role of a murderous drug addict in *The Next Three Days*.

•   •   •

In 1991, as his marriage to Gettas was crumbling, Haggis went to a Fourth of July party at the home of Scientologist friends.

Deborah Rennard, who played J. R.'s alluring secretary on *Dallas*, was at the party. Rennard had grown up in a Scientology household and joined the church herself at the age of seventeen. In her early twenties, she studied acting at the Beverly Hills Playhouse and fell in love with Milton Katselas. They had recently broken up after a six-year romance.

"When I first met Paul, he said he was having a 'crisis of faith,'" Rennard told me. "He said he'd raced up to the top of the Bridge on faith, but he hadn't gotten what he expected." Haggis admitted to her, "I don't believe I'm a spiritual being. I actually am what you see." They became a couple and married in June 1997, immediately after Haggis's divorce from Gettas became final. A son, James, was born the following year.

Rennard, concerned about her husband's spiritual doubts, suggested that he do some more study. She was having breakthroughs that sometimes led her to discover past lives. "There were images, feelings, and thoughts that I suddenly realized, That's not here. I'm not in my body, I'm in another place," she told me. For instance, she might be examining what the church calls a "contra-survival" action—"like the time I clobbered Paul or threw something at him. And I'd look for an earlier similar. Suddenly, I'd realize I was doing something negative, and I'd be in England in the eighteen-hundreds. I'd see myself harming this person. It was a fleeting glimpse at what I was doing then." Examining these moments helped the emotional charge dissipate. "Paul would say, 'Don't you think you're making this up?'" She wondered if that mattered. "If it changed me for the better, who cares?" she says. "When you are working on a scene as an actor, something similar happens. You get connected to a feeling from who knows where."

Haggis and Rennard shared a house in Santa Monica, which soon became a hub for progressive political fund raisers. Haggis lent his name to nearly any cause that espoused peace and justice: the Earth Communications Office, the Hollywood Education and Literacy Project, the Center for the Advancement of Non-

Violence. Despite his growing disillusionment with Scientology, he also raised a significant amount of money for it and made sizable donations himself, appearing frequently on an honor roll of top contributors. The Church of Scientology had recently gained tax-exempt status as a religious institution, making donations, as well as the cost of auditing, tax-deductible. (Church members had lodged more than two thousand lawsuits against the Internal Revenue Service, ensnaring the agency in litigation. As part of the settlement, the church agreed to drop its legal campaign.)

Over the years, Haggis estimates, he spent more than a hundred thousand dollars on courses and auditing, and three hundred thousand dollars on various Scientology initiatives. Rennard says that she spent about a hundred and fifty thousand dollars on coursework. Haggis recalls that the demands for donations never seemed to stop. "They used friends and any kind of pressure they could apply," he says. "I gave them money just to keep them from calling and hounding me."

.   .   .

A decade ago, Haggis moved into feature films. He cowrote the scripts for the two most recent James Bond films, *Casino Royale* and *Quantum of Solace*. He claims that Scientology has not influenced his work—there are no evident references in his movies—but his scripts often do have an autobiographical element. "I'm not good at something unless it disturbs me," he said. In *Million Dollar Baby*, he wrote about a boxing coach who pulls the plug on a paralyzed fighter. Haggis made a similar choice in real life with his best friend, who was brain dead from a staph infection. "They don't die easily," he said. "Even in a coma, he kicked and moaned for twelve hours." Haggis likes to explore contradictions, making heroes into villains and vice versa, as with the racist cop in *Crash*, played by Matt Dillon, who molests a woman in one scene and saves her life in another. In *In the Valley of Elah*, Tommy

Lee Jones plays a father trying to discover who murdered his son, a heroic soldier just returned from Iraq, only to learn that the sadism of the war had turned his son into a willing torturer.

In 2004, Haggis was rewriting *Flags of Our Fathers*, a drama about Iwo Jima, for Clint Eastwood to direct. (Haggis shared credit with William Broyles Jr.) One day, Haggis and Eastwood visited the set of *War of the Worlds*, which Steven Spielberg was shooting with Tom Cruise. Haggis had met Cruise at a fund raiser and, a second time, at the Celebrity Centre. Cruise says that he was introduced to the church in 1986 by his first wife, the actress Mimi Rogers. (Rogers denies this.) In 1992, he became the religion's most famous member, telling Barbara Walters that Hubbard's Study Tech methods had helped him overcome dyslexia. "He's a major symbol of the church, and I think he takes that very seriously," Haggis said.

Tommy Davis, at Cruise's request, was allowed to erect a tent on the set of Spielberg's *War of the Worlds*, where Scientology materials were distributed. That raised eyebrows in Hollywood. Haggis says that when he appeared on the set Spielberg pulled him aside. "It's really remarkable to me that I've met all these Scientologists, and they seem like the nicest people," Spielberg said. Haggis replied, "Yeah, we keep all the evil ones in a closet." (Spielberg's publicist says that Spielberg doesn't recall the conversation.)

A few days later, Haggis says, he was summoned to the Celebrity Centre, where officials told him that Cruise was very upset. "It was a joke," Haggis explained. Davis offers a different account. He says that Cruise mentioned the incident to him only "in passing," but that he himself found the remark offensive. He confronted Haggis, who apologized profusely, asking that his contrition be relayed to "anyone who might have been offended."

Davis has known Cruise since Davis was eighteen years old. They are close friends. The two men physically resemble each other, with long faces, strong jaws, and spiky haircuts. "I saw him hanging out with Tom Cruise after the Oscars," Haggis recalls. "At the *Vanity Fair* party, they were let in the back door. They arrived on motorcycles, really cool ones, like Ducatis." Cruise was also close to David Miscavige and has said of him, "I have never met a more competent, a more intelligent, a more tolerant, a more compassionate being outside of what I have experienced from L.R.H. And I've met the leaders of leaders."

In 2004, Cruise received a special Scientology award: the Freedom Medal of Valor. In a ceremony held in England, Miscavige called Cruise "the most dedicated Scientologist I know." The ceremony was accompanied by a video interview with the star. Wearing a black turtleneck, and with the theme music from *Mission: Impossible* playing in the background, Cruise said, "Being a Scientologist, you look at someone and you know absolutely that you can help them. So, for me, it really is K.S.W."— initials that stand for "Keeping Scientology Working." He went on, "That policy to me has really gone—*phist!*" He made a vigorous gesture with his hand. "Boy! There's a time I went through and I said, 'You know what? When I read it, you know, I just went *poo!* This is it!'" Later, when the video was posted on YouTube and viewed by millions who had no idea what he was talking about, Cruise came across as unhinged. He did not dispel this notion when, in 2005, during an interview with Oprah Winfrey, he jumped up and down on a couch while declaring his love for the actress Katie Holmes. He and Holmes married in 2006, in Italy. David Miscavige was his best man.

•   •   •

Proposition 8, the California initiative against gay marriage, passed in November 2008. Haggis learned from his daughter Lauren of the San Diego chapter's endorsement of it. He immediately sent Davis several e-mails, demanding that the church take a public stand opposing the ban on gay marriage. "I am going to an anti Prop 8 rally in a couple of hours," he wrote on November 11, after the election. "When can we expect the public statement?" In a response, Davis proposed sending a letter to the San Diego press, saying that the church had been "erroneously listed among the supporters of Proposition 8."

" 'Erroneous' doesn't cut it," Haggis responded. In another note, he remarked, "The church may have had the luxury of not taking a position on this issue before, but after taking a position, even erroneously, it can no longer stand neutral." He demanded that the church openly declare that it supports gay rights. "Anything less won't do."

Davis explained to Haggis that the church avoids taking overt political stands. He also felt that Haggis was exaggerating the impact of the San Diego endorsement. "It was *one* guy who somehow got it in his head it would be a neat idea and put Church of Scientology San Diego on the list," Davis told me. "When I found out, I had it removed from the list." Davis said that the individual who made the mistake—he didn't divulge the name—had been "disciplined" for it. I asked what that meant. "He was sat down by a staff member of the local organization," Davis explained. "He got sorted out."

Davis told me that Haggis was mistaken about his daughter having been ostracized by Scientologists. Davis said that he had spoken to the friend who had allegedly abandoned Katy, and the friend had ended the relationship not because Katy was a lesbian but because Katy had lied about it. (Haggis, when informed of this account, laughed.)

As far as Davis was concerned, reprimanding the San Diego staff member was the end of the matter: "I said, 'Paul, I've received no press inquiries. . . . If I were to make a statement on this, it would actually be *more* attention to the subject than if we leave it be.' "

Haggis refused to let the matter drop. "This is not a P.R. issue, it is a moral issue," he wrote in February 2009. In the final note of this exchange, he conceded, "You were right: nothing happened—it didn't flap—at least not very much. But I feel we shamed ourselves."

Haggis sent this note six months before he resigned. Because he stopped complaining, Davis felt that the issue had been laid to rest. But far from putting the matter behind him, Haggis began his investigation into the church. His inquiry, much of it conducted online, mirrored the actions of the lead character he was writing for *The Next Three Days*; the character, played by Russell Crowe, goes on the Internet to find a way to break his wife out of jail.

Haggis soon found on YouTube the video of Tommy Davis talking on CNN about disconnection. The practice of disconnection is not unique to Scientology. The Amish, for example, cut themselves off from apostates, including their own children; some Orthodox Jewish communities do the same. Rennard had disconnected from her parents twice. When she was a young child, her stepfather had got the family involved with Scientology. When she was in her twenties, and appearing on *Dallas*, her parents broke away from the church. Like many active members of Scientology, they had kept money in an account (in their case, twenty-five hundred dollars) for future courses they intended to take. Rennard's mother took the money back. "That's a huge deal for the church," Rennard told me. She didn't speak to her parents for several years, assuming that they had been declared Suppressive Persons.

In the early nineties, Rennard wrote to the International Justice Chief, the Scientology official in charge of such matters; she was informed that she could talk to her parents again. A decade later, however, she went to Clearwater, intending to take some upper-level courses, and was told that the previous ruling no longer applied. If she wanted to do more training, she had to confront her parents' mistakes. The church recommended that she take a course called P.T.S./S.P., which stands for "Potential Trouble Source/Suppressive Persons." "That course took a year,"

Rennard told me. She petitioned officials at the Celebrity Centre in Los Angeles for help. "They put me on a program that took two years to complete," she says. Still, nothing changed. If she failed to "handle" her parents, she would have to disconnect not only from them but also from everyone who spoke to them, including her siblings. "It was that, or else I had to give up being a Scientologist," she says.

Rennard's parents were among four hundred claimants in a lawsuit brought against Scientology by disaffected members in 1987; the case was thrown out of court the following year for lack of evidence. To make amends, Rennard's parents had to denounce the anti-Scientologist group and offer a "token" restitution. The church prescribes a seven-step course of rehabilitation, called A to E, for penitents seeking to get back into its good graces, which includes returning debts and making public declarations of error. Rennard told her parents that if they wanted to remain in contact with her they had to follow the church's procedures. Her parents, worried that they would also be cut off from their grandson, agreed to perform community service. "They really wanted to work it out with me," she says.

But the church wasn't satisfied. Rennard was told that if she maintained contact with her parents she would be labeled a "Potential Trouble Source"—a designation that would alienate her from the Scientology community and render her ineligible for further training. "It was clearly laid out for me," she says. A senior official counseled her to agree to have her parents formally branded as S.P.s. "Until then, they won't turn around and recognize their responsibilities," he said. "OK, fine," Rennard said. "Go ahead and declare them. Maybe it'll get better." She was granted permission to begin upper-level coursework in Clearwater.

In August 2006, a notice was posted at the Celebrity Centre declaring Rennard's parents Suppressive Persons, saying that they had associated with "squirrels," which in Scientology refers to people who have dropped out of the church but continue to practice unauthorized auditing. A month later, Rennard's parents sent her a letter: "We tried to do what you asked, Deborah. We worked the whole months of July & Aug. on A-E." They explained that they had paid the church the twenty-five hundred dollars. After all that, they continued, a church adjudicator had told them to hand out three hundred copies of L. Ron Hubbard's pamphlet "The Way to Happiness" to libraries; they had also been told to document the exchange with photographs. They had declined. "If this can't be resolved, we will have to say Good-Bye to you & James will lose his Grand-Parents," her mother wrote. "This is ridiculous."

In April 2007, Rennard's parents sued for the right to visit their grandson. Rennard had to hire an attorney. Eventually, the church relented. She was summoned to a church mission in Santa Monica and shown a statement rescinding the ruling that her parents were S.P.s.

Tommy Davis sent me some policy statements that Hubbard had made about disconnection in 1965. "Anyone who rejects Scientology also rejects, knowingly or unknowingly, the protection and benefits of Scientology and the companionship of Scientologists," Hubbard writes. In *Introduction to Scientology Ethics*, Hubbard defined disconnection as "a self-determined decision made by an individual that he is not going to be connected to another."

Scientology defectors are full of tales of forcible family separations, which the church almost uniformly denies. Two former leaders in the church, Marty Rathbun and Mike Rinder, told me that families are sometimes broken apart. In their cases, their wives chose to stay in the church when they left. The wives, and the church, denounce Rathbun and Rinder as liars.

.   .   .

A few days after sending the resignation letter to Tommy Davis, Haggis came home from work to find nine or ten of his Scientology friends standing in his front yard. He invited them in to talk. Anne Archer was there with Terry Jastrow, her husband, an actor turned producer and director. "Paul had been such an ally," Archer told me. "It was pretty painful. Everyone wanted to see if there could be some kind of resolution." Mark Isham, an Emmy-winning composer who has scored films for Haggis, came with his wife, Donna. Sky Dayton, the EarthLink founder, was there, along with several other friends and a church representative Haggis didn't know. His friends could have served as an advertisement for Scientology—they were wealthy high achievers with solid marriages who embraced the idea that the church had given them a sense of well-being and the skills to excel.

Scientologists are trained to believe in their persuasive powers and the need to keep a positive frame of mind. But the mood in the room was downbeat and his friends' questions were full of reproach.

Jastrow asked Haggis, "Do you have any idea that what you might do might damage a lot of pretty wonderful people and your fellow Scientologists?"

Haggis reminded the group that he had been with them at the 1985 "freedom march" in Portland. They all knew about his financial support of the church and the occasions when he had spoken out in its defense. Jastrow remembers Haggis saying, "I love Scientology."

Archer had particular reason to feel aggrieved: Haggis's letter had called her son a liar. "Paul was very sweet," she says. "We didn't talk about Tommy." She understood that Haggis was upset about the way Proposition 8 had affected his gay daughters, but she didn't think it was relevant to Scientology. "The church is not political," she told me. "We all have tons of friends and relatives who are gay. . . . It's not the church's issue. I've introduced gay friends to Scientology."

Isham was frustrated. "We weren't breaking through to him," he told me. Of all the friends present, Isham was the closest to

Haggis. "We share a common artistic sensibility," Isham said. When he visited Abbey Road Studios, in England, to record the score that he had written for *In the Valley of Elah*, Haggis went along with him. Haggis wanted him to compose the score for *The Next Three Days*. Now their friendship was at risk. Isham used Scientology to analyze the situation. In his view, Haggis's emotions at that moment ranked 1.1 on the Tone Scale—the state that is sometimes called Covertly Hostile. By adopting a tone just above it—Anger—Isham hoped to blast Haggis out of the psychic place where he seemed to be lodged. "This was an intellectual decision," Isham said. "I decided I would be angry."

"Paul, I'm pissed off," Isham told Haggis. "There's better ways to do this. If you have a complaint, there's a complaint line." Anyone who genuinely wanted to change Scientology should stay within the organization, Isham argued, not quit; certainly, going public was not helpful.

Haggis listened patiently. A fundamental tenet of Scientology is that differing points of view must be fully heard and acknowledged. When his friends finished, however, Haggis had his own set of grievances.

He referred them to the exposé in the *St. Petersburg Times* that had so shaken him: "The Truth Rundown." The first installment had appeared in June 2009. Haggis had learned from reading it that several of the church's top managers had defected in despair. Marty Rathbun had once been inspector general of the church's Religious Technology Center, which holds the trademarks of Scientology and Dianetics and exists to "protect the public from misapplication of the technology." Rathbun had also overseen Scientology's legal-defense strategy and reported directly to Miscavige. Amy Scobee had been an executive in the Celebrity Centre network. Mike Rinder had been the church's spokesperson, the job now held by Tommy Davis. One by one, they had disappeared from Scientology, and it had never occurred to Haggis to ask where they had gone.

The defectors told the newspaper that Miscavige was a serial abuser of his staff. "The issue wasn't the physical pain of it," Rinder said. "It's the fact that the domination you're getting—hit in the face, kicked—and you can't do anything about it. If you did try, you'd be attacking the COB"—the chairman of the board. Tom De Vocht, a defector who had been a manager at the Clearwater spiritual center, told the paper that he, too, had been beaten by Miscavige; he said that from 2003 to 2005 he had witnessed Miscavige striking other staff members as many as a hundred times. Rathbun, Rinder, and De Vocht all admitted that they had engaged in physical violence themselves. "It had become the accepted way of doing things," Rinder said. Amy Scobee said that nobody challenged the abuse because people were terrified of Miscavige. Their greatest fear was expulsion: "You don't have any money. You don't have job experience. You don't have anything. And he could put you on the streets and ruin you."

Assessing the truthfulness of such inflammatory statements—made by people who deserted the church or were expelled—was a challenge for the newspaper, which has maintained a special focus on Scientology. (Clearwater is twenty miles northwest of downtown St. Petersburg.) In 1998, six years before he defected, Rathbun told the paper that he had never seen Miscavige hit anyone. Now he said, "That was the biggest lie I ever told you." The reporters behind "The Truth Rundown," Joe Childs and Thomas Tobin, interviewed each defector separately and videotaped many of the sessions. "It added a measure of confidence," Childs told me. "Their stories just tracked."

Much of the alleged abuse took place at the Gold Base, a Scientology outpost in the desert near Hemet, a town eighty miles southeast of Los Angeles. Miscavige has an office there, and the site features, among other things, movie studios and production facilities for the church's many publications. For decades, the base's location was unknown even to many church insiders. Haggis visited the Gold Base only once, in the early eighties, when he was about to direct his Scientology commercial. The landscape, he said, suggested a spa, "beautiful and restful," but he found the atmosphere sterile and scary. Surrounded by a security fence, the base houses about eight hundred Sea Org members, in quarters that the church likens to those "in a convent or seminary, albeit much more comfortable."

According to a court declaration filed by Rathbun in July, Miscavige expected Scientology leaders to instill aggressive, even violent discipline. Rathbun said that he was resistant and that Miscavige grew frustrated with him, assigning him in 2004 to the Hole—a pair of double-wide trailers at the Gold Base. "There were between eighty and a hundred people sentenced to the Hole at that time," Rathbun said, in the declaration. "We were required to do group confessions all day and all night."

The church claims that such stories are false: "There is not, and never has been, any place of 'confinement' . . . nor is there anything in Church policy that would allow such confinement."

According to Rathbun, Miscavige came to the Hole one evening and announced that everyone was going to play musical chairs. Only the last person standing would be allowed to stay on the base. He declared that people whose spouses "were not participants would have their marriages terminated." The *St. Petersburg Times* noted that Miscavige played Queen's "Bohemian Rhapsody" on a boom box as the church leaders fought over the chairs, punching each other and, in one case, ripping a chair apart.

Tom De Vocht, one of the participants, says that the event lasted until four in the morning: "It got more and more physical as the number of chairs went down." Many of the participants had long been cut off from their families. They had no money, no credit cards, no telephones. According to De Vocht, many lacked a driver's license or a passport. Few had any savings or employment prospects. As people fell out of the game, Miscavige had airplane reservations made for them. He said that buses were going to be leaving at six in the morning. The powerlessness of everyone else in the room was nakedly clear.

Tommy Davis told me that a musical-chairs episode did occur. He explained that Miscavige had been away from the Gold Base for some time, and when he returned he discovered that in his absence many jobs had been reassigned. The game was meant to demonstrate that even seemingly small changes can be disruptive to an organization—underscoring an "administrative policy of the church." The rest of the defectors' accounts, Davis told me, was "hoo-ha": "Chairs being ripped apart, and people being threatened that they're going to be sent to far-flung places in the world, plane tickets being purchased, and they're going to force their spouses—and on and on and on. I mean, it's just nuts!"

Jefferson Hawkins, a former Sea Org member and church executive who worked with Haggis on the rejected Dianetics ad campaign, told me that Miscavige had struck or beaten him on five occasions, the first time in 2002. "I had just written an infomercial," he said. Miscavige summoned him to a meeting where a few dozen members were seated on one side of a table; Miscavige sat by himself on the other side. According to Hawkins, Miscavige began a tirade about the ad's shortcomings. Hawkins recalls, "Without any warning, he jumped up onto the conference-room table and he launches himself at me. He knocks me back against a cubicle wall and starts battering my face." The two men fell to the floor, Hawkins says, and their legs became entangled. "Let go of my legs!" Miscavige shouted. According to Hawkins, Miscavige then "stomped out of the room," leaving Hawkins on the floor, shocked and bruised. The others did nothing to support him, he claims: "They were saying, 'Get up! Get up!'"

I asked Hawkins why he hadn't called the police. He reminded me that church members believe that Scientology holds the key to salvation: "Only by going through Scientology will you reach spiritual immortality. You can go from life to life to life without being cognizant of what is going on. If you don't go through Scientology, you're condemned to dying over and over again in ignorance and darkness, never knowing your true nature as a spirit. Nobody who is a believer wants to lose that." Miscavige, Hawkins says, "holds the power of eternal life and death over you."

Moreover, Scientologists are taught to handle internal conflicts within the church's own justice system. Hawkins told me that if a Sea Org member sought outside help he would be punished, either by being declared a Suppressive Person or by being sent off to do manual labor, as Hawkins was made to do after Miscavige beat him. The church denies that Hawkins was mistreated and notes that he has participated in protests organized by Anonymous, a "hacktivist" collective that has targeted Scientology. The group pugnaciously opposes censorship and became hostile toward Scientology after the church invoked copyright claims in order to remove from the Internet the video of Tom Cruise extolling "K.S.W." The church describes Anonymous as a "cyber-terrorist group"; last month, the FBI raided the homes of three dozen members after Anonymous attacked the websites of corporations critical of WikiLeaks. (Two members of Anonymous have pleaded guilty to participating in a 2008 attack on a Scientology website.)

The church provided me with eleven statements from Scientologists, all of whom said that Miscavige had never been violent. One of them, Yael Lustgarten, said that she was present at the meeting with Hawkins and that the attack by Miscavige never happened. She claims that Hawkins made a mess of his presentation—"He smelled of body odor, he was unshaven, his voice tone was very low, and he could hardly be heard"—and was admonished to shape up. She says that Hawkins "wasn't hit by anyone." The defector Amy Scobee, however, says that she witnessed the attack—the two men had fallen into her cubicle. After the altercation, she says, "I gathered all the buttons from Jeff's shirt and the change from his pockets and gave them back to him."

The church characterizes Scobee, Rinder, Rathbun, Hawkins, De Vocht, Hines, and other defectors I spoke with as "discredited individuals," who were demoted for incompetence or expelled for corruption; the defectors' accounts are consistent only because they have "banded together to advance and support each other's false 'stories.'"

After reading the *St. Petersburg Times* series, Haggis tracked down Marty Rathbun, who was living on Corpus Christi Bay, in south Texas. Rathbun had been making ends meet by writing freelance articles for local newspapers and selling beer at a ballpark.

Haggis complained that Davis hadn't been honest with him about Scientology's policies. "I said, 'That's not Tommy, he has no say,'" Rathbun told me. "Miscavige is a total micromanager. I explained the whole culture." He says that Haggis was shocked by the conversation. "The thing that was most troubling to Paul was that I literally had to escape," Rathbun told me. (A few nights after the musical-chairs incident, he got on his motorcycle and waited until a gate was opened for someone else; he sped out and didn't stop for thirty miles.) Haggis called several other former Scientologists he knew well. One of them said that he had escaped from the Gold Base by driving his car—an Alfa Romeo convertible that Haggis had sold him—through a wooden fence. The defector said that he had scars on his forehead from the incident. Still others had been expelled or declared Suppressive Persons. Haggis asked himself, "What kind of organization are we involved in where people just disappear?"

•   •   •

When Haggis began casting for *The Next Three Days*, in the summer of 2009, he asked Jason Beghe to read for the part of a cop. Beghe was a gravel-voiced character actor who had played Demi Moore's love interest in *G.I. Jane*. In the late nineties, Haggis had worked with Beghe on a CBS series, *Family Law*. Like so many others, Beghe had come to the church through the Beverly Hills Playhouse. In old promotional materials for the church, he is quoted as saying that Scientology is "a rocket ride to spiritual freedom."

Beghe told Haggis, "You should know that I'm no longer in Scientology. Actually, I'm one of its most outspoken critics. The church would be very unhappy if you hire me."

Haggis responded, "Nobody tells me who I cast." He looked at a lengthy video that Beghe had posted on the Internet, in which he denounces the church as "destructive and a ripoff." Haggis thought that Beghe had "gone over the edge." But he asked if they could talk.

The two men met at Patrick's Roadhouse, a coffee shop on the beach in Pacific Palisades. Beghe was calmer than he had been in the video, which he called "a snapshot of me having been out only three months." Even though Beghe had renounced the church, he continued to use Scientology methods when dealing with members and former members. "It's almost like: 'I can speak Chinese, I understand the culture,'" he explained to me. In several meetings with Haggis, he employed techniques based on what Hubbard labeled "Ethics Conditions." These range from Confusion at the bottom and ascend through Treason, Enemy, Doubt, Liability, and Emergency, eventually leading to Power. "Each one of the conditions has a specific set of steps in a formula, and, once that formula is applied correctly, you will move up to the next-highest condition," Beghe explained. "I assumed that Paul was in a condition of Doubt."

Beghe joined Scientology in 1994. He told Haggis that, in the late nineties, he began having emotional problems, and the church recommended auditing and coursework. In retrospect, he felt that it had done no good. "I was paying money for them to fuck me up," he said. "I spent about five or six hundred thousand dollars trying to get better, and I continued to get worse." He says that when he finally decided to leave the church, in 2007, he told an official that the church was in a condition of Liability to him. Ordinarily, when a Scientologist does something wrong, especially something that might damage the image of the organization, he has to make amends, often in the form of a substantial contribution. But now the situation was reversed. Beghe recalls telling the official, "You guys don't have any policies to make up the damage." He eventually suggested to the official that the church buy property and lease it to him at a negligible rate; the church now characterizes this as an attempt at extortion.

Beghe was reluctant to use the word "brainwashing"— "whatever the fuck that is"—but he did feel that his mind had been somehow taken over. "You have all these thoughts, all these ways of looking at things, that are L. Ron Hubbard's," he explained. "You think you're becoming more you, but within that is an implanted thing, which is You the Scientologist."

Perhaps because Haggis had never been as much of a true believer as some members, he didn't feel as deeply betrayed as Beghe did. "I didn't feel that some worm had buried itself in my ear, and if you plucked it out you would find L. Ron Hubbard and his thought," he told me. But as he continued his investigation, he became increasingly disturbed. He read the church's official rebuttal to the *St. Petersburg Times* series in the Scientology magazine *Freedom*. It included an annotated transcript of conversations that had taken place between the reporters and representatives of the church, including Tommy Davis and his wife, Jessica Feshbach. In *Freedom*'s rendition of those conversations, the reporters' sources were not named, perhaps to shield Scientologists from the shock of seeing familiar names publicly denouncing the organization. Rathbun was called "Kingpin" and Scobee "the Adulteress."

At one point in the transcribed conversations, Davis reminded the reporters that Scobee had been expelled from the church leadership because of an affair. The reporters responded that she had denied having sexual contact outside her marriage. "That's a lie," Davis told them. Feshbach, who had a stack of documents, elaborated: "She has a written admission [of] each one of her instances of extramarital indiscretion. . . . I believe there were five." When Haggis read this in *Freedom*, he presumed that the church had obtained its information from the declarations that members sometimes provide after auditing. Such confessions are supposed to be confidential. (Scientology denies that it obtained the information this way, and Davis produced an affidavit, signed by Scobee, in which she admits to having liaisons. Scobee denies committing adultery, and says that she did not write the affidavit; she says that she signed it in the hope of leaving the church on good terms, so that she could stay in touch with relatives.)

In his letter to Davis, Haggis said that he was worried that the church might look through his files to smear him, too. "Luckily, I have never held myself up to be anyone's role model," he wrote.

At his house, Haggis finished telling his friends what he had learned. He suggested that they should at least examine the evidence. "I directed them to certain websites," he said, mentioning Exscientologykids.com, which was created by three young women who grew up in Scientology and subsequently left. Many stories on the site are from men and women who joined the Sea Org before turning eighteen. One of them was Jenna Miscavige Hill, David Miscavige's niece, who joined when she was twelve. For Hill and many others, formal education had stopped when they entered the Sea Org, leaving them especially ill prepared, they say, for coping with life outside the church.

The stories Haggis found on the Internet of children drafted into the Sea Org appalled him. "They were ten years old, twelve years old, signing billion-year contracts—and their parents go along with this?" Haggis told me. "Scrubbing pots, manual labor—that so deeply touched me. My God, it horrified me!" The stories of the Sea Org children reminded Haggis of child slaves he had seen in Haiti.

Many Sea Org volunteers find themselves with no viable options for adulthood. If they try to leave, the church presents them with a "freeloader tab" for all the coursework and counseling they have received; the bill can amount to more than a hundred thousand dollars. Payment is required in order to leave in good standing. "Many of them actually pay it," Haggis said. "They leave, they're ashamed of what they've done, they've got no money, no job history, they're lost, they just disappear." In what seemed like a very unguarded comment, he said, "I would gladly take down the church for that one thing."

The church says that it adheres to "all child labor laws," and that minors can't sign up without parental consent; the freeloader tabs are an "ecclesiastical matter" and are not enforced through litigation.

Haggis's friends came away from the meeting with mixed feelings. "We all left no clearer than when we went in," Archer said. Isham felt that there was still a possibility of getting Haggis "to behave himself." He said that Haggis had agreed that "it wasn't helping anyone" to continue distributing the letter and had promised not to circulate it further. Unmentioned was the fact that this would be the last time most of them ever spoke to Haggis.

I asked Isham if he had taken Haggis's advice and looked at the websites or the articles in the *St. Petersburg Times*. "I started to," he said. "But it was like reading *Mein Kampf* if you wanted to know something about the Jewish religion."

In the days after the friends visited Haggis's home, church officials and members came to his office, distracting his colleagues, particularly his producing partner, Michael Nozik, who is not a Scientologist. "Every day, for hours, he would have conversations with them," Nozik told me. It was August 2009, and shooting for *The Next Three Days* was set to start in Pittsburgh at the end of the month; the office desperately needed Haggis's attention. "But he felt a need to go through the process fully," Nozik says. "He wanted to give them a full hearing."

"I listened to their point of view, but I didn't change my mind," Haggis says, noting that the Scientology officials "became more livid and irrational." He added, "I applied more Scientology in those meetings than they did."

Davis and other church officials told Haggis that Miscavige had not beaten his employees; his accusers, they said, had committed the violence. Supposing that was true, Haggis said, why hadn't Miscavige stopped it? Haggis recalls that, at one meeting, he told Davis and five other officials, "If someone in my organization is beating people, I would sure know about it. You think I would put up with it? And I'm not that good a person." Haggis noted that, if the rumors of Miscavige's violent temper were true, it proved that everyone is fallible. "Look at Martin Luther King Jr.," he said, alluding to King's sexual improprieties.

"How dare you compare Dave Miscavige with Martin Luther King!" one of the officials shouted. Haggis was shocked. "They thought that comparing Miscavige to Martin Luther King was debasing his character," he says. "If they were trying to convince me that Scientology was not a cult, they did a very poor job of it." (Davis says that King's name never came up.)

In October 2009, Marty Rathbun called Haggis and asked if he could publish the resignation letter on his blog. Rathbun had become an informal spokesperson for defectors who believed that the church had broken away from Hubbard's original teachings. Haggis was in Pittsburgh, shooting his picture. "You're a journalist, you don't need my permission," Haggis said, although he asked Rathbun to excise parts related to Katy's homosexuality.

Haggis says that he didn't think about the consequences of his decision: "I thought it would show up on a couple of websites. I'm a writer, I'm not Lindsay Lohan." Rathbun got fifty-five thousand hits on his blog that afternoon. The next morning, the story was in newspapers around the world.

•   •   •

At the time Haggis was doing his research, the FBI was conducting its own investigation. In December 2009, Tricia Whitehill, a special agent from the Los Angeles office, flew to Florida to interview former members of the church in the FBI's office in downtown Clearwater, which happens to be directly across the street from Scientology's spiritual headquarters. Tom De Vocht, who spoke with Whitehill, told me, "I understood that the investigation had been going on for quite a while." He says Whitehill confided that she hadn't told the local agents what the investigation was about, in case the office had been infiltrated. Amy Scobee spoke to the FBI for two days. "They wanted a full download about the abuse," she told me.

Whitehill and Valerie Venegas, the lead agent on the case, also interviewed former Sea Org members in California. One of them was Gary Morehead, who had been the head of security at the Gold Base; he left the church in 1996. In February 2010, he spoke to Whitehill and told her that he had developed a "blow drill" to track down Sea Org members who left Gold Base. "We got wickedly good at it," he says. In thirteen years, he estimates, he and his security team brought more than a hundred Sea Org members back to the base. When emotional, spiritual, or psychological pressure failed to work, Morehead says, physical force was sometimes used to bring escapees back. (The church says that blow drills do not exist.)

Whitehill and Venegas worked on a special task force devoted to human trafficking. The laws regarding trafficking were built largely around forced prostitution, but they also pertain to slave labor. Under federal law, slavery is defined, in part, by the use of coercion, torture, starvation, imprisonment, threats, and psychological abuse. The California penal code lists several indicators that someone may be a victim of human trafficking: signs of trauma or fatigue; being afraid or unable to talk because of censorship by others or security measures that prevent communication with others; working in one place without the freedom to move about; owing a debt to one's employer; and not having control over identification documents. Those conditions echo the testimony of many former Sea Org members who lived at the Gold Base.

Sea Org members who have "failed to fulfill their ecclesiastical responsibilities" may be sent to one of the church's several Rehabilitation Project Force locations. Defectors describe them as punitive reeducation camps. In California, there is one in Los Angeles; until 2005, there was one near the Gold Base, at a place called Happy Valley. Bruce Hines, the defector turned research physicist, says that he was confined to RPF for six years, first in L.A., then in Happy Valley. He recalls that the properties were heavily guarded and that anyone who tried to flee would be tracked down and subjected to further punishment. "In 1995, when I was put in RPF, there were twelve of us," Hines said. "At the high point, in 2000, there were about a hundred and twenty of us." Some members have been in RPF for more than a decade, doing manual labor and extensive spiritual work. (Davis says that Sea Org members enter RPF by their own choosing and can leave at any time; the manual labor maintains church facilities and instills "pride of accomplishment.")

In 2009, two former Sea Org members, Claire and Marc Headley, filed lawsuits against the church. They had both joined as children. Claire became a member of the Sea Org at the age of sixteen, and was assigned to the Gold Base. She says she wasn't allowed to tell anyone where she was going, not even her mother, who was made to sign over guardianship. (Claire's mother, who is still in the church, has issued a sworn statement denying that she lost contact with her daughter.) The security apparatus at the Gold Base intimidated Claire. "Even though I had been in Scientology pretty much all my life, this was a whole new world," she told me. She says she was rarely allowed even a telephone call to her mother. "Every last trace of my life, as I knew it, was thrown away," she said. "It was like living in George Orwell's *1984*."

Claire met Marc Headley, also a teenager, soon after her arrival. "We had no ties to anyone not in Scientology," Claire said. "It was a very closeted and controlled existence." Marc says it was widely known around the base that he was one of the first people Tom Cruise audited. In Scientology, the auditor bears a significant responsibility for the progress of his subject. "If you audit somebody and that person leaves the organization, there's only one person whose fault that is—the auditor," Headley told me. (Cruise's attorney says that Cruise doesn't recall meeting Marc.) Claire and Marc fell in love, and married in 1992. She says that she was pressured by the church to have two abortions because of a stipulation that Sea Org members can't have children. The church denies that it pressures members to terminate pregnancies. Lucy James, a former Scientologist who had access to Sea Org personnel records, says that she knows of dozens of cases in which members were pressed to have abortions.

In 2005, Marc Headley says, he was punched by Miscavige during an argument. He and his wife quit. (The church calls Marc Headley dishonest, claiming that he kept seven hundred dollars in profits after being authorized to sell Scientology camera equipment; Headley says that shipping costs and other expenses account for the discrepancy.) In 2009, the Headleys filed their suits, which maintained that the working conditions at the Gold Base violated labor and human-trafficking laws. The church responded that the Headleys were ministers who had voluntarily submitted to the rigors of their calling and that the First Amendment protected Scientology's religious practices. The court agreed with this argument and dismissed the Headleys' complaints, awarding the church forty thousand dollars in litigation costs. The court also indicated that the Headleys were technically free to leave the Gold Base. The Headleys have appealed the rulings.

Defectors also talked to the FBI about Miscavige's luxurious lifestyle. The law prohibits the head of a tax-exempt organization from enjoying unusual perks or compensation; it's called inurement. Tommy Davis refused to disclose how much money Miscavige earns, and the church isn't required to do so, but Headley and other defectors suggest that Miscavige lives more like a Hollywood star than like the head of a religious organization—flying on chartered jets and wearing shoes custom-made in London. Claire Headley says that when she was in Scientology, Miscavige had five stewards and two chefs at his disposal; he also had a large car collection, including a Saleen Mustang, similar to one owned by Cruise, and six motorcycles. (The church denies this characterization and "vigorously objects to the suggestion that Church funds inure to the private benefit of Mr. Miscavige.")

Former Sea Org members report that Miscavige receives elaborate birthday and Christmas gifts from Scientology groups around the world. One year, he was given a Vyrus 985 C3 4V, a motorcycle with a retail price of seventy thousand dollars. "These gifts are tokens of love and respect for Mr. Miscavige," Davis informed me.

By contrast, Sea Org members typically receive fifty dollars a week. Often, this stipend is docked for small infractions, such as failing to meet production quotas or skipping scripture-study sessions. According to Janela Webster, who was in the Sea Org for nineteen years before defecting in 2006, it wasn't unusual for a member to be paid as little as thirteen dollars a week.

I recently spoke with two sources in the FBI who are close to the investigation. They assured me that the case remains open.

•   •   •

Last April, John Brousseau, who had been in the Sea Org for more than thirty years, left the Gold Base. He was unhappy with Miscavige, his former brother-in-law, whom he considered "detrimental to the goals of Scientology." He drove across the country, to south Texas, to meet Marty Rathbun. "I was there a couple of nights," he says. At five-thirty one morning, he was leaving the motel room where he was staying, to get coffee, when he heard footsteps behind him. It was Tommy Davis; he and nineteen church members had tracked Brousseau down. Brousseau locked himself in his room and called Rathbun, who alerted the police; Davis went home without Brousseau.

In a deposition given in July, Davis said no when asked if he had ever "followed a Sea Organization member that has blown"— fled the church. Under further questioning, he admitted that he and an entourage had flown to Texas in a jet chartered by Scientology and had shown up outside Brousseau's motel room at dawn. But he insisted that he was only trying "to see a friend of mine." Davis now calls Brousseau "a liar."

Brousseau says that his defection caused anxiety, in part because he had worked on a series of special projects for Tom Cruise. Brousseau maintained grounds and buildings at the Gold Base. He worked for fourteen months on the renovation of the *Freewinds*, the only ship left in Scientology's fleet; he also says that he installed bars over the doors of the Hole, at the Gold Base, shortly after Rathbun escaped. (The church denies this.)

In 2005, Miscavige showed Cruise a Harley-Davidson motorcycle he owned. At Miscavige's request, Brousseau had had the vehicle's parts plated with brushed nickel and painted candy-apple red. Brousseau recalls, "Cruise asked me, 'God, could you paint my bike like that?' I looked at Miscavige, and Miscavige agreed." Cruise brought in two motorcycles to be painted, a Triumph and a Honda Rune; the Honda had been given to him by Spielberg after the filming of *War of the Worlds*. "The Honda already had a custom paint job by the set designer," Brousseau recalls. Each motorcycle had to be taken apart completely and all the parts nickel-plated before it was painted. (The church denies Brousseau's account.)

Brousseau also says that he helped customize a Ford Excursion SUV that Cruise owned, installing features such as hand-made eucalyptus paneling. The customization job was presented to Tom Cruise as a gift from David Miscavige, he said. "I was getting paid fifty dollars a week," he recalls. "And I'm supposed to be working for the betterment of mankind." Several years ago, Brousseau says, he worked on the renovation of an airport hangar that Cruise maintains in Burbank. Sea Org members installed faux scaffolding, giant banners bearing the emblems of aircraft manufacturers, and a luxurious office that was fabricated at church facilities, then reassembled inside the hangar. Brousseau showed me dozens of photographs documenting his work for Cruise.

Both Cruise's attorney and the church deny Brousseau's account. Cruise's attorney says that "the Church of Scientology has never expended any funds to the personal benefit of Mr. Cruise or provided him with free services." Tommy Davis says that these projects were done by contractors and that Brousseau acted merely as an adviser. He also says, "None of the Church staff involved were coerced in any way to assist Mr. Cruise. Church staff, and indeed Church members, hold Mr. Cruise in very high regard and are honored to assist him. Whatever small economic benefit Mr. Cruise may have received from the assistance of Church staff pales in comparison to the benefits the Church has received from Mr. Cruise's many years of volunteer efforts for the Church." Yet this assistance may have involved many hours of unpaid labor on the part of Sea Org members.

Miscavige's official title is chairman of the board of the Religious Technology Center, but he dominates the entire organization. His word is absolute, and he imposes his will even on some of the people closest to him. According to Rinder and Brousseau, in June 2006, while Miscavige was away from the Gold Base, his wife, Shelly, filled several job vacancies without her husband's permission. Soon afterward, she disappeared. Her current status is unknown. Tommy Davis told me, "I definitely know where she is," but he won't disclose where that is.

•   •   •

The garden behind Anne Archer and Terry Jastrow's house, in Brentwood, is filled with olive trees and hummingbirds. A fountain gurgles beside the swimming pool. When I visited last May, Jastrow told me about the first time he met Archer, in Milton Katselas's class. "I saw this girl sitting next to Milton," Jastrow recalled. "I said, 'Who is *that*?'" There was a cool wind blowing in from the Pacific, and Archer drew a shawl around her.

"We were friends for about a year and a half before we ever had our first date," Archer said. They were married in 1978. "Our relationship really works," Jastrow said. "We attribute that essentially 100 percent to applying Scientology." The two spoke of the techniques that had helped them, such as never being critical of the other and never interrupting.

"This isn't a creed," Archer said. "These are basic natural laws of life." She described Hubbard as "an engineer" who had codified human emotional states, in order to guide people to "feel a zest and a love for life."

I asked them how the controversy surrounding Scientology had affected them. "It hasn't touched me," Archer said. "It's not that I'm not aware of it." She went on, "Scientology is growing. It's in a hundred and sixty-five countries."

"Translated into fifty languages!" Jastrow added. "It's the fastest-growing religion." He added, "Scientologists do more good things for more people in more places around the world than any other organization ever." He continued, "When you study the historical perspective of new faiths, historically, they've all been—"

"Attacked," Archer said. "Look what happened to the—"

"The Christians," Jastrow said, simultaneously. "Think of the Mormons and the Christian Scientists."

We talked about the church's focus on celebrities. "Hubbard recognized that if you really want to inspire a culture to have peace and greatness and harmony among men, you need to respect and help the artist to prosper and flourish," Archer said. "And if he's particularly well known he needs a place where he can be comfortable. Celebrity Centres provide that." She blamed the press for concentrating too much on Scientology celebrities. Journalists, she said, "don't write about the hundreds of thousands of other Scientologists—"

"Millions!"

"*Millions* of other Scientologists. They only write about four friggin' people!"

The church won't release official membership figures, but it informally claims eight million members worldwide. Davis says that the figure comes from the number of people throughout the world who have donated to the church. "There is no process of conversion, there is no baptism," Davis told me. It was a simple decision: "Either you are or you aren't." A survey of American religious affiliations, compiled in the *Statistical Abstract of the United States*, estimates that only twenty-five thousand Americans actually call themselves Scientologists. That's less than half the number who identify themselves as Rastafarians.

Jastrow suggested that Scientology's critics often had a vested interest. He pointed to psychiatrists, psychologists, doctors, drug makers, pharmacies—"all those people who make a living and profit and pay their mortgages and pay their college educations and buy their cars, et cetera, et cetera, based on people not being well." He cited a recent article in *USA Today* that noted that an alarmingly high number of soldiers in Iraq and Afghanistan had been hospitalized for mental illness. Drugs merely mask mental distress, he said, whereas "Scientology will solve the source of the problem." The medical and pharmaceutical industries are "prime funders and sponsors of the media," he said, and therefore might exert "influence on people telling the whole and true story about Scientology just because of the profit motive."

Scientology has perpetuated Hubbard's antagonism toward psychiatry. An organization that the church cofounded, the Citizens Commission on Human Rights, maintains a permanent exhibit in Los Angeles called "Psychiatry: An Industry of Death," which argues that psychiatry contributed to the rise of Nazism and apartheid. The group is behind an effort "to help achieve legislative protections against abusive psychiatric treatment and drugging of children." (Paul Haggis has hosted an event for the organization at his home. His defection from Scientology has not changed his view that "psychotropic drugs are overprescribed for children.")

Jastrow, in his back yard, told me, "Scientology is going to be huge, and it's going to help mankind right itself." He asked me, "What else is there that we can hang our hopes on?"

"That's improving the civilization," Archer added.

"Is there some other religion on the horizon that's gonna help mankind?" he said. "Just tell me where. If not Scientology, where?"

.   .   .

Archer and Jastrow found their way into Scientology in the mid-seventies, but Tommy Davis was reared in Archer's original faith, Christian Science. He never met L. Ron Hubbard. He was thirteen years old on January 24, 1986, the day Hubbard died. Although Davis grew up amid money and celebrity, he impressed people with his modesty and his idealism. Like Paul Haggis, Davis was first drawn to the church because of romantic problems. In 1996, he told *Details* that when he was seventeen, he was having trouble with a girlfriend and went to his mother for advice. Archer suggested that he go to the Celebrity Centre. After taking the Personal Values and Integrity course, Davis became a Scientologist.

In 1990, Davis was accepted at Columbia University. But, according to the defector John Peeler—who was then the secretary to Karen Hollander, the president of the Celebrity Centre—pressure was put on Davis to join the Sea Org. Hollander, Peeler says, wanted Tommy to be her personal assistant. "Karen felt that because of who his parents were, and the fact that he already had close friendships with other celebrities, he'd be a good fit," Peeler said. "Whenever celebrities came in, there would be Anne Archer's son." At first, Davis resisted. "He wanted to go to college," Peeler said.

That fall, Davis entered Columbia. He attended for a semester, then dropped out and joined the Sea Org. "I always wanted to do something that helped people," Davis explained to me. "I didn't think the world needed another doctor or lawyer." Archer and Jastrow say that they were surprised by Tommy's decision. "We were hoping he'd get his college education," Jastrow said.

Davis became fiercely committed to the Sea Org. He got a tattoo on one arm of its logo—two palm fronds embracing a star, supposedly the emblem of the Galactic Confederacy seventy-five million years ago. He began working at the Celebrity Centre, attending to young stars like Juliette Lewis, before taking on Tom Cruise. David Miscavige was impressed with Davis. Mike Rinder recalled, "Miscavige liked the fact that he was young and looked trendy and wore Armani suits."

Paul Haggis remembers first meeting Davis at the Celebrity Centre in the early nineties. "He was a sweet and bright boy," Haggis said.

Davis's rise within Scientology was not without difficulty. In 2005, Davis was sent to Clearwater to participate in something called the Estates Project Force. He was there at the same time as Donna Shannon, a veterinarian who had become an O.T. VII before joining the Sea Org. She had thought that she was attending a kind of boot camp for new Sea Org members and was surprised to see veterans like Davis. She says that Davis, "a pretty nice guy," was subjected to extensive hazing. "He complained about scrubbing a Dumpster with a toothbrush till late at night," she recalls. "Then he'd be up at six to do our laundry." Only later did Shannon learn that Davis was Anne Archer's son.

Shannon and Davis worked together for a while in Clearwater, maintaining the grounds. "I was supposedly supervising him," Shannon says. "I was told to make him work really hard." At one point, Shannon says, Davis borrowed about a hundred dollars from her because he didn't have money for food.

One day, according to Shannon, she and Davis were taking the bus to a work project. She asked why he was in the EPF.

"I got busted," Davis told her. Using Scientology jargon, he said, "I fucked up on Tom Cruise's lines"—meaning that he had botched a project that Cruise was involved in. "I just want to do my stuff and get back on post."

Shannon recalled that, suddenly, "it was like a veil went over his eyes, and he goes, 'I already said too much.'"

Several months later, Davis paid her back the money. (Davis says that he does not recall meeting Shannon, has never scrubbed a Dumpster, and has never had a need to borrow money.)

Davis ascended to his role as spokesman in 2007. He has since become known for his aggressive defenses of the church. In 2007, the BBC began reporting an investigative story about Scientology. From the start, the BBC crew, led by John Sweeney, was shadowed by a Scientology film crew. Davis traveled across the United States to disrupt Sweeney's interviews with Scientology dissidents. The two men had a number of confrontations. In an incident captured on video in Florida, Sweeney suggests that Scientology is "a sadistic cult." Davis responds, "For you to repeatedly refer to my faith in those terms is so derogatory, so offensive, and so bigoted. And the reason you kept repeating it is because you wanted to get a reaction like you're getting right now. Well, buddy, you got it! Right here, right now, I'm angry! *Real angry!*" The two men had another encounter that left Sweeney screaming as Davis goaded him—an incident so raw that Sweeney apologized to his viewers.

Shortly afterward, in March 2007, Davis mysteriously disappeared. He was under considerable stress. According to Mike Rinder, Davis had told Sweeney that he reported to Miscavige every day, and that angered Miscavige, who wanted to be seen as focused on spiritual matters, not public relations. According to Rinder, Davis "blew." A few days later, he surfaced in Las Vegas. Davis was sent to Clearwater, where he was "security-checked" by Jessica Feshbach, a church stalwart. A security check involves seeking to gain a confession with an E-Meter, in order to rout out subversion. It can function as a powerful form of thought control.

Davis claims that he never fled the church and was not in Las Vegas. He did go to Clearwater. "I went to Florida and worked there for a year and took some time off," he told me. "I did a lot of study, a lot of auditing." He and Feshbach subsequently got married.

·　　　·　　　·

When I first contacted Tommy Davis, last April, he expressed a reluctance to talk, saying that he had already spent a month responding to Paul Haggis. "It made little difference," he said. "The last thing I'm interested in is dredging all this up again." He kept putting me off, saying that he was too busy to get together, but he promised that we would meet when he was more available. In an e-mail, he said, "We should plan on spending at least a full day together as there is a lot I would want to show you." We finally arranged to meet on Memorial Day weekend.

I flew to Los Angeles and waited for him to call. On Sunday at three o'clock, Davis appeared at my hotel, with Feshbach. We sat at a table on the patio. Davis has his mother's sleepy eyes. His thick black hair was combed forward, with a lock falling boyishly onto his forehead. He wore a wheat-colored suit with a blue shirt. Feshbach, a slender, attractive woman, anxiously twirled her hair.

Davis now told me that he was "not willing to participate in, or contribute to, an article about Scientology through the lens of Paul Haggis." I had come to Los Angeles specifically to talk to him, at a time he had chosen. I asked if he had been told not to talk to me. He said no.

Feshbach said that she had spoken to Mark Isham, whom I had interviewed the day before. "He talked to you about what are supposed to be our confidential scriptures." Any discussion of the church's secret doctrines was offensive, she said.

In my meeting with Isham, he asserted that Scientology was not a "faith-based religion." I pointed out that, in Scientology's upper levels, there was a cosmology that would have to be accepted on faith. Isham said that he wasn't going to discuss the details of O.T. III. "In the wrong hands, it can hurt people," he said.

"Everything I have to say about Paul, I've already said," Davis told me. He agreed, however, to respond to written questions about the church.

In late September, Davis and Feshbach, along with four attorneys representing the church, travelled to Manhattan to meet with me and six staff members of *The New Yorker*. In response to nearly a thousand queries, the Scientology delegation handed over forty-eight binders of supporting material, stretching nearly seven linear feet.

Davis, early in his presentation, attacked the credibility of Scientology defectors, whom he calls "bitter apostates." He said, "They make up stories." He cited Bryan Wilson, an Oxford sociologist, who has argued that testimony from the disaffected should be treated skeptically, noting, "The apostate is generally in need of self-justification. He seeks to reconstruct his own past to excuse his former affiliations and to blame those who were formerly his closest associates."

Davis spoke about Gerry Armstrong, a former Scientology archivist who copied, without permission, many of the church's files on Hubbard and who settled in a fraud suit against the church in 1986. Davis charged that Armstrong had forged many of the documents that he later disseminated in order to discredit the church's founder. He also alleged that Armstrong had spread rumors of a 1967 letter in which Hubbard told his wife that he was "drinking lots of rum and popping pinks and grays" while researching the Operating Thetan material. Davis also noted that in 1984 Armstrong had been captured on videotape telling a friend, "I can create documents with relative ease. You know, I did for a living." Davis's decision to cite this evidence was curious—though the quote cast doubt on Armstrong's ethics, it also suggested that forging documents had once been part of a Scientologist's job.

Davis passed around a photograph of Armstrong, which, he said, showed Armstrong "sitting naked" with a giant globe in his lap. "This was a photo that was in a newspaper article he did where he said that all people should give up money," Davis said. "He's not a very sane person."

Armstrong told me that, in the photo, he is actually wearing running shorts under the globe. The article is about his attempt to create a movement for people to "abandon the use of currency." He said that he received eight hundred thousand dollars in the 1986 settlement and had given most of the money away. (The settlement prohibited Armstrong from talking about Scientology, a prohibition that he has ignored, and the church has won two breach-of-contract suits against him, including a five-hundred-thousand-dollar judgment in 2004.)

Davis also displayed photographs of what he said were bruises sustained by Mike Rinder's former wife in 2010, after Rinder physically assaulted her in a Florida parking lot. (Rinder denies committing any violence. A sheriff's report supports this.) Davis also showed a mug shot of Marty Rathbun in a jailhouse jumpsuit, after being arrested in New Orleans last July for public drunkenness. "Getting arrested for being drunk on the inter-section of Bourbon and Toulouse?" Davis cracked. "That's like getting arrested for being a leper in a leper colony." (Rathbun's arrest has been expunged.) Claire and Marc Headley were "the most despicable people in the world"; Jeff Hawkins was "an in-veterate liar."

I asked how, if these people were so reprehensible, they had all arrived at such elevated positions in the church. "They weren't like that when they were in those positions," Davis responded. The defectors we were discussing had not only risen to positions of responsibility within the church; they had also ascended Sci-entology's ladder of spiritual accomplishment. I suggested to Davis that Scientology didn't seem to work if people at the high-est levels of spiritual attainment were actually liars, adulterers, wife beaters, and embezzlers.

Scientology, Davis said, doesn't pretend to be perfect, and it shouldn't be judged on the misconduct of a few apostates. "*I* haven't done things like that," Davis said. "I haven't suborned perjury, destroyed evidence, lied—contrary to what Paul Haggis says." He spoke of his frustration with Haggis after his resigna-tion: "If he was so troubled and shaken on the fundamentals of Scientology . . . then why the hell did he stick around for thirty-five years?" He continued, "Did he stay a closet Scientologist for some career-advancement purpose?" Davis shook his head in disgust. "I think he's the most hypocritical person in the world."

We discussed the allegations of abuse lodged against Mis-cavige. "The only people who will corroborate are their fellow apostates," Davis said. He produced affidavits from other Scien-tologists refuting the accusations, and noted that the tales about Miscavige always hinged on "inexplicable violent outbursts." Davis said, "One would think that if such a thing occurred—which it most certainly did not—there'd have to be a reason."

I had wondered about these stories as well. While Rinder and Rathbun were in the church, they had repeatedly claimed that allegations of abuse were baseless. Then, after Rinder defected, he said that Miscavige had beaten him fifty times. Rathbun has confessed that in 1997 he ordered incriminating documents destroyed in the case of Lisa McPherson, the Scientologist who died of an embolism. If these men were capable of lying to protect the church, might they not also be capable of lying to destroy it? Davis later claimed that Rathbun is in fact trying to overthrow Scientology's current leadership and take over the church. (Rathbun now makes his living by providing Hubbard-inspired counseling to other defectors, but he says that he has no desire to be part of a hierarchical organization. "Power corrupts," he says.)

Twelve other defectors told me that they had been beaten by Miscavige or had witnessed Miscavige beating other church staff members. Most of them, like John Peeler, noted that Miscavige's demeanor changed "like the snap of a finger." Others who never saw such violence spoke of their constant fear of the leader's anger.

At the meeting, Davis brought up Jack Parsons's black-magic society, which Hubbard had supposedly infiltrated. Davis said, "He was sent in there by Robert Heinlein"—the science-fiction writer—"who was running off-book intelligence operations for naval intelligence at the time." Davis said, "A biography that just came out three weeks ago on Bob Heinlein actually confirmed it at a level that we'd never been able to before." The book to which Davis was referring is the first volume of an authorized Heinlein biography, by William H. Patterson Jr. There is no mention in the book of Heinlein's sending Hubbard to break up the Parsons ring, on the part of naval intelligence or any other organization. Patterson says that he looked into the matter at the suggestion of Scientologists but found nothing.

Davis and I discussed an assertion that Marty Rathbun had made to me about the O.T. III creation story—the galactic revelations that Haggis had deemed "madness." While Hubbard was in exile, Rathbun told me, he wrote a memo suggesting an experiment in which ascending Scientologists skipped the O.T. III level. Miscavige shelved the idea, Rathbun told me. Davis called Rathbun's story "libelous." He explained that the cornerstone of Scientology was the writings of L. Ron Hubbard. "Mr. Hubbard's material must be and is applied precisely as written," Davis said. "It's never altered. It's never changed. And there probably is no more heretical or more horrific transgression that you could have in the Scientology religion than to alter the technology."

But hadn't certain derogatory references to homosexuality found in some editions of Hubbard's books been changed after his death?

Davis admitted that that was so, but he maintained that "the current editions are 100 percent, absolutely fully verified as being according to what Mr. Hubbard wrote." Davis said they were checked against Hubbard's original dictation.

"The extent to which the references to homosexuality have changed are because of mistaken dictation?" I asked.

"No, because of the insertion, I guess, of somebody who was a bigot," Davis replied.

"Somebody put the material in those—?"

"I can only imagine. . . . It wasn't Mr. Hubbard," Davis said, cutting me off.

"Who would've done it?"

"I have no idea."

"Hmm."

"I don't think it really matters," Davis said. "The point is that neither Mr. Hubbard nor the church has any opinion on the subject of anyone's sexual orientation . . ."

"Someone inserted words that were not his into literature that was propagated under his name, and that's been corrected now?" I asked.

"Yeah, I can only assume that's what happened," Davis said.

After this exchange, I looked at some recent editions that the church had provided me with. On page 125 of *Dianetics*, a "sexual pervert" is defined as someone engaging in "homosexuality, lesbianism, sexual sadism, etc." Apparently, the bigot's handiwork was not fully excised.

At the meeting, Davis and I also discussed Hubbard's war record. His voice filling with emotion, he said that if it was true that Hubbard had not been injured, then "the injuries that he handled by the use of Dianetics procedures were never handled, because they were injuries that never existed; therefore, Dianetics is based on a lie; therefore, Scientology is based on a lie." He concluded, "The fact of the matter is that Mr. Hubbard was a war hero."

In the binders that Davis provided, there was a letter from the U.S. Naval Hospital in Oakland, dated December 1, 1945. The letter states that Hubbard had been hospitalized that year for a duodenal ulcer, but was "technically pronounced 'fit for duty.'" This was the same period during which Hubbard claimed to have been blinded and lame. Davis had highlighted a passage: "Eyesight very poor, beginning with conjunctivitis actinic in 1942. Lame in right hip from service connected injury. Infection in bone. Not misconduct, all service connected." Davis added later that, according to Robert Heinlein, Hubbard's ankles had suffered a "drumhead-type injury"; this can result, Davis explained, "when the ship is torpedoed or bombed."

Davis acknowledged that some of Hubbard's medical records did not appear to corroborate Hubbard's version of events. But Scientology had culled other records that *did* confirm Hubbard's story, including documents from the National Archives in St. Louis. The man who did the research, Davis said, was "Mr. X."

Davis explained, "Anyone who saw *JFK* remembers a scene on the Mall where Kevin Costner's character goes and meets with a man named Mr. X, who's played by Donald Sutherland." In the film, Mr. X is an embittered intelligence agent who explains that the Kennedy assassination was actually a coup staged by the military-industrial complex. In real life, Davis said, Mr. X was Colonel Leroy Fletcher Prouty, who had worked in the Office of Special Operations. (Oliver Stone, who directed *JFK*, says that Mr. X was a composite character, based in part on Prouty.) In the eighties, Prouty worked as a consultant for Scientology.

"We finally got so frustrated with this point of conflicting medical records that we took all of Mr. Hubbard's records to Fletcher Prouty," Davis told me. "He actually solved the conundrum for us." According to Davis, Prouty explained to the church representatives that because Hubbard had an "intelligence background," his records were subjected to a process known as "sheepdipping." Davis explained that this was military parlance for "what gets done to a set of records for an intelligence officer. And, essentially, they create two sets." He said, "Fletcher Prouty basically issued an affidavit saying L. Ron Hubbard's records were sheep-dipped." Prouty died in 2001.

Davis later sent me a copy of what he said was a document that confirmed Hubbard's heroism: a "Notice of Separation from the U.S. Naval Service," dated December 6, 1945. The document specifies medals won by Hubbard, including a Purple Heart with a Palm, implying that he was wounded in action twice. But John E. Bircher, the spokesman for the Military Order of the Purple Heart, wrote to me that the Navy uses gold and silver stars, "NOT a palm," to indicate multiple wounds. Davis included a photograph of medals that Hubbard supposedly won. Two of the medals in the photograph weren't even created until after Hubbard left active service.

After filing a request with the National Archives in St. Louis, *The New Yorker* obtained what archivists assured us were Hubbard's complete military records—more than nine hundred pages. Nowhere in the file is there mention of Hubbard's being wounded in battle or breaking his feet. X-rays taken of Hubbard's right shoulder and hip showed calcium deposits, but there was no evidence of any bone or joint disease in his ankle.

There is a "Notice of Separation" in the records, but it is not the one that Davis sent me. The differences in the two documents are telling. The St. Louis document indicates that Hubbard earned four medals for service, but they reflect no distinction or valor. In the church document, his job preference after the service is listed as "Studio (screen writing)"; in the official record, it is "uncertain." The church document indicates, falsely, that Hubbard completed four years of college, obtaining a degree in civil engineering. The official document correctly notes two years of college and no degree.

On the church document, the commanding officer who signed off on Hubbard's separation was "Howard D. Thompson, Lt. Cmdr." The file contains a letter, from 2000, to another researcher, who had written for more information about Thompson. An analyst with the National Archives responded that the records of commissioned naval officers at that time had been reviewed, and "there was no Howard D. Thompson listed."

The church, after being informed of these discrepancies, said, "Our expert on military records has advised us that, in his considered opinion, there is *nothing* in the Thompson notice that would lead him to question its validity." Eric Voelz, an archivist who has worked at the St. Louis archive for three decades, looked at the document and pronounced it a forgery.

· · ·

Since leaving the church, Haggis has been in therapy, which he has found helpful. He's learned how much he blames others for his problems, especially those who are closest to him. "I really wish I had found a good therapist when I was twenty-one," he said. In Scientology, he always felt a subtle pressure to impress his auditor and then write up a glowing success story. Now, he said, "I'm not fooling myself that I'm a better man than I am."

Recently, he and Rennard separated. They have moved to the same neighborhood in New York, so that they can share custody of their son. Rennard has also decided to leave the church. Both say that the divorce has nothing to do with their renunciation of Scientology.

On November 9, *The Next Three Days* premièred at the Ziegfeld Theatre in Manhattan. Movie stars lined up on the red carpet as photographers fired away. Jason Beghe, who plays a detective in the film, was there. He told me that he had taken in a young man, Daniel Montalvo, who had recently blown. He was placed in the Cadet Org, a junior version of the Sea Org, at age five, and joined the Sea Org at eleven. "He's never seen television," Beghe said. "He doesn't even know who Robert Redford is."

After the screening, everyone drifted over to the Oak Room of the Plaza Hotel. Haggis was in a corner receiving accolades from his friends when I found him. I asked him if he felt that he had finally left Scientology. "I feel much more myself, but there's a sadness," he admitted. "If you identify yourself with something for so long, and suddenly you think of yourself as not that thing, it leaves a bit of space." He went on, "It's not really the sense of a loss of community. Those people who walked away from me were never really my friends." He understood how they felt about him and why. "In Scientology, in the Ethics Conditions, as you go down from Normal through Doubt, then you get to Enemy, and, finally, near the bottom, there is Treason. What I did was a treasonous act."

I once asked Haggis about the future of his relationship with Scientology. "These people have long memories," he told me. "My bet is that, within two years, you're going to read something about me in a scandal that looks like it has nothing to do with the church." He thought for a moment, then said, "I was in a cult for thirty-four years. Everyone else could see it. I don't know why I couldn't."

New York

For the tenth anniversary of the events simply known as 9/11, New York *published a special issue that used the familiar and comforting format of the encyclopedia to explore what remains for many the unimaginable and baffling: the collapse of the World Trade Towers, the attack on the Pentagon, the downing of Flight 93, the decade of war that followed. "The Encyclopedia of 9/11" begins on page 36 of the September 5–11, 2011, issue with "Abbottabad" and ends on page 138 with "Zazi, Najibullah." Here are a handful of the ninety-two entries to be found in that issue, ranging from the thought-provoking ("America") to the unbearable ("Jumpers").*

Excerpts from
The Encyclopedia
of 9/11

Here in New York City, we heard it first, the drone of the plane down the West Side, surprisingly loud. Then, if we were outside, our heads pointed in the right direction, we could see it: the dull-red gash in the North Tower, smoking ominously. Just as we'd begun to absorb this strange sight, wondering what pilot could have been so dim as to steer his plane into one of those towers on what seemed the clearest, bluest September day anyone could remember, came a second plane, then a terrible blossom of flame, then the billowing smoke enshrouding downtown. There would be more, of course, two planes aimed at Washington, one that would dive into the Pentagon, the other downed in a field in Pennsylvania. But for New Yorkers, it was the most intimate of tragedies. Within weeks, the day had become a number, a kind of shorthand for a whole universe, one that hadn't existed on 9/10.

Many of us here remember going to work that week, searching for an appropriate journalistic response to a world that was changing in ways we couldn't yet see. As this anniversary loomed, we found ourselves asking the inverse of the same question: With all we now know, how to begin to address the enormity of the event? Our solution was not to shrink from its scale but to embrace it. We decided to reach back to an old form that might allow us to account for a wide assortment of what was created in the wake of the destruction: heroes and villains, great and awful ideas, twisted fates, pop songs and myths and wars. The alphabetized jumble of an encyclopedia, with its preposterous aspiration to describe whole cultures and continents and bodies of knowledge in a single place—that, we thought, might be an interesting way to take in the multiplicity of 9/11's effects. So we asked our own writers and a host of distinguished others to explore a range of subjects that might in their aggregate add up to a kind of idiosyncratic assessment. Some of the resulting ninety-two entries we kept in the vernacular of a reference book; some we allowed to deviate to accommodate remembrances and other emotional responses. We sought imagery that either felt fresh to us or hauntingly familiar—we were looking throughout to balance sentiment with distance. Borrowing from the old musty volumes on hand, we ran illustrations and data and artifacts up the margins.

In spite of its form, our encyclopedia makes no claim to be comprehensive. It's neither a first draft of history nor a verdict—just a set of impressions from some point in between. September 11, 2001, changed everything, or it did not; it will take a lot more than ten years to figure that out.

A

Airport Security

WHERE THE NEW NORMAL HAS BECOME (ALMOST) ROUTINE.
The Transportation Security Administration is for many Americans their most direct point of contact with the post-9/11 national-security state. TSA policy is built on the presumption that the public won't tolerate any risk, which is why the agency goes to great lengths to stop the terrorist threat at the familiar points—cockpit doors have been reinforced, checked baggage is now scanned, and there's real-time updating of terrorist watch lists.

But the agency has evolved like one of those creatures in Spore. Every time a bit of intel chatter picks up some new strategy to thwart the system, the system adapts, trying to neutralize the latest fear, which often has the side effect of making passengers more anxious. After shoe bomber Richard Reid, we padded through checkpoints in socks. If in 2003 you were a sufferer of obstructive sleep apnea, you were required to present your cpap machine for inspection. Thanks to the TSA body scanners and offended passenger John Tyner, *junk* is now an acceptable public word for genitalia. And there is no real consensus that those machines, or the less exhibitionistic ones introduced this summer, can detect hidden explosives or nonmetallic weapons with enough accuracy to be worth the cost and expense.

The lines themselves are a problem, too: The longer the queue of people waiting to be screened, the easier it would be for a terrorist to detonate an explosive outside the checkpoint. That's one reason so many airports have convoluted screening areas where rope-lines lead into far corners of the departure hall, vastly increasing the footprint of the security checkpoint while reducing the concentration of people at a particular place and time.

The TSA is also now training officers in behavioral profiling, which means that the officers are going to be even more vigilant about carefully screening people who seem stressed at the checkpoint. That's basically everyone.

Marc Ambinder

"America"

AN IDEA WITH MANY AUTHORS.
(i) We were attacked because we were Americans—not because we were New Yorkers or we were rich or our politics favored a diverse society—but to the terrorists themselves, "America" remained vague and abstract. The nineteen hijackers had no feeling for our culture and society and only the most general

objections to it. When they did think about America, it was as a certain kind of dupe, an overmuscled husk through which more malevolent forces moved, some of them having to do with capitalism or Christianity but most having to do with Israel. In Hamburg, as their cell arranged itself, the terrorists were all in agreement that Monica Lewinsky had been a Mossad operative, deputized to seduce President Clinton. When Ramzi Yousef was planning the World Trade Center bombing in 1993, he told an associate that he had first hoped to attack Israel but decided it was "too tough a target" and so had settled on our country instead. The *fatwas* that Al Qaeda's spiritualists issued against the United States were full of the perfidies of our policy in the Middle East—the "Zionist-Crusader alliance," the interference in Saudi and Egyptian politics—but had almost nothing about the content of our national character, the shape of our society. Next to nothing about women or about narcissism or excess or about the compulsive aspects of our infatuation with youth and modernity. In the aftermath of the attacks, we told ourselves that it must have been the things that made America exceptional—our freedoms, our liberal culture—that provoked this murderous aggression. And though this was never precisely true, it was—given everything that has followed—a propulsive misconception.

(ii) Within the United States, the political unity that existed briefly after the attacks was soon squandered, but a deeper unity, at a level of identity, remained: Both liberals and conservatives were Americans first, again. A certain conviction soon took hold that we as Americans must somehow have been betrayed by the advertisements for ourselves, as if some unscrupulous ad firm, entrusted with the "America" account, had performed sloppy work and then overbilled. If we were hated, then it was because we were misunderstood. For conservatives, as the cultural critic Susan Faludi has documented, America had been "Oprah-ized," softened and feminized—"the impotent

America," George W. Bush told Bob Woodward in 2002, describing the misimpression the Clinton years had given bin Laden. "A flaccid, you know, kind of technologically competent but not very tough country." Bush vowed virility. But along with the armies he sent to the Muslim world, he also sent a non-Arabic-speaking advertising executive, equipped with videotaped testimony from Muslim Americans, to promote the notion that the melting pot could incorporate Islam, too. Efforts at cultural evangelism gripped liberals as well. By 2003, it seemed every American music act touring Europe felt moved to apologize for the nation. "Just so you know, we're on the good side with y'all—we do not want this war, this violence, and we're ashamed that the president of the United States comes from Texas," Natalie Maines of the Dixie Chicks told a London audience.

Years earlier, as the journalist Eric Alterman noticed, Bruce Springsteen, in Paris, told a concert audience that America "held out a promise, and it was a promise that gets broken every day in the most violent way. But it's a promise that never, ever dies, and it's always inside of you." If Bush's belief was "America is great because of what makes us different," Springsteen's was "America is great because we make evident universal human hopes and universal flaws." In many ways, the politics of the past few years, with the universalist iconography of Obama on one side and a political theater of pining for the Founding Fathers on the other, has remained trapped between these two convictions.

(iii) One of these visions now seems more correct than the other. WE ARE ALL AMERICANS, the famous *Le Monde* headline read on September 12, and though as a statement of global political unity this was fleeting, it did suggest a more lasting, less sentimental realization: that the distinction between the United States and the rest of the world was eroding. Ten years later, America now looks a bit more like other countries do—our embrace of capitalism has grown more complicated, our class mobility less certain, our immigrants and our diversity less unique—and the Bush era now seems a last, angry assertion of a form of American exceptionalism that the attacks helped undo. In the military and economic disasters that have marked the past decade, it has become obvious to everyone that America cannot simply accomplish anything it wants to. The proof point of American exceptionalism had been our strength. Bin Laden got his metaphor right. He fixed his sights on a towering, singular target that he was convinced was less unique and more vulnerable than everyone else supposed.

Benjamin Wallace-Wells

Artifacts

THE THINGS LEFT BEHIND.
Among the remains: a scorched mother-of-pearl inlaid chair, its coiled guts exposed; a filing cabinet, crushed and rust-browned like a wad of chewed-up beef jerky; pieces of three Rodin sculptures, including a cast of *The Thinker*, which later went missing; election leaflets; something that resembled a meteorite; a faceless rag doll; a squeegee handle; a newly exposed slab of 450 million-year-old schist bedrock; lampposts; a small arsenal of melted handguns and rifles from the U.S. Customs office; a steel beam shaped like a cross; another, impossibly bent into the shape of a horseshoe; a 10,000-pound elevator motor; a 47,000-pound piece of the North Tower's antenna; two 110,000-pound steel tridents; 4,000 photographs; 437 watches; 77 necklaces; 379,036 ounces of gold recovered from a Bank of Nova Scotia vault (current value: $630 million); 1,358 vehicles, including a partially melted fire truck and a busted subway car; four autographed baseballs; and one uncracked glass paperweight.

Robert Moor

B

Blue

WHAT EVERYONE WOULD REMEMBER FIRST.

The morning of September 11 was, as many would observe, strikingly clear, the sky so blue it made the subsequent events that much more jarring: "A bright morning sun lit a cloudless blue sky";[1] "a beautiful blue-sky day";[2] "the kind of bright blue sky that people who love New York love best in New York";[3] "what airline pilots call 'severe clear': seemingly infinite visibility";[4] "a crystal blue bowl of morning sky";[5] "it was not just blue, it was a light, crystalline blue, cheerful and invigorating";[6] "a late-summer sky so astoundingly blue it made the whole Northeast sparkle";[7] "almost alarmingly blue";[8] "9/11 weather."[9]

C

Cheney, Dick

THE OTHER LEADER OF THE FREE WORLD, 2001–2008.

Dick Cheney is the most important government figure of the post-9/11 world. He has been called a shadow president and a war criminal. Virtually nobody had access to Bush without first going through him. But like an éminence grise out of some Graham Greene novel, he is almost impossible to apprehend, even

1. Don Brown, *America Is Under Attack, September 11, 2001: The Day the Towers Fell.* 2. John Avlon, Giuliani speechwriter, "The Resilient City," an essay in Kenneth T. Jackson and David Dunbar's *Empire City* anthology. 3. *New York Times.* 4. David Remnick, *The New Yorker.* 5. *Hartford Courant.* 6. George McKenna, *The Puritan Origins of American Patriotism.* 7. Robert Mann and Miryam Ehrlich Williamson, *Forensic Detective: How I Cracked the World's Toughest Cases.* 8. Wendy Doremus, widow of photojournalist Bill Biggart, who was killed covering the attack, *Running Toward Danger: Stories Behind the Breaking News of 9/11*, by Cathy Trost and Alicia C. Shepard; 9. Ed Park, novelist-essayist, *New York Times*, 2008.

when he is writing about himself. He reminds one of Talleyrand in that he is a master tactician and served several regimes. He seldom spoke as vice president, and when he did, it was to his wife and confrere, Lynne; or his equally veiled right-hand man, Scooter Libby (who went to prison rather than implicate his boss in the Valerie Plame business); or David Addington, consigliere. He is both an ideologue and a pragmatist, a rare and brutal combination not often found in American politics.

The core of Cheney's behavior might well be a jagged sense of helplessness and shock at the horror unfolding before him on that day. Staring at the TV in his office, taking in the carnage, he picked up the phone, trying to reach Bush in Florida. A Secret Service detail, alerted that a plane was heading for the White House, ran in, grabbed him by the shoulders, and raced him toward a bunker from which he watched the world change. Brent Scowcroft, an old friend, claimed to no longer recognize him after the terrorist attacks. In June 2007, when Bush underwent a colonoscopy, Cheney served for two hours and five minutes as acting president, and there's something of a John Ford movie about the letter he wrote to his grandchildren that afternoon: "As you grow, you will come to understand the sacrifices that each generation makes to preserve freedom and democracy for future generations, and you will assume the important responsibilities of citizens in our society. I ask of you as my grandchildren what I asked of my daughters, that you always strive in your lives to do what is right." For Cheney, this meant unceasing efforts to reassert the powers of the presidency over all other branches of government (a desire that President Obama may secretly share as of this moment).

Cheney is now very ill with a very bad heart, which, after at least five heart attacks, has finally pretty much given out. He is being kept alive by a pump that makes his blood flow. The man who championed waterboarding (and gay marriage) no longer has a pulse.

Jon Robin Baitz

Commander-in-Chief, Accidental

THE BRIEF, HARROWING ADMINISTRATION OF RICHARD A. CLARKE.
On the morning of September 11, Richard A. "Dick" Clarke
served as the de facto leader of the United States. As a national-
security and counterterrorism adviser to the last three presidents, Clarke had warned relentlessly against the looming threat
posed by Osama bin Laden (he had alerted Condoleezza Rice of
a possible al-Qaeda attack in a personal note exactly one week
before). That morning, he raced to the White House shortly after
the second plane struck the World Trade Center, arriving at Dick
Cheney's office, where Cheney and Rice were meeting alone. The
two immediately handed over significant authority to Clarke as
"crisis manager" and were escorted to a bunker. (The president,
famously reading to a kindergarten classroom in Florida, was
kept from returning to Washington.)

Clarke rapidly posited an al-Qaeda attack, the ambition
and duration of which would remain unknown to everyone—
including those at the highest levels of U.S. government—for as
long as it progressed. From a secure teleconferencing room in
the West Wing, he conferred with cabinet members across Washington. Of the 4,400 planes above the United States ordered
grounded, eleven were initially unaccounted for. From Cheney
and Bush, Clarke sought—and received—permission to shoot
down any aircraft believed to be a threat; because of a training
exercise, however, fighter jets were not immediately available
over Washington and New York.

A plane hit the Pentagon; smoke began filling the studio in
which Secretary of Defense Donald Rumsfeld sat. There were reports of a car bomb at the State Department and a fire on the Capi-
tol Mall. Clarke was told another suspected hijacked plane was
eight minutes away from the White House. Staffers were fleeing;
the Speaker of the House lifted off in a helicopter. Clarke and the
rest of those in the room wrote their names on a piece of paper,

a list e-mailed to the outside so that rescue teams could search for them.

Clarke ordered all landmark buildings across the country evacuated. The borders were closed. The Department of Defense went to DEFCON 3, alerting the Russians of the rationale. A plane was reported hijacked over Alaska. "Continuity of government" protocols, a vestige of the Cold War, were instituted. And before the first Tower had even fallen, Clarke received a secure call from the FBI: Passenger manifests showed several known al-Qaeda names.

For the rest of the day it went on like this, until both Towers had fallen and all the airplanes in the sky had landed and the president arrived back at the White House, just before seven P.M. Clarke continued on in the administration, as an adviser for Cyberspace Security, before resigning in 2003. In 2004, he published a memoir, *Against All Enemies*, in which he chastised the Bush administration for its refusal to heed his and others' pre-9/11 warnings and for the ensuing war in Iraq, which he viewed as wholly counterproductive.

Dan P. Lee

D

Dead, Accounting of the

FROM THE DUST, A NUMEROLOGY OF LOSS.
Because so many questions about the attacks were at first unanswerable, the one we kept coming back to was the one that seemed most straightforward: How many died? From among the 21,817 fragments of life eventually found in the rubble—yes, exactly that many, says the chief medical examiner's office—how many lives could be puzzled back together?

In the minutes after the collapse, rumors suggested a number in the tens of thousands. This was based on the population of the Towers at full capacity: 50,000 workers and, over the course of a day, up to 200,000 visitors. At first it seemed that those enormous numbers made sense and that most of the people in the buildings must be dead, as it was impossible to tell how many dust-covered figures were emerging. Furthermore, such a number was just large enough to match the size of the calamity as it was internalized by people watching in terror. Thinking in the upper five-figures put the loss in the mathematical range of wars (nearly 60,000 American soldiers died in Vietnam) and natural disasters (Krakatoa: 36,000). The attacks and collapse felt, in some ways, like both.

But according to later analyses, only between 14,000 and 19,000 people were in the buildings at 8:46 that morning; within a few days the city's estimate of the dead, based on missing-persons reports, accordingly shrank to about 6,700. Even that was too high. "As you recall, Mayor Giuliani told everyone to report anyone missing to the city, anyone you hadn't heard from, which led to a lot of double and triple reporting," said Ellen Borakove, director of public affairs for the medical examiner's office. "There were people who were reported missing who weren't, and people who weren't reported who were, and they had to sort that out."

They—a multidepartmental committee led by the NYPD's Missing Persons Squad—halved the figure fairly quickly. By the end of October, confirmed deaths numbered 3,478, and by the first anniversary, the official count—including the 147 victims on Flights 11 and 175 but not the 224 dead at the Pentagon and in Pennsylvania—hovered around 2,800. Thereafter, the number drifted down more slowly, to around 2,750 by November 2003, where it has pretty much stayed for eight years, occasionally creeping up by one.

But much is lost in that "pretty much." A paradox of our mostly innumerate society is that we require unreal numbers to make things real. In order to get those numbers, we are usually willing to accept certain estimates as sufficient, indulging in the fiction that we can measure, say, federal spending to the dollar, population tracts to the person. The World Trade Center attacks demanded a different kind of precision. No one could be fractionally dead; no family could be missing an approximate number of loved ones. Inaccurate, incomplete lists that floated around the Internet or that appeared, horribly enough, in overhasty memorials made the problem worse. As does the fact that only about 1,629 of the missing have been positively identified from among those 21,817 remains. The rest, some 40 percent of the total, were issued death certificates by judicial decree, with no real evidence except their absence.

So it wasn't enough to say that the largest contingent among the World Trade Center victims worked in finance (658 at Cantor Fitzgerald alone), followed by the FDNY (343). That the oldest was 85; that the youngest, not including an unborn child, was a 2-year-old on Flight 175. We must have a full accounting. Many of the dead were, after all, accountants, including Jerry J. Borg, who developed pulmonary sarcoidosis after inhaling toxins in the dust cloud that day. He died last December and was officially added to the list in June, bringing the tally to 2,753. For now.

Jesse Green

F

FDNY

WRESTLING WITH THE MYTHS OF MARTYRDOM.
JOHN CERIELLO (*then, firefighter, Squad 18, West Village, which lost seven members; now, lieutenant, Squad 252, Bushwick*): I can't stand hearing the pipes now. It's a great sound, the bagpipes, that's why I tried to learn how to play them. But now, it takes me right back to the funerals. It's not just the sadness of remembering those days, though. It's that so many people now see firefighters as the center of grief over 9/11. And the bagpipes are a symbol of us as a symbol of that grief. I understand why. And I mourn, too. But firefighters are not about grief.

SAL CASSANO (*then, FDNY assistant chief; now, fire commissioner*): Unfortunately for the department, we really got good at this business of doing funerals. We devised a book on what to do if there is a line-of-duty death in your firehouse. It talks about getting the bunting, hanging the bunting, going with the family to the funeral parlor, step by step, forty pages. It even describes what we're going to do a year later at the plaque dedication. But I don't think people look at us as a department of mourning. I think they look at us as a department that, that day, displayed strength and courage like they've never seen before.

ADRIENNE WALSH (*then, firefighter, Ladder 20, Soho, which lost seven members; now, lieutenant, Squad 18, West Village*): The thing I have a problem with is when it became a myth, the whole event, the fire department and what we did. I understand why that happened, but when you make it a myth, you take the human aspect out of it. The important thing was that when people were scared—not scared, terrified, crapping their pants—they still did their jobs.

PAUL HYLAND (*then, firefighter, Ladder 110, Downtown Brooklyn; retired March 2010*): I don't consider them nightmares, but you'd wake up just thinking about everything that happened. When we walked into the building, a woman in the lobby was severely mutilated. No legs, her arm was ripped off; her face, it looked like someone took it off with a saw. She had to be one of the jumpers.

MALACHY CORRIGAN (*then and now, director of FDNY counseling-services unit*): The No. 1 illness is anxiety. No. 2 is depression. We're seeing about 2,800 new cases a year now. That's a lot of clients. "Why did I survive?" is still a big question.

CERIELLO: Howie Scott and I had hooked up with a unit, Rescue 4, and Squad 288 in a staging area but left for a few minutes to get masks and air cylinders. While we were gone, Rescue 4 and 288 went into the South Tower. We were walking down West Street toward the Towers when it came down. Everything went to hell, went to darkness. All of those guys died, and I'm here ten years later. Why? I don't know.

HYLAND: The chief said, "Let's go," and we went up to the twenty-third floor of the North Tower. To tell you the truth, I was kind of pissed off: The fire's on the ninetieth floor, and we're going to the twenty-third? We're doing nothing! Engine 207 from our firehouse, I was talking to them in the lobby, and then I believe they went into the Marriott. None of 'em were ever found. Not even a tool. If God had a plan, I don't know what it was.

ARTIE RICCIO (*then, firefighter, Ladder 110, Downtown Brooklyn; now, lieutenant, Engine 311, Springfield Gardens, Queens*): I wished I would have died there instead of my friends with young kids. I lived with survivor's guilt for a long time. I finally went to counseling for it. I thought there was something wrong with me.

WALSH: I'm surprised more of us aren't crazy. I didn't see victims. They were dust. And I was inhaling them. So . . . you're literally taking these people in. And there's no one for us to help. When the wind blew, you couldn't grab them. They were gone.

HYLAND: We were on the twenty-third floor, searching for people, and I was standing near a window when I saw the South Tower coming down. I thought it was a partial collapse. It must have taken us twenty minutes to walk down, and when we got to the lobby, it was completely destroyed. I remember these long spears of glass hanging above us. Huge panels turned into shards. If one of these releases, you'll be killed. I have a piece of a window, glass from the World Trade Center, a small piece. I keep it above my desk. It's right here in my hands now.

CASSANO: The one thing I hold on to is a memory from that day, of meeting Father Judge on West Street. I says, "Father, you better get some help, you're gonna need it, we're gonna have a bad day here." He gave me this smile and said, "It's gonna be OK." I hold on to that memory, for sure.

RICCIO: Every year a bunch of us get together for dinner a week or so after September 11. It's weird, but it's good for us to get together and talk. I still can't look at a plane landing, though. Ten years later.

WALSH: It's always important to remember the 343, but more than 1,000 people have given their lives for the city over the years. All those deaths should be revered instead of focusing on this event as the be-all and end-all. That's why I think the tenth anniversary is going to be huge. An end point of sorts. We'll always remember. But the city can't stop.

HYLAND: There's more attention now, ten years. For me, there's no difference—seventh, eighth, eleventh. It's every day you think about it. But even the bad days—I'm thankful for those.

Chris Smith

Freedom Fries

WHAT'S IN A WORD? A CULTURE WAR.

When George W. Bush appeared before Congress on September 20, he faced a void. We barely knew the name of our enemy and hardly possessed the intellectual equipment to explain why that enemy hated us. Any president assigned to reassure the country would have invoked freedom with Bush's frequency and intensity. But Bush didn't just deploy freedom as rhetoric. He asserted it as an analysis. The attacks were the opening salvo in a long war between forces of "freedom and fear." Freedom was the reason we were attacked—and only the march of global freedom could vanquish the perpetrators. By the time Bush delivered his second inaugural address, this reasoning had bloated into grand strategy. Our "ultimate goal," he announced, was "ending tyranny in our world."

In the course of enshrining freedom at the center of American foreign policy, Bush also opened a new front in the never-ending American culture war—that battle between Manichaean moralizers and spineless relativists, to borrow the dueling caricatures. Skirmishes erupted over whether french fries, museums, and even the very building to replace the World Trade Center should now have *freedom* implanted in their monikers. But this Kulturkampf came to transcend the flash points; it would distort and hobble both conservative and liberal thinking about the world.

For conservatives, the word has particular resonances. Freedom had been their rallying cry in the Reaganite war on the state, and after September 11, it acquired theological significance. Indeed, Bush spoke of freedom in these terms: "the Almighty's gift." Because they had extended this gift to the people of Iraq, conservatives congratulated themselves in the most ostentatious terms. When Iraqi election officials required voters to dip their fingers in purple paint in the country's first free elections in the winter of 2005, congressmen painted their own fingers for the State of the Union address. The gesture didn't seem like a wholesome act of solidarity, particularly as they pointed those purple fingers across the aisle. The critics of Bush's foreign policy, after all, were nothing less than "appeasers," as the *Weekly Standard* regularly noted.

This stance invited backlash. But just as the Bush doctrine overreached, so did many of its critics. From the behavioral sciences to Fareed Zakaria's best-selling *The Future of Freedom* and, to a lesser extent, Barack Obama's presidential campaign, there were similar versions of a counterargument: that democracy is hardly an unqualified good; rather, it often bewildered citizens with a sea of choices. This was the theme of the most fêted political novel of the decade, Jonathan Franzen's *Freedom*, which suggests that our dream of "limitless freedom" has yielded a miserable consumerist society. In the end, the book's naïve idealist Walter Berglund concludes that American freedom is the "freedom to fuck up your life."

But these critics don't fully appreciate the irony of American freedom: It tolerates excesses but then punishes them. When Congressmen Bob Ney and Walter Jones wanted to punish Paris for failing to support the Iraq War, they knocked the french fry from the menu of the House of Representatives cafeterias. In its place, they unveiled the Freedom Fry. But their stunt not only failed to strike a blow against Gallic pride, it was also subjected to international ridicule. By 2006, the House restored the french fry to its rightful name. Soon after, Ney lost his own freedom, imprisoned for complicity in the Jack Abramoff scandal. Jones, for his part, came to regret the episode. In fact, he came to regret supporting Bush foreign policy. On the wall leading to his office, he has hung photos of dead soldiers from the war he once championed.

Franklin Foer

G

Good-Bye

A PHONE CALL FROM THE 105TH FLOOR.
"It was about 9:30 A.M. when he called. When I heard his voice on the phone, I was so happy. I said, 'Sean, where are you?' thinking that he had made it out and that he was calling me from the street somewhere. He told me he was on the 105th floor, and I knew right away that Sean was never coming home.

He was very calm. He told me he had been trying to find a way out and what he wanted was information. So I relayed to him what I could see on TV, what floor the flames had reached and on what side of the building. I also used my other phone, my cell phone, and called 911 and told them where Sean was and that he needed to be rescued. Sean told me that initially he was with some people that tried to escape by going down the stairs, but they had to turn back because of the smoke and the heat. They headed for the roof, but when they got there, they found that the roof doors were locked.

He told me the other people were now in a conference room and that he was alone. I asked him to go back and try the roof doors again, to pound on them, and that somebody on the other side would hear him . . .

Sean was gone for maybe five minutes, and then he came back to the phone. He hadn't had any success, and now the stairwell was full of smoke: He had actually passed out for a few minutes while pounding on the doors.

There was a building in flames underneath him, but Sean didn't even flinch. He stayed composed, just talking to me the way he always did. I will always be in awe of the way he faced death. Not an ounce of fear—not when the windows around him were getting too hot to touch; not when the smoke was making it hard to breathe.

By now we had stopped talking about escape routes. I wanted to use the precious few minutes we had left just to talk. He told me to give his love to his family, and then we just began talking about all the happiness we shared during our lives together, how lucky we were to have each other. At one point, when I could tell it was getting harder for him to breathe, I asked if it hurt. He paused for a moment, and then said, 'No.' He loved me enough to lie.

In the end, as the smoke got thicker, he just kept whispering, 'I love you,' over and over. Then I suddenly heard this loud explosion through the phone. It reverberated for several seconds. We held our breath; I know we both realized what was about to happen. Then I heard a sharp crack, followed by the sound of an avalanche. I heard Sean gasp once as the floor fell out from underneath him. I called his name into the phone over and over. Then I just sat there huddled on the floor holding the phone to my heart."

As told by Beverly Eckert, whose husband, Sean Rooney, worked at Aon in the second Tower.

Postscript

Three years after sharing her story, Eckert died when Continental Flight 3407 crashed near Buffalo in 2009. Eckert's expanded account will be published in StoryCorps's forthcoming collection, *All There Is: Love Stories From StoryCorps.*

J

Jumpers

WHY THE MOST HAUNTING IMAGES OF 2001 WERE HARDLY EVER SEEN.

On September 12, 2001, the *New York Times* printed a photograph that had been taken by Associated Press photographer Richard Drew the previous day; so did newspapers all over the country. It showed a man who, having jumped from one of the burning World Trade Center towers, was falling through the air to the pavement: an acrobatics of death. An estimated 7 percent of those who were murdered on 9/11 died by jumping; there is ample photographic documentation, taken by various witnesses from various angles, of this horrific phenomenon. But the *Times* never ran Drew's photograph, or anything like it, ever again; neither did most other American papers. Indeed, photographs of the so-called jumpers have been rendered taboo, vilified as an insult to the dead and an unbearably brutal shock to the living (though they have been printed abroad, and can be found on the Internet). And journalists who have tried to identify the falling, dying man in Drew's photograph have been met with angry rebuffs by those who might be his family, as Tom Junod documented in *Esquire* in 2009. One purported daughter told journalist Peter Cheney when confronted with Drew's photograph: "That piece of shit is not my father."

The jumper photographs make clear to us the utter vulnerability of the victims; they present us with terrorism as a human experience, not just a political crime. Those trapped in the Towers had only two choices—to jump to their deaths or to be incinerated—which is to say they had no choice at all. To moralize either "choice"—to despise one as cowardly and valorize the other as heroic—is to misunderstand both. What the 9/11 victims faced was the absence of options.

Susie Linfield

K

Kids

THE KINDERGARTEN CLASS OF P.S. 150 REMEMBERS.

TORAN: We all heard this boom, and everyone rushed to the window.

ETHAN: They announced on the intercom, "We're evacuating the building. All teachers bring your students downstairs immediately."

GLORIELA: I remember we had two hamsters in the classroom, and I took one of them and was like, "It's gonna be okay."

ROBERTO: My mom picked me up quickly, but when she was telling me about it when I was a little older she said, "Oh, I couldn't get you as quickly as I wanted to because we weren't sure if people were coming out of the plane or what was going on." So that kind of freaked me out thinking that I could have been just trapped in the school.

LUCA: My mom came and picked me up after the first plane hit, and I saw the other plane go right above me and hit the other building. I remember seeing people jumping from the windows— I remember that. And I asked my mom, "Oh, do they have a trampoline at the bottom?" She was like, "No." I'm like, "Then why are they jumping?" She's like, "I don't know." And then we started to run away.

ETHAN: We ran the whole way until we hit P.S. 3 in the Village. They brought us into the gym and gave us some paper and crayons to color with just to calm us down.

AVIYA: When we got home, me and my brother watched the news. I think it was the first time I ever watched the news.

GLORIELA: Yeah, I remember seeing the news as well. Even though I saw it myself firsthand, I saw the whole tragedy through everybody else's eyes.

ELLA: My parents decided not to tell me what happened. They wouldn't let me watch TV.

BROOK, WHO HAS CREATED A DOCUMENTARY, *THE SECOND DAY*, ABOUT HIS EXPERIENCE: Well, I was not sheltered at all. Basically, as soon as it happened, my mom was able to pick me up quickly, and she brought me about a block and a half away from the Towers and put me in a fire truck—she worked with the FDNY. She went off to run messages because the Handie-Talkies weren't working 'cause they were so overloaded. While I was in the truck, firemen were telling me messages to give to their children and their wives and everything, like, "Tell my kid I love him," "Tell my wife I love her." One fireman said to me, "Grow up and be a good man." By the time the Towers started to fall, my mom came back, grabbed me off the truck, and we started running up Greenwich Street. She was holding me so that my head was over her shoulder, and I was watching the Tower fall and people jumping off the buildings holding each other's hands. We ran north all the way to Canal Street and then that's where she put me down and started to cry.

ADELAIDE: I didn't actually remember this, but my mom told me a couple of years ago that I kept drawing the Twin Towers falling and the plane and everything, and she said it really freaked her out.

ETHAN: I think I was doing that too, actually.

TORAN: I had this phase where I would point to buildings and ask if people would fall out of those. After 9/11 my mom would have me pray every night, and she told me that one of the things I said was that I hoped that all of the terrorists would turn into babies so that they couldn't hurt anyone.

ADELAIDE: I didn't know that it was a terrorist thing until like five years ago.

MALIK: Yeah, we didn't know about terrorists.

ZACHARY: It just taught me something that I would have learned later in life, that bad things can happen.

ADELAIDE: If I'm just sitting in class and I'm bored, I'll think, *What would happen if a plane just crashed into the side of the building right now? What would everyone do?*

BEN: I think my parents kind of hope I don't remember at all, but I don't think I'll ever forget.

ETHAN: I don't want to forget it.

ADELAIDE: We're part of history.

ETHAN: Yeah, we are.

Alex Morris

M

Missing-Persons Posters

STREET ART WITH AWFUL POWER.
After what Walt Whitman called "the huge first Nothing" of annihilation, with the psychic convulsions of a demonic force still redounding in the acrid air, the spirit of the city sleepwalking in purgatorial pain, came the posters. Taped to lampposts, walls, store windows, gathered in great clusters on the sides of hospitals, they were a humble catalogue of the missing, on view for months, intense visual windows onto internal disruption and cosmic pain.

The look and feel of these flyers was unnerving. They were hastily made from whatever information could be gathered: height, weight, eye and hair color, blood type, birth date, contact numbers. There were almost no e-mail addresses, which weren't universal yet. Nearly every one listed the floor the missing person worked on, and those numbers are still terrifying: The higher the number, the deeper the pit in one's stomach. Almost all bore pictures, mostly snapshots of family gatherings, group shots, girlfriends laughing together. Most so young. All in limbo. Three weeks after 9/11, I chose three posters at random and took them home.

Rhondelle Cherie Tankard. Her flyer—on which her first name is misspelled—shows a half-length photo of a strong black woman, and tells us that she was last seen in Tower Two, on the 102nd floor. "Her family is in Bermuda and unable to come to the USA due to flight restrictions," the text reads. "Please help!" There's a pager number. Searching online today, I found pages of agonized tributes, prayers, and good-byes from Rhondelle's friends, family, and church members. One, from just last year, reads as remorseful confession: "I will forever feel responsible for you being there that day."

Leah Oliver. In her color snapshot, she is pretty, smiling, held tightly by a young man, perhaps the Eric Costa listed below as "boyfriend." Leah worked at Marsh & McLennan on the ninety-sixth floor of Tower One. She was a day shy of twenty-five. An online message about her begins, "Leah, the daughter I never had." It is signed "Godfather."

Sean Lugano. "Last seen—88th Floor—Tower 2." Today, I learn that Sean was captain of the Loyola College rugby team, a three-time All-American. In a photo of a deserted Baltimore sports stadium, the scoreboard reads SEAN LUGANO FIELD.

These flyers exude a terrible voodoo. I've never told anyone I removed them from the streets, and after I did, I immediately put them away. Their animistic power and sorrow empty the spirit still and remind me why I hadn't looked at them again until now. I could not bear to.

Jerry Saltz

Q

Quiet

THE DUMBSTRUCK CITY.

On a typical day, New York City streets register more than seventy decibels, enough to cause progressive hearing loss. The quiet that enveloped the city after the Towers fell was overwhelming. Manhattan-bound traffic was closed off to nonemergency vehicles for two days, and all commercial flights coming in and out of JFK, La Guardia, and Newark were canceled. Subways ran off and on because of power problems caused by the destruction at Chambers Street. Major League Baseball games were postponed until the seventeenth; the Stock Exchange reopened the same day. That wasn't the half of it. Whole parts of the city seemed mute—most strikingly, its typically loquacious residents, who walked the streets speechless.

Kera Bolonik

S

Surfing the Collapse

A TONY HAWK-MEETS-TOM CRUISE FANTASY, BASED PARTLY ON FACT.

In the aftermath, a fantastic action-movie-hero rumor started: Someone inside had ridden a jagged steel boogie board to safety on benevolent currents of air. *Newsweek*, in its initial coverage, quoted a doctor on the scene saying of someone found in the rubble that "he rode that"—a chunk of the building—"down all the way from the 86th floor." Though nothing of the sort was ever confirmed, one man, Pasquale Buzzelli, very nearly lived up to the role. He and his Port Authority colleagues—one of whom was Genelle Guzman-McMillan, the last survivor pulled from the wreckage—had calmly stayed put in their sixty-fourth-floor offices, then took the stairs. The North Tower began collapsing above them when they were still between thirteen and twenty-two stories up; Buzzelli, a structural engineer, knew what was happening when he heard the thunderous roar and threw himself into a fetal position. The fall reminded him of the roller coasters at Great Adventure, he would later say. He awoke three hours later, reclining atop a slab of tower, perched fifteen feet above a silent hellscape. He had a broken foot but was otherwise relatively unscathed. Somehow, the pancaking floors, which by the time they reached him had attained their terminal velocity, simply went by him. As William Langewiesche, author of *American Ground: Unbuilding the World Trade Center*, put it, "Basically the building passed him on the way to the ground. . . . He lost the race."

Nick Sywak

T

Television News

<small>THE LAST DAYS OF INTERMEDIATION.</small>
On September 11, a friend called to tell me to turn on the TV. I did, just as the second plane hit. By that afternoon, I was holed up in the West Village, desperate to escape the traumatizing loop of footage. Better to drink with friends instead.

But of course, I couldn't stop watching. Because a decade ago, television was not just one way to follow the crisis; it was the only way. In 2001, online newspapers were rudimentary, with no blogs, video, or comments; most people had dial-up. There were cell phones, but texting wasn't widespread, and camera phones were rare. Facebook launched in 2004, and Twitter in 2006. While you could e-mail or instant-message people you knew well, only technically adroit geeks could speak easily to a wider audience. We needed the professionals to fill us in: Peter Jennings, Diane Sawyer, Aaron Brown, Charles Gibson, Katie Couric, Matt Lauer, Tom Brokaw, Paula Zahn, not to mention Ashleigh Banfield, who ran forty blocks down Sixth Avenue, reported the falling of the first Tower from her cell phone, then got caught in the mêlée when the second Tower fell.

Luckily, they came through. Because in those first hours, TV news—however briefly—became news again. The anchors reacted to events as they happened, with recognizable emotions, yet keeping panic in check. Gibson warned several times: "We are dealing purely in the realm of speculation here." Field reporters were no longer voyeurs; they were downtown themselves, struggling to find context in the chaos. Peter Jennings was on the air for seventeen hours straight, his deep voice and intelligent notes of caution far more comforting than the clichés of President Bush. Twelve hours in, Jennings took a break to call his children, then offered personal advice, acknowledging the unusual break in rhetoric. "If you're a parent, you've got a kid in some other part of the country, call them up. Exchange observations."

Much of the information from those first hours turned out to be useless, like instructions about where to give blood. There were rumors about hijacked planes and bomb threats that didn't exist, as producers struggled to gauge what was real. Reporters held up missing posters to the cameras, encouraging strangers to read descriptions of loved ones who would never be found.

And it wasn't long—a day or two—before the scrim rose back up, the stirring theme songs and patriotic slogans like "America Under Attack" that would continue into the Iraq War. TV news became what it had always been—ideology and entertainment—but with even greater intensity, and more open cynicism, with the rise of Fox News. These days, we all ride the cycle of immediacy, from Anderson Cooper's reports during Hurricane Katrina, to the tweets from Haiti, to the Facebook rebels in Egypt and the comments appended to every article, daggers stabbing through news copy that was once untouchable, authoritative. Some of this new style is radical and democratic, an improvement over the phony "truth" of the past; just as often it is merely exploitative, a performance of feeling as fake as any Sam the Eagle gravitas ever was.

It wasn't until 2005 that YouTube was created, lending us access to what is now a fetishized archive of 9/11 footage, available any hour, spattered with conspiracy theories. "Oh, this is terrifying, awful," says Gibson, witnessing the second plane hitting. "To watch powerless, it's a horror," responds Sawyer. My heart beat faster as I watched, no matter how I tried to keep myself at a distance, even a decade later. But I also found that it was possible to feel a kind of perverse nostalgia, a tenderness for TV news trying its best.

Emily Nussbaum

Torture

ONCE ANATHEMA, NOW A CHOICE.

In the weeks after 9/11, Americans began torturing prisoners. At first, spurred on by fear, panic, guilt, and desperation, they improvised—stripping a wounded John Walker Lindh, the so-called American Taliban, taping him naked to a stretcher and leaving him bleeding and untreated for days in a freezing shipping container. But even in this early case, it was powerful people in the office of the Secretary of Defense who ordered those interrogating Lindh to "take the gloves off." Soon that phrase— "After 9/11, the gloves came off "—would be used by the head of counterterrorism in testifying before the Senate, and by then what had come off, for the first time since George Washington insisted his soldiers treat all prisoners humanely at the Battle of Trenton, was systematic protections governing Americans' treatment of prisoners of war. President George W. Bush stripped those captured in the war on terror of the protection of the Geneva Conventions and, indeed, of their very status as prisoners of war. Those captured after September 11 were deemed "unlawful combatants": As "combatants," they would be denied the legal rights due civilians under the Constitution; as "unlawful," they would be denied the protections conferred on soldiers by the laws of war. Detainees in the war on terror were thus cast into—as an eminent British jurist characterized Guantánamo, where nearly a thousand were interned—"a legal black hole."

What is undeniable, as we gaze back on the decade separating us from 9/11, is that thousands of these prisoners were mistreated and hundreds were tortured. American military officers and soldiers tortured prisoners in Guantánamo; in Abu Ghraib and other prisons and military bases in Iraq; and in Kandahar, Bagram, and other prisons in Afghanistan. American intelligence officers tortured prisoners at so-called black sites, secret prisons set up in Pakistan, Afghanistan, Thailand, Morocco, Poland,

Romania, and Lithuania. The methods they used—the "alternative set of procedures," in President Bush's preferred phrasing—were developed and refined within the offices of the American government, debated in memoranda that traveled between military departments and government bureaus, debated and parsed by clever lawyers, and approved and initialed by high officials who inscribed personal recommendations in the margins. ("I stand for eight to ten hours a day," scrawled Donald Rumsfeld. "Why is standing limited to four hours?")

The documentary record of how these "enhanced interrogation techniques" were developed, debated, and approved is voluminous. In documents from the CIA, the Pentagon, and the Department of Justice, we read precise descriptions of "the abdominal slap" and "the cold cell" and "the use of noise to induce stress," of "forced nudity" and "longtime standing," of "cramped confinement" in small boxes and "walling" (repeated smashing of the naked, hooded detainee against a wall by means of a collar about the neck), of sleep deprivation (not to exceed eleven days) and of "simulated drowning"—the infamous waterboarding. CIA medical experts prescribe the precise amount of water needed to achieve suffocation and its temperature; Justice Department lawyers obligingly respond that while such suffocation does produce "a controlled acute episode"—it is not torture. Beside these bureaucratic euphemisms, the detailed and extensive descriptions of how torture was used, including methodical first-person accounts compiled by investigators of the International Committee of the Red Cross that recount the effect of torture on detainees—one subjected to suffocation by water 183 times, another 83 times—are vivid, shocking, and revolting.

That these activities constituted torture and thus violated not only the Geneva Conventions but also the War Crimes Act and the Convention Against Torture is disputed by almost no legal authorities beyond those officials personally responsible for approving them. The American military prosecuted waterboarding as a war crime in the Spanish-American War and in World War II, and American courts prosecuted and convicted civilian police officers of waterboarding as recently as 1983. Yet in the wake of September 11, the highest officials of the American government personally approved torture, among them the former president, vice president, and secretary of defense. (By his own account, George W. Bush, when asked by his director of central intelligence whether Khalid Shaikh Mohammed should be waterboarded, had an immediate and dramatic response: "Damn right!")

Among those who have affirmed publicly that waterboarding constitutes torture and violates U.S. and international law are the current highest law-enforcement officer of the land, Attorney General Eric Holder, and his boss, President Barack Obama. On his second full day in office, President Obama ordered the black sites closed and torture stopped. But in hoping to break cleanly with torture, the new president proved reluctant to confront it directly. His very words point up the deep moral quandary that Americans—who see themselves as leaders in advancing human rights—find themselves mired in after 9/11: "Where force is necessary," President Obama told the Nobel Committee in December 2009, "we have a moral and strategic interest in binding ourselves to certain rules of conduct. . . . That is what makes us different from those whom we fight. That is a source of our strength. That is why I prohibited torture."

This bold statement brought vigorous applause in Oslo. The plain truth, though, is that torture is illegal, by international treaty and federal statute. President Obama has no more power to prohibit torture than President Bush had to order it. President Obama does have the power, indeed the obligation, to enforce the law and to investigate and punish those who violate it. And in this he has gone only partway. It is this dilemma, ten years after 9/11, in which the country is still caught.

Must we—can we—return to the rule of law? Can we not, as President Obama has urged, simply "look forward and not backward"? The president has once again supplied his own answer. "America—in fact, no nation—can insist that others follow the rules of the road if we refuse to follow them ourselves," he said in Oslo. "Those regimes that break the rules must be held accountable."

Apart from a few low-level soldiers foolish enough to pose for grotesque photographs at Abu Ghraib, no one has been held accountable for torture—not those who designed the methods, nor those who ordered them used, nor those who applied them in secret rooms. Americans have lived with the reality of torture for many years now, and many say they support its use. Though Americans may still believe it is their adherence to "certain rules of conduct" that makes them "different from those whom we fight," one of the saddest consequences of 9/11 is that a great many Americans now say they believe that the country can't protect itself from terrorism while following the law. We have learned, ten years on, the limits of American exceptionalism. President Obama has "prohibited torture." In the wake of the next terrorist attack, a future president, or perhaps even this one, might well approve it. Torture, once anathema, has become a policy choice.

Mark Danner

Total Progressive Collapse

WHY, PRECISELY, THE TOWERS FELL.

From the moment when video of the Towers' collapse appeared, conspiracy theorists began to speculate that the buildings had been brought down by explosives. Using as evidence the puffs of dust and debris that shot out of the buildings' sides and the speed at which the structures fell, truthers saw a secret government demolition plot.

The Towers failed, however, not because of C-4 or any other explosive but because of "total progressive collapse," an engineering phenomenon first identified in the late sixties after the partial destruction of a twenty-two-story apartment complex in East London. A gas explosion on the eighteenth floor damaged a load-bearing support, causing the top four floors to fall, crushing the ones beneath.

In total progressive collapse, a structure incurs extreme localized damage, and significant elements of the building are weakened. If the damage is not contained, structures elsewhere in the building give way and cause a catastrophic failure. In the case of the North and South Towers, the buildings' design called for the core columns, through a series of steel floor trusses and concrete blocks, to support the load of the floors. On September 11, the impact of the aircraft blasted off the spray-on fireproofing that had been applied to the buildings' core columns; 128,000 pounds of burning, loose fuel began superheating them to temperatures up to 1,500 degrees Fahrenheit. Although the steel didn't melt, it greatly softened, and buckled; as the floors began to sag, the exterior columns were pulled inward. The combination of gravity and the downward kinetic force of the higher floors caused the floors below to successively collapse (causing the puffs of dust and debris) until they hit the ground. The top floors then collapsed on top of the already-reduced-to-rubble pile, causing further wreckage.

Seismograph readings taken by Columbia University indicate two events registering 2.1 and 2.3 on the Richter scale—one for each building's collapse. The spikes started small and then grew as the buildings toppled, evidence that contradicts claims of an explosion: If the Towers' collapse had been a controlled demolition, the spikes would have been sharper and more sudden.

Matthew Giles

Rolling Stone

FINALIST—COMMENTARY,
DIGITAL MEDIA

To describe Matt Taibbi as a polemicist is an understatement bordering on absurdity. His columns for the print edition of Rolling Stone and his "Taibblog" for the magazine's website seethe with righteous anger. Or as one reader commented on the website: "I've never seen the f-word used so beautifully." Yet Taibbi's writing is also consistently eloquent and insightful. Inspired by the Occupy Wall Street movement, the three pieces collected here were described by the National Magazine Awards judges as "truth-seeking and inspiring journalism." Taibbi's work for Rolling Stone won the publication a National Magazine Award for Columns and Commentary in 2008.

Matt Taibbi

Wall Street Isn't Winning—It's Cheating *and* Mike Bloomberg's Marie Antoinette Moment *and* How I Stopped Worrying and Learned to Love the OWS Protests

Wall Street Isn't Winning—It's Cheating

I was at an event on the Upper East Side last Friday night when I got to talking with a salesman in the media business. The subject turned to Zuccotti Park and Occupy Wall Street, and he was chuckling about something he'd heard on the news.

"I hear [Occupy Wall Street] has a CFO," he said. "I think that's funny."

"Okay, I'll bite," I said. "Why is that funny?"

"Well, I heard they're trying to decide what bank to put their money in," he said, munching on hors d'oeuvres. "It's just kind of ironic."

Oh, Christ, I thought. He's saying the protesters are hypocrites because they're using banks. I sighed.

"Listen," I said. "Where else are you going to put three hundred thousand dollars? A shopping bag?"

"Well," he said, "it's just, their protests are all about . . . You know . . ."

"Dude," I said. "These people aren't protesting *money*. They're not protesting *banking*. They're protesting corruption on Wall Street."

"Whatever," he said, shrugging.

These nutty criticisms of the protests are spreading like cancer. Earlier that same day, I'd taped a TV segment on CNN with Will Cain from the *National Review,* and we got into an argument on the air. Cain and I agreed about a lot of the problems on Wall Street, but when it came to the protesters, we disagreed on one big thing.

Cain said he believed that the protesters are driven by envy of the rich.

"I find the one thing [the protesters] have in common revolves around the human emotions of envy and entitlement," he said. "What you have is more than what I have, and I'm not happy with my situation."

Cain seems like a nice enough guy, but I nearly blew my stack when I heard this. When you take into consideration all the theft and fraud and market manipulation and other evil shit Wall Street bankers have been guilty of in the last ten-fifteen years, you have to have balls like church bells to trot out a propaganda line that says the protesters are just jealous of their hard-earned money.

Think about it: there have always been rich and poor people in America, so if this is about jealousy, why the protests now?

The idea that masses of people suddenly discovered a deep-seated animus/envy toward the rich—after keeping it strategically hidden for decades—is crazy.

Where was all that class hatred in the Reagan years, when openly dumping on the poor became fashionable? Where was it in the last two decades, when unions disappeared and CEO pay relative to median incomes started to triple and quadruple?

The answer is, it was never there. If anything, just the opposite has been true. Americans for the most part love the rich, even the obnoxious rich. And in recent years, the harder things got, the more we've obsessed over the wealth dream. As unemployment skyrocketed, people tuned in in droves to gawk at Evrémonde-heiresses like Paris Hilton, or watch bullies like Donald Trump fire people on TV.

Moreover, the worse the economy got, the more being a millionaire or a billionaire somehow became a qualification for high office, as people flocked to voting booths to support politicians with names like Bloomberg and Rockefeller and Corzine, names that to voters symbolized success and expertise at a time when few people seemed to have answers. At last count, there were 245 millionaires in Congress, including 66 in the Senate.

And we hate the rich? Come on. Success is the national religion, and almost everyone is a believer. Americans *love* winners. But that's just the problem. These guys on Wall Street are not winning—they're cheating. And as much as we love the self-made success story, we hate the cheater that much more.

In this country, we cheer for people who hit their own home runs—not shortcut-chasing juicers like Bonds and McGwire, Blankfein and Dimon.

That's why it's so obnoxious when people say the protesters are just sore losers who are jealous of these smart guys in suits who beat them at the game of life. This isn't disappointment at having lost. It's anger because those other guys didn't really win. And people now want the score overturned.

All weekend I was thinking about this "jealousy" question, and I just kept coming back to all the different ways the game is rigged. People aren't jealous and they don't want privileges. They just want a level playing field, and they want Wall Street to give up its cheat codes, things like:

FREE MONEY. Ordinary people have to borrow their money at market rates. Lloyd Blankfein and Jamie Dimon get billions of dollars for free, from the Federal Reserve. They borrow at zero and lend the same money back to the government at 2 or 3 percent, a valuable public service otherwise known as "standing in the middle and taking a gigantic cut when the government decides to lend money to itself."

Or the banks borrow billions at zero and lend mortgages to us at 4 percent, or credit cards at 20 or 25 percent. This is essentially an official government license to be rich, handed out at the expense of prudent ordinary citizens, who now no longer receive much interest on their CDs or other saved income. It is virtually impossible to not make money in banking when you have unlimited access to free money, especially when the government keeps buying its own cash back from you at market rates.

Your average chimpanzee couldn't fuck up that business plan, which makes it all the more incredible that most of the too-big-to-fail banks are nonetheless still functionally insolvent, and dependent upon bailouts and phony accounting to stay above water. Where do the protesters go to sign up for their interest-free billion-dollar loans?

CREDIT AMNESTY. If you or I miss a $7 payment on a Gap card or, heaven forbid, a mortgage payment, you can forget about the great computer in the sky ever overlooking your mistake. But serial financial fuckups like Citigroup and Bank of America overextended themselves by the hundreds of billions and pumped trillions of dollars of deadly leverage into the system—and got rewarded with things like the Temporary Liquidity Guarantee

Program, an FDIC plan that allowed irresponsible banks to borrow against the government's credit rating.

This is equivalent to a trust fund teenager who trashes six consecutive off-campus apartments and gets rewarded by having Daddy co-sign his next lease. The banks needed programs like TLGP because without them, the market rightly would have started charging more to lend to these idiots. Apparently, though, we can't trust the free market when it comes to Bank of America, Goldman, Sachs, Citigroup, etc.

In a larger sense, the TBTF banks all have the implicit guarantee of the federal government, so investors know it's relatively safe to lend to them—which means it's now cheaper for them to borrow money than it is for, say, a responsible regional bank that didn't jack its debt-to-equity levels above 35-1 before the crash and didn't dabble in toxic mortgages. In other words, the TBTF banks got *better credit* for being *less responsible.* Click on free-creditscore.com to see if you got the same deal.

STUPIDITY INSURANCE. Defenders of the banks like to talk a lot about how we shouldn't feel sorry for people who've been foreclosed upon because it's their own fault for borrowing more than they can pay back, buying more house than they can afford, etc. And critics of OWS have assailed protesters for complaining about things like foreclosure by claiming these folks want "something for nothing."

This is ironic because, as one of the *Rolling Stone* editors put it last week, "something for nothing is Wall Street's official policy." In fact, getting bailed out for bad investment decisions has been de rigueur on Wall Street not just since 2008, but for decades.

Time after time, when big banks screw up and make irresponsible bets that blow up in their faces, they've scored bailouts. It doesn't matter whether it was the Mexican currency bailout of 1994 (when the state bailed out speculators who gambled on the peso) or the IMF/World Bank bailout of Russia in 1998 (a bailout of speculators in the "emerging markets") or the

Long-Term Capital Management Bailout of the same year (in which the rescue of investors in a harebrained hedge-fund trading scheme was deemed a matter of international urgency by the Federal Reserve), Wall Street has long grown accustomed to getting bailed out for its mistakes.

The 2008 crash, of course, birthed a whole generation of new bailout schemes. Banks placed billions in bets with AIG and should have lost their shirts when the firm went under—AIG went under, after all, in large part *because* of all the huge mortgage bets the banks laid with the firm—but instead got the state to pony up $180 billion or so to rescue the banks from their own bad decisions.

This sort of thing seems to happen every time the banks do something dumb with their money. Just recently, the French and Belgian authorities cooked up a massive bailout of the French bank Dexia, whose biggest trading partners included, surprise, surprise, Goldman, Sachs and Morgan Stanley. Here's how the *New York Times* explained the bailout:

> To limit damage from Dexia's collapse, the bailout fashioned by the French and Belgian governments may make these banks and other creditors whole—that is, paid in full for potentially tens of billions of euros they are owed. This would enable Dexia's creditors and trading partners to avoid losses they might otherwise suffer . . .

When was the last time the government stepped into help you "avoid losses you might otherwise suffer?" But that's the reality we live in. When Joe Homeowner bought too much house, essentially betting that home prices would go up, and losing his bet when they dropped, he was an irresponsible putz who shouldn't whine about being put on the street.

But when banks bet billions on a firm like AIG that was heavily invested in mortgages, they were making the same bet that

Joe Homeowner made, leaving themselves hugely exposed to a sudden drop in home prices. But instead of being asked to "suck it in and cope" when that bet failed, the banks instead went straight to Washington for a bailout—and got it.

UNGRADUATED TAXES. I've already gone off on this more than once, but it bears repeating. Bankers on Wall Street pay lower tax rates than most car mechanics. When Warren Buffet released his tax information, we learned that with taxable income of $39 million, he paid $6.9 million in taxes last year, a tax rate of about 17.4 percent.

Most of Buffet's income, it seems, was taxed as either "carried interest" (i.e. hedge-fund income) or long-term capital gains, both of which carry 15 percent tax rates, half of what many of the Zucotti park protesters will pay.

As for the banks, as companies, we've all heard the stories. Goldman, Sachs in 2008—this was the same year the bank reported $2.9 billion in profits, and paid out over $10 billion in compensation—paid just $14 million in taxes, a 1 percent tax rate.

Bank of America last year paid not a single dollar in taxes— in fact, it received a "tax credit" of $1 billion. There are a slew of troubled companies that will not be paying taxes for years, including Citigroup and CIT.

When GM bought the finance company AmeriCredit, it was able to marry its long-term losses to AmeriCredit's revenue stream, creating a tax windfall worth as much as $5 billion. So even though AmeriCredit is expected to post earnings of $8–$12 billion in the next decade or so, it likely won't pay any taxes during that time, because its revenue will be offset by GM's losses.

Thank God our government decided to pledge $50 billion of your tax dollars to a rescue of General Motors! You just paid for one of the world's biggest tax breaks.

And last but not least, there is:

GET OUT OF JAIL FREE. One thing we can still be proud of is that America hasn't yet managed to achieve the highest incarceration rate in history—that honor still goes to the Soviets in the Stalin/Gulag era. But we do still have about 2.3 million people in jail in America.

Virtually all 2.3 million of those prisoners come from "the 99 percent." Here is the number of bankers who have gone to jail for crimes related to the financial crisis: 0.

Millions of people have been foreclosed upon in the last three years. In most all of those foreclosures, a regional law enforcement office—typically a sheriff's office—was awarded fees by the court as part of the foreclosure settlement, settlements which of course were often rubber-stamped by a judge despite mountains of perjurious robosigned evidence.

That means that every single time a bank kicked someone out of his home, a local police department got a cut. Local sheriff's offices also get cuts of almost all credit card judgments, and other bank settlements. If you're wondering how it is that so many regional police departments have the money for fancy new vehicles and SWAT teams and other accoutrements, this is one of your answers.

What this amounts to is the banks having, as allies, a massive armed police force who are always on call, ready to help them evict homeowners and safeguard the repossession of property. But just see what happens when you try to call the police to prevent an improper foreclosure. Then, suddenly, the police will not get involved. It will be a "civil matter" and they won't intervene.

The point being: If you miss a few home payments, you have a very high likelihood of colliding with a police officer in the near future. But if you defraud a pair of European banks out of a billion dollars—that's a *billion*, with a b—you will never be arrested, never see a policeman, never see the inside of a jail cell.

Your settlement will be worked out not with armed police, but with regulators in suits who used to work for your company or one like it. And you'll have, defending you, a former head of that regulator's agency. In the end, a fine will be paid to the government, but it won't come out of your pocket personally; it will be paid by your company's shareholders. And there will be no admission of criminal wrongdoing.

The Abacus case, in which Goldman helped a hedge fund guy named John Paulson beat a pair of European banks for a billion dollars, tells you everything you need to know about the difference between our two criminal justice systems. The settlement was $550 million—just over half of the damage.

Can anyone imagine a common thief being caught by police and sentenced to pay back *half* of what he took? Just one low-ranking individual in that case was charged (case pending), and no individual had to reach into his pocket to help cover the fine. The settlement Goldman paid to the government was about 1/24th of what Goldman received *from* the government just in the AIG bailout. And that was the toughest "punishment" the government dished out to a bank in the wake of 2008.

The point being: we have a massive police force in America that outside of lower Manhattan prosecutes crime and imprisons citizens with record-setting, factory-level efficiency, eclipsing the incarceration rates of most of history's more notorious police states and communist countries.

But the bankers on Wall Street don't live in that heavily policed country. There are maybe 1,000 SEC agents policing that sector of the economy, plus a handful of FBI agents. There are nearly that many police officers stationed around the polite crowd at Zuccotti park.

These inequities are what drive the OWS protests. People don't want handouts. It's not a class uprising and they don't want civil war—they want just the opposite. They want everyone to live in the same country, and live by the same rules. It's amazing that some people think that that's asking a lot.

Mike Bloomberg's Marie Antoinette Moment

Last year I had a chance to see New York Mayor Mike Bloomberg up close at the Huffington Post's "Game Changers" event. I was standing right behind the guy when he was introduced by Nora Ephron and watched as the would-be third party powerhouse wowed the liberal crowd with one zinger after another.

He started off with a crack about Ephron, saying he had agreed to say something nice about her book, which he blithely noted he hadn't read. Still, he knew the title, *I Remember Nothing*, which he said he'd "heard is also the title of a new book by Charlie Sheen." (He pronounced Sheen like "Shine").

From there he cracked that he was honored to be a "Game Changer," although he was only the last-minute replacement for Snooki. (*Zing!*) Then he went into a riff about Halloween.

"Does everyone have their costume?" he asked. (This is the old "Did you hear this? Have you heard about this?" Jimmy-Vulmer-style standup routine). "I thought about going in a . . . dress," he began. "But then I decided I would just go as the fiscally conservative, pro-choice, anti-smoking, anti-trans-fat Jewish billionaire mayor of the World's Greatest City."

The crowd roared. Bloomberg smiled, looked up, extended his hands, and said, "Maybe that's just too much of a stretch, I don't know."

Man, I thought. This guy is really sure of himself. If there is such a thing as infinite self-satisfaction, he was definitely approaching it that night.

And it wasn't hard to see why. Bloomberg's great triumph as a politician has been the way he's been able to win over exactly the sort of crowd that was gathering at the *HuffPost* event that night. He is a billionaire Wall Street creature with an extreme deregulatory bent who has quietly advanced some nastily regressive police policies (most notably the notorious "stop-and-frisk" practice) but has won over upper-middle-class liberals with his stances on choice and gay marriage and other social issues.

Bloomberg's main attraction as a politician has been his ability to stick closely to a holy trinity of basic PR principles: bang heavily on black crime, embrace social issues dear to white progressives, and in the remaining working hours give your pals on Wall Street (who can raise any money you need, if you somehow run out of your own) whatever they want.

He understands that as long as you keep muggers and pimps out of the prime shopping areas in the Upper West Side, and make sure to sound the right notes on abortion, stem-cell research, global warming, and the like, you can believably play the role of the wisecracking, good-guy-billionaire Belle of the Ball for the same crowd that twenty years ago would have been feting Ed Koch.

Anyway, I thought of all of this this morning, when I read about Bloomberg's latest comments on Occupy Wall Street. I remembered how pleased Bloomberg looked with himself at the *HuffPost* ball last year when I read what he had to say about the anticorruption protesters now muddying his doorstep in Zuccotti Park:

Mayor Michael Bloomberg said this morning that if there is anyone to blame for the mortgage crisis that led the collapse of the financial industry, it's not the "big banks," but congress.

Speaking at a business breakfast in midtown featuring Bloomberg and two former New York City mayors, Bloomberg was asked what he thought of the Occupy Wall Street protesters.

"I hear your complaints," Bloomberg said. "Some of them are totally unfounded. It was not the banks that created the mortgage crisis. It was, plain and simple, congress who forced everybody to go and give mortgages to people who were on the cusp. Now, I'm not saying I'm sure that was terrible policy, because a lot of those people who got homes still have them and they wouldn't have gotten them without that."

To me, this is Michael Bloomberg's Marie Antoinette moment, his own personal "Let Them Eat Cake" line. This one series of comments allows us to see under his would-be hip centrist Halloween mask and look closely at the corrupt, arrogant aristocrat underneath.

Occupy Wall Street has not yet inspired many true villains outside of fringe characters like Anthony Bologna. But Bloomberg, with this preposterous schlock about Congress forcing banks to lend to poor people, may yet make himself the face of the 1 percent's rank intellectual corruption.

This whole notion that the financial crisis was caused by government attempts to create an "ownership society" and make mortgages more available to low-income (and particularly minority) borrowers has been pushed for some time by dingbats like Rush Limbaugh and Sean Hannity, who often point to laws like the 1977 Community Reinvestment Act as signature events in the crash drama.

But Rush Limbaugh and Sean Hannity are at least dumb enough that it is theoretically possible that they actually believe the crash was caused by the CRA, Barney Frank, and Fannie and Freddie.

On the other hand, nobody who actually understands anything about banking or has spent more than ten minutes inside a Wall Street office believes any of that crap. In the financial world, the fairy tales about the CRA causing the crash inspire a sort of chuckling bemusement, as though they were tribal bugaboos explaining bad rainfall or an outbreak of hoof-and-mouth, ghost stories and legends good for scaring the masses.

But nobody actually *believes* them. Did government efforts to ease lending standards put a lot of iffy borrowers into homes?

Absolutely. Were there a lot of people who wouldn't have gotten homes twenty or thirty years ago who are now in foreclosure thanks to government efforts to make mortgages more available? Sure—no question.

But did any of that have anything at all to do with the explosion of subprime home lending that caused the gigantic speculative bubble of the mid-2000s, or the crash that followed?

Not even slightly. The whole premise is preposterous. And Mike Bloomberg knows it.

In order for this vision of history to be true, one would have to imagine that all of these banks were dragged, kicking and screaming, to the altar of home lending, forced against their will to create huge volumes of home loans for unqualified borrowers.

In fact, just the opposite was true. This was an orgiastic stampede of lending, undertaken with something very like bloodlust. Far from being dragged into poor neighborhoods and forced to give out home loans to jobless black folk, companies like Countrywide and New Century charged into suburbs and exurbs from coast to coast with the enthusiasm of Rwandan machete mobs, looking to create as many loans as they could.

They lent to anyone with a pulse and they didn't need Barney Frank to give them a push. This was not social policy. This was greed. They created those loans not because they had to, but because it was profitable. Enormously, gigantically profitable— profitable enough to create huge fortunes out of thin air, with a speed never seen before in Wall Street's history.

The typical money-machine cycle of subprime lending took place without any real government involvement. Bank A (let's say it's Goldman, Sachs) lends criminal enterprise B (let's say it's Countrywide) a billion dollars. Countrywide then goes out and creates a billion dollars of shoddy home loans, committing any and all kinds of fraud along the way in an effort to produce as many loans as quickly as possible, very often putting people who shouldn't have gotten homes into homes, faking their income levels, their credit scores, etc.

Goldman then buys *back* those loans from Countrywide, places them in an offshore trust, and chops them up into securities. Here they use fancy math to turn a billion dollars of subprime junk into different types of securities, some of them AAA-rated, some of them junk-rated, etc. They then go out on the open market and sell those securities to various big customers—pension funds, foreign trade unions, hedge funds, and so on.

The whole game was based on one new innovation: the derivative instruments like CDOs that allowed them to take junk-rated home loans and turn them into AAA-rated instruments. It was not Barney Frank who made it possible for Goldman, Sachs to sell the home loan of an occasionally employed janitor in Oakland or Detroit as something just as safe as, and more profitable than, a United States Treasury Bill. This was something they cooked up entirely by themselves and developed solely with the aim of making more money.

The government's efforts to make home loans more available to people showed up in a few places in this whole tableau. For one thing, it made it easier for the Countrywides of the world to create their giant masses of loans. And second, the Fannies and Freddies of the world were big customers of the banks, buying up mortgage-backed securities in bulk along with the rest of the suckers. Without a doubt, the bubble would not have been as big, or inflated as fast, without Fannie and Freddie.

But the bubble was overwhelmingly built around a single private-sector economic reality that had nothing to do with any of that: new financial instruments made it possible to sell crap loans as AAA-rated paper.

Fannie and Freddie had nothing to do with Merrill Lynch selling $16.5 *billion* worth of crap mortgage-backed securities to the Connecticut Carpenters Annuity Fund, the Mississippi Public Employees' Retirement System, the Connecticut Carpenters

Pension Fund, and the Los Angeles County Employees Retirement Association. Citigroup and Deutsche Bank did not need to be pushed by Barney Frank and Nancy Pelosi to sell hundreds of millions of dollars in crappy MBS to Allstate.

And Goldman, Sachs did not need Franklin Raines to urge it to sell $1.2 billion in designed-to-fail mortgage-backed instruments to two of the country's largest corporate credit unions, which subsequently went bust and had to be swallowed up by the National Credit Union Administration.

These banks did not need to be dragged kicking and screaming to make the billions of dollars in profits from these and other similar selling-baby-powder-as-coke transactions. They did it for the money, and they did it because they did not give a fuck who got hurt.

Who cares if some schmuck carpenter in Connecticut loses the pension he's worked his whole life to save? Who cares if he's now going to have to work until he's seventy, instead of retiring at fifty-five? It's his own fault for not knowing what his pension fund manager was buying.

And, of course, in a larger sense, the entire crisis was the fault of that janitor in Oakland, who took out too big of a loan, with the help of do-gooder liberals in Congress and their fans in bleeding-heart liberal la-la land—you know, the same people Bloomberg wowed with his hep jokes about Snooki and Charlie Sheen.

This is the evil lie Bloomberg is now trying to dump on the Occupy movement; this is where he's choosing to spend all that third-way cred he built up over the years with the HuffPost sect. And the mayor put a cherry on the top of his Marie Antoinette act with the rest of his speech:

> "But [Congress] were the ones who pushed Fannie and Freddie to make a bunch of loans that were imprudent, if you will. They were the ones that pushed the banks to loan to everybody. And now we want to go vilify the banks because it's one

> target, it's easy to blame them and Congress certainly isn't going to blame themselves. At the same time, Congress is trying to pressure banks to loosen their lending standards to make more loans. This is exactly the same speech they criticized them for."
>
> Bloomberg went on to say it's "cathartic" and "entertaining" to blame people, but the important thing now is to fix the problem.

Jesus . . . I mean, for one thing, Fannie and Freddie don't even make loans. That's how absurd this whole thing is.

And the condescension levels here are unbelievable, his air of aristocratic superiority almost breathtaking to behold. Listen to Bloomberg paternally conceding in one breath that it is certainly nice that some struggling people now have homes ("I'm not saying I'm sure that was terrible policy, because a lot of those people who got homes still have them and they wouldn't have gotten them without that"), just before chiding us with the next that there are sometimes negative consequences to doing something that sounds like goodness, like giving people a place of their own to live.

And then there's this whole line in which he professes to indulgently understand the need for the "catharsis" and "entertainment" of protest, again almost like a dad who tells his idiot teenage son that he understands the need to sow a wild oat or two, but please don't wreck the family Mercedes next time.

Well, you know what, Mike Bloomberg? FUCK YOU. People are not protesting for their own entertainment, you asshole. They're protesting because millions of people were robbed, by your best friends incidentally, and they want their money back. And you're not everybody's dad, so stop acting like you are.

How I Stopped Worrying and Learned to Love the OWS Protests

I have a confession to make. At first, I misunderstood Occupy Wall Street.

The first few times I went down to Zuccotti Park, I came away with mixed feelings. I loved the energy and was amazed by the obvious organic appeal of the movement, the way it was growing on its own. But my initial impression was that it would not be taken very seriously by the Citibanks and Goldman Sachs of the world. You could put 50,000 angry protesters on Wall Street, 100,000 even, and Lloyd Blankfein is probably not going to break a sweat. He knows he's not going to wake up tomorrow and see Cornel West or Richard Trumka running the Federal Reserve. He knows modern finance is a giant mechanical parasite that only an expert surgeon can remove. Yell and scream all you want, but he and his fellow financial Frankensteins are the only ones who know how to turn the machine off.

That's what I was thinking during the first few weeks of the protests. But I'm beginning to see another angle. Occupy Wall Street was always about something much bigger than a movement against big banks and modern finance. It's about providing a forum for people to show how tired they are not just of Wall Street, but *everything*. This is a visceral, impassioned, deepseated rejection of the entire direction of our society, a refusal to take even one more step forward into the shallow commercial abyss of phoniness, short-term calculation, withered idealism, and intellectual bankruptcy that American mass society has become. If there is such a thing as going on strike from one's own culture, this is it. And by being so broad in scope and so elemental in its motivation, it's flown over the heads of many on both the right and the left.

The right-wing media wasted no time in cannon-blasting the movement with its usual idiotic clichés, casting Occupy Wall Street as a bunch of dirty hippies who should get a job and stop chewing up Mike Bloomberg's police overtime budget with their urban sleepovers. Just like they did a half-century ago, when the debate over the Vietnam War somehow stopped being about why we were brutally murdering millions of innocent Indochinese civilians and instead became a referendum on bralessness and long hair and flower-child rhetoric, the depraved flacks of the right-wing media have breezily blown off a generation of fraud and corruption and market-perverting bailouts, making the whole debate about the protesters themselves—their hygiene, their "envy" of the rich, their "hypocrisy."

The protesters, chirped Supreme Reichskank Ann Coulter, needed three things: "showers, jobs and a point." Her colleague Charles Krauthammer went so far as to label the protesters hypocrites for having *iPhones*. OWS, he said, is "Starbucks-sipping, Levi's-clad, iPhone-clutching protesters [denouncing] corporate America even as they weep for Steve Jobs, corporate titan, billionaire eight times over." Apparently, because Goldman and Citibank are corporations, no protester can ever consume a corporate product—not jeans, not cell phones, and definitely not coffee—if he also wants to complain about tax money going to pay off some billionaire banker's bets against his own crappy mortgages.

Meanwhile, on the other side of the political spectrum, there were scads of progressive pundits like me who wrung our hands with worry that OWS was playing right into the hands of assholes like Krauthammer. *Don't give them any ammunition!* we counseled. *Stay on message! Be specific!* We were all playing the Rorschach-test game with OWS, trying to squint at it and see what we wanted to see in the movement. Viewed through the prism of our desire to make near-term, within-the-system changes, it was hard to see how skirmishing with cops in New York would help foreclosed-upon middle-class families in Jacksonville and San Diego.

What both sides missed is that OWS is tired of all of this. They don't care what we think they're about, or should be about. They just want something different.

We're all born wanting the freedom to imagine a better and more beautiful future. But modern America has become a place so drearily confining and predictable that it chokes the life out of that built-in desire. Everything from our pop culture to our economy to our politics feels oppressive and unresponsive. We see 10 million commercials a day, and every day is the same life-killing chase for money, money, and more money; the only thing that changes from minute to minute is that every tick of the clock brings with it another space-age vendor dreaming up some new way to try to sell you something or reach into your pocket. The relentless sameness of the two-party political system is beginning to feel like a *Jacob's Ladder* nightmare with no end; we're entering another turn on the four-year merry-go-round, and the thought of having to try to get excited about yet another minor quadrennial shift in the direction of one or the other pole of alienating corporate full-of-shitness is enough to make anyone want to smash his own hand flat with a hammer.

If you think of it this way, Occupy Wall Street takes on another meaning. There's no better symbol of the gloom and psychological repression of modern America than the banking system, a huge heartless machine that attaches itself to you at an early age, and from which there is no escape. You fail to receive a few past-due notices about a $19 payment you missed on that TV you bought at Circuit City, and next thing you know a collector has filed a judgment against you for $3,000 in fees and interest. Or maybe you wake up one morning and your car is gone, legally repossessed by Vulture Inc., the debt-buying firm that bought your loan on the Internet from Chase for two cents on the dollar. This is why people hate Wall Street. They hate it because the banks have made life for ordinary people a vicious tightrope act; you slip anywhere along the way, it's 10,000 feet down into a vat of razor blades that you can never climb out of.

That, to me, is what Occupy Wall Street is addressing. People don't know exactly what they want, but as one friend of mine put it, they know one thing: *FUCK THIS SHIT!* We want something different: a different life, with different values, or at least a *chance* at different values.

There was a lot of snickering in media circles, even by me, when I heard the protesters talking about how Liberty Square was offering a model for a new society, with free food and health care and so on. Obviously, a bunch of kids taking donations and giving away free food is not a long-term model for a new economic system.

But now, I get it. People want to go someplace for at least five minutes where no one is trying to bleed you or sell you something. It may not be a real model for anything, but it's at least a place where people are free to dream of some other way for human beings to get along, beyond auctioned "democracy," tyrannical commerce and the bottom line.

We're a nation that was built on a thousand different utopian ideas, from the Shakers to the Mormons to New Harmony, Indiana. It was possible, once, for communities to experiment with everything from free love to an end to private property. But nowadays even the palest federalism is swiftly crushed. If your state tries to place tariffs on companies doing business with some notorious human-rights-violator state—like Massachusetts did, when it sought to bar state contracts to firms doing business with Myanmar—the decision will be overturned by some distant global bureaucracy like the WTO. Even if 40 million Californians vote tomorrow to allow themselves to smoke a joint, the federal government will never permit it. And the economy is run almost entirely by an unaccountable oligarchy in Lower Manhattan that absolutely will not sanction any innovations in banking or debt forgiveness or anything else that might lessen its predatory influence.

And here's one more thing I was wrong about: I originally was very uncomfortable with the way the protesters were focusing on the NYPD as symbols of the system. After all, I thought, these are just working-class guys from the Bronx and Staten Island who have never seen the inside of a Wall Street investment firm, much less had anything to do with the corruption of our financial system.

But I was wrong. The police in their own way are symbols of the problem. All over the country, thousands of armed cops have been deployed to stand around and surveil and even assault the polite crowds of Occupy protesters. This deployment of law-enforcement resources already dwarfs the amount of money and manpower that the government "committed" to fighting crime and corruption during the financial crisis. One OWS protester steps in the wrong place, and she immediately has police roping her off like wayward cattle. But in the skyscrapers above the protests, anything goes.

This is a profound statement about who law enforcement works for in this country. What happened on Wall Street over the past decade was an unparalleled crime wave. Yet at most, maybe 1,500 federal agents were policing that beat—and that little group of financial cops barely made any cases at all. Yet when thousands of ordinary people hit the streets with the express purpose of obeying the law and demonstrating their patriotism through peaceful protest, the police response is immediate and massive. There have already been hundreds of arrests, which is hundreds more than we ever saw during the years when Wall Street bankers were stealing billions of dollars from retirees and mutual-fund holders and carpenters unions through the mass sales of fraudulent mortgage-backed securities.

It's not that the cops outside the protests are doing wrong, per se, by patrolling the parks and sidewalks. It's that they should be somewhere else. They should be heading up into those skyscrapers and going through the file cabinets to figure out who stole what, and from whom. They should be helping people get their money back. Instead, they're out on the street, helping the Blankfeins of the world avoid having to answer to the people they ripped off.

People want out of this fiendish system, rigged to inexorably circumvent every hope we have for a more balanced world. They want major changes. I think I understand now that this is what the Occupy movement is all about. It's about dropping out, if only for a moment, and trying something new, the same way that the civil rights movement of the 1960s strived to create a "beloved community" free of racial segregation. Eventually the Occupy movement will need to be specific about how it wants to change the world. But for right now, it just needs to grow. And if it wants to sleep on the streets for a while and not structure itself into a traditional campaign of grassroots organizing, it should. It doesn't need to tell the world what it wants. It is succeeding, for now, just by being something different.

GQ

FINALIST—ESSAYS AND
CRITICISM

Weaving together personal memoir and critical theory, John Jeremiah Sullivan seized on the posthumous publication of David Foster Wallace's Pale King *to explore—with characteristic audacity—the novelist's life and legacy. Sullivan's story "You Blow My Mind. Hey, Mickey!" for the* New York Times Magazine *was also nominated for a National Magazine Award this year; his "Mister Lytle: An Essay" for* The Paris Review *won the award for Essays and Criticism last year; and his "Horseman, Pass By" for* Harper's Magazine *won the award for Feature Writing in 2003. And in a sign of the times, "Too Much Information" was published on the* GQ *iPad app, not in print.*

John Jeremiah Sullivan

Too Much Information

One of the few detectable lies in David Foster Wallace's books occurs in his essay on the obscure '90s-era American tennis prodigy Michael Joyce, included in Wallace's first nonfiction anthology, *A Supposedly Fun Thing I'll Never Do Again*. Apart from some pages in his fiction, it's the best thing he wrote about tennis—better even than his justly praised but disproportionately famous piece on Roger Federer[1]—precisely

1. This is not or not purely a tribute footnote but an actual editorially defensible appendage to this piece: I was supposed to write that Federer essay, for *Play*, the sports magazine published for too few years by the *New York Times*. Like Wallace, I played tennis in school and had continued to follow the game. It was an easy answer when *Play* called saying they had access to Federer at Wimbledon. *GQ* wouldn't let me do it, though. Turns out I'd signed something my agent described as a "contract" that forbade me from writing for other mags. Also, in fairness to *GQ*, I'd been slacking for a couple of months, maybe blew an assignment or two, couldn't really argue. At the end of the last conversation with the guy who would have been my editor, after telling him it was a no-go, I suggested he contact Wallace, which to me was like saying, "Why don't you call the White House?" The editor was forced into an awkwardness. "Well," he said, "actually, we called him first. He couldn't do it." Wallace must have had a change of heart, however. Several months later, there was his essay on my kitchen table. Reading it gave me complicated feelings. On one level it was gratifying to see that he'd made a case I had vaguely imagined making,

because Joyce was a journeyman, an unknown, and so offered Wallace's mind a white canvas. Wallace had almost nothing to work with on that assignment:[2] ambiguous access to the qualifying rounds of a Canadian tournament, a handful of hours staring through chain link at a subject who was both too nice to be entertaining and not especially articulate. Faced with what for most writers would be a disastrous lack of material, Wallace looses his uncanny observational powers on the tennis complex, drawing partly on his knowledge of the game but mainly on his sheer ability to *consider* a situation, to revolve it in his mental fingers like a jewel whose integrity he doubts. In the mostly empty stadium he studies the players between matches. "They all have the unhappy self-enclosed look of people who spend huge amounts of time on

---

that the greatness of Federer lay in how he evolved his elegant all-court game from inside the unforgiving speed and brutality of the power-baseline game. But Wallace had explained it all with an accuracy and effortlessness that I knew I wouldn't have achieved or seen as possible. In this humbling there was a strange intimacy. I got to feel, for a woozy instant, exactly how Wallace's brain would handle a subject I'd held in my own, in a vacuum, before knowing that he would take it up. Anyway, that's my contribution to the Wallace oeuvre, his last magazine piece. I don't begrudge the reader for feeling the world of letters benefited by the substitution. Just saying you're welcome.

2. Wallace often preferred it that way. Recall that he got himself invited onto a David Lynch film set by assuring Lynch's people that he had no actual desire to interview the director. Early in 2008, *GQ* asked him to write about Obama's speeches or, more largely, about American political rhetoric. It was still a somewhat gassy idea as presented to him, but Wallace saw the possibilities, so we started making inquiries to the Obama campaign, and even made reservations for him to be in Denver during the convention. Our thought was to get him as close to the head speechwriters (and so as close to Obama) as possible. But Wallace said, very politely, that this wasn't what interested him. He wanted to be with a worker bee on the speechwriting team—to find out how the language was used by, as he put it, "the ninth guy on the bench." It also seemed like maybe a temperament thing, that he would be more comfortable reporting away from the glare.

planes and waiting around in hotel lobbies," he writes, "the look of people who have to create an envelope of privacy around them with just their expressions." He hears the "authoritative pang" of tour-tight racket strings and sees ball boys "reconfigure complexly." He hits the practice courts and watches players warm up, their bodies "moving with the compact nonchalance I've since come to recognize in pros when they're working out: the suggestion is one of a very powerful engine in low gear."

The lie comes at the start of the piece, when Wallace points out a potential irony of what he's getting ready to do, namely write about people we've never heard of, who are culturally marginal, yet are among the best in the world at a chosen pursuit. "You are invited to try to imagine what it would be like to be among the hundred best in the world at something," Wallace says. "At anything. I have tried to imagine; it's hard."

What's strange is that this was written in 1996—by then, Wallace had completed his genre-impacting second novel, *Infinite Jest*, as well as the stories, a couple already considered classic, in the collection *Girl with Curious Hair*. It's hard to believe he didn't know that he was indeed among the hundred best at a particular thing, namely imaginative prose, and that there were serious people ready to put him among an even smaller number. Perhaps we should assume that, being human, he knew it sometimes and at other times feared it wasn't true. Either way, the false modesty— asking us to accept the idea that he'd never thought of himself as so good and had proposed the experiment naively—can't help reading as odd. Which may itself be deliberate. Not much happens by accident in Wallace's stuff; his profound obsessive streak precluded it. So could it be there's something multilayered going on with sport as a metaphor for writing—even more layers than we expect? It does seem curious that Wallace chose, of all the players, one named Joyce, whose "ethnic" Irishness Wallace goes out of his way to emphasize, thereby alluding to an artist whose own fixation on technical mastery made him a kind of grotesque, dazzling but isolated from healthful, human narrative concerns. Certainly Wallace played textual games on that level.

Here's a thing that is hard to imagine: being so inventive a writer that when you die, the language is impoverished. That's what Wallace's suicide did, two and a half years ago. It wasn't just a sad thing, it was a blow.

.   .   .

It's hard to do the traditional bio-style paragraph about Wallace for readers who, in this oversaturated mediascape, don't know who he was or why he mattered because you keep flashing on his story "Death Is Not the End," in which he parodies the practice of writing the traditional bio-style paragraph about writers, listing all their honors and whatnot, his list becoming inexplicably ridiculous as he keeps naming the prizes, and you get that he's digging into the frequent self-congratulating silliness of the American literary world, "a Lannan Foundation Fellowship, . . . a Mildred and Harold Strauss Living Award from the American Academy and Institute of Arts and Letters . . . a poet two separate American generations have hailed as the voice of their generation." Wallace himself had many of the awards on the list, including "a 'Genius Grant' from the prestigious MacArthur Foundation." Three novels, three story collections, two books of essays, the Roy E. Disney Professorship of Creative Writing at Pomona College . . .

When they say that he was a *generational* writer, that he "spoke for a generation," there's a sense in which it's almost scientifically true. Everything we know about the way literature gets made suggests there's some connection between the individual talent and the society that produces it, the social organism. Cultures extrude geniuses the way a beehive will make a new queen when its old one dies, and it's possible now to see Wallace as one of those. I remember well enough to know it's not a trick of hindsight, hearing about and reading *Infinite Jest* for the first time, as a twenty-year-old, and the immediate sense of: This is it. One of us is going to try it. The "it" being all of it, to capture the sensation of being alive in a fractured superpower at the end of the twentieth century. Someone had come along with an intellect potentially strong enough to mirror the spectacle and a moral seriousness deep enough to want to in the first place. About none of his contemporaries—even those who in terms of ability could compete with him—can one say that they risked as great a failure as Wallace did.

People who've never read a word he wrote know his style, the so-called quirks, a bag of typographical tricks ripped from the eighteenth-century comic novel and recontextualized: the footnotes and skeptical parentheticals, clauses that compulsively double back, feeling for weaknesses in themselves. It's true these match the idiosyncrasies of his manner of speech and thought. (We know this especially well now that all those YouTube videos of him at readings and in interviews have become familiar—oddly so: For someone who clearly squirmed under the eye of scrutiny like a stuck bug, Wallace *submitted* and subjected himself to so much of it. He had more author photos than any of his peers. He was nothing if not a torn person.)

The point is that his style did more than reflect his habit of mind; it was an expression of an unusually coherent sensibility. Wallace was a relentless reviser and could have streamlined all of those syntactically baroque paragraphs. He didn't think the world worked that way. The truth, or rather truth seeking, didn't sound like that. It was self-critical—self-interrogating, even—on the catch for its own tricks of self-evasion. It's worth noting, in that regard, that *The New Yorker*, which published some of his best fiction, never did any of his nonfiction. No shame to Wallace or *The New Yorker*, it's simply a technically interesting fact: He *couldn't* have changed his voice to suit the magazine's famous house style. The "plain style" is about erasing yourself as a writer and laying claim to a kind of invisible narrative authority, the idea being that the writer's mind and personality are manifest in every line, without the vulgarity of having to tell the reader it's happening. But Wallace's relentlessly first-person strategies didn't proceed from narcissism, far from it—they were signs of philosophical stubbornness. (His father, a professional philosopher, studied with Wittgenstein's last assistant; Wallace himself as an undergraduate made an actual intervening contribution—recently published as *Fate, Time, and Language*—to the debate over free will.) He looked at the plain style and saw that the impetus of it, in the end, is to sell the reader something. Not in a crass sense, but in a rhetorical sense. The well-tempered magazine feature, for all its pleasures, is a kind of fascist wedge that seeks to make you forget its problems, half-truths, and arbitrary decisions and swallow its nonexistent imprimatur. Wallace could never exempt himself or his reporting from the range of things that would be subject to scrutiny.

The one time I met him, at a reception before a reading, I spoke to him only to mumble stock phrases about "admire your work," etc. But the visual impression has remained strong, because in that cocktail-party atmosphere (Tom Wolfe was ten feet away, in his white suit), Wallace was possibly the most physically uncomfortable-looking person I've ever seen. If you have, at any point in your life, been trapped in a room in a mountain house with a forest animal, a raccoon or a bobcat, that's how Wallace seemed, frozen like that. He had a smile on his face like he was waiting for someone to punch him. Yet was polite and shoulder-shruggy when he spoke to you. Everyone was all dressed up except Wallace, who had on a kind of Russian-peasant's shirt and was in a full-on "I have long hair like a lady but also a beard" phase. It gave him a homeless-person vibe, like he'd seen the food table and decided to join the party. Yet when he got up onstage in the end, alongside George Plimpton and Seymour Hersh among others, he not only held his own but held the theater spellbound and more than once had to stop and let laughter pass, enunciating those roundly nasal vowels.

His voice was regional in more than one sense—the fastidiousness about usage, for instance. Only Midwesterners will waste time over the grammar of small talk with you; nowhere else, when you ask, "Can I get an iced tea?" does anyone ever say, "I don't know . . . *can* you?" And Wallace did think of himself as in some ways a regional writer—else he'd never have let the über-author photographer Marion Ettlinger take the well-known trench-coat-lion shot of him smiling wryly beside a waving cornfield. He knew that he came, as he said in the essay he read that night, from a landscape "whose emptiness is both physical and spiritual." The very "maximalism" of his style, which his detractors claimed to find self-indulgent, suggests an environment with space to fill. In one of his earliest essays—about playing junior tennis in tornado alley—he mythologizes his relationship with the plains:

> I liked the sharp intercourse of straight lines more than the other kids I grew up with. I think this is because they were natives, whereas I was an infantile transplant from Ithaca, where my dad had Ph.D.'d. So I'd known, even horizontally and semiconsciously as a baby, something different, the tall hills and serpentine one-ways of upstate NY. I'm pretty sure I kept the amorphous mush of curves and swells as a contrasting backlight somewhere down in the lizardy part of my brain, because the . . . children I fought and played with, kids who knew and had known nothing else, saw nothing stark or new-worldish in the township's planar layout . . .

New-worldish: It was like Wallace to sound informal when he was abandoning rigor and making claims that weren't quite defensible—a way to get you on his side.

He's maybe the only notoriously "difficult" writer who almost never wrote a page that wasn't enjoyable, or at least diverting, to read. Yet it was the theme of loneliness, a particular kind of postmodern, information-saturated loneliness, that, more than anything, drew crowds to his readings who looked in size and excitement level more like what you'd see at an in-store for a new band. Many of Wallace's readers (this is apparent now that every single one of them has written an appreciation of him somewhere on the Internet) believed that he was speaking to them in his work—that he was one of the few people alive who could help them navigate a new spiritual wilderness, in which every possible source of consolation had been nullified. And Wallace was speaking to them; his native conscientiousness prevented him from shirking the role of sage altogether. It's in this way that we can understand his frequent and uncharacteristically Pollyanna statements about the supposed power of fiction against solipsism, i.e., that only in literature do we know for sure we're having "a deep, significant conversation with another consciousness."

Wallace knew that this was a bromide. (There can be no better proof than how it was picked up as a thing to say about him, in pieces after his death.) Fiction can only substitute the chaos of text for the chaos of talk. It replaces the mirrors in the hall with other mirrors. He didn't want to be a total bummer, though; plus, it gave him something to say in interviews. In his books, so fluffy an idea would never survive the withering storm of pan-optical analysis. It's right there in "Good Old Neon," a story about a golden boy who kills himself, as remembered by his classmate David Wallace, who is "fully aware that the cliché that you can't ever truly know what's going on inside somebody else is hoary and insipid and yet at the same time trying very consciously to prohibit that awareness from mocking the attempt or sending the whole line of thought into the sort of inbent spiral that keeps you from ever getting anywhere . . ."

•   •   •

One feels that Wallace himself couldn't pull up from some kind of inbent spiral. We know now—though he tended to keep it private in life—that he had suffered from severe clinical depression and anxiety disorders from his teenage years and had been fighting valiantly against his own brain chemistry the whole time. When he died, we lost a writer who kept the landscape of American literature in a state of energized flux because he was so clearly playing for keeps and, technically speaking, had proved himself capable of almost anything. The last story collection he published during his life, *Oblivion*, is correctly considered his blackest and least amusing book, but it contained stories that showed a new mastery and concision, including the one-paragraph masterpiece, "Incarnations of Burned Children." The notion that Wallace didn't have future masterpieces in him seemed crazy, like anticipating a change in the laws of nature.

It helps to know all of that, or to know at any rate that a population of people feels this way, if you want to understand the hubbub around *The Pale King*, the novel Wallace left unfinished, now being published by Little, Brown. Rumors of posthumous work started almost immediately after his death, and it's safe to say that loyal readers have been clinging to the promise of this new book over the last couple of years, almost as a means of fending off the reality and violence of what happened. Some of the collective grief for the man got sublimated into excitement for the book. I myself was surprised, on finishing the review copy, to have the wind sucked out of me by the thought—long delayed—that there would be no more Wallace books. Not that we won't be treated to a whole half-shelf of volumes: his letters, his uncollected stuff, a best of, a collected works. That's only proper.

·　　·　　·

The Pale King is different. He left us this book—the people closest to him agree that he wanted us to see it. This is not, in other words, a classic case of Posthumous Great Novel, where scholars have gone into an estate and unearthed a manuscript the author would probably never want read. Wallace seems to have laid this book before us in an all but do-with-it-what-you-will sort of way. Supposedly one of his last acts on earth was to arrange the most-ready pages and leave them in a place where his wife, the artist Karen Green, could find them. His notebooks led to the identification of partial chapters, which his longtime editor Michael Pietsch has assembled into something like a draft of the novel as it might have looked in Wallace's head—more polished than that, in places, less so in others. Think of a big mural that was half done.

The Pale King (the title of which may or may not refer to a nineteenth-century folk expression, "the pale king of terrors," meaning the melancholy fear of death) is about a group of people, all of whom work at a particular IRS processing station in Illinois. Some of the characters get involved with one another in various, not obviously consequential ways. Two of them are named David Wallace. That's the whole plot. It never progresses.[3] It never really seems to begin.

You'd be forgiven for suspecting that a book about random people who work for the government sounds insufferably tedious. The reason it's not has to do with the word *about*—it's the wrong word, the wrong preposition. Wallace doesn't write *about* his characters; he hadn't in a long time. He writes *into* them. That thing he could do on a tennis court or a cruise ship, or at a porn convention, that made him both an inspiration and a madden-

---

3. Actually, something does change. Things get spooky, there are doublings. Ghosts appear. One of the characters, it turns out, is clairvoyant. A note at the end of the book suggests that a team of X-Agents, as it were, all of whom possess different unusual qualities, is being assembled by a small group of supervisors. The whole story is apparently taking place in a world where Bush, and not Reagan, got elected in 1980 (Reagan was his vice president). But these intrusions of mysticism don't otherwise trouble the fabric of the novel's reality.

ing, envy-making presence for the scores like me who learned to do "magazine writing" in his shadow (he was one of those writers who, even when you weren't sounding like him, made you think about how you weren't sounding like him)—Wallace liked to do that, in his fiction, with his characters' interior lives.

Imagine walking into a place, say a mega-chain copy shop in a strip mall. It's early morning, and you're the first customer. You stop under the bright fluorescents and let the doors glide closed behind you, look at the employees in their corporate-blue shirts, mouths open, shuffling around sleepily. You take them in as a unified image, with an impenetrable surface of vague boredom and dissatisfaction that you're content to be on the outside of, and you set to your task, to your copying or whatever. That's precisely the moment when Wallace hits pause, that first little turn into inattention, into self-absorption. He reverses back through it, presses play again. Now it's different. You're in a room with a bunch of human beings. Each of them, like you, is broken and has healed in some funny way. Each of them, even the shallowest, has a novel inside. Each is loved by God or deserves to be. They all have something to do with you: When you let the membrane of your consciousness become porous, permit osmosis, you know it to be true, we have something to do with one another, are part of a narrative—but what? Wallace needed very badly to know. And he sensed that the modern world was bombarding us with scenarios, like the inside of the copy shop, where it was easy to forget the question altogether. We "feel lonely in a crowd," he writes in one of his stories, but we "stop not to dwell on what's brought the crowd into being," with the result that "we are, always, faces in a crowd."

That's what I love in Wallace, noticed details like that, microdescriptions of feeling states that seem suggestive of whole branching social super-systems, sentences that make me feel like, *Anyone who doesn't get that is living in a different world*. He was the closest thing we had to a recording angel. There are paragraphs in

Infinite Jest where he's able to *trap* things, fleeting qualities of our "moment," things that you weren't sure others felt but suspected they might. To read these is like watching X-rays of the collective unconscious develop:

> Arm out like a hack's arm, Gately blasts through B.U. country. As in backpack and personal-stereo and designer-fatigues country. Soft-faced boys with backpacks and high hard hair and seamless foreheads. Totally lineless untroubled foreheads like cream cheese or ironed sheets. . . . Gately's had lines in his big forehead since he was about twelve. . . . Girls who look like they've eaten nothing but dairy products their whole lives. Girls who do step-aerobics. Girls with good combed long clean hair. Nonaddicted girls. The weird *hopelessness* at the heart of lust.

The Pale King has much in common with *Infinite Jest*, which also took a set group of people, unified in a circumstantial way—in that earlier case, the residents of an addiction halfway house, or the student body of a tennis academy—then reeled off into their lives, creating in the end a kind of spoked wheel of interconnected stories. But *The Pale King* is not really reminiscent of *Infinite Jest*, doesn't put you in mind of it, that is. To read it is in part to feel how much Wallace had changed as a writer, compressed and deepened himself.

There are lots of characters, including several of what can be called main characters. Claude Sylvanshine is one. He's a "fact psychic." He knows things about people, but his knowledge comes in tiny bursts of disconnected information, which he can't turn off. (Wallace hands parts of himself to different characters, so that at times the edges blur.) There's Lane Dean Jr., the new guy, onetime high school super-Christian. Also Meredith Rand, office hottie—Wallace's beat-by-beat breakdown of what happens to a table full of ordinary men and women when an extremely physically attractive person sits down (in this case, at the bar where the IRS workers hang out) is both painful and darkly humorous, an example of what I was trying to say about his observational power, and of how discouraging it must have often been to find yourself stuck in Wallace's head, not in the illness of it, but in the clarity of it:

> Suffice it that Meredith Rand makes the . . . males self-conscious. They thus tend to become either nervous and uncomfortably quiet, as though they were involved in a game whose stakes have suddenly become terribly high, or else they become more voluble and conversationally dominant and begin to tell a great many jokes, and in general appear deliberately unself-conscious, whereas before Meredith Rand had arrived and pulled up a chair and joined the group there was no real sense of deliberateness or even self-consciousness among them. Female examiners, in turn, react to these changes in a variety of ways, some receding and becoming visually smaller (like Enid Welch and Rachel Robbie Towne), others regarding Meredith Rand's effect on men with a sort of dark amusement, still others becoming narrow-eyed and prone to hostile sighs or even pointed departures. . . . Some of the male examiners are, by the second round of pitchers, performing for Meredith Rand, even if the performance's core consists of making a complex show of the fact that they are not performing for Meredith Rand or even especially aware that she's at the table. Bob McKenzie, in particular, becomes almost manic, addressing nearly every comment or quip to the person on either the right or left side of Meredith Rand.

Imagine flat being able to dissect us like that, with that grain of detail—as primates, if you like—and worse, being unable to stop. A person would have to maintain tremendous stores of sympathy to keep the world from turning into a constant onslaught of Swiftian grotesquerie. Wallace didn't seek to escape it, either—he cultivated it, as his art demanded. It ought to remind us of the psychic risk involved in writing at the level he sought. Like all good citizens, I'm with those who wish to resist romanticizing his suicide, but there remains a sense in which artists do expose themselves to the torrents of their time, in a way that can't help but do damage, and there's nothing wrong with calling it noble, if they've done it in the service of something beautiful. Wallace paid a price for traveling so deep into himself, for keeping his eye unaverted as *long* as it takes to write passages like the one just quoted, for finding other people *interesting* enough to pay attention to them long enough to write scenes like that. It's the reason most of us can't write great or even good fiction. You have to let a lot of other consciousnesses into your own. That's bad for equilibrium.

·　　·　　·

Wallace's choice of the IRS as a setting makes sense when you consider that he's doing something theological in this novel, and the "service," as the employees call it, provides him with convenient Jesuitical overtones. He was using the IRS the way Borges used the library and Kafka used the law-courts building: as an analogy for the world. He implies a connection between a subterranean shift in IRS policy that turned the agency from one entrusted with collecting our taxes (i.e., enforcing the law) to one charged with maximizing revenue, or as Wallace says in one of the marginal notes he left behind with the manuscript, "Big Q is whether IRS is to be essentially a corporate entity or a moral one." Through various faint hints (the mentioning of obscure lawsuits), Wallace connects the notion of the IRS becoming a corporate agency with the older idea, introduced into American life in the late nineteenth century, that in the eyes of the law, a corporation was the same as an individual, with the same rights. Wallace hadn't worked it all out, but suffice it to say, a finished Pale King might have operated by a symbolic logic in which, if IRS = corporation, and corporation = individual, then IRS = individual. The agency would be a metaphor for America's political soul.

The novel repeats a certain move, zooming into the childhood or youth of a character, whose adult self we encounter elsewhere in the book, in the orbit of the IRS office. It's in juxtaposition with these glimpses of their earlier selves that the characters' inward complexity builds. Wallace is working to prove to us that everyone's complicated, that when people seem simple and dull, it's we who aren't paying attention enough, it's our stubborn inborn tendency to see other people as major or minor characters in our story.

It's easy to make the book sound heavy, but it's often very funny, and not politely funny, either. We meet the excruciatingly upbeat Leonard Stecyk, his "smile so wide it almost looked like it hurt," a version of whom each of us knows or to some extent is. As a child he was such a do-gooder, everyone who met him instantly loathed him. "A teacher in whose homeroom the boy suggests a charted reorganization of the coat hooks and boot boxes lining one wall . . . ends up brandishing blunt scissors and threatening to kill both the boy and then herself." (I won't ruin a good scene by telling you what a high school shop teacher thinks of him.)

Unhappily, it's with this aspect of the book—the back-and-forth between recent past (at the IRS center) and deeper past (the characters' formative years)—that we come to know what the publisher means about "unfinished." The patterning isn't right. It's hardly even present. Wallace was struggling to compose the themes of these lives in a symphonic way, but he didn't get there or, it has to be said, anywhere near.

And yet even in its broken state, *The Pale King* contains what's sure to be some of the finest fiction of the year. It's intimidating to have to describe the excellence of some of these set pieces, among them the chapter (excerpted in *The New*

Yorker) in which Lane Dean Jr. tries to figure out whether or not to say he loves his junior-college girlfriend, Sheri, who's pregnant with their child. If he says he loves her, she'll keep it, and they'll spend their lives together (as happens). Neither of them has the slightest idea what love is or how to read each other's use of the word: They're relying on a bad translation. Yet what they say in the moment will determine their lives. Wallace treats teen romance with such seriousness and fidelity to emotional consciousness that the scene takes on a sort of *Bovary*-esque grandeur. Throughout are strewn the little descriptive nails that he drove home at will—that, for instance, the stick figures on the airplane's laminated safety-instruction cards are "crossing their arms funereally," or that from the plane's window, traffic seems to crawl "with a futile pointless pathos you could never sense on the ground." These aren't showy passages. Just unusually precise descriptions of things we all do and see. We enter and recognize the modern-day office environment: "the desk practically an abstraction. The whisper of sourceless ventilation." Friends left behind in a small town are imagined "selling each other insurance, drinking supermarket liquor, watching television, awaiting the formality of their first cardiac." Michael Pietsch, the book's editor, pointed me toward a late, surreal chapter in which Lane Dean Jr., an adult now, working for the IRS, has a conversation with one of the dead agents' ghosts who hang around the office. Pietsch called it the novel's "fullest flowering," and "as densely woven and tight-wound as anything he has written." It's a miniature tour de force, not even twenty pages, done all in dialogue, in places reminiscent of the "Nighttown" chapter in Ulysses. When I asked Pietsch how he imagined a finished *Pale King*, he said, "A book in which even more chapters are as full and tight as this," which describes a book devoutly to be missed.

•   •   •

The most remarkable pages in *The Pale King*—they steal the novel, in an interesting way—have to do with the girlhood of Toni Ware, a character who barely impinges on the IRS parts of the novel. She's in the periphery; Wallace hadn't got to her yet. But the chapters dealing with her memories of growing up in a gothic trailer park, with a mentally ill mother who brought home abusive boyfriends on a serial basis, are staggering runs of prose. What's more, they don't sound like anything else Wallace wrote. For lack of a better term, they're unselfaware. He's letting himself overwrite in a way that great writers will do, when the story doesn't have time for all of your inner quibbles. If it's true, as has been said, that Wallace was striving with *The Pale King* to find some other level, to go beyond *Infinite Jest*, he finds it here if anywhere.

They drove then once more at night. Below a moon that rose round before them. What was termed the truck's backseat was a narrow shelf on which the girl could sleep if she arranged her legs in the gap behind the real seats whose headrests possessed the dull shine of unwashed hair. The clutter and yeast smell bespoke a truck that was or had been lived in; the truck and its man smelled the same. The girl in cotton bodice and her jeans gone fugitive at the knees. The mother's conception of men was that she used them as a sorceress will dumb animals, as sign and object of her unnatural powers. Her spoken word aloud for these at which the girl gave no reproof, *familiar.* Swart and sideburned men who sucked wooden matches and crushed cans with their hands. Whose hats' brims had sweatlines like the rings of trees. Whose eyes crawled over you in the rearview. Men inconceivable as ever themselves being children or looking up naked at someone they trust, with a toy. To whom the mother talked like babies and let them treat her like a headless doll, *manhandle.*

At times, even in the midst of their beauty and terror, there's a whiff of parody or pastiche to the Toni Ware sections. Wallace seems to be making fun of bad Cormac McCarthy, the incorrigible McCarthy who, when he wants to write "toadstools," writes "mushrooms with serrate and membraneous soffits where-under toads are reckoned to siesta." Wallace has Toni Ware remember boys who "wore wide rimpled hats and cravats of thong and some displayed turquoise about their person, and of these one helped her empty the trailer's sanitary tank and then pressed her to fellate him in recompense." This strange uncertainty of tone is heightened when Toni's harrowing past recurs later in the book, but in another character's voice, one that starts out, "Toni's mom was a bit nuts . . . Blah Blah," as if anyone's story were just a matter of technique. And yet this later, at first flippant-sounding chapter *also* slips back into the same strong third-person style, in fact it leads to the most memorable page in the book, the scene of the death of Toni Ware's mother. It's as if this new voice were something Wallace couldn't resist. Perhaps we can conclude, then, that he was groping for something more satisfyingly conventional, more *adult*, in his work, and that these chapters are tantalizing flashes of a new, tragically stillborn Wallace . . .

·   ·   ·

Hold on—we're talking about *David Foster Wallace*. Things could never be that straightforward, much less that sappy. Sure enough, immediately following the last sentence of the Toni Ware chapter, as if to punish us for having loved it better than the rest of the book, Wallace does something that can only be described as delivering a formal chest slap. Having just handed us a serving of the old-fashioned virtues, pages and pages of writing writing, he goes into the most arch-meta, most heavily footnoted, winky-winky, self-conscious-about-its-winky-winkyness, too-clever-by-half, drunk-on-postmodern-hijinks chapter he's ever written. It's perverse. It's as if Wallace can hear us, in his head, writing to him the same letter he wrote to Eggers about *A Heartbreaking Work of Staggering Genius*, that Eggers put on the back cover as a blurb, which said, in part, "I admired many of the headier, more po-mo comic bits," but "the places where you cut loose and did arias of grief . . . were the book's best art." He can hear us saying something like that, after having just had our minds blown by Toni Ware, and he's saying back to us, pretty emphatically, Sorry, but this textual business is part of what it's about. Without this, I'm playing chamber music.

It will be for future critics to debate the aesthetic merits of that decision. Wallace was by no means at peace with it. Often while reading *The Pale King* I was pulled up by thoughts of the essay he wrote about Dostoevsky:

> [This new] bio prompts us to ask ourselves why we seem to require of our art an ironic distance from deep convictions or desperate questions, so that contemporary writers have to either make jokes of them or else try to work them in under cover of some formal trick like intertextual quotation or incongruous juxtaposition, sticking the really urgent stuff inside asterisks as part of some multivalent defamiliarization-flourish or some such shit. Part of the explanation for our own lit's thematic poverty obviously includes our century and situation.

He might as well be describing *The Pale King*. It's as if he had inside his head a fully formed hostile critic who despised his own work. All writers have these voices, but Wallace's were practically additional personalities. In the trick chapter we're told that the novel we think we've been reading is actually a "first-person memoir," the true story of a man named David Foster Wallace.

And there's another character named David F. Wallace in the book. As well as a character named David Cusk, who shares things, biographically, with the real David Foster Wallace.

It isn't gamesmanship, exactly. Nor is it even a question of what Wallace intended, since we don't know what he intended. Michael Pietsch has done yeoman's work as an editor here—as readers, we're in his debt—but there wasn't enough to edit. It would be dishonest to say otherwise. The story never really attains what Poe called "unity of impression" in the way that *Infinite Jest*, even with all its poly-skeinedness, did, or did at times. Also, there's something about the posthumous thing. It robs you of a certain pleasure that you take in reading, of being in dialogue with the author's decisions, judging them and at the same time having the excitement of witnessing them, which is part of the drama of a book. Here you don't know what they were. Every word you read and don't like, you think, "Well, he would have changed that." Whereas everything that does work, that's the real Wallace. Yet even major choices, such as what to use for the novel's ending, were made, out of necessity, not by Wallace but by Pietsch. "There was no outline or chapter sequence," he told me, "and no indication of what should be the opening or closing chapter." At that point, the whole question of whether we can call this "a Wallace novel" becomes unsolvable.

If we want another ending, we could say this: *The Pale King*, as we have it, is true to Wallace in a very important respect. He himself was unfinished, unresolved. There's a great Stevie Smith poem called "Was He Married?" It's her argument that normal human beings are more heroic than gods. Their difficulties are much greater, she says, "because they are so mixed." Wallace was so mixed. He was ambivalent and conflicted, about, among other things, the difference between the kinds of writing in this novel. He wasn't sure which he preferred, or how they might go together. And what if the one he wound up valuing most wasn't the one he was best at, by nature?

To give up these contradictions would've been to give up his source of power. They saved him from self-righteousness. He was a writer who in fighting to rise above the noise of his time remained hopelessly of it, susceptible to its voices even while trying to master them. His reality, as he once wrote, had been "MTV'd." This is why, like no one else, he seems to speak from inside the tornado. (A symbol that haunted his work, and that reappears in *The Pale King*.) It's this quality, of being inwardly divided, that risks getting flattened and written out of Wallace's story by his postmortem idolization, which would make of him a dispenser of wisdom. We should guard against that. We'll lose the most essential Wallace, the one that is forever wincing, reconsidering, wishing he hadn't said whatever he just said. Those were moments when his voice was most authentically of our time, and they are the reason people will one day be able to read him and feel what it was like to be alive now.

Wallace's work will be seen as a huge failure, not in the pejorative sense, but in the special sense Faulkner used when he said about American novelists, "I rate us on the basis of our splendid failure to do the impossible." Wallace failed beautifully. There is no mystery whatsoever about why he found this novel so hard to finish. The glimpse we get of what he wanted it to be—a vast model of something bland and crushing, inside of which a constellation of individual souls would shine in their luminosity, and the connections holding all of us together in this world would light up, too, like filaments—this was to be a novel on the highest order of accomplishment, and we see that the writer at his strongest would have been strong enough. He wasn't always that strong.

The Atlantic

FINALIST—REPORTING

Abdul Raziq, the police chief of Kandahar province and one of the most powerful men in Afghanistan, had long dismissed rumors that he was involved in smuggling, kidnapping, torture, and murder. Matthieu Aikins—who speaks Dari, the most widely spoken language in Afghanistan—spent two years investigating those rumors. As a result, we now know the truth about Raziq—and also understand the moral compromises made by the United States in its pursuit of victory in Afghanistan. Already one of the most honored magazines in the history of the National Magazine Awards before James Bennet was named editor in 2006, The Atlantic *has received twenty-five nominations since then.*

Matthieu Aikins

Our Man in Kandahar

S hyly, at times smiling with weak adolescent bravado, the two young men recounted to me how they were beaten and tortured. It was July, and we were sitting at a table in the cavernous restaurant where they both work, in the stupefying summer heat. They slouched forward with their arms on their knees, frequently glancing down toward their open sandals, at toes where livid burns from the electrical wires were still visible.

I will call them Najib and Ahmad, though their names, like others in this article, have been changed to protect their safety. Both twenty-three years old, they looked like gangly young men who should be playing basketball on the street outside their house, or perhaps video games inside. But here in Kandahar City, the linchpin of the U.S. military's campaign against the Taliban in southern Afghanistan, they had found themselves the victims of America's Afghan allies.

One afternoon in June, two younger boys who worked at the restaurant, ages twelve and fourteen, had been stopped by the Afghan National Police while carrying home leftovers from an afternoon wedding. The boys, who were each paid about $60 a month, explained that they always took home leftover meals for their families. But this time they were arrested and accused of bringing food to insurgent fighters hiding outside the city.

Around eleven o'clock that night, police showed up at the restaurant and arrested Najib and Ahmad as well, accusing them of having sent the younger boys out to feed the Taliban. They were taken to police headquarters, where they were handed over to men wearing the mottled gray-green uniforms of the Border Police.

"They said, 'We are going to beat you,'" Ahmad recalled.

The Border Police were a new sight in the city: rough-looking types with wraparound shades and bandoliers of grenades, who could be seen lounging at checkpoints throughout the city and guarding installations such as the governor's palace. Though restricted by Afghan law to operate only in international airports or within fifty kilometers of the border, they'd entered the city on May 29 when their boss, Brigadier General Abdul Raziq, was appointed acting chief of police in Kandahar province, following the assassination of his predecessor. Raziq was well known as a warlord and suspected drug trafficker who had waged a brutal campaign against the Taliban. He was also a close ally of both President Hamid Karzai and the U.S. military.

Inside the station, the policemen tied a scarf to Najib's handcuffs and hung him from the ceiling until he felt as if his arms were being pulled from their sockets. Then two men—one in uniform and holding a black metal baton, the other in plain clothes and wielding a length of cable—began beating him across his hips and thighs. A third man, also in plain clothes, questioned Najib: "What was the name of the commander you were bringing food to? How often do you bring food to the enemy?" Sobbing, Najib pleaded his innocence. In a nearby room, Ahmad could hear his friend's screams, though he was spared for the time being.

When the beating was over, Najib and Ahmad were taken outside and thrown into the back of an armored Humvee, where they lay all night with their wrists still tightly cuffed, suffocating in the stiflingly hot, enclosed interior.

Early the next morning, they were taken to the governor's palace, a long, low white compound fronted by a series of arches, jointly guarded by American soldiers and Border Police, where U.S. and Afghan officials meet on a daily basis. The police brought them around the back, to a filthy room that smelled of human waste, where they were shackled to the wall next to two other prisoners. Then, one at a time, they were taken to a second room, empty except for a gas-powered generator.

Najib went first. He was forced to lie on his back, and wires leading to the generator were attached to toes on both his feet. A group of Border Police crowded around him, jeering and spitting snuff on his face. "Tell us the truth," they commanded. Then they switched on the power. "It felt," Najib told me, "like my whole body was filled with moving knives."

After he passed out from the pain, it was Ahmad's turn to be tortured. When the two awoke from the ordeal, they were placed in separate rooms. In the evening, they were taken to police headquarters to see Abdul Raziq himself.

Raziq is just thirty-three years old, slender and boyish-looking, with a square jaw and a widow's peak that tufts up beneath the embroidered pillbox cap he favors when he's not in uniform. Uneducated but clever and charismatic, he is, despite his youth, one of the most powerful warlords in southern Afghanistan. He controls a militia of several thousand men, as well as the lucrative drug-smuggling routes that pass through his territory, which includes a key trading town called Spin Boldak, near the border with Pakistan.

That June evening, Najib and Ahmad were seated facing Raziq, who asked them to explain why they had been arrested. They told him about the younger boys who would take leftover food home to their families, and whether it was because they had not confessed or because their stories had checked out, Raziq ordered them released.

Najib and Ahmad complained to me of suffering nerve damage in their wrists from being cuffed for two days, and both said they'd had problems with their kidneys since the electrocutions:

Ahmad, who had the more-severe burns, urinated blood for three days afterward. I examined the wounds on Ahmad's and Najib's toes—distinct circular burn marks that were still raw and unhealed—and I spoke with a number of their coworkers, who corroborated their claims. I was also given photos of their injuries taken immediately after they were released and was told their story independently by a source inside the Kandahar police department unhappy with the abuses taking place under Raziq. "That's what happened to them when they were innocent," this official said. "Think of what they do to the guilty."

.   .   .

What happened to Ahmad and Najib is not an isolated incident, but part of a larger pattern of abuse that has occurred wherever Raziq has been in power, first in his outpost of Spin Boldak and now in Kandahar City. Raziq has long been publicly suspected of drug trafficking and corruption; allegations that he and his men have been involved in extrajudicial killings, torture, and illegal imprisonment have been trickling out for years. Raziq categorically denies all such charges, telling *The Atlantic*, "When someone works well, then he finds a lot of enemies who try to ruin his name."

Last fall, Raziq and his militia were given a starring role in the U.S.-led military offensive into Taliban-controlled areas west of Kandahar City, a campaign that boosted his prestige immensely. Mentored by an American Special Forces team, Raziq's fighters won public praise from U.S. officers for their combat prowess. After the offensive, Raziq was promoted to brigadier general—a rank requiring a direct order from President Karzai—in a January ceremony at the governor's mansion. As Ben Moeling, who was until July the State Department's senior official in Kandahar province, explained to me at the time, the promotion was "an explicit recognition of his importance."

Nor was that promotion the only evidence of Raziq's continuing ascent. In May, when Karzai appointed him chief of police for Kandahar province, Raziq accepted only on the condition that he also remain in charge of Spin Boldak, the seat of his economic and tribal power. So, in a move that enabled him to retain both jobs, Raziq was appointed "acting" police chief in Kandahar.

While beatings in police custody have been common in Kandahar for as long as there have been police, a number of Afghan and international officials familiar with the situation there told me that Raziq has brought with him a new level of brutality. Since his arrival, Raziq has launched a wave of arrests across the city in coordination with the government intelligence agency, the National Directorate of Security. One human-rights official who has conducted prison visits in Kandahar told me that the number of prisoners is up more than 50 percent since Raziq's arrival. In July, even the U.S. military seemed to have realized that the situation was out of hand, when American and NATO forces quietly halted the transfer of detainees to Afghan authorities in southern Afghanistan, because of credible allegations that prisoners had been severely abused while in police and NDS custody.

Though Raziq has risen in large part through his own skills and ambition, he is also, to a considerable degree, a creation of the American military intervention in Afghanistan. (Prior to 2001, he had worked in a shop in Pakistan.) As part of a countrywide initiative, his men have been trained by two controversial private military firms, DynCorp and Xe, formerly known as Blackwater, at a U.S.-funded center in Spin Boldak, where they are also provided with weapons, vehicles, and communications equipment. Their salaries are subsequently paid through the Law and Order Trust Fund for Afghanistan, a UN-administered international fund, to which the U.S. is the largest contributor. Raziq himself has enjoyed visits in Spin Boldak from such senior U.S. officials as Ambassador Karl Eikenberry and Generals Stanley McChrystal and David Petraeus.

In public, American officials had until recently been careful to downplay Raziq's alleged abuses. When I met with the State Department's Moeling at his Kandahar City office in January, he told me, "I think there is certainly a mythology about Abdul Raziq, where there's a degree of assumption on some of those things. But I have never seen evidence of private prisons or of extrajudicial killings directly attributable to him."

Yet, as a 2006 State Department report shows, U.S. officials have for years been aware of credible allegations that Raziq and his men participated in a cold-blooded massacre of civilians, the details of which have, until now, been successfully buried. And this, in turn, raises questions regarding whether U.S. officials may have knowingly violated a 1997 law that forbids assistance to foreign military units involved in human-rights violations.

·   ·   ·

Among a certain group of Kandaharis, the rough outlines of the massacre in question are well known. But nailing down a consistent, detailed version of what took place required two years of cross-checking with a diverse set of sources, including tribal elders, human-rights workers, police officers, and government officials. Most important, I was eventually given direct access to information and photos from a suppressed police investigation into the episode.

On March 20, 2006, Shin Noorzai, a burly smuggler in his midthirties, arrived with fifteen companions at the guesthouse of an acquaintance, Zulmay Tufon, in Kabul. It was the eve of Nowruz, the Persian New Year, occasion for Afghanistan's biggest festivities, and the capital city's bedraggled trees were strung with fallen kites and the first buds of spring.

Shin had grown up in southern Afghanistan during the violent, turbulent times of the anti-Soviet and civil wars, and had once been jailed in Pakistan for kidnapping a man. His companions, though, were a mixed group. Some were smugglers, but others were simply friends from the vicinity of the Afghan-Pakistani border, farmers or traders accompanying him on a trip to Mazar-e Sharif, a northern city famous for its new-year celebrations.

According to an acquaintance of Shin's who was also present at the gathering, he and his friends had arrived at the invitation of another man, Mohammed Naeem Lalai, an old friend of Shin's who was then working as an officer in the Border Police. It was Lalai who had persuaded Shin and his friends to stop in Kabul on their way to Mazar. As the group sat down to dinner, Shin's acquaintance, a fellow tribesman, watched uneasily, nervous about the company Shin was keeping. He offered to make the trip with Shin instead. "Come with me to Mazar," he said to him.

Shin replied that he was going to travel up to Mazar with Lalai. But first, he said, Lalai was taking him to another house where music and entertainment were promised. That night, as darkness fell over Kabul, Shin and his fifteen companions left the house with Lalai. Their friends and families would never see them alive again.

At the second house, Shin and his friends were apparently drugged. Unconscious, they were bound and gagged, then loaded into vehicles with official plates, one of them a green Ford Ranger with the seal of the Border Police on its doors.

Driving along back roads, the cars made their way 500 kilometers south to Kandahar province, and by the next morning arrived at Spin Boldak, where Abdul Raziq, then a Border Police colonel in his midtwenties, was waiting for them.

Raziq and Lalai had together lured Shin and his associates to Kabul. The tribes to which Raziq and Shin belonged had been feuding over smuggling routes, and Raziq held Shin responsible for the 2004 killing of his brother. Shin had been a marked man ever since. His fifteen companions were just going to be collateral damage.

Raziq and his men loaded their captives into a convoy of Land Cruisers and headed out to a parched, desolate stretch of the Afghan-Pakistani border. About ten kilometers outside of town, they came to a halt. Shin and the others were hauled out of the trucks and into a dry river gully. There, at close range, Raziq's forces let loose with automatic weapons, their bullets tearing through the helpless men, smashing their faces apart, and soaking their robes with blood. After finishing the job, they unbound the corpses and left them there.

Arriving back in Spin Boldak, Raziq reported to his superiors and to the press that he had intercepted "at least fifteen" Taliban fighters infiltrating from Pakistan, led by the "mid-level Taliban commander Mullah Shin," and had killed them in a gun battle. "We got a tip-off about them coming across the border. We went down there and fought them," Raziq told the Associated Press the next day. It was the beginning of a cover-up that would go all the way up to President Karzai in Kabul.

· · ·

Last January, I followed a turbaned old man down an alley off the bustling Char Suq Bazaar in Kandahar City. The man, whom I will call Waheed, was a relative of one of the men who was killed in the gully outside Spin Boldak. I was dressed in local garb—I speak Dari and, with my half-Asian features, can pass for Afghan—and was carrying photos from the suppressed police investigation of the massacre.

As Waheed and I passed children kicking a soccer ball, he beckoned to me and ducked inside a doorway. He led me into a tiny guest room, where he clicked on a low-watt bulb and his adolescent son brought us tea. In the dim light, the three of us went through the series of twenty-one photos taken by crime-scene investigators. The bodies, lying close together in the gully, had been numbered by the investigators. One had had his neck blown apart;

another was unrecognizable, his face a mass of charred flesh. Yet another photo was of a young boy, seemingly untouched, his smooth, skinny neck sticking out of a baggy tunic. He might have been asleep, were it not for his sightless eyes gazing skyward.

"There, Father. That's Tooryalai," Waheed's son said, pointing at the picture of a rotund, walrus-mustached man, his face scrunched in agony, the white fabric around his midsection drenched with blood. Waheed nodded. "That's him."

Tooryalai had been about thirty-five years old, and had worked as an occasional taxi driver and laborer. He had known Shin for years, and the invitation to accompany him to the Nowruz festivities in Mazar had seemed a welcome chance to escape the stultifying rural backwater of Kandahar province. Waheed, his relative, had advised against it. "I said, 'Don't go with him, you are a poor man, and you should stay at home,'" Waheed told me.

But Tooryalai went. They found his vehicle later, abandoned in Kabul. Tooryalai's wife and children moved in with her father. Two of his brothers joined the Afghan National Police in hopes of one day avenging Tooryalai, but both were killed in the war before they had the chance. Their father had since gone mad, and Tooryalai's youngest brothers were now picking rags in the street.

"It was a tribal conflict," Waheed said, shaking his head, his long fingers trembling as they tapped against his cheek. "Raziq had a problem with Shin, but why did he have to kill all the others?"

As Raziq intended, the victims were framed as Taliban in the Afghan press. There was an outcry across the border in Pakistan, however, where many of the victims' families lived. On March 23, two days after the murders, the Pakistani Foreign Office lodged a protest with the Afghan ambassador in Islamabad. Yet it is likely that Raziq and Lalai would have kept the truth hidden, were it not for an Afghan official working for the European Union who had happened to be in Spin Boldak at the time of the murders.

When he heard of the suspicious killings, this official called his boss, Michael Semple, who was then the deputy to Francesc Vendrell, the European Union's special representative to Afghanistan. "He had real-time information and alerted me," said Semple, who noticed the discrepancy between word-of-mouth reports in Spin Boldak and the official line. "It was being sold as a heroic defense of Afghanistan against the Taliban."

A tall Irishman with a flaming-red beard, fluent in Dari and Pashto, Semple was known as a foreigner who didn't hesitate to get directly involved in Afghan politics. That hands-on attitude would later get Semple in trouble, when he was caught up in a 2007 dispute over a local cease-fire with the Taliban and was kicked out of the country by Karzai. He's now a fellow at Harvard University's Carr Center for Human Rights Policy and a widely respected expert on Afghanistan and Pakistan.

Concerned that a massacre by Afghan security forces had just occurred, Semple got in touch with a senior Afghan official at the Interior Ministry, who was able to get a team from the Criminal Investigations Department sent to Spin Boldak from Kandahar City.

One of the members of that CID team, whom I will call Mohammad, met with me earlier this year in Kabul. As he described it, the team drove to Spin Boldak on March 22, the day after the killings. After asking around among the local villagers, the investigators realized that the victims' bodies were still out there, and drove to a Border Police outpost near the site. "We asked the local police what happened, and they said that Abdul Raziq came in five or six vehicles, and then they heard firing," Mohammad told me.

The CID team found the sixteen corpses lying a meter or two apart in a ravine near the Pakistani border. Mohammad told me that it was immediately obvious that Raziq's story of a fierce battle with Taliban fighters could not have been true. The men had clearly been killed at close range. They were clumped together at the bottom of a steep-walled gully, an improbable place for a gun battle. Their wrists bore bind marks, and their clothes were clean and new, more suitable for a party than for a Taliban incursion.

As an investigative officer in one of the most violent provinces in Afghanistan, Mohammad had seen hundreds of dead bodies. But this time, he was overcome with emotion by the corpse of a boy who could not have been more than sixteen—the same boy whose picture I had looked at with Waheed. "He was a lovely boy. I wept for him as I lifted his body," Mohammed said, his voice thickening. "For one person, Raziq killed fifteen innocents."

Raziq refused to meet with the CID team and went to stay in the house of his friend Asadullah Khalid, then the governor of Kandahar province and now the minister of tribal and border affairs; it was announced in the press that Raziq had been "taken into custody and temporarily replaced in his job pending an investigation." Khalid, though, would hardly seem to be one to call Raziq to account: in 2007, while Khalid was governor, the Canadian military temporarily ceased detainee transfers after persistent allegations of torture by security forces, including Khalid's notorious palace-guard force, Brigade 888.

The CID team reported its findings to Kabul, and a larger investigation was launched, interviewing scores of witnesses and establishing the identities of the murdered men, the fact that they had been lured to Kabul and drugged, and the involvement of Mohammed Naeem Lalai. (Lalai, now a member of the Afghan Parliament, denied any involvement to me.)

At the behest of President Karzai, a delegation of senior officials was sent to Kandahar, led by Major General Abdur Rahman, who was the deputy director of the Border Police. The delegation interviewed the Kandahar CID team, a variety of witnesses, and Raziq himself, before returning to Kabul.

There, according to a senior Interior Ministry official who is directly familiar with the events, President Karzai and other top officials were briefed by Rahman on the CID investigation.

Semple, who was later shown the contents of the report, said that it was an open-and-shut case. "They documented the killings in such a way that would leave no reasonable person in doubt that these were summary executions carried out by the Border Police," he said.

Yet after the CID file was handed over to the attorney general's office, no prosecution was ever initiated. And on April 6, well after he had presented the CID's evidence to Karzai, Rahman gave an interview to the Afghan station Tolo TV in which he backed up Raziq's version of the story, claiming that the murdered men had been Taliban infiltrators. Raziq was soon back in charge of his post at the border.

Not long after, in one of their meetings with Karzai, Semple and his boss, Vendrell, raised the issue of the killings. "We informed Karzai that we were aware of the incident in Spin Boldak and we considered that the evidence pointed to summary executions by [Raziq's] forces, and that they had sufficient evidence of it to mount a prosecution," Semple told me. "And he said something to the effect of 'Abdul Raziq is a special case.' The implication that I understood from that was that he was saying that Abdul Raziq was an essential ally against whom he was not prepared to take action, irrespective of the nature of the allegations or the evidence."

Vendrell didn't recall Karzai's exact response, but he remembered the incident clearly. "It was pretty shocking, in the sense that one of the tasks of my office was to ensure that there would be no gross violations of human rights after the Bonn accord," he told me. He reported the incident to his headquarters in Brussels, which meant that all members of the EU were made aware of it.

For Semple, it felt like a watershed moment for impunity under the Karzai regime. "It wasn't a case of 'Everybody's up to it, and only poor Abdul Raziq got caught,'" he said. "Whatever may be the sins of post-2001 security forces in Afghanistan, a propensity to indulge in multiple summary executions is not among them."

A spokesman for the Karzai administration declined to comment. Raziq himself continues to maintain that the men killed outside of Spin Boldak were Taliban. "In the past five years, a lot of soldiers have been killed, and our enemies have also been killed," he told *The Atlantic*. "And those who have been killed, they were terrorists."

· · ·

The U.S. embassy was also aware of the killings of Shin and his companions. Each year, with the help of embassy staffers around the world, the State Department's Bureau of Democracy, Human Rights, and Labor produces an annual report on every country's human-rights situation. In the 2006 report for Afghanistan, the bureau notes:

> In March Commander Abdul Razaq of Kandahar province was removed from his post for allegedly attacking 16 rivals under the pretext that they were Taliban militants. The 16 men were Pakistani citizens who had traveled to Afghanistan for Afghan New Year celebrations. They belonged to a clan in Pakistan that Razaq blamed for the death of his brother two years earlier.

Nor was that the only time Raziq's force was featured in the human-rights report. Last year's report referred to an incident in February 2010, noting that "Afghan Border Police mistakenly killed seven civilians who were collecting firewood near a checkpoint in the border town of Spin Boldak." As reported in the press, the seven victims were from the remote village of Sortano, near the border. In an exchange remarkably similar to that which followed the Shin Noorzai killings, Raziq claimed they had been mistaken for Taliban infiltrators, while the Pakistani press reported simply that they were "Pakistani drivers" who had been killed over "old differences."

Other episodes have been reported as well. In January 2010, Nader Nadery, a commissioner of the Afghan Independent Human Rights Commission, held a press conference to denounce abuses in Kandahar. One of the subjects he brought up was Raziq. "In at least three cases where the chief of the Border Police in Spin Boldak was involved, people gave testimonies that they were illegally imprisoned and tortured," Nadery told me. The victims claimed to have been beaten with cables and held incommunicado, one of them for three months. According to Nadery, they were simple men who had not been accused of serious crimes. Their detentions may have been politically motivated, or related to conflicts over business.

Given the level of violence in Kandahar, confirming these sorts of claims is extraordinarily difficult and dangerous. According to Mohammad, who was part of the CID team that investigated the deaths of Shin Noorzai and his companions in 2006, a comparable government investigation of allegations against Raziq would be unthinkable today. He has grown too powerful.

I was, however, able to speak with multiple sources about the deaths of two young men, whom I will call Sediq and Faizullah. The two were allegedly killed by the Border Police on September 7, 2010, at the height of the U.S.-led military offensive. Their deaths, among others, strongly suggest that the murders of Shin Noorzai and his friends were not an isolated incident, but rather part of a pattern of private detention and extrajudicial killing overseen by Raziq.

Both men, according to family members, had been in custody in one of Raziq's private prisons in Spin Boldak, before being pulled from jail and shot in the last days of Ramadan, possibly in retaliation for the assassination on August 31 of one of Raziq's favorite commanders. Faizullah had been from a family of taxi drivers, and was about twenty-one years old. He had been arrested by the Border Police in Spin Boldak three months earlier. Sediq, around the same age, was a madrasa student who had been arrested a month before that. Though they hadn't known each other, they wound up sharing a grave in a remote area near the village of Katsai Ziarat.

"Their hands were tied, in a dried gully, far from the village," one of their relatives, who recovered the bodies, told me. "The shepherds from the village had seen dead bodies, and so the locals took us there."

It is impossible now to tell whether the men had any involvement with the Taliban, or worked for rival smuggling gangs, or were, as their relatives claimed, truly innocent. Regardless, though, they were, according to these sources, summarily and illegally executed. And the desperation and fear of their relatives was palpable. "We went so many times to the Americans," another relative claimed. "They did nothing. What else can we do?"

Since then, thanks in part to the support and forbearance of the United States, Raziq has become the acting police chief of Kandahar province, which includes Afghanistan's second-largest city, and he seems to have brought with him the brutal methods of the borderlands. In July, I spoke with a man who told me that his son, an eighteen-year-old shopkeeper, after being seen with a man the police suspected of being an insurgent, was detained by police and beaten so badly in custody that he died of internal injuries. And I saw with my own eyes the round burn marks on Najib's and Ahmad's toes, where, they told me, they had been electrocuted during questioning about crimes they did not commit.

•   •   •

Moral questions aside, Raziq's record of reported human-rights abuses should make it illegal for the U.S. to train and assist his forces. In 1997, in response to abuses by the Colombian army, Congress passed the Leahy Amendment, named after its sponsor and most vocal advocate, Senator Patrick Leahy, a Democrat from Vermont. The law prohibits State Department or Defense

Department assistance or training to a foreign military unit where there is "credible evidence that such unit has committed gross violations of human rights."

The State Department's Bureau of Democracy, Human Rights, and Labor—which put out the 2006 report citing Raziq's alleged involvement in the massacre of civilians—is also the group responsible for overseeing compliance with the Leahy Amendment. Yet, incredibly, U.S. support for Raziq seems never to have triggered Leahy concerns. "No Leahy Amendment issues have come to me," Ben Moeling, the State Department official in Kandahar, told me in January.

The question is whether Raziq's apparent exclusion from Leahy vetting represents a baffling oversight, or a deliberate evasion. In August, WikiLeaks released hundreds of classified, Leahy-related cables from the U.S. embassy in Kabul that revealed that, from 2006 to 2010, the U.S. vetted thousands of Afghan security officials before training them. In one instance, on September 29, 2007, the embassy vetted 251 midlevel and senior officers in the Border Police. Raziq's name was conspicuously absent.

"U.S. training of Afghan security forces is covered by the Leahy Amendment," Leahy, who chairs the Senate Judiciary Committee, told me. "I'm concerned about the effectiveness of the vetting, and that the amendment isn't being applied as vigorously as it should be." (A State Department spokesman said the department cannot comment on whether it has investigated an individual over Leahy concerns.)

Now that Raziq has moved to a higher-profile job, as the acting police chief of Kandahar, the American military seems finally to have become concerned about being complicit in his abuses. The decision to bar all units in NATO's International Security Assistance Force from transferring detainees into police or NDS custody in southern Afghanistan, pending resolution of concerns over the allegations, was quietly issued in a classified report on July 12.

The problem of the human-rights abuses by America's Afghan allies is broader than just Raziq. A UN report drafted in September interviewed hundreds of detainees held in police and NDS detention facilities and found that more than half reported that they had been tortured. Though the Afghan government rejected the report, ISAF halted detainee transfers to several additional prisons based on its findings.

But the abuses seem likely to continue, as long as those ordering the torture do so with impunity. On August 22, Karzai appointed Asadullah Khalid—the former governor who protected Raziq in 2006 and whose personal guard unit had been implicated in torture—as his special representative to oversee all security forces in southern Afghanistan.

The halting of detainee transfers in Kandahar province might well result in Raziq's returning, for now, to his fiefdom on the border. But this is not the first time that the United States and ISAF have considered withdrawing their support for him. Toward the end of 2009, senior ISAF officials reportedly thought about pushing for Raziq to be replaced. According to leaked cables, a high-level meeting was convened in Kabul, chaired by Deputy Ambassador Earl Wayne and Major General Michael Flynn, to discuss the problematic behavior of Raziq, among others. "Nobody, including his US military counterparts," one cable noted, "is under any illusions about his corrupt activities." Ultimately, however, General McChrystal, who was then the commander of ISAF and U.S. forces, decided that Raziq was too useful to cut loose, according to an article in the *Washington Post*. (McChrystal, through a spokesperson, declined to comment.) Cables also reveal that an American information-operations team even proposed a plan, "if credible," for "the longer-term encouragement of stories in the international media on the 'reform' of Razziq."

For his part, Raziq continues to deny all allegations of wrongdoing. "We have told the world and the media," he said, "that if you have any proof regarding this matter, come and drag us to court."

That has been America's balancing act in Kandahar—weighing the allegations of abuse and criminality that have been raised regarding Raziq against his effectiveness as an ally in the war on the Taliban. Or, as Moeling told me back in January, before the most recent round of allegations: "At the moment, I think we have to take a look at what he's been able to achieve. For us, trying to see the negative doesn't really get us anywhere."

Rolling Stone

FINALIST—FEATURE
WRITING

In "Arms and the Dudes," Guy
Lawson recounts the bizarre tale
of two stoner kids from Miami
Beach, David Packouz and Efraim
Diveroli, who managed to land a
$300 million contract from the
Pentagon to supply the Afghan
army with ammunition. Having
gathered an extraordinary trove of
narrative detail, Lawson wisely
decided to tell the story straight.
Which is to say: this is a story that
clips along, in the end unveiling
the shadowy but—in this telling—
hilarious world of gunrunning.
Lawson is now writing a book
based on this article—and of
course there's a movie in the
works.

Guy Lawson

Arms and the Dudes

The e-mail confirmed it: everything was finally back on schedule after weeks of maddening, inexplicable delay. A 747 cargo plane had just lifted off from an airport in Hungary and was banking over the Black Sea toward Kyrgyzstan, some 3,000 miles to the east. After stopping to refuel there, the flight would carry on to Kabul, the capital of Afghanistan. Aboard the plane were eighty pallets loaded with nearly 5 million rounds of ammunition for AK-47s, the Soviet-era assault rifle favored by the Afghan National Army.

Reading the e-mail back in Miami Beach, David Packouz breathed a sigh of relief. The shipment was part of a $300 million contract that Packouz and his partner, Efraim Diveroli, had won from the Pentagon to arm America's allies in Afghanistan. It was May 2007, and the war was going badly. After six years of fighting, al-Qaeda remained a menace, the Taliban were resurgent, and NATO casualties were rising sharply. For the Bush administration, the ammunition was part of a desperate, last-ditch push to turn the war around before the U.S. presidential election the following year. To Packouz and Diveroli, the shipment was part of a major arms deal that promised to make them seriously rich.

Reassured by the e-mail, Packouz got into his brand-new blue Audi A4 and headed home for the evening, windows open, the stereo blasting. At twenty-five, he wasn't exactly used to the pressures of being an international arms dealer. Only months earlier, he had been making his living as a massage therapist; his studies at the Educating Hands School of Massage had not included classes in military contracting or geopolitical brinkmanship. But Packouz hadn't been able to resist the temptation when Diveroli, his twenty-one-year-old friend from high school, had offered to cut him in on his burgeoning arms business. Working with nothing but an Internet connection, a couple of cell phones and a steady supply of weed, the two friends—one with a few college credits, the other a high school dropout—had beaten out Fortune 500 giants like General Dynamics to score the huge arms contract. With a single deal, two stoners from Miami Beach had turned themselves into the least likely merchants of death in history.

Arriving home at the Flamingo, his sleek condo with views of the bay, Packouz packed the cone of his Volcano, a smokeless electronic bong. As the balloon inflated with vapors from the high-grade weed, he took a deep toke and felt the pressures of the day drift away into a crisp, clean high.

Dinner was at Sushi Samba, a hipster Asian-Latino fusion joint. Packouz was in excellent spirits. He couldn't believe that he and Diveroli were actually pulling it off: Planes from all over Eastern Europe were now flying into Kabul, laden with millions of dollars worth of grenades and mortars and surface-to-air missiles. But as Packouz's miso-marinated Chilean sea bass arrived, his cell phone rang. It was the freight forwarder he had employed to make sure the ammunition made it from Hungary to Kabul. The man sounded panicked.

"We've got a problem," he told Packouz, shouting to be heard over the restaurant's thumping music. "The plane has been seized on the runway in Kyrgyzstan."

The arms shipment, it appeared, was being used as a bargaining chip in a high-stakes standoff between George W. Bush and

Vladimir Putin. The Russian president didn't like NATO expanding into Kyrgyzstan, and the Kyrgyz wanted the U.S. government to pay more rent to use their airport as a crucial supply line for the war in Afghanistan. Putin's allies in the Kyrgyz KGB, it seemed, were holding the plane hostage—and Packouz was going to be charged a $300,000 fine for every day it sat on the runway. Word of the seizure quickly reached Washington, and Defense Secretary Robert Gates himself was soon on his way to Kyrgyzstan to defuse the mounting tensions.

Packouz was baffled, stoned, and way out of his league. "It was surreal," he recalls. "Here I was dealing with matters of international security, and I was half-baked. I didn't know anything about the situation in that part of the world. But I was a central player in the Afghan war—and if our delivery didn't make it to Kabul, the entire strategy of building up the Afghanistan army was going to fail. It was totally killing my buzz. There were all these shadowy forces, and I didn't know what their motives were. But I had to get my shit together and put my best arms-dealer face on."

Sitting in the restaurant, Packouz tried to clear his head, cupping a hand over his cell phone to shut out the noise. "Tell the Kyrgyz KGB that ammo needs to get to Afghanistan!" he shouted into the phone. "This contract is part of a vital mission in the global war on terrorism. Tell them that if they fuck with us, they are fucking with the government of the United States of America!"

.   .   .

Packouz and Diveroli had picked the perfect moment to get into the arms business. To fight simultaneous wars in both Afghanistan and Iraq, the Bush administration had decided to outsource virtually every facet of America's military operations, from building and staffing army bases to hiring mercenaries to provide security for diplomats abroad. After Bush took office, private military contracts soared from $145 billion in 2001 to $390 billion in 2008. Federal contracting rules were routinely ignored or skirted, and military-industrial giants like Raytheon and Lockheed Martin cashed in as war profiteering went from war crime to business model. Why shouldn't a couple of inexperienced newcomers like Packouz and Diveroli get in on the action? After all, the two friends were after the same thing as everyone else in the arms business—lots and lots and lots of money.

"I was going to make millions," Packouz says. "I didn't plan on being an arms dealer forever—I was going to use the money to start a music career. I had never even owned a gun. But it was thrilling and fascinating to be in a business that decided the fate of nations. Nobody else our age was dealing weapons on an international level."

Packouz and Diveroli met at Beth Israel Congregation, the largest Orthodox synagogue in Miami Beach. Packouz was older by four years, a skinny kid who wore a yarmulke and left his white dress shirts untucked. Diveroli was the class clown, an overweight kid with a big mouth and no sense of fear. After school, the pair would hang out at the beach with their friends, smoking weed, playing guitar, sneaking in to swim in the pools at five-star hotels. When Packouz graduated, his parents were so concerned about his heavy pot use that they sent him to a school in Israel that specialized in handling kids with drug problems. It turned out to be a great place to get high. "I took acid by the Dead Sea," Packouz says. "I had a transcendental experience."

Returning home, Packouz drifted through two semesters at the University of Florida. Short of cash, he studied massage because it seemed like a better way to make money than flipping burgers. Nights, he sat around with his high school buddies getting high and dreaming of becoming a pop star. He wrote angsty rock ballads with titles like "Eternal Moment"—but it was hard to get a break in the music industry. With a shaved head and intense blue eyes, Packouz was plenty smart and plenty ambitious, in his slacker fashion, but he had no idea what to do with his life.

Efraim Diveroli, by contrast, knew exactly what he wanted to be: an arms dealer. It was the family business. His father brokered Kevlar jackets and other weapons-related paraphernalia to local police forces, and his uncle B. K. sold Glocks, Colts, and Sig Sauers to law enforcement. Kicked out of school in the ninth grade, Diveroli was sent to Los Angeles to work for his uncle. As an apprentice arms dealer, he proved to be a quick study. By the time he was sixteen, he was traveling the country selling weapons. He loved guns with a passion—selling them, shooting them, talking about them—and he loved the arms industry's intrigue and ruthless amorality. At eighteen, after a dispute with his uncle over money, Diveroli returned to Miami to set up his own operation, taking over a shell company his father had incorporated called AEY Inc.

His business plan was simple but brilliant. Most companies grow by attracting more customers. Diveroli realized he could succeed by selling to one customer: the U.S. military. No government agency buys and sells more stuff than the Defense Department—everything from F-16s to paper clips and front-end loaders. By law, every Pentagon purchase order is required to be open to public bidding. And under the Bush administration, small businesses like AEY were guaranteed a share of the arms deals. Diveroli didn't have to actually make any of the products to bid on the contracts. He could just broker the deals, finding the cheapest prices and underbidding the competition. All he had to do was win even a minuscule fraction of the billions the Pentagon spends on arms every year and he would be a millionaire. But Diveroli wanted more than that: His ambition was to be the biggest arms dealer in the world—a young Adnan Khashoggi, a teenage Victor Bout.

To get into the game, Diveroli knew he would have to deal with some of the world's shadiest operators—the war criminals, soldiers of fortune, crooked diplomats, and small-time thugs who keep militaries and mercenaries loaded with arms. The vast aftermarket in arms had grown exponentially after the end of the Cold War. For decades, weapons had been stockpiled in warehouses throughout the Balkans and Eastern Europe for the threat of war against the West, but now arms dealers were selling them off to the highest bidder. The Pentagon needed access to this new aftermarket to arm the militias it was creating in Iraq and Afghanistan. The trouble was, it couldn't go into such a murky underworld on its own. It needed proxies to do its dirty work—companies like AEY. The result was a new era of lawlessness. According to a report by Amnesty International, "Tens of millions of rounds of ammunition from the Balkans were reportedly shipped—clandestinely and without public oversight—to Iraq by a chain of private brokers and transport contractors under the auspices of the U.S. Department of Defense."

This was the "gray market" that Diveroli wanted to penetrate. Still a teenager, he rented a room in a house owned by a Hispanic family in Miami and went to work on his laptop. The government website where contracts are posted is fbo.gov, known as "FedBizOpps." Diveroli soon became adept at the arcane lingo of federal contracts. His competition was mostly big corporations like Northrop Grumman, Lockheed, and BAE Systems. Those companies had entire departments dedicated to selling to the Pentagon. But Diveroli had his own advantages: low overhead, an appetite for risk, and all-devouring ambition.

In the beginning, Diveroli specialized in bidding on smaller contracts for items like helmets and ammunition for U.S. Special Forces. The deals were tiny, relatively speaking, but they gave AEY a history of "past performance"—the kind of track record the Pentagon requires of companies that want to bid on large defense contracts. Diveroli got financing from a Mormon named Ralph Merrill, a machine-gun manufacturer from Utah who had worked for his father. Before long, Diveroli was winning Pentagon contracts.

Like all the kids in their pot-smoking circle, Packouz was aware that Diveroli had become an arms dealer. Diveroli loved to brag about how rich he was, and rumors circulated among the stoners about the vast sums he was making, at least compared with their crappy part-time jobs. One evening, Diveroli picked Packouz up in his Mercedes, and the two headed to a party at a local rabbi's house, lured by the promise of free booze and pretty girls. Diveroli was excited about a deal he had just completed, a $15 million contract to sell old Russian-manufactured rifles to the Pentagon to supply the Iraqi army. He regaled Packouz with the tale of how he had won the contract, how much money he was making, and how much more there was to be made.

"Dude, I've got so much work I need a partner," Diveroli said. "It's a great business, but I need a guy to come on board and make money with me."

Packouz was intrigued. He was doing some online business himself, buying sheets from textile companies in Pakistan and reselling them to distributors that supplied nursing homes in Miami. The sums he made were tiny—a thousand or two at a time—but the experience made him hungry for more.

"How much money are you making, dude?" Packouz asked.

"Serious money," Diveroli said.

"How much?"

"This is confidential information," Diveroli said.

"Dude, if you had to leave the country tomorrow, how much would you be able to take?"

"In cash?"

"Cold, hard cash."

Diveroli pulled the car over and turned to look at Packouz. "Dude, I'm going to tell you," he said. "But only to inspire you. Not because I'm bragging." Diveroli paused, as if he were about to disclose his most precious secret. "I have $1.8 million in cash."

Packouz stared in disbelief. He had expected Diveroli to say something like $100,000, maybe a little more. But nearly $2 million?

"Dude," was all Packouz said.

•   •   •

Packouz started working with Diveroli in November 2005. His title was account executive. He would be paid entirely in commission. The pair operated out of a one-bedroom apartment Diveroli had by then rented in Miami Beach, sitting opposite each other at a desk in the living room, surrounded by stacks of federal contracts and a mountain of pot. They quickly fell into a daily routine: wake up, get baked, start wheeling and dealing.

Packouz was about to get a rare education. He watched as Diveroli won a State Department contract to supply high-grade FN Herstal machine guns to the Colombian army. It was a lucrative deal, but Diveroli wasn't satisfied—he always wanted more. So he persuaded the State Department to allow him to substitute Korean-made knockoffs instead of the high-end Herstals—a swap that instantly doubled his earnings. Diveroli did the same with a large helmet order for the Iraqi army, pushing the Pentagon to accept poorer-quality Chinese-made helmets once he had won the contract. After all, it wasn't like the military was buying weapons and helmets for American soldiers. The hapless end-users were foreigners, and who was going to go the extra mile for them?

The Pentagon's buyers were soldiers with little or no business experience, and Diveroli knew how to win them over with a mixture of charm, patriotism, and a keen sense of how to play to the military culture; he could *yes sir* and *no sir* with the best of them. To get the inside dirt on a deal, he would call the official in charge of the contract and pretend to be a colonel or even a general. "He would be toasted, but you would never know it," says Packouz. "When he was trying to get a deal, he was totally convincing. But if he was about to lose a deal, his voice would start shaking. He would say that he was running a very small business, even though he had millions in the bank. He said that if the deal fell through he was going to be ruined. He was going to lose his house. His wife and kids were going to go hungry. He would literally cry. I didn't know if it was psychosis or acting, but he absolutely believed what he was saying."

Above all, Diveroli cared about the bottom line. "Efraim was a Republican because they started more wars," Packouz says. "When the United States invaded Iraq, he was thrilled. He said to me, 'Do I think George Bush did the right thing for the country by invading Iraq? No. But am I happy about it? Absofuckinglutely.' He hoped we would invade more countries because it was good for business."

That spring, when mass protests broke out in Nepal, Diveroli frantically tried to put together a cache of arms that could be sold to the Nepalese king to put down the rebellion—heavy weapons, attack helicopters, ammo. "Efraim called it the Save the King Project, but he didn't give a shit about the king," Packouz says. "Money was all he talked about, literally—no sports or politics. He would do anything to make money."

To master the art of federal contracts, Packouz studied the solicitations posted on fbo.gov. The contracts often ran to thirty or forty pages, each filled with fine print and legalese. As Diveroli's apprentice, Packouz saw that his friend never read a book or a magazine, never went to the movies—all he did was pore over government documents, looking for an angle, a way in. Diveroli called it *squeezing into a deal*—putting himself between the supplier and the government by shaving a few pennies off each unit and reselling them at a markup that undercut his competitors. Playing the part of an arms dealer, he loved to deliver dramatic one-liners, speaking as if he were the star of a Hollywood blockbuster. "I don't care if I have the smallest dick in the room," he would say, "as long as I have the fattest wallet." Or: "If you see a crack in the door, you've got to kick the fucker open." Or: "Once a gun runner, always a gun runner."

"Efraim's self-image was as the modern merchant of death," says Packouz. "He was still just a kid, but he didn't see himself that way. He would go toe-to-toe with high-ranking military officers, Eastern European mobsters, executives of Fortune 500 companies. He didn't give a fuck. He would take them on and win, and then give them the finger. I was following in his footsteps. He told me I was going to be a millionaire within three years—he guaranteed it."

At first, Packouz struggled to land his own deals. Bidding on contracts on fbo.gov was an art; closing a deal was a science. At one point, he spent weeks obsessing over an $8 million contract to supply SUVs to the State Department in Pakistan, only to lose the bid. But he finally won a contract to supply 50,000 gallons of propane to an Air Force base in Wyoming, netting a profit of $8,000. "There were a lot of suppliers who didn't know how to work FedBizOpps as well as we did," he says. "You had to read the solicitations religiously."

Once a week or so, the pair would hit the clubs of South Beach to let off steam. Karaoke in a basement bar called the Studio was a favorite. Packouz took his performances seriously, choosing soulful music like U2's "With or Without You" or Pearl Jam's "Black," while Diveroli threw himself into power ballads and country anthems, tearing off his shirt and pumping his fists to the music. Between songs, the two friends would take hits of the cocaine that Diveroli kept in a small plastic bullet with a tiny valve on the top for easy access. Packouz was shy around girls, but Diveroli cut right to the chase, often hitting on women right in front of their boyfriends.

All the partying wasn't exactly conducive to running a small business, especially one as complicated and perilous as arms dealing. As AEY grew, it defaulted on at least seven contracts, in one case failing to deliver a shipment of 10,000 Beretta pistols for the Iraqi army. Diveroli's aunt—a strong-willed and outspoken woman who fought constantly with her nephew—joined the two friends to provide administrative support. She didn't approve of their drug use, and she talked openly about them on the phone, as if they weren't present.

"Mark my words," she told Diveroli's mother repeatedly, "your son is going to crash and burn."

"Shut up!" Diveroli would shout, the coldblooded arms dealer giving way to the pissed-off teenager. "You don't know what you're talking about! I made millions last year!"

"Crash and burn," the aunt would say. "Mark my words—crash and burn."

·   ·   ·

In June, seven months after Packouz started at AEY, he and Diveroli traveled to Paris for Eurosatory, one of the world's largest arms trade shows. Miles of booths inside the Paris Nord Villepinte exhibition center were filled with arms manufacturers hawking the latest instruments of death—tanks, robots, unmanned drones—and serving up champagne and caviar to some of the most powerful political and military officials on the planet. Packouz and Diveroli were by far the youngest in attendance, but they tried to look the part, wearing dress pants, crisp shirts and sales-rep ties. "Wait until I am really in the big time," Diveroli boasted. "I will *own* this fucking show."

At a booth displaying a new robotic reconnaissance device, Diveroli and Packouz met with Heinrich Thomet, a Swiss arms dealer who served as a crucial go-between for AEY. Tall and suave, with movie-star looks and an impeccable sense of fashion, Thomet had blond hair, light-blue eyes and an eerily calm demeanor. He spoke fluent English with a slight German accent, adding "OK" to the beginning and end of every sentence ("OK, so the price on the AKs is firm, OK?"). He seemed to have connections everywhere—Russia, Bulgaria, Hungary. Serving as a broker, Thomet had created an array of shell companies and offshore accounts to shield arms transactions from official scrutiny. He had used his contacts in Albania to get Diveroli a good price on Chinese-made ammunition for U.S. Special Forces training in Germany—a deal that was technically illegal, given the U.S. embargo against Chinese arms imposed after the Tiananmen Square massacre in 1989.

"Thomet could get body armor, machine guns, anti-aircraft rockets—anything," Packouz recalls. "He was one of the best middlemen in the business, a real-life Lord of War."

Like Diveroli, Thomet had been in the business since he was a teenager, and he recognized that the two young upstarts could be useful to him. Thomet was singled out by Amnesty International for smuggling arms out of Zimbabwe in violation of U.S. sanctions. He was also under investigation by U.S. law enforcement for shipping weapons from Serbia to Iraq, and he was placed on a "watch list" by the State Department. Given the obstacles to selling directly in the United States, Thomet wanted to use AEY as a front, providing him an easy conduit to the lucrative contracts being handed out by the Pentagon.

With Thomet on their side, Diveroli and Packouz soon got the break they were looking for. On July 28, 2006, the Army Sustainment Command in Rock Island, Illinois, posted a forty-four-page document titled "A Solicitation for Nonstandard Ammunition." It looked like any other government form on fbo.gov, with blank spaces for names and telephone numbers and hundreds of squares to be filled in. But the document actually represented a semicovert operation by the Bush administration to prop up the Afghan National Army. Rather than face a public debate over the war in Afghanistan, which was going very badly indeed, the Pentagon issued what is known as a "pseudo case"— a solicitation that permitted it to allocate defense funds without the approval of Congress. The pseudo case wasn't secret, precisely, but the only place it was publicized was on fbo.gov. No press release was issued, and there was no public debate. The money was only available for two years, so it had to be spent quickly. And unlike most federal contracts, there was no dollar limit posted; companies vying for the deal could bid whatever they wanted.

Based on the numbers, it looked like it was going to be a *lot* of money. The Army wanted to buy a dizzying array of weapons—ammunition for AK-47 assault rifles and SVD Dragunov sniper rifles, GP 30 grenades, 82 mm Russian mortars, S-KO aviation rockets. The quantities were enormous—enough ammo to literally create an army—and the entire contract would go to a single bidder. "One firm fixed-price award, on an all-or-none basis, will be made as a result of this solicitation," the tender offer said.

The solicitation was only up for a matter of minutes before Diveroli spotted it, reading the terms with increasing excitement. He immediately called Packouz, who was driving along the interstate.

"I've found the perfect contract for us," Diveroli said. "It's enormous—far, far bigger than anything we've done before. But it's right up our alley."

•　　•　　•

The pair met at Diveroli's apartment to smoke a joint and discuss strategy. Supplying the contract would mean buying up hundreds of millions of dollars worth of ammunition for the kind of Eastern Bloc weapons that the Afghans used. Because such weapons were traded in the gray market—a world populated by illegal arms dealers, gun runners, and warlords—the Pentagon couldn't go out and buy the ammo itself without causing a public relations disaster. Whoever won the contract to arm the Afghans would essentially be serving as an official front operation, laundering shady arms for the Pentagon.

Normally, a small-time outfit like AEY wouldn't have a shot at such a major defense contract. But Diveroli and Packouz had three advantages. First, the Bush administration had started its small-business initiative at the Pentagon, mandating that a certain percentage of defense contracts go to firms like AEY. Second, the fledgling arms dealers specialized in precisely the sort of Cold War munitions the Pentagon was looking for: They had the "past performance" required by the contract, and they could fulfill the order using the same supply lines Diveroli had developed through Thomet. Third, the only requirement in the contract was that the ammunition be "serviceable without qualification." As Diveroli and Packouz interpreted it, that meant the Pentagon didn't care if they supplied "shit ammo," as long as it "went bang and went out of the barrel."

For the two friends, it was a chance to enter a world usually reserved for multinational defense contractors with armies of well-connected lobbyists. "I knew it was a long shot," recalls Packouz. "But it seemed like we might be able to actually compete with the big boys. I thought we actually had a chance. If we worked hard. If we got lucky."

Bidding on defense contracts is a speculative business—laborious, time-consuming, with no prize for second place. As they passed a joint back and forth, Diveroli decided it was time for Packouz to step up and take on a larger role.

"I don't really have time to source all these things," he told Packouz. "But I've got good contacts for you to start with. I want you to get on the Internet and get a price from everyone and his mother. Any new sources you bring to the table, I'll give you 25 percent of the profit."

This was Packouz's big chance. That night, he went online and searched defense databases for every arms manufacturer in Eastern Europe he could find—Hungary, Bulgaria, Ukraine, any place that might deal in Soviet-era weapons. He e-mailed or faxed or called them all. The phone connection was often bad, and Packouz had to shout to be heard. If the person who answered didn't speak English, he would say "English! English! English!" and then spend minutes on hold while they tracked down the one guy in the outfit who spoke a few words. "*Da, da,*" they would tell Packouz. "You buy, you buy." When he managed to make himself understood, he told the manufacturers that the ammunition had to "work." It also had to "look good," and not be in rusty boxes or exposed to the elements.

For six weeks, Packouz worked through the night, sleeping on Diveroli's couch and surviving on weed and adrenaline. He located stockpiles of ammunition in Eastern Europe at good prices. At the same time, Heinrich Thomet sourced a massive amount of ammunition through his Albanian connections. As the date for the final bid neared, Diveroli agonized. He paced day and night, a cloud of smoke over his head as he smoked joint after joint, muttering, worrying, cursing.

"Efraim was conflicted about whether to put a 9 percent or 10 percent profit margin on top of our prices," Packouz recalls. "The difference was more than $3 million in cash, which was huge—but with either margin, profits were going to be more than $30 million. He figured everyone else was going to take 10 percent, but what if another bidder had the same idea as him and put in 9 percent? So maybe he should go with 8 percent. But then we might be leaving money on the table—God forbid!"

Finally, at the last possible moment, Diveroli went for 9 percent. He scribbled a number on the form: $298,000,000. It was an educated guess, one he prayed wouldn't be undercut by the big defense contractors. There were just ten minutes left before the application deadline. The two friends jumped in Diveroli's car and sped through the quiet residential streets of Miami Beach, making it to the post office with only seconds to go.

•   •   •

The Pentagon can be a slow-moving bureaucracy, a place where paperwork goes to die. But because the Afghanistan solicitation was a "pseudo case," it had been designed to move swiftly. On the evening of January 26, 2007, Packouz was parking his beat-up old Mazda Protege when Diveroli called.

"I have good news and bad news," Diveroli said.

"What's the bad news?" Packouz asked.

"Our first order is only for $600,000."

"So we won the contract?" Packouz asked in disbelief.

"Fuck yeah!" said Diveroli.

The two friends, still in their early twenties, were now responsible for one of the central elements of the Bush administration's foreign policy. Over multiple bottles of Cristal at an upscale Italian restaurant, the pair toasted their amazing good fortune. Throughout the meal they passed Diveroli's cocaine bullet back and forth under the table, using napkins to pretend to blow their noses.

"You and me, buddy," Diveroli said. "You and me are going to take over this industry. I see AEY as a $10 billion company in a few years. These fat cats in their boardrooms worrying about the stock prices of their companies have no idea what is about to hit them."

"General Dynamics isn't going to be too happy right now," Packouz agreed.

Despite the celebratory air, they both knew that their work had just begun. They had already managed to clear three different government audits, hiring an accountant to establish the kind of basic bookkeeping systems that any cafe or corner store would have. Now, a few weeks after winning the contract, AEY was suddenly summoned to a meeting with the purchasing officers at Rock Island.

Diveroli asked Ralph Merrill, the Mormon gun manufacturer from Utah, to come along. An experienced businessman in his sixties, Merrill had provided the financial backing needed to land the contract, pledging his interest in a piece of property in Utah. Diveroli had also shown auditors his personal bank balance, by then $5.4 million.

The meeting with army officials proved to be a formality. Diveroli had the contracting jargon down, and he sailed through the technical aspects of the transaction with confidence: supply sources, end-user certificates, AEY's experience. No one ever asked his age. "We were supremely confident," says Packouz. "I just think it never occurred to the army people that they were dealing with a couple of dudes in their early twenties."

In reality, the Pentagon had good reason to disqualify AEY from even vying for the contract. The company and Diveroli had both been placed on the State Department "watch list" for importing illegal firearms. But the Pentagon failed to check the list. It also ignored the fact that AEY had defaulted on prior contracts. Initially rated as "unsatisfactory" by the contracting office, AEY was upgraded to "good" and then "excellent."

There was only one explanation for the meteoric rise: Diveroli had radically underbid the competition. In private conversations, the army's contracting officers let AEY know that its bid was at least $50 million less than its nearest rival. Diveroli's anxiety that his bid of nearly $300 million would be too high had failed to consider the corpulent markups employed by corporate America when it deals with the Pentagon. For once, at least, taxpayers were getting a good deal on a defense contract.

The first Task Order that AEY received on the deal was for $600,000 worth of grenades and ammunition—a test, Diveroli surmised, to make sure they could deliver as promised. Make a mistake, no matter the reason, and the Pentagon might yank the entire $298 million contract.

After their celebratory dinner the night they received the contract, the two friends headed for Diveroli's brand-new Audi. As Diveroli arranged a line of coke on the dashboard, he warned Packouz not to make any mistakes with the grenades.

"You've got the bitch's panties off," Diveroli said, adopting his best movie-star swagger. "But you haven't fucked her yet."

    •   •   •

Diveroli and Packouz needn't have worried. They had barely gotten started on the order for grenades when the second Task Order arrived. This time, it was for more than $49 million in ammunition—including 100 million rounds of AK ammo and more than a million grenades for rocket launchers. There was no question now. The Pentagon was ecstatic to award the contract to a tiny company like AEY, which helped fulfill the quota set by Bush's small-business initiative.

Packouz calculated that even with the tight margins, he stood to make as much as $6 million on the contract. But he wasn't so sure that AEY was going to be able to deliver. Diveroli had already hit the road, traveling to the Ukraine, Montenegro, and the Czech Republic in search of suppliers. So Packouz would have to tend to most of the Afghanistan contract by himself—a job that any conventional defense contractor would have assigned to dozens of full-time, experienced employees.

In February 2007, saddled with a gargantuan task, Packouz went by himself to the annual International Defense Exhibition in Abu Dhabi to look for suppliers. "It was bizarre," he says. "I was just a kid, but I was probably the single biggest private arms dealer on the planet. It was like Efraim had put me into the movie he was starring in." To look the part of an international arms dealer, Packouz carried a silver aluminum briefcase and wore wraparound shades. He also had business cards printed up with an impressive new title, considering he was part of a two-man operation: vice president.

In Abu Dhabi, Packouz hoped to find a single supplier big enough to meet most of AEY's demands. The obvious candidate was Rosoboron Export, the official dealer for all Russian arms.

The company had inherited the Soviet Union's global arms-exporting empire; now, as part of Vladimir Putin's tightly held network of oligarchic corporations, Rosoboron sold more than 90 percent of Russia's weapons. The firm was so big that Packouz could have just given them the list of ammunition he needed and they could have supplied the entire contract, a one-stop weapons shop.

But there was a catch, the kind of perversity common in the world of arms dealing: Rosoboron had been banned by the State Department for selling nuclear equipment to Iran. The U.S. government wanted Russian ammo, just not from the Russians. AEY couldn't do business with the firm—at least, not legally. But for gun runners, this kind of legal hurdle was just that—a hurdle to be jumped.

Packouz went to the main Russian pavilion every day to try to get an appointment with the deputy director of Rosoboron. The giant exhibit was like a souk for arms dealers, with scores of Russian generals in full-dress uniform meeting with businessmen and sheiks. Finally, on the last day, Packouz was given an appointment. The deputy director looked like he was ex-KGB—big and fat, in his sixties, with thick square glasses. As Packouz spoke, the man kept surveying the pavilion out of the corner of his eye, as if he were checking to see if he was being watched. Packouz showed him the list of munitions he needed, along with the quantities. The director raised his eyebrows, impressed by the scale of the operation.

"We have very good interest in this business," he said in a thick Russian accent. "You know we are only company who can provide everything."

"I'm aware of that," Packouz said. "That's why we want to do business with you."

"But as you know, there is problem. State Department has blacklist us. I don't understand your government. One month is OK to do business, next month is not OK. This is very not fair. Very political. They just want leverage in dealing with Kremlin."

"I know we can't do business with you directly," Packouz said. Then he hinted that there was a way to get around the blacklist. "If you can help us do business with another Russian company, then we can buy from them."

"Let me talk to my people," the Russian said, taking one of Packouz's newly printed business cards.

It was the last Packouz ever heard from the Russian. Several weeks later, as he was arranging supply routes for the deal, Packouz was informed that AEY would not be given overflight permission for Turkmenistan, a former Soviet satellite that had to be crossed to reach Afghanistan. "It was clear that Putin was fucking with us directly," Packouz says. "If the Russians made life difficult for us, they would get taken off the American blacklist, so they could get our business for themselves."

Packouz managed to obtain the overflight permission through a Ukrainian airline—but the episode was an ominous reminder of how little he understood about the business he was in. "There was no way to really know why the heads of state were doing things, especially when it came to something like invading Iraq," he says. "It was such a deep game, we didn't know what was really happening."

· · ·

With the flights to Kabul arranged, Packouz hit the phones looking for more ammunition. The cheaper the better: The less the ammo cost, the more he and Diveroli would pocket for themselves. They didn't need quality; antique shells, second-rate mortar rounds—all of it was fine, as long as it worked. "Please be advised there is no age restriction for this contract!!!" AEY advised one potential supplier in an e-mail. "ANY age ammunition is acceptable."

Of course, if the Pentagon really cared about the Afghan National Army, it could have supplied them with more expensive, and reliable, state-of-the-art weapons. The Bush administration's ambivalence about Afghanistan had manifested itself in the terms of the contract: The soldiers of Kabul and Kandahar would not be abandoned in the field, but nor would they be given the tools to succeed.

Packouz sat on the couch in Diveroli's apartment, bong and lighter handy, and called U.S. embassies in the "stans"—the former Soviet satellites—and asked to speak to the defense attaché. Deepening his voice and adopting a clipped military inflection, Packouz chatted them up, made them laugh, asked about how things were in Kazakhstan, described how sunny it was in Miami. Whenever possible, he threw in military lingo designed to appeal to the officers: He was working on an essential contract in the War on Terror, he explained, and the United States military was counting on AEY to complete the mission. "I said it was part of the vital process of nation building in the central front of the War on Terror," Packouz recalls. "Then I would tell them the specifics of what I was after—mortar rounds, the size of ammo, the amount. They were all eager to help."

Every day, Packouz spoke with military officials, sending volleys of e-mails to Kabul and Kyrgyzstan and the army depot in Rock Island. The contracting officers he dealt with told him that there was a secret agenda involved in the deal. The Pentagon, they said, was worried that a Democrat would be elected president in 2008 and cut the funding for the war—or worse, pull U.S. troops out of Afghanistan entirely.

"They said Bush and Rumsfeld were trying to arm Afghanistan with enough ammo to last them the next few decades," Packouz recalls. "It made sense to me, but I didn't really care. My main motivator was making money, just like it was for General Dynamics. Nobody goes into the arms business for altruistic purposes."

It didn't take long for AEY to strike cut-rate deals that vastly improved its profit margin. The 9 percent planned for in the original bid was soon pushing toward 25 percent—enough to provide Packouz and Diveroli with nearly $85 million in profits. But even such a jaw-dropping sum didn't satisfy Diveroli. He scoured FedBizOpps for even more contracts and landed a private deal to import Lithuanian ammo, determined to turn AEY into a multi-billion-dollar company.

To cope with the increased business, AEY leased space in a larger and more expensive office building in Miami Beach. The company hired an office manager and two young secretaries they found on Craigslist. Diveroli brought in two more friends from the synagogue, including a guy fluent in Russian, to help fulfill the contracts. "Things were rolling along," Packouz recalls. "We were delivering on a consistent basis. We had suppliers in Hungary and Bulgaria and other countries. I had finally arranged all the overflight permits. We were cash positive."

Packouz had yet to be paid a cent, but he was convinced he was about to be seriously rich. Anticipating the big payday, he ditched his beater Mazda for a brand-new Audi A4. He moved from his tiny efficiency apartment to a nice one-bedroom overlooking the pool at the Flamingo in fashionable South Beach. Diveroli soon followed, taking a two-bedroom in the central tower. It was convenient for both—their drug dealer, Raoul, lived in the complex.

"The Flamingo was a constant party," Packouz says. "The marketing slogan for the building was 'South Beach revolves around us,' and it was true. There was drinking, dancing, people making out in the Jacuzzi—sometimes more than just making out. Outside my balcony there was always at least a few women sunbathing topless. People at parties would ask us what we did for a living. The girls were models or cosmetologists. The guys were stockbrokers and lawyers. We would say we were international arms dealers. 'You know the war in Afghanistan?' we would say. 'All the bullets are coming from us.' It was heaven. It was wild. We felt like we were on top of the world."

In the evenings, Packouz and Diveroli would get high and go to the American Range and Gun Shop—the only range near Miami that would let them fire off the Uzis and MP5s that Diveroli was licensed to own. "When we let go with our machine guns, all the other shooters would stop and look at us like, 'What the fuck was that?' Everyone else had pistols going *pop pop*. We loved it. Shooting an automatic machine gun feels powerful."

•   •   •

The biggest piece of the Afghan contract, in terms of sheer quantity, was ammunition for AK-47s. Packouz had received excellent quotes from suppliers in Hungary and the Czech Republic. But Diveroli insisted on using the Swiss arms dealer Heinrich Thomet's high-level contacts in Albania. The move made sense. The Albanians didn't require a large deposit as a down payment, which made it easier for AEY to place big orders. And Albania's government could certainly handle the volume: Its paranoid communist leaders had been so convinced they were going to be attacked by foreign powers that they had effectively transformed the nation into a vast military stockpile, with bunkers scattered throughout the countryside. In fact, AK-47 ammunition was so plentiful that Albania's president had recently flown to Baghdad and offered to donate millions of rounds to Gen. David Petraeus.

The structure for AEY's purchase of the Albanian ammo was standard in the world of illegal arms deals, where the whole point is to disguise origins and end-users. It was perfectly legal, but it had the stench of double-dealing. A shell company called Evdin, which Thomet had incorporated in Cyprus, would buy the ammo from Albania's arms-exporting company. Evdin would then resell the rounds to AEY. That way Thomet got a cut as broker, and AEY and the U.S. government were insulated from any legal or moral quandaries that came with doing business in a country as notoriously corrupt and unpredictable as Albania.

There was only one snag: When Diveroli bid on the contract, he had miscalculated the cost of shipping, failing to anticipate the rising cost of fuel. The army had given him permission to repackage the rounds into cardboard boxes, but getting anything done in a country as dysfunctional as Albania wasn't easy. So Diveroli dispatched another friend from their synagogue, Alex Podrizki, to the capital city of Tirana to oversee the details of fulfilling the deal.

Despite the hands-on approach, signs of trouble emerged immediately. When Podrizki went to look at a cache of ammunition in one bunker, it was apparent that the Albanians had a haphazard attitude about safety; they used an ax to open crates containing live rounds and lit cigarettes in a room filled with gunpowder. The ammunition itself, though decades old, seemed to be in working order, but the rounds were stored in rusty cans and stacked on rotting wooden pallets—not the protocol normally used for such dangerous materiel. Worst of all, Podrizki noticed that the steel containers holding the ammunition— known as "sardine cans"—were covered in Chinese markings. Podrizki called Packouz in Miami.

"I inspected the stuff and it seems good," Podrizki told him. "But dude, you know this is Chinese ammo, right?"

"What are you talking about?" Packouz said.

"The ammo is Chinese."

"How do you know it's Chinese?"

"There are Chinese markings all over the crates."

Packouz's heart sank. There was not only an embargo against selling weapons manufactured in China: The Afghan contract specifically stipulated that Chinese ammo was not permitted. Then again, maybe AEY could argue that the ammunition didn't violate the ban, since it had been imported to Albania decades before the embargo was imposed, back when Albania's communist government had forged an alliance with Mao. There was precedent for such an argument: Only the year before, the Army had been delighted with Chinese ammo that AEY had shipped from Albania. But this time, when Diveroli wrote the State Department's legal advisory desk to ask if he could use Chinese rounds made prior to the embargo, he received a curt and unequivocal reply: not without a presidential decree.

Given the deadline on the contract, there was no time to find another supplier. The Hungarians could fill half the deal, but the ammunition would not be ready for shipment until the fall; the Czechs could fill the entire order, but they wanted $1 million. Any delay would risk losing the entire contract. "The army was pushing us for the ammo," says Packouz. "They needed it ASAP."

So the two friends chose a third option. As arms dealers, subverting the law wasn't some sort of extreme scenario—it was a routine part of the business. There was even a term of art for it: *circumvention.* Packouz e-mailed Podrizki in Albania and instructed him to have the rounds repackaged to get rid of any Chinese markings. It was time to circumvent.

Alone in a strange city, Podrizki improvised. He picked up a phone book and found a cardboard-box manufacturer named Kosta Trebicka. The two men met at a bar near the Sky Tower in the center of town. Trebicka was in his late forties, a wiry and intense man with thick worker's hands. He told Podrizki that he could supply cardboard boxes strong enough to hold the ammunition, as well as the labor to transfer the rounds to new pallets. A week later, Podrizki called to ask if Trebicka could hire enough men to repack 100 million rounds of ammunition by taking them out of metal sardine cans and placing them in cardboard boxes. Trebicka thought the request exceedingly odd. Why go to all that trouble? Podrizki fibbed, saying it was to lighten the load and save money on air freight. After extended haggling with Diveroli back in Miami, Trebicka agreed to do the job for $280,000 and hired a team of men to begin repackaging the rounds.

As he worked at the warehouse, however, Trebicka grew even more suspicious. Concerned that something nefarious was happening, he called the U.S. embassy and met with the economic attaché. Over coffee at a cafe called Chocolate, Trebicka confided that the ammunition was covered in Chinese markings. Was that a problem? Not at all, the U.S. official replied. The embassy had been trying to find the money to pay for demolishing the ammunition, so sending the rounds to Afghanistan would actually do them a favor. AEY appeared to be in the clear.

But greed got the better of Diveroli. In a phone call from Miami, he asked Trebicka to use his contacts in the Albanian government to find out how much Thomet was paying the Albanians for the ammunition. AEY was giving the Swiss arms broker just over four cents per round and reselling them to the Pentagon for ten cents. But Diveroli suspected that Thomet was ripping him off.

He turned out to be right. A few days later, Trebicka reported that Thomet was paying the Albanians only two cents per round—meaning that he was charging AEY double the asking price, just for serving as a broker. Diveroli was enraged. He asked Trebicka to meet with his Albanian connections and find a way to cut Thomet out of the deal entirely.

Trebicka was happy to help. The Albanians, he thought, would be glad to deal with AEY directly. After all, by doing an end run around Thomet, there would be more money for everyone else. But when Trebicka met with the Albanian defense minister, his intervention had the opposite effect: The Albanians cut him out of the deal, informing AEY that the repackaging job would be completed instead by a friend of the prime minister's son. What Trebicka had failed to grasp was that Thomet was paying a kickback to the Albanians from the large margin he was making on the deal. Getting rid of Thomet was impossible, because that was how the Albanians were being paid off the books.

Diveroli flew to Albania and tried to intervene to help Trebicka keep the job, but he didn't have enough clout to get the decision reversed. Trebicka was stuck with the tab for the workers he had hired to repackage the rounds, along with a warehouse full of useless cardboard boxes he had printed to hold the ammo. Furious at being frozen out, he called Diveroli and secretly recorded the conversation, threatening to tell the CIA what he knew about the deal. "If the Albanians want to still work with me, I will not open my mouth," he promised. "I will do whatever you tell me to do."

Diveroli suggested that Trebicka try bribing Ylli Pinari, the head of the Albanian arms-exporting agency that was supplying the ammunition. "Why don't you kiss Pinari's ass one more time," Diveroli said. "Call him up. Beg. Kiss him. Send one of your girls to fuck him. Let's get him happy. Maybe we can play on his fears. Or give him a little money, something in his pocket. And he's not going to get much—$20,000 from you."

When Trebicka complained about being muscled out of the deal, Diveroli said there was nothing he could do about it. There were too many thugs involved on the Albanian end of the deal, and it was just too dangerous. "It went up higher, to the prime minister and his son," Diveroli said. "This mafia is too strong for me. I can't fight this mafia. It got too big. The animals just got too out of control."

•　　•　　•

With things up in the air in Albania, Packouz was starting to feel the pressure. He was stressed out, working around the clock, negotiating multi-million-dollar purchases and arranging for transportation. It felt like AEY was under siege from all directions. So when the cargo plane had finally taken off from Hungary on its way to Kabul loaded with 5 million rounds of ammunition, Packouz had breathed a sigh of relief. Then the plane had been abruptly seized in Kyrgyzstan—and Packouz had been forced to swing into action once more, working the phones for weeks to get the ammo released. Fortunately, AEY had friends in high places. When Packouz contacted the U.S. embassy in Kyrgyzstan, the military attaché immediately wrote to the Kyrgyz government, explaining that the cargo was "urgently needed for the war on terrorism being fought by your neighboring Afghan forces." Two weeks later, Defense Secretary Robert Gates traveled to Kyrgyzstan on a mission to keep supplies flowing through the airport there. Under pressure from top U.S. officials, the ammo was eventually released.

"I never did find out what really happened, or why the plane was seized," says Packouz. "It was how things were done in international arms dealing. The defense industry and politics were extremely intertwined—you couldn't do business in one without dealing with the other. Your fate depended on political machinations behind the scenes. You don't even know whose side you were on—who you were helping and who you were hurting."

With the plane released and the Albanian supply line secured, Packouz and Diveroli thought they finally had everything under control. Cargo planes filled with ammunition were taking off from airports across Eastern Europe. The military officials receiving the ammo in Kabul had to know it was Chinese: Every round is stamped with the place of manufacture, as any soldier knows. But the shipments were routinely approved, and there were no complaints from the Afghans about the quality of the rounds. The ammo worked, and that was all that mattered. Millions of dollars were being transferred via wire from the Pentagon into AEY's accounts, and the $300 million contract was moving along smoothly. Diveroli was rich. Packouz was going to be rich. They had it made.

But it didn't take long for success to drive a wedge between the two friends. The exhausted Packouz no longer had to work eighteen hours a day to track down suppliers. He started coming in late and knocking off early. Diveroli, who owed him commission but had yet to cut a check to his partner, started to argue with him about his hours.

"Efraim started looking at me differently," Packouz says. "I could tell he was working things over in his head. There was real money in the bank—millions and millions. He was about to be forced to pay me a huge chunk of change. He said he didn't want to 'give' me all that money. That was how he put it. Not like I had earned the money."

One day, Diveroli finally made his move. He wanted to renegotiate the deal. Packouz knew he was in a bad bargaining position. The money coming in from the army went directly to AEY. Packouz had no written contract with Diveroli, only an oral agreement. The handshake deal they had made was worth just that—a handshake.

In an effort to protect his interests, Packouz demanded a meeting with lawyers present. Before the session, the two friends had a quick exchange.

"Listen, dude, if you fuck me, I'm going to fuck you," Packouz warned.

"Whatever," said Diveroli.

"It's going to be war," Packouz said. Then he played his trump card. "You don't want the IRS starting to come and look around."

Diveroli's face went white.

"Calm down," Diveroli said. "Don't throw around three-letter words like IRS. We can find a settlement."

"I know all of your contacts, and I can send them the actual documents showing what the government is paying," Packouz said. "You'll lose your entire profit margin."

"Take it easy," said Diveroli.

"We both know you're delivering Chinese," Packouz said.

A deal was struck, with Packouz agreeing to a fraction of the commission he had been promised. He figured he had something more precious than money: He knew how to work FedBizOpps. To compete with his former partner, he opened up his own one-man shop, Dynacore Industries, claiming on his website that his "staff" had done business with the State Department, the Pentagon, and the Iraqi and Afghan armies. "Sometimes you have to fake it until you make it," Packouz says. "People won't do business with you unless you have experience, but how can you get experience if they won't do business with you? Everyone has got to lie sometimes." Fearing that Diveroli might decide it was cheaper to have him killed than to pay him, Packouz also bought a .357 revolver as insurance.

·   ·   ·

It turned out that Packouz had bigger things to worry about. Winning the Afghan contract had earned AEY powerful enemies in the industry. One American arms dealer had complained to the State Department, claiming that AEY was buying Chinese-made AK-47s and shipping them to the Iraqi army. The allegation was false, but it had apparently triggered a criminal investigation by the Pentagon. On August 23, 2007—the very day Packouz was supposed to sign the settlement papers with Diveroli—federal agents raided AEY's offices in Miami Beach. Ordering everyone to step away from their computers, the agents seized all of the company's hard drives and files.

The raid led agents directly to the e-mails about the Chinese markings on the ammunition from Albania, and the conspiracy to repackage it. "The e-mails were incredibly incriminating—they spelled out everything," Packouz says. "I knew once they saw them we were in trouble. We were so stupid. If we didn't e-mail, we could probably have denied the whole thing. But there were the names and dates. It was undeniable. I realized I was going to get caught no matter what I did, so I turned myself in. When the agents came to my lawyer's office to interview me, they were joking about how they had seen all the e-mails and notes. They were laughing."

To avoid indictment, Packouz agreed to cooperate, as did Alex Podrizki. But Diveroli went right on shipping Chinese ammo to

Afghanistan—and the Army went right on accepting it. By now, though, the repackaging being done in Albania was getting even sloppier. Some of the crates were infested with termites, and the ammunition had been damaged by water. Tipped off by an attorney for Kosta Trebicka, who had begun a crusade against corruption in Albania, the *New York Times* ran a front-page story in March 2008 entitled "Supplier Under Scrutiny on Arms for Afghans."

Before the *Times* story ran, Packouz had been led to believe that he wasn't going to be charged for shipping pre-embargo Chinese ammunition. But after the article appeared, he and Podrizki and Diveroli were indicted on seventy-one counts of fraud. Faced with overwhelming evidence, all pleaded guilty. The Mormon gun manufacturer from Utah, Ralph Merrill, pleaded not guilty and was convicted in December. Heinrich Thomet simply vanished; according to rumors, he was last seen somewhere in Bosnia.

After the story broke, Kosta Trebicka traveled to the United States to talk to congressional investigators and federal prosecutors in Miami. He soon became terrified that the U.S. government was going to indict him as well. But back in Albania, he also became the lead witness in a case that targeted Albanian thugs and gangsters with ties to the prime minister. Then one afternoon in September 2008, Trebicka was killed in a mysterious "accident" when his truck somehow managed to flip over on a flat stretch of land outside Tirana. He was found alive by villagers, but medical crews and the police were slow to arrive. One of the first officials on the scene, in fact, was the Albanian prime minister's former bodyguard. "If it was an accident," says Erion Veliaj, an Albanian activist who worked with Trebicka, "it was a very strange kind."

Through all the chaos, Diveroli and Packouz had done a huge amount of business with the U.S. military. All told, AEY made eighty-five deliveries of munitions to Afghanistan worth more than $66 million, and had already received orders for another

$100 million in ammunition. But the fiasco involved more than a couple of stoner kids who made a fortune in the arms trade. "The AEY contract can be viewed as a case study in what is wrong with the procurement process," an investigation by the House Committee on Oversight and Government Reform later concluded. There was a "questionable need for the contract," a "grossly inadequate assessment of AEY's qualifications," and "poor execution and oversight" of the contract. The Bush administration's push to outsource its wars in Iraq and Afghanistan, in short, had sent companies like AEY into the world of illegal arms dealers—but when things turned nasty, the federal government reacted with righteous indignation.

In January, Packouz was sentenced to seven months of house arrest after he stood before a federal judge in Miami and expressed his remorse for the "embarrassment, stress, and heartache that I have caused." But his real regret is political: He believes that he and Diveroli were scapegoats, prosecuted not for breaking the law but for embarrassing the Bush administration. No one from the government has been charged in the case, even though officials in both the Pentagon and the State Department clearly knew that AEY was shipping Chinese-made ammunition to Afghanistan.

"We were the army's favorite contractors when we got the deal—poster boys for President Bush's small-business initiative," Packouz says. "We would have saved the government at least $50 million. We were living the American dream, until it turned into a nightmare."

●   ●   ●

In January, dressed in a tan prison-issued jumper, Diveroli came before Judge Joan Lenard for sentencing at Miami's gleaming new federal courthouse. The court was packed with his friends and relatives, but they didn't exactly give him the support he was hoping for. "Efraim needs to go to jail," a local rabbi told the judge. Even Diveroli's mother concurred. "I know you hate me for saying this," she said, addressing her son directly, "but you need to go to jail." Diveroli's shoulders slumped.

Diveroli described his contrition to Judge Lenard. When prison guards saw his file, he said, they asked in amazement how such a young person had managed to win such a huge military contract. "I have no answer," Diveroli told the court. "I have had many experiences in my short life. I have done more than most people can dream of. But I would have done it differently. All the notoriety in my industry and all the good times—and there were some—cannot make up for the damage."

Judge Lenard gazed at Diveroli for a long time. "If it wasn't so amazing, you would laugh," she said. Then she sentenced him to four years.

The hearing was not the end of Diveroli's woes. As a convicted felon, he was barred from so much as holding a gun, let alone selling arms. But while he was awaiting sentencing on the fraud charges, Diveroli couldn't stay out of the business he loved. He contrived to act as a consultant to a licensed importer who wanted to buy Korean-made ammunition magazines. The deal was technically legal—the magazines only fed ammo into the guns, so Diveroli wasn't actually selling weapons—but it put him in the cross hairs of another federal sting operation.

An ATF agent posing as an arms dealer spent weeks trying to wheedle Diveroli into selling arms. Diveroli refused, but he couldn't resist bragging about his exploits; as agents recorded his every word, he talked about hunting alligators and hogs in the Everglades with a .50-caliber rifle. Finally, the ATF agent lured Diveroli to a meeting, asking him to bring along a gun so they could go shooting together. Diveroli didn't bring a weapon—he knew that would constitute a felony. But the ATF agent, who had thoughtfully brought along a gun of his own, handed Diveroli a Glock to try out.

The temptation was too much. Adopting his best tough-guy swagger, Diveroli cleared the chamber and inspected the weapon. As always, the twenty-four-year-old arms dealer was the star of his own Hollywood movie. No matter what happened, he told the agent moments before his arrest, he would never leave the arms business.

"Once a gun runner," he boasted," always a gun runner."

The New Yorker

WINNER—PUBLIC INTEREST

Based on more than a year of reporting, "The Invisible Army" uncovered the mistreatment of tens of thousands of foreign workers on military bases in Iraq and Afghanistan. Sarah Stillman documented the existence of a corrupt system of labor supply that recruited foreign workers with promises of high-paying jobs and consigned them to what was in effect indentured servitude. "The Invisible Army" won The New Yorker its seventh National Magazine Award for Public Interest since 2000; the judges described themselves as being "wowed by Stillman's in-depth reporting and riveting but sober storytelling." Sarah Stillman was twenty-six when this story was published.

Sarah Stillman

The Invisible Army

I t was lunchtime in Suva, Fiji, a slow day at the end of the tourist season in September of 2007, when four men appeared in the doorway of the Rever Beauty Salon, where Vinnie Tuivaga worked as a hair stylist. The men wore polished shoes and bright Hawaiian shirts, and they told Vinnie about a job that sounded, she recalls, like "the fruits of my submission to the Lord all these years." How would she like to make five times her current salary at a luxury hotel in Dubai, a place known as the City of Gold? How would she like to have wealthy Arab customers, women who paid ridiculous fees for trendy cut-and-color jobs?

"I'll talk it over with my husband," she replied, coolly, but her pulse was racing. Vinnie, who was forty-five, had never worked abroad, but she often dreamed of it while hearing missionaries' lectures at her local church. Nearly six feet tall and two hundred and thirty pounds, Vinnie moved with an arthritic gait. But she took care with her appearance. She wore shiny slacks, with a gold pageboy cap on her perfectly coiffed frosted black hair, and carried a bright-red faux-leather purse, stuffed with silver eyeshadow. She could see herself working in one of the great cosmopolitan capitals. The offer seemed like her big break, the chance to send her teenage daughter to hospitality college and to pay her youngest son's fees for secondary school.

Later that week, at a salon around the corner, Lydia Qeraniu, thirty-two, heard a similar offer. A quick-witted woman with a coquettish smile and a figure that prompted Fijian men to call out "*uro, uro!*"—slang for "yummy"—Lydia was thrilled by the prospect of a career in Dubai. So were many other women in beauty shops and beachside hotels across Fiji. A Korean Air flight to Dubai would be leaving from Nadi International Airport in a few days. The women just had to deliver their résumés, hand over their passports, submit to medical tests, and pay a commission of five hundred dollars to a local recruitment firm called Meridian Services Agency.

Soon, more than fifty women were lined up outside Meridian's office to compete for positions that would pay as much as thirty-eight hundred dollars a month—more than ten times Fiji's annual per-capita income. Ten women were chosen, Vinnie and Lydia among them. Vinnie lifted her arms in the air and sang her favorite gospel song: "We're gonna make it, we're gonna make it. With Jesus on our side, things will work out fine." Lydia raced home to tell her husband and explain things to her five-year-old son. "Mommy's going to be OK," she recalls telling him. "Dubai, it's a rich country. Only good things can happen."

On the morning of October 10, 2007, the beauticians boarded their flight to the Emirates. They carried duffel bags full of cosmetics, family photographs, Bibles, floral sarongs, and chambas, traditional silky Fijian tops worn with patterned skirts. More than half of the women left husbands and children behind. In the rush to depart, none of them examined the fine print on their travel documents: their visas to the Emirates weren't employment permits but thirty-day travel passes that forbade all work, "paid or unpaid"; their occupations were listed as "Sales Coordinator." And Dubai was just a stopping-off point. They were bound for U.S. military bases in Iraq.

Lydia and Vinnie were unwitting recruits for the Pentagon's invisible army: more than seventy thousand cooks, cleaners, construction workers, fast-food clerks, electricians, and beauticians from the world's poorest countries who service U.S. military logistics contracts in Iraq and Afghanistan. Filipinos launder soldiers' uniforms, Kenyans truck frozen steaks and inflatable tents, Bosnians repair electrical grids, and Indians provide iced mocha lattes. The Army and Air Force Exchange Service (AAFES) is behind most of the commercial "tastes of home" that can be found on major U.S. bases, which include jewelry stores, souvenir shops filled with carved camels and Taliban chess sets, beauty salons where soldiers can receive massages and pedicures, and fast-food courts featuring Taco Bell, Subway, Pizza Hut, and Cinnabon. (AAFES's motto: "We go where you go.")

The expansion of private-security contractors in Iraq and Afghanistan is well known. But armed security personnel account for only about 16 percent of the overall contracting force. The vast majority—more than 60 percent of the total in Iraq—aren't hired guns but hired hands. These workers, primarily from South Asia and Africa, often live in barbed-wire compounds on U.S. bases, eat at meager chow halls, and host dance parties featuring Nepalese romance ballads and Ugandan church songs. A large number are employed by fly-by-night subcontractors who are financed by the American taxpayer but who often operate outside the law.

The wars' foreign workers are known, in military parlance, as "third-country nationals," or TCNs. Many of them recount having been robbed of wages, injured without compensation, subjected to sexual assault, and held in conditions resembling indentured servitude by their subcontractor bosses. Previously unreleased contractor memos, hundreds of interviews, and government documents I obtained during a yearlong investigation confirm many of these claims and reveal other grounds for concern. Widespread mistreatment even led to a series of food riots in Pentagon subcontractor camps, some involving more than a thousand workers.

Amid the slow withdrawal of U.S. forces from Iraq and Afghanistan, TCNs have become an integral part of the Obama administration's long-term strategy, as a way of replacing American boots on the ground. But top U.S. military officials are seeing the drawbacks to this outsourcing bonanza. Some argue, as retired General Stanley McChrystal did before his ouster from Afghanistan, last summer, that the unregulated rise of the Pentagon's Third World logistics army is undermining American military objectives. Others worry that mistreatment of foreign workers has become, as the former U.S. representative Christopher Shays, who cochairs the bipartisan Commission on Wartime Contracting, describes it, "a human-rights abuse that cannot be tolerated."

·　　·　　·

The extensive outsourcing of wartime logistics—first put to the test during the Clinton administration in Somalia and the Balkans—was designed to reduce costs while allowing military personnel to focus on combat. In practice, though, military privatization has produced convoluted chains of foreign subcontracts that often lead to cost overruns and fraud. The Commission on Wartime Contracting recently warned of the dangers associated with "poorly conceived, poorly structured, poorly conducted, and poorly monitored subcontracting," particularly noting the military's "heavy reliance on foreign subcontractors who may not be accountable to any American governmental authority."

The process of outsourcing begins at major government entities, notably the Pentagon, which awarded its most recent prime logistics contract (worth as much as fifteen billion dollars a year) to three U.S.-based private military behemoths: KBR (the former Halliburton subsidiary), DynCorp International, and Fluor. These "prime venders" then shop out the bulk of their contracts to hundreds of global subcontractors, many based in Middle

Eastern countries that are on the U.S. State Department's human-trafficking noncompliance list. Finally, these firms call upon thousands of Third World "manpower agencies"—small recruiting operations like Meridian Services.

A common recruiting story involves a tempting ad for Middle East "Salad Men" torn out of a newspaper, or an online job posting that promises "openings for cooks/chefs/master chefs for one of the best . . . middle east jobs." Given the desperate circumstances of many applicants, few questions are asked, and some subcontractors sneak workers to U.S. bases without security clearances, seeking to bypass basic wage and welfare regulations. "No one plays straight here," a foreign concession manager with six years of experience in Iraq told me. He introduced me to three young Nepali and Bangladeshi workers in a nearby Popeye's and Cinnabon, each of whom had paid a smuggler between three hundred and four hundred dollars to bring them onto the base with a fake letter of authorization. That's in addition to the money—an average of three thousand dollars—they had paid a recruiter in their home country to get the job.

Such sums are hardly unusual. A typical manpower agency charges applicants between two thousand and four thousand dollars, a small fortune in the countries where subcontractors recruit. To raise the money, workers may pawn heirlooms, sell their wedding rings or land or livestock, and take out high-interest loans. U.S. military guidelines prohibit such "excessive" fees. But in hundreds of interviews with TCNs, I seldom met a worker who had paid less than a thousand dollars for his or her job, and I never learned of a case in which anyone was penalized for charging these fees.

It's equally uncommon to meet a worker who receives the salary he or she was promised. A twenty-five-year-old Taco Bell employee on a major U.S. base in Iraq told me that he had paid a recruiting agency in Nepal four thousand dollars. "You'll make the money back so quick in Iraq!" he was assured. When he arrived in Baghdad in May 2009, he was housed in a shipping container behind the U.S. embassy, in the Green Zone, where he slept on soiled mattresses with twenty-five other migrants from Nepal, India, and Bangladesh. Many learned that they were to earn as little as two hundred and seventy-five dollars a month as cooks and servers for U.S. soldiers—a fraction of what they'd been promised and a tiny sliver of what U.S. taxpayers are billed for their labor.

So he paid another agent three hundred dollars to drive him in a taxi to a U.S. base in northern Iraq. There, an Indian smuggler charged an additional three hundred dollars to help him get a five-hundred-dollar-a-month job making burritos. "I am safe now," he said, tearfully, from the food-delivery window. "That is past, yeah? The army is my father and my mother."

For those familiar with the service economies of the Gulf states, this labor pipeline is simply the latest extension of a transnational system that for decades has supplied Kuwait, Saudi Arabia, Jordan, and the United Arab Emirates with low-wage workers. It's just that these employees face mortar fire, rocket attacks, improvised explosive devices, and other risks of war— and that they are working, albeit through intermediaries, for the United States government.

·　　·　　·

Vinnie, Lydia, and the other Fijian beauticians landed in Dubai just before dawn in October 2007. At the airport, they say, they were met by someone associated with Kulak Construction Company, a Turkish firm with millions of dollars in Pentagon subcontracts to do everything from building bowling alleys for troops to maintaining facilities on bases. The women were driven to a private hospital in the heart of the city. "It was very quiet there, because it was Ramadan," Vinnie recalls. In a small examination room, nurses gave them a series of blood tests and vaccinations.

Vinnie asked what all the poking and prodding was for. "You'll need these for Iraq," one of the nurses explained.

"Oh, we went crazy when we heard that," the youngest of the Fijian women, a petite twenty-two-year-old former resort hostess named Melanie Gonebale, told me later. We spoke in her flimsy living quarters on Forward Operating Base Sykes, near Tal Afar, in northern Iraq. A Kevlar helmet and bulletproof vest sat at the foot of her bed. "We'd watched on TV every day about Iraq—the bombs, people dying." That night, the women contemplated running away. But a number of them had taken out loans to cover their recruiting fees, and Meridian had reportedly threatened some with more than a thousand dollars in early-termination fines if they left.

A couple of nights later, a few of the women slipped out to a pay phone to call their families. "You take a big breath, honey," Vinnie told her husband, holding back tears. "I'm not working here in Dubai. A bus is going to take us to the airport, and we're going to go straight to Iraq." After Kie Puafomau, another of the Fijians, reached her husband, he went to the Fijian police, the Ministry of Labor, and the national press. The *Fiji Times* ran a story exposing Meridian Services Agency's recruiting fraud. But even as the police pledged to investigate, they could do little to help the beauticians some nine thousand miles away.

The next morning, Vinnie, Lydia, and the other women flew to Iraq and found themselves on a convoy bound for Balad, forty miles north of Baghdad. There, on a U.S. base called Camp Anaconda—and known to soldiers as Mortaritaville, for its constant barrage of incoming mortar fire—they got more bad news. Instead of earning between fifteen hundred and thirty-eight hundred dollars a month, as they had been promised, the women were told that they would make only seven hundred dollars a month, a sum that was later reduced, under another subcontractor, to three hundred and fifty. "We were just all dumbstruck," Chanel Joy, who had earned several times as much working as a certified beauty therapist at a Fijian resort, recalled. "It was ridiculous, really, slave labor, absolutely ridiculous out here in a war zone." In the contract they signed in Iraq, their working hours were specified as "Twelve (12) hours per day and seven (7) days a week." Their "vacation" was a "Return ticket after the completion of the service." Appended to the contract was a legal waiver: "I am willingly and of my own free will have decided to go and work in Iraq, and I declare that no one in Fiji or out of Fiji has approach me to work in Iraq. . . . I am contented with my job. . . . I want to complete my contract, till then, I will not go back home." (A lawyer for Kulak Construction denied that the company had ever employed any women from Fiji, although the company's name appears on the women's contracts. He added, "Kulak has a good reputation for sixty years.")

For nearly two weeks, the ten women refused to do any work. "We decided we had to stick together," Chanel, a dignified older woman with a mane of auburn curls, recounted. "Desert Sisters—that's what we called each other." Eventually, they agreed to a revised deal offering them eight hundred dollars a month. It was better than being stranded with no pay. The next morning, the beauticians were separated, and sent to different military camps. Two stayed at Camp Anaconda; three were flown to Tikrit; two went to Camp Diamondback, in Mosul; and three—Vinnie, Lydia, and Melanie—ended up in Tal Afar, after stints in Tikrit and Mosul. Before boarding their flights, the women received body armor and a tutorial on rocket attacks: how to duck and dive, then sprint to the nearest bunker until the "all clear" sirens sounded.

Only then, Vinnie told me, did her situation truly sink in. Climbing into a military helicopter in her weighty new gear, she decided that she would have to pray each night that the Lord would send her home alive. "Am I going to get hurt?" she wondered, as the Black Hawk took off. "Am I going to get killed? Who's going to take care of my family, my children? Please, God, give me protection."

.   .   .

Not every third-country national makes it home safely. Since 2001, more than two thousand contractor fatalities and more than fifty-one thousand injuries have been reported in Iraq and Afghanistan. For the first time in American history, private-contractor losses are now on a par with those of U.S. troops in both war zones, amounting to 53 percent of reported fatalities in the first six months of 2010. Since many TCN deaths and injuries are never tallied—contractors are expected to self-report, with spotty compliance—the actual numbers are presumed to be higher.

Constantine Rodriguez, a soft-spoken thirty-eight-year-old from the former Portuguese colony of Goa, was working at a Pizza Hut at Camp Taji, Iraq, when an insurgent's rocket struck. Two of his Bangladeshi co-workers died, according to a former boss, and Rodriguez lost an eye and a leg. Disabled, he was sent back to southern India, where he had a young wife and a baby to support. Although employees who are injured on U.S. bases are usually entitled to medical care and disability compensation, few foreign workers are aware of their rights, and fewer still are able to navigate the byzantine process required to receive payment.

If most Americans know nothing about this foreign workforce on U.S. bases, al-Qaeda and other extremist groups have taken notice. As early as 2004, Sunni militants launched a campaign to kill TCNs. Their goal was to disrupt American supply chains by blowing up truckers, and to punish Third World Muslims who collaborated with "the infidels" and pressure governments to prevent their citizens from going abroad to work for Coalition troops. Over the summer and the early fall of 2004, the list of those kidnapped by insurgents included Turks, Pakistanis, Indonesians, Indians, Egyptians, Macedonians, Bulgarians, and Kenyans. In one particularly bloody incident, a caravan of Nepalese workers bound for a major U.S. airbase was taken captive. Eleven were shot dead, and one man was beheaded.

Despite these risks and harsh conditions, many TCNs are grateful for their jobs. In my travels through Iraq and Afghanistan, I met dozens of workers like Paz Dizon, a Filipina cleaning woman employed by G3 Logistics at the hospital on Kandahar Airfield. ("Paz?" I repeated when she introduced herself, to which she replied, cheerfully, "Yes, like 'Pass away!'") She feels that she's contributing something important to the war effort while earning a wage that far exceeds what she could make back home. At night, she snacks on Twinkies with the other Filipinas in her barracks; after rocket attacks, they sing eighties pop songs on a dust-covered karaoke machine. "We keep on teasing that the G3 ladies will die happy, singing and dancing," her colleague Rey Villa Cacas told me with a giggle, describing how their boss belted out the lyrics to "Soldier of Fortune" during the previous night's mortar shelling.

At first, Vinnie, Lydia, and Melanie got along well in Iraq, too. After several months, the three were flown northwest to Forward Operating Base Sykes, where I first met them. They were working for another Turkish subcontractor, and were put under the supervision of a chain-smoking Turkish man in his twenties. They lived in air-conditioned shipping containers, played pool in the "morale, welfare, and recreation" hall, sang in Sunday church services, and ate meals in the main dining facility, which included a hot-sandwich bar, a wings-and-burgers grill, a "healthy choice" line, and an assortment of Baskin-Robbins ice cream. The AAFES beauty salon turned out to be pleasant, filled with soldiers in vinyl chairs, M-16 rifles at their feet, flipping through copies of *Maxim* as they awaited seven-dollar pedicures or five-dollar straight-razor shaves. Dated fashion posters hung on the walls, with eighties-style Madonna look-alikes (hoop earrings, feathered bangs) and inspirational words, like "Simplicity Is the Essence of Beauty" and "We're Here for You!"

The three women had a knack for setting customers at ease. Vinnie would joke with soldiers about "putting the 'man' in manicure" or show off snapshots of her twelve-year-old son, Samuel, who liked to eat trays of her stir-fried chicken with cashew nuts. Lydia, as she worked, asked soldiers about their lives in the States: any girlfriends, kids, Harleys? Melanie, the shyest of the three, ended her pedicure sessions by inquiring, like a peppy travel agent, "Have you thought about taking your holiday in Fiji? You should come. It's a beautiful place, like paradise, really. You can have your honeymoon there someday." (She regularly extolled the virtues of Fiji-brand artesian bottled water, to the point that she came to be known around the base as "the Fiji Water lady.")

Some customers would tease back, asking, "Why'd you choose to leave a nice place like Fiji for a shit-hole like this?" If the boss was out for a smoke and the man in the lavender swivel chair seemed trustworthy, the women would tell him. One sympathetic customer, an American private contractor, got in touch with associates in New York; a letter was sent to the Defense Department, requesting an official investigation into whether the women's recruitment and working conditions were "exploitative." Soon thereafter, the AAFES Inspector General dispatched a business manager to interview the beauticians. But the manager determined that, because the three had their passports and had known their ultimate destination after arriving in Dubai, AAFES was not in violation of anti-trafficking regulations. (The organization did note that, in general, "better safeguards and improvements were necessary to protect contract workers.")

Late one night in early April 2008, I knocked on the door of Lydia and Vinnie's shipping container to find Lydia curled up on the floor, knees to chest, chin to knees, crying. Vinnie told me, after some hesitation, that a supervisor had "had his way with" Lydia. According to the two women's tearful account, nonconsensual sex had become a regular feature of Lydia's life. They said the man would taunt Lydia, calling her a "fucking bitch" and describing the various acts he would like to see her perform.

Lydia trembled, her normally confident figure crumpled inward. "If he comes tonight, you have to scream," Vinnie told Lydia, tapping her fist against the aluminum siding of the shipping container. "Bang on this wall here and scream!"

The next day, I dialed the U.S. Army's emergency sexual-assault hot line, printed on a pamphlet distributed across the base that read, "Stand Up Against Sexual Assault . . . Make a Difference." Nobody answered. Despite several calls over several days, the number simply rang and rang. (A U.S. Central Command spokesman, when later reached for comment, noted, "We do track and investigate any report of criminal activity that occurs on our military bases.")

·　　·　　·

Abuses like these weren't supposed to be happening. In early 2006, after reports of human trafficking, the Department of Defense launched an investigation into subcontractors' working conditions. Government inspectors listed "widespread" abuses, including the illegal confiscation of workers' passports, "deceptive hiring practices," "excessive recruiting fees," and "substandard worker living conditions."

That April, George W. Casey, then the commanding general for Iraq, issued an order to private contractors and subcontractors there, seeking to establish guidelines for humane treatment. For the first time, TCNs were entitled to "measurable, enforceable standards for living conditions (e.g. sanitation, health, safety, etc.)," including "50 feet as the minimum acceptable square footage of personal living space per worker." All U.S. troops would receive training to help them recognize human trafficking and abuse, and major contractors were ordered to design a mandatory anti-trafficking awareness session for their employees.

But the Pentagon's "zero tolerance" policy for violators proved largely toothless. In one incident in December 2008, U.S. military personnel discovered that a warehouse operated off the base by a KBR subcontractor, Najlaa International Catering, was filled with more than a thousand workers who appeared to be human-trafficking victims. Many of the men were sent home, but Najlaa retained its service contracts and won a new multi-million-dollar deal for operating a USAID dining facility in the Green Zone.

A representative of Najlaa's associate firm in Amman, Jordan, told me that the workers' mistreatment had been due to a temporary "cash money problem," and a KBR spokesman said that the company "fully disclosed the incident to our U.S. government clients including all remedial actions taken by both KBR and Najlaa." What's more, a KBR spokesman said that "we actively encourage our employees to raise issues of concern through the proper channels and processes the company has in place."

However, in some cases managers have clearly been dissuaded by their superiors from taking an interest in such matters. Soon after Mike Land, an American who was a KBR foreman, complained about the living conditions of his Filipino and Indian men, he received an official reprimand: "You are expected to refrain from further involvement regarding the working and living conditions of the sub-contract workers as that is not your responsibility. . . . Any future interference with [the subcontractor's] operations will result in additional action up to and including termination." In Afghanistan, one high-ranking contracting officer told me that labor law "doesn't exist here," and that enforcement would be hard to prioritize if it did: the job "is to get the war fighters what they need."

Still, the Obama administration has made a point of talking about contractor accountability. Not long after taking office, in 2009, President Obama pledged to make good on his campaign promise to end the "lack of planning, oversight, and management of these contractors," which "has repeatedly undermined our troops' efforts in the field." When General McChrystal assumed command of U.S. and NATO forces in Afghanistan in June

2009, he set out to reduce the role of TCNs. He pushed a policy of "Afghanization," bringing in local Afghan workers to replace third-country nationals whenever possible. Conventional wisdom held that allowing Afghans—or, in Iraq, Iraqis—to work on U.S. bases posed a grave security threat to troops. But the military's new counter-insurgency doctrine turned this logic on its head. What if bringing in workers from Sierra Leone and Bangladesh rendered U.S. bases less safe, by alienating locals and occupying jobs they could perform? McChrystal saw an opportunity to make inroads with Afghanistan's unemployed masses.

"Afghanization" turned out to be a tall order. Corruption meant that U.S. tax dollars were soon funneling into the hands of Taliban insurgents. Even the process of getting Afghans on and off the bases proved exhausting, slowing down vital construction projects. By March 2010, at the height of the Afghan First initiative, the number of third-country nationals counted by the Department of Defense in Afghanistan had actually increased by nearly 50 percent from the previous June, reaching 17,512.

The "drawdown" of operations in Iraq, on the other hand, has created new difficulties for TCNs there. Last summer, Colonel Richard E. Nolan, of the military's contracting office, expressed concern that TCNs were being abandoned on U.S. bases when their companies lost contracts or were ordered to shed numbers. I met several such workers, one of whom, a Popeye's employee, had been told by a sympathetic boss to pack his bags, carry them to the office of a U.S. commander, and fall to his knees weeping, in the hope of being granted a ticket home.

At Kandahar Airfield, in Afghanistan, I talked to Joel Centeno, a Filipino who sat with his head buried in his hands on a picnic bench behind a T.G.I. Friday's. A Pentagon subcontractor had laid him off but refused to provide him with a return ticket. ("Thank you and appreciated your contribution to the team," his termination letter read.) Centeno was among the war's new breed of workers: adrift on U.S. bases, searching for work, unable to afford the ticket home, and fearful of loan sharks who await them there.

•   •   •

In early April 2008, Vinnie and Lydia were told that they would be flying back to Fiji. (Not long after I began conducting interviews with the women, U.S. military personnel complained that they were "making trouble" on the base.) For them, the prospect of returning home was a godsend. "We're just counting the days," Lydia told customers. "Fresh fruit and beaches and our families." After boarding a U.S. military aircraft, they flew to Mosul to await processing. They said that they were held there for more than a month, and that their passports and identification badges were confiscated by their Turkish subcontractor. This meant they had no right of mobility; without an ID, the U.S. military could detain them simply for going to the latrine or walking to the AT&T phone booth to call their families. Even so, Lydia managed to get in touch with her husband and son on occasion. "Don't worry, Mommy's doing all right, I'll be home soon," she told them, to which her five-year-old responded, "Will you buy me a big gun?"

Finally, in the first week of May, they boarded a homebound flight. They carried a few souvenirs: their AAFES nametags, snapshots in front of a sandbagged bunker, perfume from an Iraqi contractor, and an oversized black T-shirt for Lydia's son that read, in both English and Arabic, "Caution Stay 100 Meters Back or You Will Be Shot."

When Vinnie arrived home, she found her whole family waiting up by a lantern on a big ceremonial *kuta* mat on the living-room floor—all but her youngest, Samuel, who hid under a blanket in a nearby room, ashamed that he'd grown chubbier in her absence, and frightened that his mother wouldn't recognize him. "It's your mama," Vinnie coaxed him. "Come out from under there!" When he finally emerged, Vinnie held him in her arms.

Vinnie passed several weeks with her children and her husband, cooking big meals and singing gospel tunes. Eventually, she went back to work styling hair at the Rever Beauty Salon. Lydia and her husband had a baby girl. "It took me, like, four months to get away from my own head," she recalls. "I was sleeping in the day and waking up in the night, so many negative stories. . . . I just wanted to take my son to school and pick him up." Melanie arrived home a few months later, equally relieved. She busied herself with wedding plans and got a job at the Pure Fiji Spa, where customers are instructed to "step lightly over running waters . . . leaving behind cares and the outside world as if on a far distant shore."

Then one afternoon in the fall of 2009, Vinnie heard on the radio that the police were calling for people who had been defrauded by Meridian Services Agency to come forward with their stories. She learned that the company had reportedly conned more than twenty thousand Fijian workers into paying large fees for fraudulent "Middle East jobs." Meridian's director, a portly local named Timoci Lolohea, had, according to the *Fiji Times*, extracted more than $1.6 million from his victims over the previous five years; they included not only poor workers but also church congregations, tribal elders, and village community centers seeking overseas employment for their constituents. In the lush farming region of Waimaro, one village spokesman produced receipts to show that Lolohea had collected the equivalent of as much as twenty-seven thousand dollars—a Fijian windfall—from thirteen impoverished villages in exchange for jobs in Kuwait which never materialized. The devastation from Lolohea's recruiting scheme was so widespread that the deputy director of the Fijian police created a special task force to investigate it.

When several human-rights litigators in Washington, D.C., learned, through my investigation, of the beauticians' experiences, they flew Vinnie to the United States to hear the details of her case. I sat in on several days of interviews with labor experts. Her trip culminated in a meeting with State Department officials, at which Vinnie spoke with purpose about her false recruitment and subsequent mistreatment. She spoke, too, of her children and the months she'd spent away from them while serving U.S. soldiers in the salon.

After the meeting, Ambassador at Large Luis CdeBaca, the director of the State Department's Office to Monitor and Combat Trafficking in Persons, notified officials at AAFES and the Office of the Secretary of Defense about the allegations, and urged them to investigate. "We're going to make sure that Secretary Clinton is aware of these allegations," he wrote in a February 2010 e-mail to Defense Department officials, first obtained by the Project on Government Oversight. Soon thereafter, the women's story began to circulate among army officials in a classified PowerPoint presentation, distributed by the U.S. Army Inspector General School. "Army policy opposes any and all activities associated with human trafficking," the briefing notes, adding, in red ink, "No leader will turn a blind eye to this issue!"

Yet when reporters asked the U.S. Army's Criminal Investigation Command (CID) for details last summer, they were told that allegations of the women's mistreatment had been investigated earlier and were "not substantiated." (According to an internal AAFES report, "allegations of rape never surfaced" in the organization's prior investigation of the women's recruitment.) CID officials declined to say whether any victims had been interviewed, and, when reached recently, a CID spokesman apologized for being unable to locate any record of the case. According to the spokesman, "CID takes allegations of sexual assault very seriously and fully investigates allegations where there is credible information that a crime may have occurred involving army personnel or others accompanying the force." Lydia and Vinnie both say that no one from the military or AAFES spoke with them about the sexual-assault claims.

. . .

In the three years since Vinnie and Lydia returned from Iraq, thousands of third-country nationals have tried to make their grievances known, sometimes spectacularly. Previously unreported worker riots have erupted on U.S. bases over issues such as lack of food and unpaid wages. On May 1, 2010, in a labor camp run by Prime Projects International (PPI) on the largest military base in Baghdad, more than a thousand subcontractors—primarily Indians and Nepalis—rampaged, using as weapons fists, stones, wooden bats, and, as one U.S. military policeman put it, "anything they could find."

The riot started as a protest over a lack of food, according to a whippet-thin worker in the camp named Subramanian. A forty-five-year-old former rice farmer from the Indian state of Tamil Nadu, Subramanian worked twelve-hour days cleaning the military's fast-food court. Around seven o'clock on the evening of the riot, Subramanian returned to the PPI compound and lined up for dinner with several thousand other workers. But the cooks ran out of food with at least five hundred left to feed. This wasn't the first time; empty plates had become common in the camp during the past year. Several of the men stormed over to the management's office, demanding more rice. When management refused, he recalls, dozens more entered the fray, then hundreds, and ultimately more than a thousand. Employees started to throw gravel at the managers. Four-foot pieces of plywood crashed through glass windows. Workers broke down the door to the food cellar and made off with as much as they could carry.

The riot spread through the vast camp. At one point, as many as fourteen hundred men were smashing office windows, hurling stones, destroying computers, raiding company files, and battering the entrance to the camp where a large blue-and-white sign reads "Treat others how you want to be treated. . . . No damaging P.P.I. property that has been built for your comfort." (According to an investigation conducted by KBR, "P.P.I. employees . . . became agitated after being told they'd experience a delay while additional food was prepared." "Upon full assessment of the incident," a company spokesperson relayed in a written statement, "KBR notified P.P.I. management of the need for changes to prevent any recurrence and worked with the subcontractor to implement those corrective actions.")

Only when U.S. military police arrived—followed by Ugandan security guards—did the camp fall quiet. Some workers attempted to hide, though there wasn't anywhere to go—just a sea of gravel dotted by an archipelago of dismal white shipping containers, in which workers slept in tightly packed rows of creaky bunks with colorful towels draped between them for privacy.

"Almost every window in the camp was destroyed, food everywhere," Sergeant Jonathan Trivett, one of the first U.S. military policemen to the scene, recalls. "They pretty well destroyed the entire camp. . . . It was shocking." Trivett, a handsome twenty-five-year-old with an aw-shucks Indiana smile, later gave me a tour of the camp, which MPs now patrol twice daily to insure that nothing "out of the ordinary" is taking place. ("Lotta love, buddy," he greets the guards at the gate.) His police team did its best to investigate the rioters' motives, but most workers, including Subramanian, were too terrified to talk, and the majority spoke little or no English. Three military policemen under Sergeant Trivett's supervision that night later received Army Achievement Medals for their role in quelling the rampage.

Several weeks after the riot, the defiant mood spread to other parts of the base. Workers in the neighboring camp of Gulf

Catering Company (GCC), another subcontractor, staged a copy-cat riot, pelting their bosses with stones and accusing the company of failing to pay them their proper wages. That same week, more GCC employees en route from a base in Balad set fire to their barracks to protest unpaid wages. Several buildings burned to the ground.

This was not unprecedented. In 2008, in another nearby labor compound, a rumpled Iraqi businessman named Alaa Noori Habeb faced a similar horde of rioting workers. At the time, he ran a Baghdad warehouse for a company called Elite Home Group, which sheltered and fed hundreds of foreign KBR subcontractors in conditions that were, he admitted, foul. As Habeb flipped through photos of the incident, he told me how Nepalis in his compound erupted in rage—ripping up mattresses, tearing out electrical boxes, and destroying company computers. A manager at yet another KBR subcontractor camp in Baghdad, Ziad Al Karawi, described how a thousand Indian and Sri Lankan men under his supervision slept on crowded floors: "rats and flies attacked us. . . . We had no beds to sleep at or tables to eat at. . . . No communication, no TV, no soap to wash or bathe, no visits from anyone from the company or KBR. . . . The workers had no choice except going out in a protest."

In the wake of various uprisings, workers have been reprimanded and sent home. KBR insists that its "business ethics and values" require that employees and subcontractors are treated with "dignity and respect," that it adheres to U.S. government guidelines for the treatment of workers, and that it "follows rigorous policies, procedures, and training," to protect the welfare of foreign-national workers. But, even after investigations by KBR and the military, little seems to change. A spokesman for U.S. Central Command acknowledged that it "does not play a formal role in the monitoring of living conditions on U.S. bases," although each base has a military chain of command responsible for "working with the entities involved to insure minimum standards are met." Government officials rarely learn of these riots, most of which take place in compounds watched over by private guards. Nor do major media outlets. "We thought the journalists would come," Imtiyas Sheriff, a thirty-eight-year-old GCC bus driver and father from Sri Lanka, told me. "They call this Operation Iraqi Freedom, but where is our freedom?" Still, many of the workers have faith that the U.S. military wants to do right by them. In fact, the majority view American soldiers and marines as their sole protectors. "The American people are a good people," the round-faced Sheriff said to me more than once, as we crouched in a sweltering bunker. "They will help us, if they know what is happening."

•   •   •

Back in Fiji, Vinnie and Lydia's quest for accountability has proved fruitless. Spotting one of her "lying bastard" recruiters on the street not long ago, Vinnie ran up to him, scolding, "How can you show your face around here?" Lydia and several of the other women stormed the offices of Meridian Services, demanding that the men answer for their actions and take down a photograph they'd posted, from a Fijian social-networking website, of Lydia, Vinnie, and three other beauticians on a U.S. base emblazoned with the words "Salsa Nite! Mosul, Iraq. No wonder I haven't been seeing them in town. Lovely hairdressers . . . Take care ladies!" Before she left, Lydia warned the men that it's a small world. "Next time," she told them, "don't you take all these ladies and fool them."

The Fijian press has denounced Timoci Lolohea, Meridian's director, as a "fraudster" and "con artist." But some Fijian officials seemed to have condoned such activities, in the hope of bringing remittances from U.S. military operations. "The government knows that more men are leaving for Kuwait and Iraq and it is a good thing, because it is providing employment for the unemployed," Fiji's minister for labor, Kenneth Zinck, said back in 2005. Zinck was initially assigned to lead the government investigation into Meridian's practices. In July of 2010, Lolohea (who did not respond to requests for comment) pleaded not guilty to charges of unlawful recruiting.

Through it all, Lolohea's employment empire has remained. Recently, he put up a placard outside his house advertising jobs in Dubai. He also opened a new office in Suva, where, each morning, throngs of workers have been lining up outside his gate. They bring their passports and pockets stuffed with borrowed cash. They are undeterred by the large white sign at the entrance, which the police have ordered Lolohea to post, reading, "NO Recruitment Until Further Notice." Most have heard the rumors about Lolohea's shady past, and they know that he was long denounced in the local newspapers as one of "Fiji's most wanted men." But they've also heard that he's offering a starting salary of six thousand dollars a month to prospective security guards and military logistics workers for his new company, Phoenix Logistics Corporation Limited. And so the crowds keep flocking to his illicit office in the midst of the rainy season—most of them eager young men in baggy jeans and baseball caps, or in traditional *sulu* skirts, but also the occasional woman, her head filled with dreams of a life in the City of Gold.

Glamour

Four women are killed every day in the United States by their partners. Yeardley Love was a twenty-two-year-old college student whose boyfriend shook her so hard that her head repeatedly hit the wall. Samantha Miller, thirty-four, was shot in the head on Christmas Day. Courtney Delano, nineteen, was killed when she was six months pregnant. Sarah Coit, twenty-three, was stabbed repeatedly in her apartment on the very day this story went to press. This year more than 1,400 women will be murdered by someone they once loved. Why is relationship violence so frighteningly common? Glamour *not only explained but told readers what they could do about it.*

Liz Brody

The Secret That Kills Four Women a Day

Not long before sunrise on a Midwestern Friday, college student and part-time waitress Alexandra Briggs sat in her one-bedroom apartment, meticulously applying thick makeup all over her face, neck, and arms. It took two coats to cover her boyfriend's teeth marks and the cigarette burns he'd inflicted, along with her newly purpling bruises; her pants hid the spot on her thigh where he'd stabbed her with a fork. When she finished, he drove her to the Original Pancake House for her seven A.M. shift. "I'm sick," she told her boss as she clocked in and headed to the restroom.

Briggs, a freckled, blue-eyed Beatles fan who was studying criminal justice, had first chatted with Matthew Hubbard over instant messenger five months earlier. After their first date, she hadn't been interested, but when Hubbard, a fellow student, begged her to give him a chance, she did.

By that morning, she was barely a whisper of herself. As Hubbard would later admit in court, before Briggs had gone to work he'd hit her repeatedly with a small bat and strangled her until she slumped, unconscious—typical of the violence that had started a month into the relationship. "He had me in a choke hold against the wall, saying, 'I'm going to kill you. No one will find your body; no one cares about you,'" Briggs, now twenty-six, recalls. Dazed, she had agreed to Hubbard's order to go to work, fake the stomach flu, and return home with him. She was huddled over the toilet when her manager, Shea Duymovic, pushed her way into the stall and sat on the floor. "Look at me," Duymovic said, her face next to Briggs's. "I know what he's doing to you. And I can't stand to see this happen anymore."

A moment passed. When Briggs finally turned, she saw her boss's eyes filled with tears. She remembers thinking one simple thought: *Someone cares?* Overwhelmed, she began to sob. "Do you want me to call your parents?" Duymovic asked gently. Briggs could only nod.

That day wasn't the first time Duymovic, then thirty-three, had worried about her employee. She'd weathered a violent relationship herself, swept into it young, as Briggs had been. "I knew Alex's situation was getting really bad," Duymovic recalls. She had seen the bruises on Briggs's arms and noticed that she'd begun wearing glasses and heavy foundation; once bubbly, Briggs now spent most breaks tethered to her cell phone. "She came in and I could just tell," Duymovic says. "I think she would have died if she had left with him." And so Duymovic stepped in: staying by Briggs' side until her father arrived, keeping in touch as Briggs recovered from her injuries—including a broken nose and ruptured eardrum. And the day that Hubbard was sentenced to ten years in prison and the details of Briggs's abuse went on record, Duymovic was there, cheering her on. As Briggs says today, "Shea was my angel."

Duymovic *is* a hero. But what she did is something each and every one of us can do—and must do. Because the violence Briggs kept secret is much too common.

•　　　•　　　•

The truth is, four women are killed *every single day* in the United States by someone they're involved with. One year ago, on May 3, the world lost Yeardley Love, a twenty-two-year-old University of Virginia lacrosse player whose boyfriend now faces trial for her murder; he told police he shook her so hard her head repeatedly hit the wall. And the headlines kept coming, telling the horror stories of New York swimsuit designer Sylvie Cachay, thirty-three, strangled and left in her hotel bathroom, allegedly by her boyfriend; Samantha Miller, thirty-four, shot in the head on Christmas near a Tennessee army base; Courtney Delano, nineteen, killed in Michigan when she was six months pregnant. The very day *Glamour* went to press with this story, Sarah Coit, twenty-three, was stabbed multiple times, reportedly by her boyfriend, in their Manhattan apartment. "I knew he was going to kill her," a former neighbor told the *New York Post.* And that's just the tip of the iceberg: Over the course of an average year in twenty-first-century America, more than 1,400 women will be murdered by someone they've loved.

Most alarming, things are only getting *more* dangerous for some women: While overall female "intimate partner homicides," as these deaths are called, have dropped almost 20 percent since domestic violence awareness began in the 1970s, a closer look at data from the Bureau of Justice Statistics reveals that, frighteningly, among women who are dating—as opposed to married—the homicide rate is *climbing.* "For girlfriends killed by boyfriends, especially white girlfriends, the homicide rates have actually risen slightly," says James Alan Fox, Ph.D., a criminology expert at Northeastern University and former fellow of the Bureau of Justice Statistics, who analyzed the government data for *Glamour.* And the rates of violence for young married women are still unacceptably high as well: In an exclusive *Glamour*/Harris Interactive random survey of 2,542 women ages eighteen to thirty-five—single, living together, and married—a full 29 percent said they'd been in an abusive relationship. Another 30 percent said they'd never been abused but then went on to acknowledge that, at some point, a partner had viciously hurt them: from verbal degradation to being strangled or threatened with a knife. That means more than half of all women have been harmed by their partner.

Why is this still happening in 2011? After all, as women, we're clearly no longer second-class citizens, so dependent on men's earnings and support that we must put up with brutal relationships simply because we have no choices. We have more choices than ever—and men are surely more enlightened. So why are women more likely to be killed by their boyfriend than they were thirty-five years ago? And what can we do to reverse the trend?

Glamour is hoping to answer those questions. To honor the one-year anniversary of Yeardley Love's death, we're encouraging women to talk about relationship violence—both to ask for help and to offer it without judgment. Our campaign starts on these pages—full of real stories, hard science, and guidance about exactly what to say and do. The most important step: Tell Somebody.

Why Young Women Are More at Risk Now

We've come a long way since the 1980s, when movies like Farrah Fawcett's *The Burning Bed* helped break decades of silence about relationship abuse. Back then "everyone thought that domestic violence and rape were rare occurrences," says Patricia Tjaden, Ph.D., who headed the acclaimed National Violence Against Women Survey ten years ago. "Now there is a consensus among practitioners, policy makers, researchers and the public that these types of violence are widespread." And yet it seems that greater awareness hasn't translated into a public condemnation of these crimes—instead, some days, our reaction looks like one giant cultural shrug. Consider Charlie Sheen, who apparently spent two decades pushing, shoving, threatening, and, on one occasion, even accidentally shooting the women in his life— much of the time while enjoying his role as TV's highest-paid actor. ("I will cut your head off, put it in a box, and send it to

your mom!" he reportedly said to his third wife, Brooke Muel-
ler.) Mel Gibson pleaded no contest to charges stemming from
hitting his girlfriend, Oksana Grigorieva ("You f—king deserved
it," he ranted), and then went on to star in *The Beaver*, one of his
biggest films in years. Over in the sports world, at least three
players in the NFL alone were accused of domestic violence last
year. It all maddens attorney Gael Strack, cofounder of the National Family Justice Center Alliance. "It's like, 'I just got charged
with DV, what's the big deal?'" she says. "In a lot of cases, there
are few or no consequences."

But cultural complacency may be only one reason relationship violence persists. New technology is playing a part too. For
years experts have known—and told victims—that any partner
who constantly needs to know where you are and what you're
doing is a dangerous partner, that such "monitoring" often leads
to physical violence. But these days it's become so acceptable for
couples, colleagues, and friends to text and e-mail one another
at any given moment that women may miss those early danger
signs. What's more, GPS and computer spyware are cropping up
increasingly in stalking and dating violence cases. "Abusers can
now be on you 24/7," says Cindy Southworth, founder of the
Safety Net Project, a team of experts on digital abuse at the National Network to End Domestic Violence.

And believe it or not, in a hookup culture, some advocates
worry that young women may be brushing off "bad boy" behavior. "A major misperception is that if the relationship isn't serious, the abuse can't be serious," says Cristina Escobar, a spokes-
woman for Break the Cycle, a dating violence organization for
teens and twentysomethings. "Just because you're hooking up
doesn't mean you're not experiencing violence." In fact, says
Tjaden, "there's more intimate violence reported in cohabiting
couples than in marriages."

Perhaps most surprising, some researchers believe that because young women today feel invulnerable in relationships,

they may actually try to tough it out themselves rather than ask for help when things turn bad. "We've grown up in a different generation, where women are leaders, we have careers, children—we break glass ceilings," one twenty-four-year-old student tells *Glamour*, explaining why she spent two and a half years with a boyfriend who called her "bitch" and "whore" and, according to her police report, hit her and threatened her. "We expect to be strong and independent. When the abuse began, I thought, I can handle this on my own."

In other words, it's hard for young women to see themselves as victims at the hands of a man. "They don't believe they'll ever be an Ike and Tina Turner story," says Kenya Fairley, program manager for the National Resource Center on Domestic Violence, "because they see the initial incidents of abuse in the same way they see obstacles they're tackling at work. So if a boyfriend criticizes her, she thinks, I can handle it, just like she does with her boss. Women today keep managing the abuse until they're so far in they need help getting out."

That's exactly what happened to April Singiser, twenty-two, a San Diego nursing student. Over the course of three years, she says, her then boyfriend threw food at her and held her hostage in his apartment when she wanted to leave. She told no one—not her family, not her friends, not her coworkers—because "I was ashamed and embarrassed," she says. "I am not that type of person. I'm the person who always says, 'I don't care how big you are.'" But after she tried to break up with him, he forced her into her Honda Civic at knifepoint, and she had to face it: She might be strong, but at 6'5" and 300 pounds with a switchblade in his hand, he was stronger.

"He was telling me, 'You shouldn't have left me; I'm going to take you to an Indian reservation where I can kill you and no one will find you,' and holding the knife to my throat," she recalls. "I was driving on the 805 North, bawling, thinking, How am I going to get out of this? Should I just crash the car on his side?" When, at his direction, she got off the freeway, they hit a red light. Singiser sprang out, raced to the car behind her and banged on the windows. "He's going to kill me!" she screamed. It was literally the first time she'd ever asked for help.

Singiser's ex is now in jail; he gets out next February. She is worried—on his Facebook profile, his interests include "Gettin Even"—but she's also thriving, going to school and working as a medical assistant. "Even though I thought I could handle it," she says of her early reluctance to talk about her situation, "I obviously couldn't."

Why Doesn't She Just Leave?

Perhaps the most nagging question about this issue is, Why do women stay? Some of the reasons are the age-old ones: Love, as uncomfortable as it is to confront, was the top answer from women in our survey when asked why they had not left an abusive partner. And research is proving exactly how emotional and physical abuse physiologically changes the brain. Using MRI scans, neuroscientists like Alan Simmons, Ph.D., an assistant professor of psychiatry at the University of California, San Diego, have found that repeated abuse makes a victim more prone to being withdrawn, forgetful, and so stuck in negative thinking that she can't even see how a situation could improve. Many survivors look back and say they were in a fog; often the phrase is "I lost myself." "There is something biological," says Simmons. "It's not a sign of weakness. It's akin to what happens to the brain during war."

This rings true for Reena Becerra, thirty-eight, a Ph.D. student in clinical psychology, whose then boyfriend, Mike Vargas, once bashed her head against the linoleum floor and strangled her. (Despite that and his eighteen prior incidents, he got five years' probation and no jail time—shockingly not atypical in these cases.) "People think, You don't have kids, you're a beautiful girl—what's keeping you with him?" she says. "Well, I started out a confident, strong girl. Five years of someone telling me, 'If you just shut up, I wouldn't have to hit you,' and I started thinking, Maybe I *should* shut up."

Rene Renick, a vice president at the National Network to End Domestic Violence and a counselor for twenty years, sees women like Becerra all the time. "You become isolated, and the only feedback you're getting is from this guy who's giving *really* distorted messages, like 'You caused this,' which gets inside your head," Renick says. "You fall in this cycle of believing that if you caused the violence, you can stop it, which you can't—only he can."

Speak Up—It Really Matters

Vanessa Saulter, thirty-seven, thanks God every day that she told her friends about the violence her on-again, off-again boyfriend put her through and that they stuck by her. Longtime pal thirty-two-year-old Janet McKnight may have even saved her life one night.

As Saulter remembers it, that early spring evening started off well enough. She and her boyfriend were hanging out at her apartment, but his mood veered after an argument in which he accused her of cheating. In what became a deranged marathon of violence, he punched and choked Saulter until at one point she looked out the window of her third-story bedroom and—fell? jumped? she's not sure—but somehow found herself, one sneaker on, plunging three stories through the midnight air.

When she came to on the parking lot cement, "he told me, 'I can leave you here, or I can take you back upstairs,'" says Saulter, now a resident director at Bennett College in Greensboro, North Carolina. "I couldn't feel my legs. I knew I needed help." He carried her to her bed but instead of calling 911, continued to torture her for another twelve hours. Sometime the next morning, he hacked off her hair.

Meanwhile, McKnight was trying desperately to reach Saulter; knowing about the violence, she always worried when Saulter didn't answer her calls immediately. Frantic, she phoned Saulter's parents and urged them to hurry to the apartment. When McKnight got there herself, she says, "I saw her hair everywhere, holes in the wall, blood. And I was thinking, What *happened* to her?"

Saulter's family rushed their daughter to the hospital; she had multiple rib fractures, a collapsed lung and "she'd broken her back in two bad places," says her doctor, Leonard Nelson, M.D. "It takes an unusual amount of force to do that."

After more than a year, Saulter got back on her feet, both physically and emotionally. "Honestly, I thought I would *never* get to the point where I could leave," she says, giving full credit to her friends for their support. "They saw the signs from the beginning. They would tell me I would go missing and my picture would end up on a milk carton. Over time, it slowly sank in."

It *does* sink in, say experts. "If others can continually counter with messages like 'It's not you. You didn't cause this. This is not a normal relationship,'" says Renick, "they can help women escape the abuser's reality."

That's exactly the script Ashia Troiano, twenty-one, a recent Swarthmore College graduate, used with her best friend, Quasona Cobb, also twenty-one. "There were plenty of times where I was like, 'This isn't healthy—you're not even happy,'" she says of Cobb's relationship with boyfriend Keith Bailey and his ongoing brutality.

Cobb, a hotel administrative assistant and college student in New York, eventually came to the same conclusion herself; last December, she demanded that Bailey move out. Troiano stood by her—and is still her rock through the even darker time that has followed. One night before Bailey left, as Cobb later told police, he pulled out a chunk of her hair and dragged her down the hall; then, planting his foot on her stomach and holding a lighter in one hand, he started dousing her with her own aromatherapy oil. Vanilla, maybe, or grapefruit. She realized, with horror, what he was about to do. "I was screaming. I was begging, 'Please do not set me on fire. I'll do anything you want, OK? I'll stay with you,'" she recalls. He finally calmed down and fell asleep. Immediately, Cobb texted Troiano: *Be here at 7:30 in the morning to help me move out.* Bailey would leave for work by then.

When Troiano arrived, the two threw some clothes in a bag for Cobb and went straight to the Forty-second Precinct to file a police report. And then Cobb called her mom, Arlene Gordon, a forty-two-year-old assistant analyst for Con Edison. Although they talked five times a day, Cobb had never told her mother about Bailey's rages. Now she did, and they agreed that Cobb shouldn't see her boyfriend again; instead, Gordon, a fierce mama-bear type, would supervise Bailey as he cleared his belongings out of her daughter's apartment. Cobb urged her to go with a male relative, but Gordon said no, she could take care of this herself. Cobb called and talked to her mother at the apartment around 4:30. When she phoned again at 5:01, no answer; 5:10, nothing. So Cobb dialed 911.

At 7:30 she heard. Cobb says police had found her mother facedown on the bed, set afire—the heat so intense, a garbage bag over her head had melted into her hair. She was alive, but barely. Her head had been crushed by a heavy object, Cobb says. The only thing untouched were her perfectly pedicured red toes.

"That was the hardest night," says Cobb. "I wanted to die myself. You go through the blame—Why didn't I go with her?"

Five months later, Gordon remains in the hospital. At press time, she has said just two words, but two words of a fighting spirit: "I want." Bailey, for his part, faces ten counts, including arson and attempted murder of Gordon.

The two friends are still in constant contact. They're struggling with their guilt, but Cobb reassures Troiano that she's saved at least one life. "Ashia is my she-ro," she says. "I tell her every day: 'You are the best friend in the whole wide world.'"

Here's What *You* Can Say

Over the five years that Cobb stayed with her boyfriend, Troiano never stopped talking to her about what was going on. But many people—37 percent in *Glamour*'s survey—don't reach out to a friend or acquaintance if they suspect abuse. It is hard to know what to say, but here are some of the exact phrases that helped fifty survivors we interviewed with the help of the National Family Justice Center Alliance:

"I am afraid for you." Nicole Van Winkle, twenty-four, heard these words after confiding to an old friend that she worried her boyfriend would hit her if she didn't return his calls. "She said it wasn't OK, but she didn't judge me," says Van Winkle. "She just listened—and that really helped."

"You're not leaving until I take pictures." A friend said this to Yvonne Coiner, forty-four, after she spotted Coiner's bruises one day. The friend gave the photos to a counselor, who told Coiner that she wasn't safe. "I needed to hear that," Coiner says, "because when you're in the abuse, you're paralyzed."

"I am proud of you." After Petra Johansson, thirty-nine, filed for divorce from her abusive husband, her friend sent her that text. "I'll never forget it," she says, "and during bad times I'd pull it up again, reread it and be able to go on."

"I'm sorry, but honey, if he's hit you once, he'll hit you again." A friend said this to Jennica Tulao, twenty-five, after noticing her bruises. "I'd told her I wanted to give him another chance," says Tulao. "That's when she said the thing about hitting. It was one of the turning points for me."

"Do you want your kids to go through that?" Ashley Raymer's dad asked that question when she came back home after a fight

with her boyfriend. "I really wanted to be a mom," says Raymer, twenty-four, "and that stayed with me."

"I can prosecute a felony DV charge with you alive—or wait until you're dead and prosecute a felony murder charge." Reena Becerra, thirty-eight, was considering going back to her abuser when the district attorney said this. "It was the wake-up call I needed," she says. "I thought I was in danger; I just didn't know how much."

Many of the survivors we spoke to acknowledged just how tough it is for a friend to step in but said that having a caring, nonjudgmental supporter was nothing short of lifesaving. "Even if it doesn't happen overnight," stresses Renick, "the victim will say, 'You know, someone told me, "That isn't OK," and it took me six months, but it planted a seed.' It helps women begin to think about leaving a relationship."

And saying something—even an awkward, uncomfortable something—is always better than saying nothing. "So many women think there's no way out," says Sue Else, president of the National Network to End Domestic Violence. "If every woman who reads this says something, the ripple effect will be unbelievable."

As Vanessa Saulter, whose circle of female friends never gave up on her, puts it: "Along with my family and faith, my close friends are 100 percent responsible for the fact that I'm finally free."

Men's Health

FINALIST—PUBLIC
INTEREST

In this searing story, Men's Health's contributing editor Bob Drury exposes the effect of a previously neglected injury of the wars in Iraq and Afghanistan: genital damage caused by improvised explosive devices. With incisive reporting and riveting vignettes, Drury sheds light on this most personal of all war wounds, and the article incited significant changes in military policy. Although this was Men's Health's first nomination in the Public Interest category, it had previously won awards in Personal Service both in print and digital media. And in an indication of the changes taking place in the distribution of magazine content, "The Signature Wound" was also published by Amazon Kindle Singles.

Bob Drury

The Signature Wound

In the diabolical scheme of things, it's a minor detail, but it still eats at Tom Bertelsmann: He had already walked the same damn stretch of trail twice.

The first time was immediately after his platoon's forward observer had been vaporized by an improvised explosive device, or IED, that had been planted under a narrow footbridge leading into a pomegranate grove. Another platoon in the area had also lost a man to an IED, and the two deaths had scotched the afternoon's pincer movement into the orchard, a known insurgent stronghold. His commanding officer ordered the entire Stryker Company, in country for just over a month, to fall back into the adjacent village to reorganize.

They were west of Kandahar City in Afghanistan, and the taut, dark-eyed Bertelsmann,* a twenty-five-year-old lieutenant out of West Point, was leading his first combat command. That evening he barely had time to post his sentries and contemplate the loss of his man—all they had found were a twisted rifle barrel and fingernail-size fragments of flesh, bone, and uniform—when the company commander radioed for a meeting with the three platoon leaders. Bertelsmann grabbed his rifle and made his way through the now-deserted hamlet to the CO's compound,

*Note: This name has been changed to protect the soldier's privacy.

perhaps twenty yards down the dusty path. By the time the parley broke, it was past midnight on a starless night. But Bertelsmann knew the way back. After twelve hours, the Afghan village was beginning to feel like home.

He was not particularly worried about IEDs. Sure, the insurgents came out after dark to plant their bombs. But nobody would be sneaking through the perimeter to lay a mine tonight. That would be insane.

It was August, hot and humid, and Bertelsmann was mere paces from the entrance to his own compound when he stepped on the pressure plate. It must have been buried there all day, a couple of inches below the dirt. He realized immediately what had happened. There was no sensation of being thrown into the air. It was more like the hand of God had come down and squashed him like a bug.

After the explosion he remained conscious, lying on a slant in the crater, his head below his shoulders. He let his head tilt back into the moist soil, wet with his own blood, and he knew. Just knew. He fought the urge to check below his waist, but he couldn't help himself. His left arm and hand were shredded, so he reached down with his right hand, which was still intact. Where his right thigh should have been there was . . . space. He fingered a hard nub, inches long with a jagged point—all that was left of his femur protruding from his pelvis socket. He moved his right hand across his midsection and ran it down his left leg. That limb was a big longer, although it, too, disappeared above the knee.

"I knew my guys were just on the other side of the compound wall," Bertelsmann, who's since been promoted to captain, tells me now. He shifts slightly in his wheelchair and brushes his broad forehead with his left hand. The pinkie is missing. "So I call out, 'Guys! Guys! I need your help. I hit a bomb. I don't have any legs.' I knew I was hurt other places too." Here Bertelsmann pauses. He slowly twists the cap from a plastic water bottle, takes a swig, and falls silent.

We're in the coffee shop at the Walter Reed National Military Medical Center in Bethesda, Maryland. The other customers pay no attention to him; in this place, the sight of a gravely wounded soldier is sadly common.

To break the silence in our conversation, I mention that earlier this morning I'd visited with two soldiers and a marine, all in their twenties, in the hospital's vast physical therapy wing. Each man had lost a leg to an IED in Afghanistan. This elicits a grim smile from Bertelsmann.

"AK or BK?" he asks. Above the knee or below the knee?

"One AK and two BKs."

He laughs. "Paper cuts."

"The marine told me that the first thing you do after the blast is a facial check," I tell Bertelsmann. I feel my head with both hands, mimicking what the marine had shown me. "You see if your eyes, your nose, your mouth, your ears are still there. Then you grab your dick. He said if you got that—a face and a dick—you're fine. Everything else is manageable."

Bertelsmann ponders this. He says finally, "Nah. Ears and noses can be put back together, or you can live without them. You can even get by without legs. Trust me, the first thing you check is your dick."

Back in that nondescript Afghan village two years ago, surrounded by his company's three medics, that had indeed been Bertelsmann's instinct. "I don't remember speaking, but apparently at some point I said, 'I have no dick.' But it wasn't true. I lost both testicles, injured beyond repair. But my penis is fine; it still works, thank God. Does everything I want it to. Still . . ."

The medics pulled him from the crater by his chest rig, drew tight flex tourniquets around his stumps to prevent him from bleeding out, jabbed him with morphine, bandaged his mangled arm, and began an IV drip. All the while, Bertelsmann could make out three voices—his first sergeant's, his company commander's, and his staff sergeant's, each one pleading, demanding, that he open his eyes. A memory intruded, from war movies Bertelsmann had watched as a kid. Wounded soldiers who did not open their eyes died; the ones who did, lived. He would not open his eyes, he decided.

"But then I thought about my parents and my brother." He takes another long swig, draining the water bottle. "Man, my dad would have been so pissed if I had died in Afghanistan. I didn't want to disappoint my family. And then there were the company medics. I was the first living guy they worked on. I remember thinking, *I don't want these medics to have to work on me and have me die. I don't want to let them down.*

"So I thought, *Okay, I'll open my eyes. I'll give it a shot.*"

"You Can't Shoot Back at an IED."

The signature physical wound of the war in Afghanistan begins when you step on a homemade bomb. Most of these are built with the fertilizer ammonium nitrate, an ingredient widely available throughout Afghanistan. The detonation, triggered either by a buried pressure plate or, less often, a command wire operated by a nearby enemy, instantly pulverizes the flesh, bone, tissue, and muscle of one or both of your lower limbs. In all likelihood the force of the explosion will sever the nerves in your leg or legs, and yet you will experience little pain. Surprisingly, as shock sets in and you lie in your pooling blood, you may not feel anything but a vague sense of pressure, as if a strong man were wrapping both hands around one of your calves and squeezing as hard as he could.

In many cases, the force of the explosion also travels straight up into your genital and pelvic area, blasting tiny shards of rock and dirt into your torso between your front and rear Kevlar body-armor flaps. If all or part of your "package" is not blown off by the detonation itself, the flying debris from the blast often penetrates soft tissue, leaving you vulnerable to penile, scrotal, testicular, and rectal infections. If the damage is bad enough, it could even lead to a full or partial amputation of your genitals.

Unlike in Iraq, where the most prevalent IEDs are rigged from artillery shells designed to bust up vehicles, the mines in Afghanistan are, in the words of army combat engineer Command Sergeant Major Todd Burnett, "much more personal." Iraq has roads. Afghanistan, for the most part, does not. Not good ones, anyway. That means more dismounted American patrols, and more amputees and genital injuries.

In 2010, the number of U.S. troops in Afghanistan who lost at least one limb was double that of either 2008 or 2009, according to casualty data compiled by surgeons at the Landstuhl Regional Medical Center, a U.S. military hospital in Germany. And three times as many have lost more than one limb—usually both legs. Moreover, the number of severe genital wounds has tripled, causing Pentagon and Department of Veterans Affairs officials to scramble to review insurance packages that assess, for instance, the value of a severed thumb at $50,000 but assign no dollar value on damage to a penis or testicles. (The serviceman may receive monthly disability payments for a genital injury, if the VA deems it serious enough.)

"Everybody was taken aback by the frequency of these injuries," says John B. Holcomb, MD, a trauma surgeon who contributed to the report. "The double amputations, the injuries to the penis and testicles. Nothing like this had been seen before in such numbers."

Burnett, forty-six, has served in both of our current wars. For the past three years, as part of the Department of Defense's Joint IED Defeat Organization, he has taken quarterly trips to Afghanistan. He says there's a big difference between IED incidents in Iraq and those in Afghanistan. "In Iraq, the IED was the event. In Afghanistan, the IED either begins or ends the event." In other words, it's used in ambushes.

As most soldiers can tell you, a firefight is almost preferable to a mine blast. It's rare when any U.S. outfit loses a straight-up battle. The physical and psychological tolls of an IED attack, however, linger past detonation.

"The insurgents are adapting their techniques to counter our technology," writes U.S. Army First Lieutenant Matthew Roll in an e-mail from Afghanistan, where he leads an IED-clearance unit. "Some pressure plates are very hard to detect, even with a Husky [a mine-detecting vehicle] or a handheld mine detector. You can't shoot back at an IED. How do you deal with an enemy you can't see or shoot at?"

Ronald Glasser, MD, who served in Vietnam as a physician, has studied the psychological and physical trauma of war for his recent book, *Broken Bodies, Shattered Minds: A Medical Odyssey from Vietnam to Afghanistan*. He tells me that during Vietnam there were 2.4 U.S. troops injured for every death. In Afghanistan, current Department of Defense numbers yield a ratio of 8 to 1—largely a result of improved combat medical treatment.

"Everyone talks about the large number of amputations during the Civil War," Dr. Glasser says. "But the percentage of all our servicemen and women in Afghanistan who have lost limbs could be equal to or even greater than the percentage of limb loss that occurred as a result of the Civil War. And genital wounds. Jeez, almost everybody.

"You can't get your legs blown off without suffering genital and/or perineum injuries," he says, referring to the groin region. "You mention infections? All kinds of shit gets blown into the wounds from these blasts. How do you clean them out? And because of the initial swelling and such, you don't know for a day or two, probably longer, how much tissue is damaged. The more time it takes to glean this information and make the proper medical decisions, the higher the probability of long-lasting damage.

"The army doesn't like it," he continues. "Nor does the army like anybody hearing about it. And there's just so much we don't know yet in terms of treatment. Take testosterone. You need it. For maintaining muscle mass. For sexual desire. A lot of these kids with damaged or lost testicles are looking at a lifetime of hormone treatments. Yet each patient has different dosage needs. How much should you give them? Well, we're still trying to figure that out. Common sense says, 'Declining testosterone? Amp up the levels.' Except that there might be other complications. If you add testosterone to a patient who might be developing prostate cancer, for instance, it's like throwing gasoline on a fire. Nobody knows how to do this yet.

"But I'll tell you one thing. We're going to have to learn pretty quickly. That's one thing wars do—turn medical techniques honed on the battlefield into standard civilian medical practice. Different wars, different tactics, different injuries. Walter Reed, a military doctor, discovered that yellow fever was transferred by mosquitoes and not person-to-person contact; that breakthrough allowed the building of the Panama Canal. One of the great advances in burn care came out of the sinking of our ships in the Pacific during World War II, when oil burned on the sea's surface. And because of the number of wounded returning from Afghanistan with their genitals blown off, well, we will surely learn from this also. But at what price?"

One immediate cost: These wounded have given our enemies a terribly effective physical and psychological weapon to use against us. Our men who serve are young and able-bodied, and the double threat to their mobility and their masculinity speaks precisely to their greatest dread. I've heard reports of marines winding loose tourniquets around their thighs before going on foot patrols so they could cinch them if they lost a leg. So has Dr. Glasser. "Their officers don't like it because they view it as a sign of defeat, but the marines don't care," he says. "They basically say, 'The hell with it, we're going to wear them anyway. If our legs are blown off, at least we'll survive.'"

In informal conversations, including dozens of interviews for this story, many servicemen said they had also heard of men banking sperm before shipping out to Afghanistan. "The guys who have been deployed to Afghanistan are telling others about to be deployed to store their sperm," says Bertelsmann. "It had never occurred to me. But I tell my friends going on their second or third deployments, 'Hey, store some in case.' I wish I had. I wish the army had made me."

"Your Junk Is the First Thing You're Looking Out For. You Gotta Keep the Important Things."

Losing a penis is a delicate subject in and out of the service. Military brass, in general, are reluctant to discuss this particular wound. But through a mutual friend, I made contact with a veteran whose penis was so wounded by an IED detonation that it had to be partially amputated. The phone conversation was brief, halting, and uncomfortable for both of us. After telling me he did not wish to be identified in the pages of a national magazine, he said that the realization that his manhood had been compromised was "worse than death . . . at first."

"Why live if you can't walk and you can't, well . . . you know," he said. A young single man, he also lost both of his legs and his testicles. "I got some of the [penile] shaft left—less than half. One side and most of the tip were gone. But my nerves were really damaged. At least in my case, they kind of rebuilt it for me using tissue and flesh from other parts of my body. And they can implant this thing to get you hard. But without the nerves, the sensation just isn't there. Or it's there only a little. You remember what it was like and you think you feel that . . . and then you don't. Sometimes I don't even realize that I'm sitting on this kind of bobbly thing hanging between my legs.

"The docs aren't done with me," he continued. "But it will take a special girl to understand all of this. I'm not ready for that yet. I don't know if I'll ever be ready for that. And that sucks."

Walter Reed's chief urologist, Colonel James Jezior, MD, tells me that more and more such patients are arriving at the medical center. "There are areas that we're trying to improve as these guys have gotten further and further out from their injuries. They are going to have to tell *us* what works. We don't have as much data on this type of injury as we want to have. We've had our own learning curve."

Just under a dozen men have lost all of their genital organs either through IED detonation or subsequent amputation, according to a Walter Reed administrator. And medical center data presented earlier this year at a national urology meeting pin the blame for more than three out of every four cases of genital injuries on IEDs. From October 2003 to February of this year, Walter Reed doctors have seen almost forty servicemen with injuries to or loss of their penis, and nearly sixty with injuries to or loss of one or both testicles.

Dr. Jezior says the medical science involved in penile and scrotal reconstruction is similar to that of gender reassignment surgery. "The new organ is certainly nothing like the original penis," he says. "It doesn't have the ability on its own to become erect. And if the nerves are not intact after the injury, [the patient] will have less chance of having a good sensation down the shaft. And that's tough. If they are successful in getting even a little bit of sensation back, however, then we'll implant a prosthesis in the penis."

There are additional difficulties. Some men cannot adjust to a rebuilt penis and find it difficult even to urinate. Moreover, a lifetime of complicated and delicate hormone treatments follow the loss of testicles. And even if a man's ability to have sex is technically restored, his experience will vary from past performance; results vary from patient to patient as well. Says Dr. Jezior, "There is such a wide range of injuries to the lower extremities, genitals, perineum, and scrotum that an understanding of how to help men physically have intercourse—what methods work for someone with this kind of injury as opposed to that kind of injury—is still being sought."

As you would expect, a genital wound causes massive damage to the psyche of a serviceman. This, too, requires further study. Dr. Jezior recalls that early on, surgeons at Walter Reed talked to patients more about the positive aspects of their progress: They were healing. But that reassurance didn't address their main worry. "Their expectations were . . . uh . . . higher."

Now servicemen who arrive at the medical center with severe genital trauma are prepped to expect a second devastation soon after regaining consciousness and finding their penis damaged or missing. Says Marine Lance Corporal Michael Martinez, who lost both legs to an IED blast in Helmand province, "Your junk is the first thing you're looking out for. You gotta keep the important things."

He was lucky. His groin was spared.

"Let's Face It: You Either Die of It or You Learn to Live with It."

Martinez's war story is typical. Fifteen months ago, as his unit was returning from reinforcing another marine outfit that had walked into an ambush, he found what he calls "my mine."

"I was the fourth guy in the patrol. The guys in front of me all stepped on the IED, but nothing happened. I was the lucky one."

Martinez related his tale over dinner at white-tablecloth restaurant in Bethesda. When he'd walked through the door in his sharp blue business suit, black dress shoes, and striped red tie, several pretty women sitting in a corner booth snapped their heads in his direction. His prostheses were undetectable.

Over coffee he made an interesting observation: "At the hospital I've noticed that the worse the injury, the better the attitude. There are some guys who, say, have been shot or blown up, but they only have shrapnel wounds . . . and they don't think their lives will go on. But then there are guys who are missing both legs and an arm, and they have the best attitude. The worse off we are, the more we're thankful for what we have."

I'm thinking about those words the next morning as I sit with U.S. Army Captain Bradley Ritland, DPT, chief of the physical therapy amputee section at Walter Reed. The sun has only just risen, and Martinez is hard at work. He has one end of a leash-like elastic cord attached to his prosthetic left leg; the other end is hooked onto a physical therapist. Martinez looks like a sled dog as he pulls the therapist around a carpeted track.

"Of the nearly 200 amputees in various stages of rehab that we manage, we always know Mike will be the first one here, and always with a smile," says Ritland, a long, lean twenty-nine-year-old from Minnesota.

Ritland and his staff of twelve physical therapists and two technician assistants preside over a huge state-of-the-art facility on the ground floor of the medical center. The oval track encircles scores of treadmills, free weights, treatment tables, and stair-stepping machines. Ritland had earlier reviewed with me the most recent hospital report on the number of patients with limb loss who are receiving treatment here at Walter Reed and at other U.S. military medical facilities. (The current count includes a staggering thirty-two new patients from June, when IED attacks in Afghanistan hit an all-time high of 1,600.) I was struck by the number of multiple amputees; more than half of the marines who'd lost limbs in Afghanistan had lost more than one.

Thanks to a change in VA regulations, the government now reimburses most travel expenses to Walter Reed for amputees returning for "tuneups." As prosthetics technology improves—and Walter Reed is already recognized for having state-of-the-art equipment and one of the best prosthetics programs of any hospital in the United States—so will treatment. Ritland nods toward Martinez, who is struggling to maintain his balance as he drags his therapist around the track with the elastic cord, which is now attached to his prosthetic right knee joint.

"You cannot imagine the advances made with prosthetics," says Ritland. "Mike's knee emulates his natural walking motion. The microprocessor knows where he is in his gait pattern and can make adjustments from the feedback it receives from its sensors. Our prosthetics team fine-tunes each leg to accommodate each patient's progress."

•   •   •

The hours pass, and the Walter Reed physical therapy center fills with more young men missing body parts. As this small but exclusive club has grown over the past months, so too has an informal mentoring program—old-timers working out with new arrivals who have sustained similar wounds. They're careful with each other, though. "I pretty much leave the new guys alone unless they approach me to talk," says Malik, a twenty-one-year-old army sergeant from New Jersey who lost his left leg above the knee to an IED in Afghanistan's eastern Wardak province. "I don't want to invade their space. If they ask, I tell them my rehab story, help them out."

Sometimes, says Martinez, a physical therapist or one of the staff psychologists will ask him to help new arrivals. "I remember when I first came in. Sometimes you want to talk to somebody. And there are other times when you just want to be left alone."

And what, I ask, would he say to a fellow veteran who had lost his penis?

For once the voluble Martinez has no answer. "What do you say to a kid who hasn't even hit the crest of his life and that happens? I don't know."

One morning at Walter Reed, someone told me about a wounded soldier who had recently been provided with prosthetic testicles—"the biggest pair they make, good only for aesthetic purposes." It reminded me of a demonstration I'd attended at the Pentagon, where officers and civilians from the Department of Defense and the army who are charged with protecting soldiers were reviewing prototype ballistic underwear and Kevlar codpieces. They laid them out on a conference table so we could inspect them.

The program's manager, Colonel William Cole, explained the differences between fire-resistant Kevlar boxer shorts and a variety of armored jockstrap-type inventions. In field tests on U.S. bases, he said, soldiers and marines much preferred the underwear to the chafing codpieces, and 800 pairs had recently been supplied to an army unit in Afghanistan. Some marines have received the boxers as well.

A senior navy corpsman attached to one of the marine outfits told me in an e-mail, "From every report I have read, the boxer shorts are stopping shrapnel and saving genitalia. A navy nurse I know told our captain that the shorts are the main reason many of the casualties she is seeing are keeping their genitalia, thighs, and sometimes femoral arteries intact. I know I will be wearing mine on every single mission we run."

Could this protection have saved Bertelsmann from injury? I think about this during our final encounter. We'd talked about the long-term psychological strain these wounds induce. "There were some dark days," he says, even though his penis still functions normally. "This is a huge lifestyle change."

Then he makes the observation that not every wounded warrior is created equal: "Here at Walter Reed I'm surrounded by the other men going through the exact same trials I am," he says. He is "constantly uncomfortable" sitting on his pelvis socket. And he is still learning to walk on the bucketlike contraption he attaches by carbon-fiber waist belts to a prosthetic hip joint that is vacuum-sealed onto his right butt cheek. "If I woke up in this much pain back before the explosion, I'd have been complaining all day.

"But I'm also a realist. Sure, I can't play soccer anymore. I can't be a ranger anymore. [My] hormones are all messed up. But I'm twenty-seven, and I can still have a great life. I can travel, and I do. I have a wonderful girlfriend. I can drive a car. And then I look at the other wounded guys—a lot of these kids are eighteen or twenty. They're barely out of high school. They have young wives, sometimes young children. They're not officers, they don't have the military degree and the school network hooking them up with jobs."

Bertelsmann is applying to graduate business schools at Stanford, Harvard, Berkeley, and MIT. He hopes to use his education to make a difference in the field of prosthetics. And as long as he remains at Walter Reed as an outpatient, he adds, he will be on call 24/7 to offer assistance to any fellow patients who ask, and sometimes to those who don't.

"I'll see a BK guy in the gym whose therapist is telling him to work harder and the guy wants to take a break. I'll yell across the room, 'Are you kidding me? You have two knees and an ankle. I don't have any of that and you don't see me taking a break.'"

"Let's face it: You either die of it or you learn to live with it," he says finally. "You'd better learn to accept who you are now: this different person. I have, and I'd like to help others who aren't there yet. Lighten things up."

To that end, Bertelsmann and his girlfriend have already planned their perfect Halloween costumes. They are dressing as Lieutenant Dan and the hippie chick Jenny, Forrest Gump's one true love.

Good Housekeeping

FINALIST—PERSONAL
SERVICE

Women's magazines had been writing about osteoporosis for decades, but "Fractured" was the story that hadn't been told. With thorough reporting and thoughtful analysis, Susan Ince demonstrates what was wrong with traditional treatments and describes the steps women should take to ensure proper diagnosis and care. The article tells the stories of women who had been prescribed questionable bone-building drugs and documents the neglect of older women with obvious signs of osteoporosis. In publishing this story, Good Housekeeping *risked its relationship with an important advertiser by criticizing its business practices, but the magazine fulfilled its duty to its readers by helping them understand a disease that is routinely misdiagnosed and mistreated.*

Susan Ince

Fractured

Shortly before eight A.M. on a sunny spring morning in Rome, Ga., Jeanne Mathews stepped outside to retrieve her newspaper from the driveway. It was Mother's Day 2009, and Mathews was looking forward to attending church with her mom, her adult children, and her grandchildren, then having lunch with the family. But when her foot landed on the first brick step, her thighbone snapped completely in two, the jagged ends pointing in opposite directions. Mathews, sprawled in agony across the steps, hadn't even tripped.

She cried out for help, and eventually a neighbor—one she'd never met but now will never forget—found her and called 911. It took forty-five minutes, and a lot of morphine, to ease Mathews into the ambulance while she clung to her leg bones so they wouldn't pop through the skin.

At the hospital, surgeons inserted a rod into Mathews's broken thighbone. But a year later, she was still in pain and unable to walk normally. Last November, doctors inserted a new rod and started her on daily injections of bone-building teriparatide (brand name: Forteo).

Mathews, who is assistant vice president of public relations and marketing at Berry College in nearby Mount Berry, was dumbfounded by what had happened. About four months before the break, she had started having pain in that thigh. She'd tried seven different office chairs, put heat on the leg at night, and finally con-sulted an orthopedist, who X-rayed her hip for arthritis and found nothing. He had prescribed rigorous physical therapy, but all the pushing and pulling was probably the worst thing Mathews could have done, her surgeon later said. Her pain, it turned out, stemmed from an undiagnosed stress fracture, not visible on a regular X-ray, that finally cracked the bone clear through.

Usually, it takes severe trauma, like a car crash, to break the femur, the body's longest and strongest bone. So why would Mathews's thighbone have snapped like that, especially since she had taken medication—alendronate (Fosamax) and then iban-dronate (Boniva)—for almost six years to reduce her fracture risk?

Mathews wasn't the only one asking that question. She learned of a support group whose members had stories that were re-markably similar to hers—largely women who'd broken a thigh-bone when they were in their fifties and sixties while they were walking or bending to pick up something or simply rolling over in bed. Some of the members had osteoporosis, but others, like Mathews, then fifty-seven, had been perfectly healthy. (That was the case, too, with the group's founder, Jennifer Schneider, MD, a physician whose thighbone broke when, at age fifty-nine, she was jolted on a New York City subway.) Most had been told they had osteopenia, or low bone density, after a routine scan and, like Mathews, had been prescribed bisphosphonates, a class of drugs that includes Fosamax, Boniva, Actonel (risedronate), and the once-yearly infusion, Reclast (zoledronic acid). In fact, the common denominator for all the women in the group was that they had been taking one of these drugs.

·   ·   ·

For nearly a decade, federal guidelines have called for physicians to offer bone-density testing to all women age sixty-five and older. But no doctor had ever suggested it to Peggy Keenan, although she had regular medical visits to monitor her blood pressure, cholesterol, and other vital stats. And Keenan, who was on her feet all day as a beautician in Grand Rapids, Mich., and was a regular on the treadmill and weight machines at the gym, never worried about her bones or asked about a screening. Then, in 2006, at age seventy-two, while walking her shih tzu, she slipped on an icy patch and went down hard, breaking her shoulder.

Keenan has nothing but praise for the doctor who treated her fracture without surgery and got her back to exercising right away. Still, he never brought up the possibility of osteoporosis, and it didn't occur to her to ask. *With that fall, anyone would have broken something*, she thought.

But then, two years later at a family picnic, Keenan broke two bones in her wrist when she fell while climbing down from a tree house with her grandson Mitchell. This time, a hand specialist recommended she have a bone-density scan immediately, and Keenan learned she had severe osteoporosis. Now seventy-six, she took Forteo injections for two years and has just started on Reclast. "I tell Mitchell, 'If it hadn't been for you, I wouldn't have found out I have osteoporosis and gotten treated,'" Keenan says. Still, she's angry at herself for not having been a better advocate for her own health. And she also wonders about her medical care. "I'm not blaming my doctor, but he dropped the ball where I'm concerned," she observes.

Jeanne Mathews and Peggy Keenan: two women, two very different stories—and textbook examples of how dangerously skewed the American approach to bone health has become. Pharmaceutical companies have spent millions trying to persuade midlife women (and their doctors) that they need to protect themselves against broken bones. Meanwhile, older women, who are at the greatest risk, are often overlooked. Even when a sixty-five- or seventy-five-year-old woman breaks a hip or sustains a fracture after a low-impact fall—in medical-speak, a "fragility fracture"—as few as one in five are evaluated for osteoporosis or started on treatment. "We have women in their forties and fifties taking pills they really don't need, and at the same time, we have women in their sixties and seventies who have had a fracture and no one has paid attention to why it happened," says Anna Tosteson, Sc.D., professor of medicine and an expert in bone-health policy issues at the Dartmouth Institute for Health Policy and Clinical Practice.

     •   •   •

As late as the 1980s, osteoporosis was a relatively neglected disease. Diagnosis was after the fact: If you were elderly and broke a hip, you had it—and you faced up to a 25 percent chance of dying from complications within the next year. It wasn't until 1992 that a group of experts met in Rome under the auspices of the World Health Organization (WHO) to consider ways to best identify women at risk *before* a fracture. A significant part of the discussion focused on how to use the amount of mineral in bones to identify fracture-prone people (X-ray machines that could measure bone-mineral density had been developed, though they were expensive and relatively few medical centers had them). "We had to draw the line somewhere," says Tosteson, who participated in the meeting. "There's a discussion like this in every field. To prevent heart attacks, for example, you have to ask, 'At what point does higher blood pressure become hypertension?'"

The doctors were grappling with fracture risk, trying to set thresholds of density scores to identify the group at higher risk. Finally, they settled on the T-score, a commonly used statistical calculation. In this case, the T-score indicates how an individual's bone density compares with that of a young, healthy adult woman, whose bones should be at their peak density and strength. A score could fall into one of several categories: normal, osteoporosis (or severe osteoporosis), or a middle range between osteoporosis and normal that has caused untold difficulties. "We could have simply called that middle range 'low bone density,' but we gave it the name 'osteopenia,'" Tosteson recalls.

It was a decision she and other experts now deem "unfortunate," because in the minds of many physicians and patients, the designation of osteopenia (literally, "deficiency of bone") created a new disease—and ultimately new drugs to treat it. The purpose of the T-score cutoffs set at the WHO meeting was simply to help investigators conducting prevention studies to compare groups with regard to bone density. "None of the people in those studies would know what category they were in," says Nelson Watts, MD, director of the University of Cincinnati Bone Health and Osteoporosis Center.

What they were *not* trying to do, stresses Tosteson, was suggest who needed drugs. But soon, that's exactly how the new classifications would be used.

Three years after the WHO meeting, in 1995, anticipating FDA approval of its drug Fosamax, Merck prepared for the launch of what would be the first nonhormonal treatment okayed for osteoporosis. The company established a nonprofit Bone Measurement Institute to encourage screening. To make scans more widely available, it promoted doing the procedure in doctors' offices, working with manufacturers to help physicians afford the machines. Many of these were low-end scanners. Unlike the pricey models that measure density in the hips or spine, these cheaper scanners examine the heel, forearm, or wrist, providing results that don't always reflect what's going on in the areas of biggest fracture concern.

The marketing worked: Women got tested, and often their bone-density reports displayed where they fell in the WHO classifications—normal, osteopenia, or osteoporosis—sometimes even color-coded in green, yellow, or red to drive home the point. And soon, Fosamax was a big seller for Merck.

It was about to become even bigger. In 1997, the drug company submitted studies to the FDA in support of marketing a lower-dose version of Fosamax as a *preventive* drug for post-menopausal women at risk of osteoporosis—and got approval. Now there was a huge new market for the drug: middle-aged women at increased fracture risk because of family history, small size, lifestyle (smoking, excess drinking), medications, or certain diseases—or often just because they had received an osteopenia rating on a bone-density scan. Osteoporosis affects more than 10 million people in the United States, but osteopenia occurs in more than three times as many—34 million.

One major problem: An osteopenia "score," because of its wide range, can mean anything from close to normal to just shy of osteoporosis. Take Denise Boba, a magazine circulation specialist in Bloomingdale, Ill., who scored a –1.1 in one hip on a bone-density test in 2009. Although Boba was only forty-eight and followed a healthy diet, exercised, and took vitamins, her physician, knowing her mother had osteoporosis, immediately prescribed Fosamax. "The doctors make you so frightened about brittle bones," says Boba.

And if doctors weren't scaring women, promotions for Fosamax drove the message home, targeting *all* women at menopause—or at least trying to until the FDA stepped in. For example, in a patient brochure that Merck produced in 1997, one headline read: "Menopause is the single most important cause of osteoporosis." The FDA, calling the statement "false" and "misleading," told Merck to stop distributing brochures containing that headline. At the same time, observes Susan Ott, MD, a bone-health expert and professor of medicine at the University of Washington, "You never saw ads for women who were bent over with osteoporosis and truly needed the drug."

By 2005, Fosamax sales reached almost $3.2 billion. The company had gotten the word out. But too often, it was to the wrong women.

New Worries

No matter what your age, no one disputes the benefits of bone-smart choices in diet, exercise, and medical care. But bisphosphonates have some experts wondering whether the drugs have become this generation's hormone therapy: Women start on them as a menopausal rite of passage, and then, after millions of patients have been popping them for years, the pills are found to pose frightening risks.

All drugs have downsides, of course. But, says Dr. Ott, women with osteopenia get the risks of treatment without evidence that it reduces fractures. In fact, many women with osteopenia have a very low fracture risk. The average age for breaking a hip is about eighty, and no research shows that starting bisphosphonates at fifty will help keep a bone from breaking thirty years later—or even after ten. The best fracture prevention, she adds, is achieved when women only take the drugs if they develop osteoporosis (though she and other doctors might advise going on them if your T-scores are near the cutoff and you have significant risk factors).

Meanwhile, as many women will attest, the side effects of bisphosphonates can be miserable. Stomach pain and heartburn are major complaints. When Boba, who had doubts that she needed to be on medication, started taking Fosamax, she was ultracareful to try to avoid the digestive problems that had plagued her mother. After taking a pill, she waited sixty minutes rather than the prescribed thirty before eating anything or lying down. Still, she developed heartburn, acid reflux, and stomach pains. After eight weeks, her doctor sent her to a gastroenterologist to look for any unrelated cause for her symptoms. The specialist didn't find anything, but did note that she was seeing at least one new bisphosphonate user each week. Boba's doctor prescribed once-a-month Boniva instead, but for now, Boba's not taking any medication for her barely-below-normal bone density.

Beyond heartburn and other GI problems, side effects of bisphosphonates include severe muscle and joint pains. And now that the drugs have been in use for over a decade, new problems have begun to emerge that have some experts very worried.

Esophageal Cancer

Comparing bisphosphonate use in some 93,000 patients, British researchers found that taking the drugs for three to five years roughly doubled the risk of esophageal cancer—from about 1 in 1,000 to 2 in 1,000. Although that's still rare, researchers are worried that they don't know enough about what these drugs could do after that time. "We're particularly concerned about women after menopause who are at risk of a fracture. In the past, they would have been given hormone therapy; now they're being put on bisphosphonates, and we don't know what the long-term effects will be," says lead author Jane Green, MD, Ph.D., of the University of Oxford.

Fractured Femurs

Jeanne Mathews's orthopedic surgeon had no doubt that her unusual fracture had resulted from using osteo drugs. Bisphosphonates work by reducing the activity of cells called osteoclasts, which normally break down bone. But suppressing the bone's normal cycle of breakdown and buildup may not be healthy in the long run. The tiny areas that are damaged in daily life may never get repaired, and accumulated minerals can make the bone abnormal and more prone to breaking. "There's good evidence that with the drugs, your bones become stronger for five years, but we're really worried that after ten years, they will get more brittle," says Dr. Ott.

It's been understandably tough to establish direct cause and effect in a group of patients already considered more likely to suffer a bone break. But last October, after patients passionately argued for a strong warning and the American Society for Bone Mineral Research weighed in with its data, the FDA acknowledged the connection and issued a warning to physicians and patients about the possible risk. As is standard, the agency left prescribing decisions up to doctors.

And then in May, Swedish researchers reported the clearest link yet between the drugs and thigh fractures: In a review of data on 1.52 million women, 78 percent of those who'd had unusual thigh fractures like Mathews's (admittedly rare) were taking bisphosphonates. Only 10 percent of the women with ordinary thigh breaks were on the drugs. Those taking bisphosphonates the longest had the highest risk. Women on these drugs need to be vigilant about stress fractures, advises the National Osteoporosis Foundation. "If you're taking bisphos phonates and develop pain in your muscles or bones, you need to be checked for stress fractures," says Robert R. Recker, M.D., president of the foundation. "That means a nuclear bone scan—stress fractures won't show up on a regular X-ray." And if you have one? "You should switch from bisphosphonates to a medication that stimulates bone formation—Forteo—and seriously limit physical activity till you heal."

Infected Jaws

In a University of Southern California dental program where the tough cases are treated, Parish Sedghizadeh, DDS, frequently sees women whose jawbone tissue has died and who have suffered nasty infections after tooth extractions or other invasive procedures, such as bone surgery. Most cases occur in patients who have certain types of cancer and, as a part of treatment, take a higher dose of bisphosphonates intravenously. But in a 2009 review of cases, Sedghizadeh found that 9 of 208 oral bisphosphonate users on the patient rolls had developed such osteonecrosis, or death of jaw tissue.

While these numbers may be somewhat high because the dental school program serves such serious cases, new research confirms the link: An April study of more than half a million HMO members revealed that while osteonecrosis is quite rare, it is nonetheless 9.2 times more likely to occur in someone taking oral bisphosphonates. Why a bone medication might increase tissue death and infection risk is still unclear. Salvatore L. Ruggiero, MD, DMD, the New York oral surgeon who first alerted his profession to the problem, suspects these drugs may have a bigger impact on the jawbone because that part of the skeleton has a high rate of bone turnover and they therefore may interfere with the normal healing process.

If you're about to start on a bisphosphonate, check in with your dentist to see if you need any major work. Or, if you're already on the medication, ask your doctor if taking a "drug holiday" makes sense. But don't skip needed work—if you have an abscessed tooth, for example, you could risk a life-threatening infection. Better to tell the dentist about your drugs so she or he can take extra precautions.

Over the years, there have been multiple lawsuits filed against drug companies by patients who have suffered jaw problems and other complications they believe stem from their use of bisphosphonates. So far, in suits against Merck, the drugmaker has prevailed in several cases, but had a judgment against it in another, which Merck is now in the process of appealing. The vast majority of cases are still pending trial. When asked for comment, the companies selling these medications pointed to their success in helping prevent fractures and their commitment to patient safety.

The Invisible Patient

Here's the kicker: For all the women who are suffering from the effects of taking these drugs too soon and for too long, there are untold thousands who truly need them—and aren't getting them.

Almost nine out of ten hip fractures occur in people sixty-five or older, yet fewer than half of older women have had even one bone-density screen reports Herbert Muncie, MD, professor of family medicine and a specialist in geriatrics at the LSU Health Sciences Center School of Medicine in New Orleans. Don't blame Medicare: It covers testing every two years—with no copay.

And the tests are far more helpful in older women. You and your mom may have matching T-scores, but your chances of breaking a bone aren't even in the same ballpark. "Density is just one of the ways bones change with age and become more prone to fracture," says Dr. Recker. Older bones also differ in their proteins, their supporting scaffolding, and the hormones that determine when and where minerals are deposited. "If a woman in her forties and a woman in her late sixties or early seventies both have a T-score of −2.5, the older woman has ten times the risk of fracture," he notes.

Even when an older woman breaks a bone, her doctor may not think of osteoporosis. "I've frequently seen patients who have had three, four, or five fractures—it's painful just to listen to their stories—but weren't being tested or treated for osteoporosis," says geriatrician Beatrice Edwards, MD, who is director of the Fracture, Osteoporosis and Metabolic Bone Disease Program at Northwestern University's Feinberg School of Medicine in Chicago.

Most of these women had fragility fractures, which signal that you need not just evaluation but treatment. "If you've broken a bone from day-to-day activities or a simple fall, you have osteoporosis, no matter what your bone-density score is," says Dr. Watts. "If someone has a heart attack, you treat them to reduce the chance of another, even if they don't have high blood pressure or high cholesterol. People who've already had a 'bone attack' also need therapy."

To figure out *why* doctors weren't taking action when treating fracture patients, Dr. Edwards assembled focus groups of hospital-based physicians in Chicago. Their responses: They felt unprepared to deal with the condition, or they didn't consider it an acute problem. Tellingly, they also admitted they were reluctant to enter the turf of primary-care doctors. But primary-care docs often don't get the chance to help, either: after a fracture, only one in ten patients who had been treated in the ER went back to her regular doctor or to a specialist afterward for a bone check and treatment, Dr. Edwards found in a survey of seventy patients. Like Peggy Keenan, the seventy-six-year-old Michigan woman who endured two serious breaks, all figured that anyone who had a similar fall would have broken something.

More frightening, not enough doctors are making sure patients understand their risk: In a large 2010 international study led by Ethel Siris, MD, director of the Toni Stabile Osteoporosis Center of Columbia University Medical Center in New York City, only one-third of women who had broken a bone after age forty-five considered themselves to be at even a slightly higher risk of having another fracture compared with other women their age. And, inexplicably, one in five thought she was at *less* risk. In reality, such women's odds are doubled.

Maybe if this survey is given again in a few years, patients (and their doctors) will be more knowledgeable. The American Orthopaedic Association has launched "Own the Bone," a program for doctors to reinforce that fracture care includes follow-up so patients with low bone mass or osteoporosis have every chance to avoid a future fracture.

For many women, that will mean taking bisphosphonates—and in this case, the benefits may well outweigh the risks. "Every single drug and medical treatment has potential complications," says Andrew D. Bunta, MD, an orthopedic surgeon at Northwestern's Feinberg School of Medicine. "Compared with the number of fractures that are prevented and the ability of people to stay active in their senior years, the risks of complications are minimal."

Even Dr. Ott, the Seattle bone specialist who sounded some of the earliest and loudest warnings about the long-term risks of bisphosphonates, prescribes them—and often. "For the right people, these drugs really prevent fractures," she says.

Now, as women push health agencies to recognize the risks of prescription bone protection, and as professionals finally begin targeting the patients who truly need attention, the dangerously distorted priorities in bone health are slowly beginning to change. But whether you're at risk of too much treatment or too little, you have to advocate for your own best care.

When the FDA warnings on femur fractures came out last October, Joy Vogelgesang, fifty-six, co-owner of a bookstore in Keauhou, Hawaii, had been on bisphosphonates for five years. At her next doctor's appointment, her MD reviewed her medication list and didn't suggest any changes. But when Vogelgesang asked about the bone drug, the doctor readily said it was OK to stop. "She acknowledged that after five years, I'd probably gotten all the benefit I was likely to. But if I hadn't raised the issue, I could have been taking it forever," says Vogelgesang.

Peggy Keenan has become a fiery advocate for self-help, encouraging friends to keep up their strength and balance exercises and urging older women to demand bone testing: "You can't just put this in the hands of your doctor—you have to know the facts, ask questions, and make sure you get the right treatment for you."

Sports Illustrated

FINALIST—PROFILE WRITING

Dewayne Dedmon was a naturally gifted athlete on his way to being seven feet tall. He had always dreamed of playing basketball, but his mother, a devout member of the Jehovah's Witnesses, had forbidden it. At eighteen, he defied her. In "Dewayne Dedmon's Leap of Faith," Chris Ballard meticulously tracked Dedmon's growth from guileless boy to budding superstar. This is a story of faith—in God but also in personal transformation. The author of Hoops Nation, Ballard is a senior writer at Sports Illustrated—a magazine honored more than a dozen times by the National Magazine Awards for its narrative journalism.

Chris Ballard

Dewayne Dedmon's Leap of Faith

Thou wilt show me the path of life.

—Psalm 16:11

Dieter Horton first caught sight of the skinny kid with the long arms one afternoon in April 2008. The boy was sitting in the first row of the bleachers in the small gym at Antelope Valley College, waiting silently, his knees together. Only when he stood up, thirty minutes later, did Horton realize just how tall he was. At least 6'8", Horton thought. Then he looked closer: Who the hell *is* this kid?

After all, AVC is located in Lancaster, Calif., in the heart of the Antelope Valley, only an hour's drive north of Los Angeles over the San Gabriel Mountains but in a world of its own. If there was a teenager within a nose of 6'6" in the valley, Horton could tell you his home address, his girlfriend's name, and what he liked on his pizza. In eleven years as a junior college basketball coach in California, Horton had won a state title, sent nearly twenty kids to Division I schools, and set a state juco record by finishing 37-0 at Fullerton College in 2005–06. Young, ambitious, and handsome in a clean-cut way, Horton scouted so relentlessly that his phys-ed students had grown accustomed to his teaching with a cell phone pressed to his ear. Yet here was a towering kid unfamiliar to the coach from local high schools or the AAU circuit or even city rec leagues.

When Horton finished talking with one of his players, the boy walked over. He wore an enormous pair of beat-up hightops, ratty shorts and a white T-shirt so large it looked like a muu-muu. He hunched over, as if trying to shrink to standard proportions. "Coach," he said, "my name is Dewayne Dedmon. I want to play basketball."

Instantly Horton recognized the name. For years stories had floated around the valley about a tall kid who wasn't allowed to play basketball, but the coach had never believed them. He heard lots of stories. Most came from the kids themselves. Every year dozens of cocky teenagers approached Horton and assured him they'd score twenty a game if only he'd give them a uniform and the rock. To weed out the dreamers and boasters, he told them, "Come back next week." Only one in ten ever did.

"O.K., Dewayne Dedmon, how about we see what you got," Horton said. "Show up next Tuesday at three P.M., and we'll work you out."

Dedmon nodded. "Yes, sir," he said. "I'll see you then."

Within a few days, Horton had forgotten all about him.

.   .   .

Gail Lewis was so proud she felt like crying. She stared at the letters on the notepaper stuck to the wall and read along. She knew the line, from Proverbs. Then she looked down at her nine-year-old son, sitting on his bed in their sparsely furnished three-bedroom apartment in Lancaster. Here he was, only halfway grown up and already disciplining himself.

It wasn't the first time he'd had to. Dewayne was a gentle boy with a big heart, but he struggled to contain an independent streak. When he spoke disrespectfully to an adult or used a bad word, he would retreat to his room. There he'd look through his Bible until he found a relevant scripture and carefully copy the passage. In moments such as these, Gail knew her decision had been the right one.

She'd joined the Truth four years earlier, in 1995. At the time she'd needed structure—for herself and for the three young children she was raising alone on her income as a receptionist in a doctor's office. She took Dewayne and his older sisters, Sabrina and Marina, to Kingdom Hall for an hour of Bible study on Tuesday, two hours of ministry school on Thursday, and a two-hour public meeting on Sunday. On Saturday they all performed their most important duty as Jehovah's Witnesses: spreading the word. If the people whose doors they knocked on sometimes looked at them scornfully, Gail felt only pity for them.

She knew her family was on the right side of the Lord, along with so many others. She could recite the stats: There were several million Jehovah's Witnesses worldwide, and over a million in more than 10,000 congregations in the United States. Like Gail, Jehovah's Witnesses believe that we are living in the end days of a wicked world, and that when the Apocalypse comes, only true believers will be granted eternal life. They recognize not the Holy Trinity but only the Father, and they take the Bible as his literal word. You can serve only one master, the Bible says; allegiance to anyone or anything but Jehovah is forbidden. So like all Witnesses, Gail was expected not to vote in elections or salute the flag. She could not run for public office or serve in the armed forces. Her family celebrated neither birthdays nor holidays. Gail could not receive a blood transfusion, even if refusing one could be fatal, because the Bible says one must "abstain from blood."

Then there was the matter of sports. Though not expressly forbidden, playing on a team encouraged children to show allegiance to something other than Jehovah and challenged their other priorities: Afternoons were for meetings, not practices, and weekends for service, not games. Even though Gail had been a talented volleyball player and quite a dancer, she knew sports were not right for her children now.

So, in a country in which parents put basketballs in their sons' cribs, in which fathers such as Earl Woods and Marv Marinovich trained their offspring to be sports stars from birth, Gail Lewis did the opposite. She forbade her tall, athletic son to play sports.

．　　　．　　　．

On Tuesday, Horton walked into the Antelope Valley gym at two-thirty P.M. He was on his way to work out in the dingy weight room, which housed rusted dumbbells and ancient Nautilus equipment. AVC, founded in 1929 in a sprawling desert populated by alfalfa farmers, had grown from a tiny adjunct to a high school into an institution with a student body of more than 12,000. Like many other California schools, AVC struggled with funding. Its classrooms were cramped and facilities outdated. The locker room was so small that during football season the players lined up around a corner to use the shower. That the basketball program had enjoyed so much success in such conditions was something of which Horton and his predecessor, Newton Chelette, were rightly proud.

As Horton hurried across the warped gym floor, he noticed someone watching him. Later it would strike him as unusual that the boy had arrived thirty minutes early. At the time, though, Horton was just surprised to see Dedmon at all.

Well, the coach figured, he's here. He grabbed a ball and passed it to Dedmon. "OK, let's go," he said. "Start with Mikan drills."

Dedmon stared back at him.

"You know what those are, right?" Horton said.

"No, sir," Dedmon replied.

So Horton took back the ball and demonstrated the simplest drill: Stand on the right side of the basket, take one step, and lay the ball in right-handed. Catch the ball as it exits the net, move to the left side, and do the same thing left-handed.

Dedmon took an ungainly step and muffed the layup. As the workout proceeded, he botched his footwork on post moves, fumbled the ball while dribbling, and fired his jump shot from so far behind his head that it seemed he might topple over.

After half an hour Horton was tempted to end the workout. But then he told Dedmon to go through the Mikan drills one more time. Slowly at first, Dedmon moved from side to side, catching the ball and laying it in. It wasn't pretty, but Horton noticed something remarkable: Dedmon was already 50 percent better than the first time he had performed the drills.

Still, Horton couldn't get a read on the kid. Dedmon was shy and awfully skinny for an eighteen-year-old, no more than 190 pounds, and had never really been coached. But he had potential, and you couldn't be picky at a place like AVC, especially when it came to 6'8" kids. Horton told Dedmon he would gray-shirt him. It was a no-risk move—the kid would keep his eligibility but wouldn't use up a roster spot—even if in Horton's experience only one in three grayshirts ever panned out.

Dedmon seemed puzzled by the term *grayshirt*. So the pair headed to Horton's office, a small corner room in a trailer with fake-wood walls that looked out on a vacant lot. Horton sat behind his old metal desk and explained college basketball: how eligibility worked and the difference between a juco and a Division I school. He was amazed at how little Dedmon knew. He had never heard of the Big Ten or even the Pac-10.

By the end of the afternoon, however, Dedmon understood the most important thing: He could attend AVC as a part-time student and practice with the team. He'd receive a small amount of financial aid, but the rest—transportation, getting a job, improving his game—would be up to him.

•   •   •

To Gail Lewis's children, the world was a small place. Its borders were the dusty slopes and the desert on the horizons. From the San Gabriel Mountains, Antelope Valley appears to be a flat plain upon which man has tried to impose his will with mixed results. There are shopping malls, highways, and a manmade lake watched over by a lone windmill. Everything feels tenuous. Tumbleweeds roll onto the highway; backyards abut rocky desert where cacti provide the only hint of green. Towns sprawl, their highway exits marked by the letters of the alphabet. Street numbers rise past 40000. There is no center to anything; in Lancaster, 145,000 people live in 94 square miles.

Though Gail moved her family often, it was always within the valley, from Palmdale north to Lancaster, one condo or apartment to the next. They hardly ever went Down Below, as the locals called L.A., other than to visit friends in suburban Long Beach. Money was tight. Life consisted of church, school, and family.

Here Gail could maintain order, though occasionally she relented. After Dewayne pleaded, she told him he could play one season of volleyball, in the eighth grade. It didn't seem a huge risk—the practices didn't conflict with meetings, and she hoped playing would burn off some of his energy.

Then one day the team was losing a match and an assistant coach yelled at Dewayne. Really yelled at him. He'd been scolded before, but not like this. He yelled back. And that, Gail decided, was that. You are never playing again, she declared. As she would later say, "No boy of mine was going to embarrass me like that. He needed to learn."

•   •   •

How do you win a race in which everyone else has an eighteen-year head start? The day after that first workout with Horton, Dedmon started with the basics, stuff most kids learned in junior high. Drop steps, pivots, box outs. Horton reconstructed

Dedmon's jumper and forbade him to shoot from outside the key. Start at your hip, then make an L with your arm and push it up into an I, Horton said. One-two-three, he counted with every shot, one-two-three. In one sense Dedmon was a coach's nightmare; in another he was a coach's dream. He had no bad habits to correct because he had no habits. He was a blank slate.

One day Horton showed up with a pair of size-eighteen Adidas hightops he'd ordered for $35 off Eastbay.com. Dedmon was ecstatic—"like it was Christmas," Horton remembers. In the fall, when Dedmon received his uniform and warmups, he was overjoyed. He wore them everywhere: to class, on the bus, while studying.

Not only did Dedmon have new clothes, he had a dozen new friends. He became particularly close with fellow grayshirts Edwin Herrera and Jason Logan. They ate burgers at Primos and called themselves the Three Amigos. Logan liked Dedmon, who was funny and gentle, but didn't think much of his basketball ability. "You could tell he'd never played," Logan remembers. "He couldn't jump. He couldn't even dunk some days."

In October, after six months of working out with Horton and on his own, Dedmon joined the team for its first practices. They were brutal. Drills were performed until perfected. If a player didn't go hard, everyone ran sprints. Whole afternoons were spent solely on defense. Dedmon loved it. He raced up and down the floor as if in an Olympic trial. He dived after loose balls. His teammates stared; didn't the new kid understand this was just *practice*? As AVC assistant coach Tim Atkerson puts it, Dedmon "defied all the things that [kids just out of] high school are supposed to be."

Whatever was needed, Dedmon did it. He helped clean the gym. After games he stuck around and let elementary school kids throw him alley-oops. The assistant coaches' children particularly took to him. He put them on his shoulders, remembered their names, made them feel special. They saw him as just another kid, if an enormous one.

There was only one problem: attendance. Dedmon missed class repeatedly and fared poorly in his studies; he missed some practices, too. Horton was annoyed until he learned that Dedmon lived in southeast Palmdale, fifteen miles away, and had no regular ride to school. His family had one car, and his mom needed it for work most days. So Dedmon relied on friends with cars or took forty-five-minute bus rides.

Horton didn't get it. Here was a kid who needed to make up a lot of ground, and yet for some reason he was having trouble just getting to school.

•   •   •

It began with the shoes. One afternoon when he was a boy, Dewayne announced that he couldn't find his. And without shoes, how could he go to Kingdom Hall? "Too bad, then you're going without them," Gail said.

"But Mom—"

"No buts. We're going."

She made him get into the car in his socks. In Gail Lewis's house, you didn't miss meetings.

It got worse. Dewayne became insubordinate. He began hanging out with boys she didn't like, boys who were rude and got him into trouble. But now, when she got mad at him, instead of writing scripture, he jumped on his bike and rode away, sometimes from Seventeenth Street west all the way to Seventieth Street, to a family friend's house. One time Gail locked him out for an afternoon. When she returned home, she found him sitting on the porch, fuming. "Boy, get in the house," she said. "You have to learn."

This defiance bled into school. As the family moved, Dewayne attended three schools. He kept talking about sports—not volleyball but basketball now. He pleaded to play. Gail held firm. She saw herself as a one-woman team: mother, father, uncle, and aunt. She knew boys get to an age at which they're susceptible to influences and can take the wrong path. It was up to her to hold the line. It would be different if Dewayne's father were in the picture.

Thomas Dewayne Dedmon had been easy to spot at 6'3" and 210 pounds. But his was a transient life. He worked in the military for a while and fathered six children, three with one woman and three with Gail, whom he never married. Gail thought Thomas was giving and caring but also lazy and a bad influence on their kids. When she started to make changes in her life, trying to do the right thing and show more self-respect, she knew he couldn't be part of it.

A few years later she heard the news: At age thirty-four, Thomas had taken his own life, according to Gail. Their youngest child, Dewayne, was three years old.

• • •

Horton couldn't believe it: Dedmon had grown again. Here it was, December 2008, early in his grayshirt season, and he was nearly 6'10"—almost two inches taller than when he'd first shown up in the AVC gym.

Dedmon was transforming himself in other ways too. Thanks to financial aid and part-time jobs, he had more money to eat, and he ate nonstop—even it was mostly fast food. When he didn't eat, he slept. For the first time in his life he was lifting weights, and slowly the muscle accreted. He drew his shoulders back, puffed out his chest, became more confident. On the practice court his footwork improved and with it his explosiveness. His jump shot remained erratic, but his form was textbook: one-two-three, L to I. "I've never seen a kid with that high a learning curve," says Atkerson. "If you saw him one week and came back two weeks later, you could see a significant improvement in all facets."

It was time to challenge the kid. AVC had a hugely athletic player named Kyisean Reed, who would go on to sign with Utah

State. Reed was 6'6" and could touch the box on the backboard from a standing jump. For months he and Dedmon had matched up in practice. One day in late December, Horton gathered the team together and announced, "If at any point during practice Kyisean dunks on Dewayne, I'll end practice. Even if it's the first play."

Given an opportunity to free their teammates for an afternoon, most kids would allow themselves to be dunked on right away. Not Dedmon. Three times that day Reed rose up for a jam, and three times Dedmon met him at the basket with tremendous force. The same thing happened the next day, and the day after that. If Reed got a step on him, Dedmon came flying in from behind, nearly decapitating his teammate. At times Reed looked at Horton for help—"He's killing me here!"—but Horton let them play on. Reed never got that dunk.

Dedmon's energy began changing the tenor of the team. His teammates gravitated to him. As Horton puts it, "Here's this 6'10" kid playing harder than anyone they'd ever seen, playing so hard he's almost hurting himself. People respect that."

There is a price for such rapid development, though. Dedmon grew so fast that his body balked. His hamstrings tightened, his knees ached, his back got sore. The only solution was to freeze away the pain. So Dedmon, at the coaches' suggestion, lowered himself into a 57° whirlpool, where he sat for twenty minutes at a time, perched on an orange Home Depot bucket. Even though his body went numb from the waist down, he didn't complain. Tell Dedmon to do something, and he did it.

• • •

He came to her the fall of his senior year of high school, a few months after he turned eighteen. I'm going to play basketball, Dewayne said, and there's nothing you can do about it. I'm my own man now.

Absolutely not, said Gail. The Bible says you can't serve two masters.

I can do both, he said.

Gail knew he wouldn't listen to her. What Dewayne needed was a male influence. So she called upon the men at Kingdom Hall. Two of them came to the house and sat down in the small kitchen across from Dewayne. Gail put out snacks, and the men explained how basketball could take Dewayne away from his Christian upbringing. How it could corrupt him.

Dewayne sat and listened to the men. There was a lot at stake. He would be going against not just his mother's wishes but also the churchmen's. Among Jehovah's Witnesses, even minor infractions such as saluting the flag or dating a nonbeliever can lead to punishment by a judicial committee. Drifting away from the Truth can result in "disassociation": A member is disavowed by loved ones and shunned by friends. Then there was a more profound risk. If Dewayne still believed in the Truth and continued to defy his church, he might eventually face divine execution at the Battle of Armageddon. All for playing a game.

His whole life, his mother had been his world and the church his guide. The instructions were clear. "Avoid independent thinking," it said in a 1983 *Watchtower* magazine, and "questioning the counsel that is provided by God's visible organization."

And yet Dewayne knew that this was likely his last chance to play ball. When he graduated in the spring, he'd need to get a job, probably something minimum wage. That's what kids like him did in Lancaster—that is, if they didn't get involved in drugs or worse. He knew plenty headed that way. He didn't want to join them.

He told the men and his mother that he'd made his decision, and it was final: He was going to play. Gail was crushed. Still, she hoped it was only a dalliance, and as the year went on she became hopeful. After all, Dewayne hardly ever played. His few minutes in games were mop-up duty and an occasional call to clog up the middle on defense. Almost all he did during his senior year at Lancaster High was sit—on the bus, on the bench, on the sideline. The coach, David Humphreys, didn't have much use for a skinny kid with no discernible skills, even if he was 6'7". Humphreys was trying to win a Golden League title.

When the season was over, though, instead of giving up on sports and returning to the church, Dewayne did the opposite. One day in the spring he came home and told Gail he was going to go to college. To play basketball.

· · ·

The text pinged onto Horton's phone one morning in the fall of 2009. It was from the school janitor, Herman Mena. *Dedmon was just in here for an hour and a half*, it read. The time stamp was 12:45 A.M.

Moving out of the house had changed Dedmon's world. One day at the start of the semester Mena had come by with a borrowed truck and helped Dedmon load up his belongings: one mattress, an old TV, a dresser and some clothes. They'd moved him into a sublet a few blocks from AVC. From that point on Dedmon had practically lived on campus. He showed up at seven in the morning to lift, often arriving on his foot-propelled Razor scooter, looking like a giraffe on wheels. He stuck around after his evening classes; Mena opened the gym for him, and Dedmon lifted weights and worked on his game. "I'm going to be a point guard!" he shouted, and Mena laughed and shook his head. Eventually Dedmon would take a work-study job alongside Mena, cleaning the cafeteria four or five times a week at midnight, the tallest janitor you've ever seen.

That fall Dedmon finally got a chance to play in a real game. It was ugly. A whistle a couple of minutes in, another not long after, and then he was on the bench. The next game was worse: He grappled for position, challenged every shot and flew around the court, but he finished with four fouls and only two points. It was the Kyisean Reed approach—cede nothing, challenge everything—only it doesn't work in a real game. The next time out he got three fouls in the first half. Horton had to yank him again. Dedmon jogged to the bench, where he sat down next to Mike Rios, the school's athletic academic adviser. "Coach, why'd I come out?" Dedmon asked.

"You have three fouls," said Rios.

"Well, how many do I get?"

Rios chuckled and put his arm around Dedmon. "You only get five, my man, only five."

The breakthrough came against Fullerton College on November 21, the sixth game of the season. One of Fullerton's players bumped Dedmon repeatedly, then finally threw an elbow at his head. It was the ultimate honor: Fullerton was trying to get Dedmon out of the game. Of course, Dedmon didn't see it that way. He shoved the Fullerton player and drew a technical foul. But Dedmon stayed in the game and something changed. Energized, he became more aggressive on offense. He finished tied for the team lead in points (fourteen) and rebounds (eight) in an overtime win. Better yet, he didn't foul out.

The kid was improving by the day, and he seemed to retain everything. One morning AVC's point guard was late to a walkthrough, and Dedmon volunteered to take his place. Horton stared in disbelief while Dedmon ran the offense as if he'd been doing it all year. "We had probably fifty plays, and he could run point through five on every play perfectly—the timing and nuance, baseline out-of-bounds, half-court, you name it," says Horton. "Here was this 6'10" kid who'd hardly even played, and he had the best basketball IQ I'd seen. I was taken aback."

In games Dedmon scored his points on offensive rebounds and monstrous putback dunks and became so good at converting lobs that Horton installed four plays for him, his favorite being X, a back-pick against a zone in which Dedmon soared in from the right side. Defense was still his forte, though. He pulled down fourteen boards in one game, blocked seven shots in another. Logan was not only losing to his friend in one-on-one but was also finding it hard to even score.

As fond as coaches and teammates were of Dedmon, he was even more popular with the fans. AVC is something of an anomaly among junior colleges: Its games are so popular that certain fans have reserved seats, while residents, students, and alumni crowd the 828-seat gym, standing and stomping on the bleachers. They loved how Dedmon hustled, how he made the rim shake on follow dunks, how he yelled after big plays. That kid plays with joy, they said.

· · ·

Gail hardly ever went to her son's games. Not during his senior year in high school and not now, in 2009, his first season of playing significant minutes. After all, games were often during meetings or community outreach, which took up seventy hours a month.

It hurt Gail that she was losing touch with Dewayne, just as it hurt him that she never met his teammates or knew what he was doing. When they spoke on the phone, they often argued. Again and again, the same loop:

"Mom, you're not listening," he would say.

"You never call me," she would reply.

One time they really got into it. Finally, Gail said, "You know something . . ." but then, before she said something she would regret, she caught herself and hung up.

She called back early that evening because the Bible says, "Don't let the sun go down on your wrath." When he answered, she said, "You know, Dewayne, I love you, I'm your mom, and you're still my son, but we need to come to an agreement."

He loved her too, he said. But things were about to change even more. It was time to tell her about the recruitment process that had begun over the summer and about USC.

·　　·　　·

Bob Cantu had been an assistant at USC for eight years by the fall of 2009. He'd helped recruit Derrick Williams (though Williams went on to play at Arizona when coach Tim Floyd left the Trojans) and other big-time players. Even so, Cantu still dreamed about finding an Ervin Johnson.

The legend of Johnson is oft told in coaching circles: how in 1988 a 6'11" player walked into Floyd's office at New Orleans after spending the previous two years working at a grocery store in Baton Rouge; how he went on to lead the American South Conference in blocks, rebounds and shooting percentage and to play thirteen years in the NBA.

There have been just a handful of others like Johnson—seven-footer Michael Olowokandi didn't play basketball until he was eighteen, when he cold-called the University of the Pacific. So catalogued and cross-referenced was every young big man in the country that it seemed there were no undiscovered gems. Yet when Cantu first saw Dewayne Dedmon in July 2009, months before he played his first official game for AVC, he didn't see a gangly kid who'd never played in a college game. He saw Ervin Johnson.

The setting was a junior college showcase at USC's Galen Center. It was essentially a window-shopping event for big schools: About thirty jucos from around California brought their teams and played two days' worth of games so coaches could scout transfer prospects. For Horton, the exposure would help his players get Division I scholarships, and those scholarships would help sell his program to future recruits.

Dedmon arrived as an afterthought; he had no stats, no scouting file, and no buzz. Then, thirty seconds into his first game, he pinned a shot against the glass. Then another. Then he ran the floor and got a dunk. He missed a lot of easy shots, and he looked lost at times, but it didn't matter. Cantu and new Trojans coach Kevin O'Neill were standing on the baseline, smitten.

By the second day so were plenty of others. USC had an advantage, though: Cantu and Horton were old friends. "Are you friggin' kidding me?" Cantu said when he called Horton a couple of days after the event. "Have you been holding out on me with this kid?"

"No, Bob, I told you about him. You just didn't believe me, remember?" Cantu had to give him that: It had been an unlikely story.

By fall the word was out: There was a tall, raw kid at Antelope Valley with an incredible motor who was still growing. That Dedmon was nowhere near graduating didn't seem to matter, nor did the fact that he still hadn't played a college game. The coaches had begun showing up en masse during the recruiting period: Clemson, USC, Texas, Washington, West Virginia, LSU. There were so many that Atkerson and fellow AVC assistant Brad Wiggs felt more like bellhops than coaches. Line up the chairs, get water, make small talk.

Dedmon was shocked at first. He hadn't thought he was any good. Now, after the Fullerton game, he felt as if he belonged. It was time to commit. He thought about all those schools, all those faraway places. He wanted to stay near his sisters, the two people to whom he was closest. That narrowed the list considerably. Then he visited USC. Riding shotgun in a golf cart with Horton, he toured the campus, awed by the buildings, dorm rooms, and giant auditoriums. What really got him, though, was the training room in Little Galen, where the football players ate. Dedmon stared at the menu: tri-tip steak, chicken, pasta. "You mean I get to eat all that?" he asked, incredulous.

"Yeah, Dewayne, you get to eat as much as you want," said Horton.

This was Shangri-la. The way Dedmon's body had been growing, he couldn't take in calories fast enough. He'd probably been eating only 3,000 or so a day, many of them empty, when his body needed 5,000. Just the idea of being on scholarship overwhelmed him; add to that the quality of the school and the coaching staff, and he was sold. Though he wouldn't officially sign for another five months, he verbally committed to USC that November.

From that day, whether it was freezing or 90° out, Dedmon wore his USC sweatshirt. Around town he became a hero. The *Antelope Valley Press* wrote about him. Students high-fived him. His teachers marveled at how he'd changed and what an unlikely path he had taken. After all, most of the time we hear about wayward young men who one day find God. Dedmon, however, was the opposite. As history professor Cynthia Lehman says, "He just walked into the gym one day and found basketball."

•   •   •

It is a warm afternoon in July 2011 at Los Angeles Trade Technical College (LATTC) in downtown L.A., and the Say No Classic summer league is in full swing. Rap music booms from the speakers, roughly seventy-five fans lounge in the wooden bleachers, and tall young men wander around in shorts, athletic sandals and hoodies, waiting for their games. The court is filled with top Division I players. Larry Drew of UCLA is here, as are Malik Story of Nevada and Quincy Lawson of Loyola Marymount. And, wearing a mini-mohawk and towering over the rest of the players at just over seven feet, Dewayne Dedmon.

So much has happened in the last year and a half. After signing with USC, Dedmon celebrated his first Christmas, watching *How the Grinch Stole Christmas* at the Hortons' house with Dieter's five-year-old son, Charles. Then Dedmon suffered a gruesome injury late in AVC's 2009–10 season—his forehead was fractured and his sinus cavity was partially collapsed by an elbow—and missed the last seven Pioneer Conference games. In April 2010, Horton was hired as an assistant by USC, and not long after that the Trojans' coaches asked if Dedmon could arrive by New Year's and redshirt the second half of the '10–11 season. That meant cramming in all his units, taking an online course, and graduating from AVC early, all without the help of the coach who'd mentored him, because Horton's contact with Dedmon was now severely limited by NCAA rules. So Dedmon applied the discipline he'd learned during his days at Kingdom Hall and succeeded with the help of flash cards and study sessions with Lehman. He even made the Dean's List one semester.

When he arrived at USC in January for the second half of the basketball season, he once again treated practices like games, sprinting and banging. Starting forwards Nikola Vucevic and Alex Stepheson weren't quite sure what to make of the new seven-foot maniac, but one thing was clear: He pushed them. When USC made a surprising run to qualify for the NCAA tournament, the coaches cited Dedmon's influence in practice as one reason why.

Provided access to the training table, Dedmon ate five times a day and chugged protein shakes. His weight rose to 258 pounds from 222. In workouts he began knocking down jumpers, extending his range beyond the three-point line. He became a savvy passer, added post moves, and proved to be the second-fastest player on the team in length-of-the-court races, behind only point guard Maurice Jones.

"For a big guy he has the best motor I've seen," says O'Neill, who has more than twenty years of coaching experience in college and the NBA. He compares Dedmon's desire with Ben Wallace's and his potential skill set with Kevin Garnett's. O'Neill intended to bring Dedmon along slowly, but when Vucevic declared for the NBA draft, the coach had no choice: Dedmon's learning curve had to be shortened again.

Despite being a seven-footer at a Pac-12 school, Dedmon remained off the radar of collegiate pundits and NBA recruiting experts throughout the spring and into the summer of 2011. After all, most kids transferred from jucos with gaudy numbers; Dedmon averaged 6.6 points and 7.8 rebounds in his 23 games at AVC. Asked about Dedmon last April, Jonathan Givony of DraftExpress offered only, "Can't say I've seen him play."

Even now, at LATTC, Dedmon is playing in only his third summer league game and remains something of a mystery to opponents. Though not for long. His team scores its first basket when Dedmon rises up for a resounding tip dunk. The team's next bucket comes when he makes a nice slip cut, catches a bounce pass, and throws it down again. When he gets his third dunk of the quarter, it's after dropping down to the baseline, and this one has the whole stanchion rocking. He runs the floor as if each fast break is a kamikaze mission to the rim. On defense, his legs splay like a spider's as he scurries around swatting at shots. When he connects, he roars, "*Nooooo!*" You wonder when he will run out of energy—but then you remember that he's spent a lifetime waiting for this. As he says, "I'm so far behind, I can't stop running."

A night later Dedmon will hit a sixteen-foot jump shot to win the game. In August he will travel to Brazil on an exhibition tour and score a team-high nineteen points and block four shots for USC against a Brazilian professional squad, then Skype his sisters to talk about it. By the end of August he will have gone from unknown to known. The Spurs and the NBA's head scout, Ryan Blake, will have called the AVC offices asking for information. Dedmon will be projected as a power forward who can face up, hit the trail three-pointer, and block a ton of shots. He will be mentioned as a first-round, perhaps even lottery, pick. That he will break his right hand during practice in October will only heighten the interest—for, Dewayne being Dewayne, he will keep playing with the hand in a soft cast and begin focusing obsessively on improving his left hand, leaving himself on track to play in the season opener.

On this July day, though, Dedmon is still just a thoughtful, playful boy who lists his activities on Facebook as *basketball* and *sleep* and says he still doesn't think he's that good. He remains torn between two worlds. He says he still accepts some of the religious doctrine he was raised to believe—he won't take a blood transfusion, for example—only now, "I'm just not so much into it." He is amazed at the turn his life has taken, at the ripple effects of his decision to play a game. "Since basketball came, it helped me out with [the church] so I didn't have to be completely immersed," he says. "I don't know where my life would be, I don't know what I'd be doing." He pauses. "That's crazy."

•　　　•　　　•

What is more important than faith and family?

To get to Gail Lewis's house in southeast Palmdale, you drive down Highway 138, past the fish fry and the soul-food grocery store and the wig shop. A right turn takes you past vacant lots and condo complexes to Longhorn Pavilion Apartments, where 160 small units are encircled by a metal gate. Behind the complex the desert takes over again: Scrub brush and sand become rocky hills. Out front signs say NOW RENTING: LAUNDRY IN EVERY APARTMENT and placards near the office read *future resident parking*. Wet clothes hang from railings, dents are visible in the stucco walls, shirtless kids cluster in stairwells.

Gail's condo is up one flight. A brown leather-bound book titled *Holy Scriptures* sits on her kitchen table. On a wall there is a picture of the family when Dewayne was five years old, with round cheeks and a killer smile, dressed in a blue blazer. Gail welcomes a guest and offers bottled water. She is a tall, warm, pretty woman with a nice smile, and she flips her long hair when she talks. Though thin, she says she wishes she worked out more. She does not proselytize, at least not today.

She says she's trying to come to terms with Dewayne's life. It's been hard. The previous fall USC invited her down for a campus tour, and after many entreaties from the coaches she accepted. She'd never seen so many school buildings—"Gosh, they sure spend a lot of money on this school, all just for education," she says. She liked the coach, that bald man with glasses. He seemed nice, and he told her she could call any time.

There is good and bad. She's glad Dewayne is educating himself, especially since his classes will give him opportunities to make evening meetings. She's looked into it, and there are Kingdom Halls close to USC. Still, she wishes he told her more. Until a reporter called a few weeks earlier, she had no idea Dewayne was even playing in a summer league. "That is just blowing me away right now," she said then. "I wish my kids were still [young], back when they listened and did what you said. They get older and become independent and get a mind of their own."

Mother and son are on better terms now. Dewayne texts her occasionally, and they talk on the phone. She went to a couple of his games at AVC and plans on going down to USC when her schedule allows. When they talk, she reminds him of his Christian upbringing, and he says, "Mom, I think about it all the time."

"Maybe sometimes you need to act on your thinking," she replies.

She knows Dewayne might be drafted into the NBA, and she's concerned. "It would be kind of difficult, because you can't serve two masters," she says. "He would probably have to make a decision within himself. He thought he could do both, but obviously you can't."

If he decides to go to the NBA, she says, she will not stand in his way, though she hopes he will be like that one man, A. C. Green, the Lakers' forward who kept his morals and said he remained a virgin until he was married, in April 2002. For now, though, she holds out hope he will return to the fold. She tells Dewayne he has to want his faith just like he wants basketball, that he is like the prodigal son and just needs to find his way home. "I told him, 'You turned away from [your faith], but I'm gonna pray until you come back,'" she says. "I told him, 'I'm not gonna stop praying until you return.'"

Soon Gail ushers her visitor out the door, into the stifling heat of the Antelope Valley. Outside the gates of the complex the desert stretches out as far as the eye can see, hot and dry. In the cool room inside she returns to her reading, preparing for her next trip out into the community to talk to lost souls.

Gail Lewis truly believes it: Everyone can find his salvation.

New York

Deftly blending personal narrative with thorough reporting, Wesley Yang confronted a popular stereotype—the studious, successful Asian American, molded by the culture celebrated in Amy Chua's Battle Hymn of the Tiger Mother—*and blew it to pieces. Whether visiting a boot camp where young Asians are taught to be assertive or exploring the failure of the meritocratic ideal, Yang fashioned an example of essay writing at its best—cogent, surprising, universal in scope. Since the appointment of Adam Moss as editor in chief of* New York *in 2004, the magazine has won twenty National Magazine Awards, but this was its first for Essays and Criticism.*

Wesley Yang

Paper Tigers

S ometimes I'll glimpse my reflection in a window and feel astonished by what I see. Jet-black hair. Slanted eyes. A pancake-flat surface of yellow-and-green-toned skin. An expression that is nearly reptilian in its impassivity. I've contrived to think of this face as the equal in beauty to any other. But what I feel in these moments is its strangeness to me. It's my face. I can't disclaim it. But what does it have to do with me?

Millions of Americans must feel estranged from their own faces. But every self-estranged individual is estranged in his own way. I, for instance, am the child of Korean immigrants, but I do not speak my parents' native tongue. I have never called my elders by the proper honorific, "big brother" or "big sister." I have never dated a Korean woman. I don't have a Korean friend. Though I am an immigrant, I have never wanted to strive like one.

You could say that I am, in the gently derisive parlance of Asian Americans, a banana or a Twinkie (yellow on the outside, white on the inside). But while I don't believe our roots necessarily define us, I do believe there are racially inflected assumptions wired into our neural circuitry that we use to sort through the sea of faces we confront. And although I am in most respects devoid of Asian characteristics, I do have an Asian face.

Here is what I sometimes suspect my face signifies to other Americans: an invisible person, barely distinguishable from a mass of faces that resemble it. A conspicuous person standing apart from the crowd and yet devoid of any individuality. An icon of so much that the culture pretends to honor but that it in fact patronizes and exploits. Not just people "who are good at math" and play the violin, but a mass of stifled, repressed, abused, conformist quasi robots who simply do not matter, socially or culturally.

I've always been of two minds about this sequence of stereotypes. On the one hand, it offends me greatly that anyone would think to apply them to me, or to anyone else, simply on the basis of facial characteristics. On the other hand, it also seems to me that there are a lot of Asian people to whom they apply.

Let me summarize my feelings toward Asian values: Fuck filial piety. Fuck grade-grubbing. Fuck Ivy League mania. Fuck deference to authority. Fuck humility and hard work. Fuck harmonious relations. Fuck sacrificing for the future. Fuck earnest, striving middle-class servility.

I understand the reasons Asian parents have raised a generation of children this way. Doctor, lawyer, accountant, engineer: These are good jobs open to whoever works hard enough. What could be wrong with that pursuit? Asians graduate from college at a rate higher than any other ethnic group in America, including whites. They earn a higher median family income than any other ethnic group in America, including whites. This is a stage in a triumphal narrative, and it is a narrative that is much shorter than many remember. Two thirds of the roughly 14 million Asian Americans are foreign-born. There were less than 39,000 people of Korean descent living in America in 1970, when my elder brother was born. There are around 1 million today.

Asian American success is typically taken to ratify the American Dream and to prove that minorities can make it in this country without handouts. Still, an undercurrent of racial panic always accompanies the consideration of Asians, and all the more so as China becomes the destination for our industrial base and the banker controlling our burgeoning debt. But if the armies of Chinese factory workers who make our fast fashion and iPads terrify us, and if the collective mass of high-achieving Asian American students arouse an anxiety about the laxity of American parenting, what of the Asian American who obeyed everything his parents told him? Does this person really scare anyone?

Earlier this year, the publication of Amy Chua's *Battle Hymn of the Tiger Mother* incited a collective airing out of many varieties of race-based hysteria. But absent from the millions of words written in response to the book was any serious consideration of whether Asian Americans were in fact taking over this country. If it is true that they are collectively dominating in elite high schools and universities, is it also true that Asian Americans are dominating in the real world? My strong suspicion was that this was not so, and that the reasons would not be hard to find. If we are a collective juggernaut that inspires such awe and fear, why does it seem that so many Asians are so readily perceived to be, as I myself have felt most of my life, the products of a timid culture, easily pushed around by more assertive people, and thus basically invisible?

·　　·　　·

A few months ago, I received an e-mail from a young man named Jefferson Mao, who after attending Stuyvesant High School had recently graduated from the University of Chicago. He wanted my advice about "being an Asian writer." This is how he described himself: "I got good grades and I love literature and I want to be a writer and an intellectual; at the same time, I'm the first person in my family to go to college, my parents don't speak English very well, and we don't own the apartment in Flushing that we live in. I mean, I'm proud of my parents and my neighborhood and what I perceive to be my artistic potential or whatever, but sometimes I feel like I'm jumping the gun a generation or two too early."

One bright, cold Sunday afternoon, I ride the 7 train to its last stop in Flushing, where the storefront signs are all written in Chinese and the sidewalks are a slow-moving river of impassive faces. Mao is waiting for me at the entrance of the Main Street subway station, and together we walk to a nearby Vietnamese restaurant.

Mao has a round face, with eyes behind rectangular wire-frame glasses. Since graduating, he has been living with his parents, who emigrated from China when Mao was eight years old. His mother is a manicurist; his father is a physical therapist's aide. Lately, Mao has been making the familiar hour-and-a-half ride from Flushing to downtown Manhattan to tutor a white Stuyvesant freshman who lives in Tribeca. And what he feels, sometimes, in the presence of that amiable young man is a pang of regret. Now he understands better what he ought to have done back when he was a Stuyvesant freshman: "Worked half as hard and been twenty times more successful."

Entrance to Stuyvesant, one of the most competitive public high schools in the country, is determined solely by performance on a test: The top 3.7 percent of all New York City students who take the Specialized High Schools Admissions Test hoping to go to Stuyvesant are accepted. There are no set-asides for the underprivileged or, conversely, for alumni or other privileged groups. There is no formula to encourage "diversity" or any nebulous concept of "well-roundedness" or "character." Here we have something like pure meritocracy. This is what it looks like: Asian Americans, who make up 12.6 percent of New York City, make up 72 percent of the high school.

This year, 569 Asian Americans scored high enough to earn a slot at Stuyvesant, along with 179 whites, 13 Hispanics, and 12 blacks. Such dramatic overrepresentation, and what it may be read to imply about the intelligence of different groups of New Yorkers, has a way of making people uneasy. But intrinsic intelligence, of course, is precisely what Asians don't believe in. They believe—and have proved—that the constant practice of test taking will improve the scores of whoever commits to it. All throughout Flushing, as well as in Bayside, one can find "cram schools," or storefront academies, that drill students in test preparation after school, on weekends, and during summer break. "Learning math is not about learning math," an instructor at one called Ivy Prep was quoted in the *New York Times* as saying. "It's about weightlifting. You are pumping the iron of math." Mao puts it more specifically: "You learn quite simply to nail any standardized test you take."

And so there is an additional concern accompanying the rise of the Tiger Children, one focused more on the narrowness of the educational experience a non-Asian child might receive in the company of fanatically preprofessional Asian students. Jenny Tsai, a student who was elected president of her class at the equally competitive New York public school Hunter College High School, remembers frequently hearing that "the school was becoming too Asian, that they would be the downfall of our school." A couple of years ago, she revisited this issue in her senior thesis at Harvard, where she interviewed graduates of elite public schools and found that the white students regarded the Asians students with wariness. (She quotes a music teacher at Stuyvesant describing the dominance of Asians: "They were mediocre kids, but they got in because they were coached.") In 2005, the *Wall Street Journal* reported on "white flight" from a high school in Cupertino, California, that began soon after the children of Asian software engineers had made the place so brutally competitive that a B average could place you in the bottom third of the class.

Colleges have a way of correcting for this imbalance: The Princeton sociologist Thomas Espenshade has calculated that an Asian applicant must, in practice, score 140 points higher on the SAT than a comparable white applicant to have the same chance of admission. This is obviously unfair to the many qualified

Asian individuals who are punished for the success of others with similar faces. Upper-middle-class white kids, after all, have their own elite private schools, and their own private tutors, far more expensive than the cram schools, to help them game the education system.

You could frame it, as some aggrieved Asian Americans do, as a simple issue of equality and press for race-blind quantitative admissions standards. In 2006, a decade after California passed a voter initiative outlawing any racial engineering at the public universities, Asians composed 46 percent of UC-Berkeley's entering class; one could imagine a similar demographic reshuffling in the Ivy League, where Asian Americans currently make up about 17 percent of undergraduates. But the Ivies, as we all know, have their own private institutional interests at stake in their admissions choices, including some that are arguably defensible. Who can seriously claim that a Harvard University that was 72 percent Asian would deliver the same grooming for elite status its students had gone there to receive?

Somewhere near the middle of his time at Stuyvesant, a vague sense of discontent started to emerge within Mao. He had always felt himself a part of a mob of "nameless, faceless Asian kids," who were "like a part of the décor of the place." He had been content to keep his head down and work toward the goal shared by everyone at Stuyvesant: Harvard. But around the beginning of his senior year, he began to wonder whether this march toward academic success was the only, or best, path.

"You can't help but feel like there must be another way," he explains over a bowl of phô. "It's like, we're being pitted against each other while there are kids out there in the Midwest who can do way less work and be in a garage band or something—and if they're decently intelligent and work decently hard in school . . ."

Mao began to study the racially inflected social hierarchies at Stuyvesant, where, in a survey undertaken by the student newspaper this year, slightly more than half of the respondents reported that their friends came from within their own ethnic group. His attention focused on the mostly white (and Manhattan-dwelling) group whose members seemed able to manage the crushing workload while still remaining socially active. "The general gist of most high-school movies is that the pretty cheerleader gets with the big dumb jock, and the nerd is left to bide his time in loneliness. But at some point in the future," he says, "the nerd is going to rule the world, and the dumb jock is going to work in a carwash.

"At Stuy, it's completely different: If you looked at the pinnacle, the girls and the guys are not only good-looking and socially affable, they also get the best grades and star in the school plays and win election to student government. It all converges at the top. It's like training for high society. It was jarring for us Chinese kids. You got the sense that you had to study hard, but it wasn't enough."

Mao was becoming clued in to the fact that there was another hierarchy behind the official one that explained why others were getting what he never had—"a high-school sweetheart" figured prominently on this list—and that this mysterious hierarchy was going to determine what happened to him in life. "You realize there are things you really don't understand about courtship or just acting in a certain way. Things that somehow come naturally to people who go to school in the suburbs and have parents who are culturally assimilated." I pressed him for specifics, and he mentioned that he had visited his white girlfriend's parents' house the past Christmas, where the family had "sat around cooking together and playing Scrabble." This ordinary vision of suburban-American domesticity lingered with Mao: Here, at last, was the setting in which all that implicit knowledge "about social norms and propriety" had been transmitted. There was no cram school that taught these lessons.

Before having heard from Mao, I had considered myself at worst lightly singed by the last embers of Asian alienation. Indeed, given all the incredibly hip Asian artists and fashion designers and so forth you can find in New York, it seemed that this feeling was destined to die out altogether. And yet here it was in a New Yorker more than a dozen years my junior. While it may be true that sections of the Asian American world are devoid of alienation, there are large swaths where it is as alive as it has ever been.

A few weeks after we meet, Mao puts me in touch with Daniel Chu, his close friend from Stuyvesant. Chu graduated from Williams College last year, having won a creative-writing award for his poetry. He had spent a portion of the $18,000 prize on a trip to China, but now he is back living with his parents in Brooklyn Chinatown.

Chu remembers that during his first semester at Williams, his junior adviser would periodically take him aside. Was he feeling all right? Was something the matter? "I was acclimating myself to the place," he says. "I wasn't totally happy, but I wasn't depressed." But then his new white friends made similar remarks. "They would say, 'Dan, it's kind of hard, sometimes, to tell what you're thinking.'"

Chu has a pleasant face, but it would not be wrong to characterize his demeanor as reserved. He speaks in a quiet, unemphatic voice. He doesn't move his features much. He attributes these traits to the atmosphere in his household. "When you grow up in a Chinese home," he says, "you don't talk. You shut up and listen to what your parents tell you to do."

At Stuyvesant, he had hung out in an exclusively Asian world in which friends were determined by which subway lines you traveled. But when he arrived at Williams, Chu slowly became aware of something strange: The white people in the New England wilderness walked around smiling at each other. "When you're in a place like that, everyone is friendly."

He made a point to start smiling more. "It was something that I had to actively practice," he says. "Like, when you have a transaction at a business, you hand over the money—and then you smile."

He says that he's made some progress but that there's still plenty of work that remains. "I'm trying to undo eighteen years of a Chinese upbringing. Four years at Williams helps, but only so much." He is conscious of how his father, an IT manager, is treated at work. "He's the best programmer at his office," he says, "but because he doesn't speak English well, he is always passed over."

Though Chu is not merely fluent in English but is officially the most distinguished poet of his class at Williams, he still worries that other aspects of his demeanor might attract the same kind of treatment his father received. "I'm really glad we're having this conversation," he says at one point—it is helpful to be remembering these lessons in self-presentation just as he prepares for job interviews.

"I guess what I would like is to become so good at something that my social deficiencies no longer matter," he tells me. Chu is a bright, diligent, impeccably credentialed young man born in the United States. He is optimistic about his ability to earn respect in the world. But he doubts he will ever feel the same comfort in his skin that he glimpsed in the people he met at Williams. That kind of comfort, he says—"I think it's generations away."

.   .   .

While he was still an electrical-engineering student at Berkeley in the nineties, James Hong visited the IBM campus for a series of interviews. An older Asian researcher looked over Hong's résumé and asked him some standard questions. Then he got up without saying a word and closed the door to his office.

"Listen," he told Hong, "I'm going to be honest with you. My generation came to this country because we wanted better for you kids. We did the best we could, leaving our homes and going to graduate school not speaking much English. If you take this job, you are just going to hit the same ceiling we did. They just see me as an Asian Ph.D., never management potential. You are going to get a job offer, but don't take it. Your generation has to go far-ther than we did, otherwise we did everything for nothing."

The researcher was talking about what some refer to as the "Bamboo Ceiling"—an invisible barrier that maintains a pyra-midal racial structure throughout corporate America, with lots of Asians at junior levels, quite a few in middle management, and virtually none in the higher reaches of leadership.

The failure of Asian Americans to become leaders in the white-collar workplace does not qualify as one of the burning social issues of our time. But it is a part of the bitter undercur-rent of Asian American life that so many Asian graduates of elite universities find that meritocracy as they have understood it comes to an abrupt end after graduation. If between 15 and 20 percent of every Ivy League class is Asian, and if the Ivy Leagues are incubators for the country's leaders, it would stand to reason that Asians would make up some corresponding portion of the leadership class.

And yet the numbers tell a different story. According to a re-cent study, Asian Americans represent roughly 5 percent of the population but only 0.3 percent of corporate officers, less than 1 percent of corporate board members, and around 2 percent of college presidents. There are nine Asian American CEOs in the Fortune 500. In specific fields where Asian Americans are heav-ily represented, there is a similar asymmetry. A third of all soft-ware engineers in Silicon Valley are Asian, and yet they make up only 6 percent of board members and about 10 percent of corpo-rate officers of the Bay Area's twenty-five largest companies. At the National Institutes of Health, where 21.5 percent of tenure-track scientists are Asians, only 4.7 percent of the lab or branch directors are, according to a study conducted in 2005. One suc-cinct evocation of the situation appeared in the comments sec-tion of a website called Yellowworld: "If you're East Asian, you need to attend a top-tier university to land a good high-paying gig. Even if you land that good high-paying gig, the white guy with the pedigree from a mediocre state university will some-how move ahead of you in the ranks simply because he's white."

Jennifer W. Allyn, a managing director for diversity at Price-waterhouseCoopers, works to ensure that "all of the groups feel welcomed and supported and able to thrive and to go as far as their talents will take them." I posed to her the following defini-tion of parity in the corporate workforce: If the current crop of associates is 17 percent Asian, then in fourteen years, when they have all been up for partner review, 17 percent of those who are offered partner will be Asian. Allyn conceded that Pricewater-houseCoopers was not close to reaching that benchmark any-time soon—and that "nobody else is either."

Part of the insidious nature of the Bamboo Ceiling is that it does not seem to be caused by overt racism. A survey of Asian Pacific American employees of Fortune 500 companies found that 80 percent reported they were judged not as Asians but as individuals. But only 51 percent reported the existence of Asians in key positions, and only 55 percent agreed that their firms were fully capitalizing on the talents and perspectives of Asians.

More likely, the discrepancy in these numbers is a matter of unconscious bias. Nobody would affirm the proposition that tall men are intrinsically better leaders, for instance. And yet while only 15 percent of the male population is at least six feet tall, 58 percent of all corporate CEOs are. Similarly, nobody would say that Asian people are unfit to be leaders. But subjects in a re-cently published psychological experiment consistently rated hypothetical employees with Caucasian-sounding names higher in leadership potential than identical ones with Asian names.

Maybe it is simply the case that a traditionally Asian upbring-ing is the problem. As Allyn points out, in order to be a leader, you must have followers. Associates at PricewaterhouseCoopers are initially judged on how well they do the work they are as-signed. "You have to be a doer," as she puts it. They are expected to distinguish themselves with their diligence, at which point they become "super-doers." But being a leader requires different skill sets. "The traits that got you to where you are won't necessarily take you to the next level," says the diversity consultant Jane Hyun, who wrote a book called *Breaking the Bamboo Ceiling*. To become a leader requires taking personal initiative and thinking about how an organization can work differently. It also requires networking, self-promotion, and self-assertion. It's racist to think that any given Asian individual is unlikely to be creative or risk taking. It's simple cultural observation to say that a group whose education has historically focused on rote memorization and "pumping the iron of math" is, on aggregate, unlikely to yield many people inclined to challenge authority or break with inherited ways of doing things.

Sach Takayasu had been one of the fastest-rising members of her cohort in the marketing department at IBM in New York. But about seven years ago, she felt her progress begin to slow. "I had gotten to the point where I was overdelivering, working really long hours, and where doing more of the same wasn't getting me anywhere," she says. It was around this time that she attended a seminar being offered by an organization called Leadership Education for Asian Pacifics.

LEAP has parsed the complicated social dynamics responsible for the dearth of Asian American leaders and has designed training programs that flatter Asian people even as it teaches them to change their behavior to suit white-American expectations. Asians who enter a LEAP program are constantly assured that they will be able to "keep your values, while acquiring new skills," along the way to becoming "culturally competent leaders."

In a presentation to 1,500 Asian American employees of Microsoft, LEAP president and CEO J. D. Hokoyama laid out his grand synthesis of the Asian predicament in the workplace. "Sometimes people have perceptions about us and our communities which may or may not be true," Hokoyama told the audience. "But they put those perceptions onto us, and then they do something that can be very devastating: They make decisions about us not based on the truth but based on those perceptions." Hokoyama argued that it was not sufficient to rail at these unjust perceptions. In the end, Asian people themselves would have to assume responsibility for unmaking them. This was both a practical matter, he argued, and, in its own way, fair.

Aspiring Asian leaders had to become aware of "the relationship between values, behaviors, and perceptions." He offered the example of Asians who don't speak up at meetings. "So let's say I go to meetings with you and I notice you never say anything. And I ask myself, 'Hmm, I wonder why you're not saying anything. Maybe it's because you don't know what we're talking about. That would be a good reason for not saying anything. Or maybe it's because you're not even interested in the subject matter. Or maybe you think the conversation is beneath you.' So here I'm thinking, because you never say anything at meetings, that you're either dumb, you don't care, or you're arrogant. When maybe it's because you were taught when you were growing up that when the boss is talking, what are you supposed to be doing? Listening."

Takayasu took the weeklong course in 2006. One of the first exercises she encountered involved the group instructor asking for a list of some qualities that they identify with Asians. The students responded: upholding family honor, filial piety, self-restraint. Then the instructor solicited a list of the qualities the members identify with leadership, and invited the students to notice how little overlap there is between the two lists.

At first, Takayasu didn't relate to the others in attendance, who were listing typical Asian values their parents had taught them. "They were all saying things like 'Study hard,' 'Become a doctor or lawyer,' blah, blah, blah. That's not how my parents were. They would worry if they saw me working too hard." Takayasu had spent her childhood shuttling between New York and Tokyo. Her father was an executive at Mitsubishi; her mother was a concert pianist. She was highly assimilated into American culture, fluent in English, poised and confident. "But the more we got into it, as we moved away from the obvious things to the deeper, more fundamental values, I began to see that my upbringing had been very Asian after all. My parents would say, 'Don't create problems. Don't trouble other people.' How Asian is that? It helped to explain why I don't reach out to other people for help." It occurred to Takayasu that she was a little bit "heads down" after all. She was willing to take on difficult assignments without seeking credit for herself. She was reluctant to "toot her own horn."

Takayasu has put her new self-awareness to work at IBM, and she now exhibits a newfound ability for horn tooting. "The things I could write on my résumé as my team's accomplishments: They're really impressive," she says.

The law professor and writer Tim Wu grew up in Canada with a white mother and a Taiwanese father, which allows him an interesting perspective on how whites and Asians perceive each other. After graduating from law school, he took a series of clerkships, and he remembers the subtle ways in which hierarchies were developed among the other young lawyers. "There is this automatic assumption in any legal environment that Asians will have a particular talent for bitter labor," he says, and then goes on to define the word *coolie*, a Chinese term for "bitter labor." "There was this weird self-selection where the Asians would migrate toward the most brutal part of the labor."

By contrast, the white lawyers he encountered had a knack for portraying themselves as above all that. "White people have this instinct that is really important: to give off the impression that they're only going to do the really important work. You're a quarterback. It's a kind of arrogance that Asians are trained not to have. Someone told me not long after I moved to New York that in order to succeed, you have to understand which rules you're supposed to break. If you break the wrong rules, you're finished. And so the easiest thing to do is follow all the rules.

But then you consign yourself to a lower status. The real trick is understanding what rules are not meant for you."

This idea of a kind of rule-governed rule breaking—where the rule book was unwritten but passed along in an innate cultural sense—is perhaps the best explanation I have heard of how the Bamboo Ceiling functions in practice. LEAP appears to be very good at helping Asian workers who are already culturally competent become more self-aware of how their culture and appearance impose barriers to advancement. But I am not sure that a LEAP course is going to be enough to get Jefferson Mao or Daniel Chu the respect and success they crave. The issue is more fundamental, the social dynamics at work more deeply embedded, and the remedial work required may be at a more basic level of comportment.

•   •   •

What if you missed out on the lessons in masculinity taught in the gyms and locker rooms of America's high schools? What if life has failed to make you a socially dominant alpha male who runs the American boardroom and prevails in the American bedroom? What if no one ever taught you how to greet white people and make them comfortable? What if, despite these deficiencies, you no longer possess an immigrant's dutiful forbearance for a secondary position in the American narrative and want to be a player in the scrimmage of American appetite right now, in the present?

How do you undo eighteen years of a Chinese upbringing?

This is the implicit question that J. T. Tran has posed to a roomful of Yale undergraduates at a master's tea at Silliman College. His answer is typically Asian: practice. Tran is a pickup artist who goes by the handle Asian Playboy. He travels the globe running "boot camps," mostly for Asian male students, in the art of attraction. Today, he has been invited to Yale by the Asian-American Students Alliance.

"Creepy can be fixed," Tran explains to the standing-room-only crowd. "Many guys just don't realize how to project themselves." These are the people whom Tran spends his days with, a new batch in a new city every week: nice guys, intelligent guys, motivated guys, who never figured out how to be successful with women. Their mothers had kept them at home to study rather than let them date or socialize. Now Tran's company, ABCs of Attraction, offers a remedial education that consists of three four-hour seminars, followed by a supervised night out "in the field," in which J. T., his assistant Gareth Jones, and a tall blonde wing-girl named Sarah force them to approach women. Tuition costs $1,450.

"One of the big things I see with Asian students is what I call the Asian poker face—the lack of range when it comes to facial expressions," Tran says. "How many times has this happened to you?" he asks the crowd. "You'll be out at a party with your white friends, and they will be like—'Dude, are you angry?'" Laughter fills the room. Part of it is psychological, he explains. He recalls one Korean American student he was teaching. The student was a very dedicated schoolteacher who cared a lot about his students. But none of this was visible. "Sarah was trying to help him, and she was like, 'C'mon, smile, smile,' and he was like . . ." And here Tran mimes the unbearable tension of a face trying to contort itself into a simulacrum of mirth. "He was so completely unpracticed at smiling that he literally could not do it." Eventually, though, the student fought through it, "and when he finally got to smiling he was, like, really cool."

Tran continues to lay out a story of Asian American male distress that must be relevant to the lives of at least some of those who have packed Master Krauss's living room. The story he tells is one of Asian American disadvantage in the sexual marketplace, a disadvantage that he has devoted his life to overturning. Yes, it is about picking up women. Yes, it is about picking up white women. Yes, it is about attracting those women whose hair is the color of the midday sun and eyes are the color of the ocean, and it is about having sex with them. He is not going to apologize for the images of blonde women plastered all over his website. This is what he prefers, what he stands for, and what he is selling: the courage to pursue anyone you want, and the skills to make the person you desire desire you back. White guys do what they want; he is going to do the same.

But it is about much more than this, too. It is about altering the perceptions of Asian men—perceptions that are rooted in the way they behave, which are in turn rooted in the way they were raised—through a course of behavior modification intended to teach them how to be the socially dominant figures that they are not perceived to be. It is a program of, as he puts it to me later, "social change through pickup."

Tran offers his own story as an exemplary Asian underdog. Short, not good-looking, socially inept, sexually null. "If I got a B, I would be whipped," he remembers of his childhood. After college, he worked as an aerospace engineer at Boeing and Raytheon, but internal politics disfavored him. Five years into his career, his entire white cohort had been promoted above him. "I knew I needed to learn about social dynamics, because just working hard wasn't cutting it."

His efforts at dating were likewise "a miserable failure." It was then that he turned to "the seduction community," a group of men on Internet message boards like alt.seduction.fast. It began as a "support group for losers" and later turned into a program of self-improvement. Was charisma something you could teach? Could confidence be reduced to a formula? Was it merely something that you either possessed or did not possess, as a function of the experiences you had been through in life, or did it emerge from specific forms of behavior? The members of the group turned their computer-science and engineering brains to the question. They wrote long accounts of their dates and subjected them to collective scrutiny. They searched for patterns in the raw material and filtered these experiences through social-psychological research. They eventually built a model.

This past Valentine's Day, during a weekend boot camp in New York City sponsored by ABCs of Attraction, the model is being played out. Tran and Jones are teaching their students how an alpha male stands (shoulders thrown back, neck fully extended, legs planted slightly wider than the shoulders). "This is going to feel very strange to you if you're used to slouching, but this is actually right," Jones says. They explain how an alpha male walks (no shuffling; pick your feet up entirely off the ground; a slight sway in the shoulders). They identify the proper distance to stand from "targets" (a slightly bent arm's length). They explain the importance of "kino escalation." (You must touch her. You must not be afraid to do this.) They are teaching the importance of sub-communication: what you convey about yourself before a single word has been spoken. They explain the importance of intonation. They explain what intonation is. "Your voice moves up and down in pitch to convey a variety of different emotions."

All of this is taught through a series of exercises. "This is going to feel completely artificial," says Jones on the first day of training. "But I need you to do the biggest shit-eating grin you've ever made in your life." Sarah is standing in the corner with her back to the students—three Indian guys, including one in a turban, three Chinese guys, and one Cambodian. The students have to cross the room, walking as an alpha male walks, and then place their hands on her shoulder—firmly but gently—and turn her around. Big smile. Bigger than you've ever smiled before. Raise your glass in a toast. Make eye contact and hold it. Speak loudly and clearly. Take up space without apology. This is what an alpha male does.

Before each student crosses the floor of that bare white cubicle in midtown, Tran asks him a question. "What is good in life?" Tran shouts.

The student then replies, in the loudest, most emphatic voice he can muster: "To crush my enemies, see them driven before me, and to hear the lamentation of their women—in my bed!"

For the intonation exercise, students repeat the phrase "I do what I want" with a variety of different moods.

"Say it like you're happy!" Jones shouts. ("I do what I want.") Say it like you're sad! ("I do what I want." The intonation utterly unchanged.) Like you're sad! ("I . . . do what I want.") Say it like you've just won $5 million! ("I do what I want.")

Raj, a twenty-six-year-old Indian virgin, can barely get his voice to alter during intonation exercise. But on Sunday night, on the last evening of the boot camp, I watch him cold-approach a set of women at the Hotel Gansevoort and engage them in conversation for a half-hour. He does not manage to "number close" or "kiss close." But he had done something that not very many people can do.

.   .   .

Of the dozens of Asian Americans I spoke with for this story, many were successful artists and scientists; or good-looking and socially integrated leaders; or tough, brassy, risk-taking, street-smart entrepreneurs. Of course, there are lots of such people around—do I even have to point that out? They are no more morally worthy than any other kind of Asian person. But they have figured out some useful things.

The lesson about the Bamboo Ceiling that James Hong learned from his interviewer at IBM stuck, and after working for a few years at Hewlett-Packard, he decided to strike off on his own. His first attempts at entrepreneurialism failed, but he finally struck pay dirt with a simple, not terribly refined idea that had a strong primal appeal: hotornot.com. Hong and his cofounder eventually sold the site for roughly $20 million.

Hong ran hotornot.com partly as a kind of incubator to seed in his employees the habits that had served him well. "We used to hire engineers from Berkeley—almost all Asian—who were on the cusp of being entrepreneurial but were instead headed toward jobs at big companies," he says. "We would train them in how to take risk, how to run things themselves. I remember encouraging one employee to read *The Game*"—the infamous pickup-artist textbook—"because I figured growing the *cojones* to take risk was applicable to being an entrepreneur."

If the Bamboo Ceiling is ever going to break, it's probably going to have less to do with any form of behavior assimilation than with the emergence of risk takers whose success obviates the need for Asians to meet someone else's behavioral standard. People like Steve Chen, who was one of the creators of YouTube, or Kai and Charles Huang, who created Guitar Hero. Or Tony Hsieh, the founder of Zappos.com, the online shoe retailer that he sold to Amazon for about a billion dollars in 2009. Hsieh is a short Asian man who speaks tersely and is devoid of obvious charisma. One cannot imagine him being promoted in an American corporation. And yet he has proved that an awkward Asian guy can be a formidable CEO and the unlikeliest of management gurus.

Hsieh didn't have to conform to Western standards of comportment because he adopted early on the Western value of risk taking. Growing up, he would play recordings of himself in the morning practicing the violin, in lieu of actually practicing. He credits the experience he had running a pizza business at Harvard as more important than anything he learned in class. He had an instinctive sense of what the real world would require of him, and he knew that nothing his parents were teaching him would get him there.

You don't, by the way, have to be a Silicon Valley hotshot to break through the Bamboo Ceiling. You can also be a chef like Eddie Huang, whose little restaurant on the Lower East Side, Bao-Haus, sells delicious pork buns. Huang grew up in Orlando with a hard-core Tiger Mom and a disciplinarian father. "As a kid, psychologically, my day was all about not getting my ass kicked," he says. He gravitated toward the black kids at school, who also knew something about corporal punishment. He was the smallest member of his football team, but his coach named him MVP in the seventh grade. "I was defensive tackle and right guard because I was just mean. I was nasty. I had this mentality where I was like, 'You're going to accept me or I'm going to fuck you up.'"

Huang had a rough twenties, bumping repeatedly against the Bamboo Ceiling. In college, editors at the *Orlando Sentinel* invited him to write about sports for the paper. But when he visited the offices, "the editor came in and goes, 'Oh, no.' And his exact words: 'You can't write with that face.'" Later, in film class at Columbia, he wrote a script about an Asian American hot-dog vendor obsessed with his small penis. "The screenwriting teacher was like, 'I love this. You have a lot of Woody Allen in you. But do you think you could change it to Jewish characters?'" Still later, after graduating from Cardozo School of Law, he took a corporate job, where other associates would frequently say, "You have a lot of opinions for an Asian guy."

Finally, Huang decided to open a restaurant. Selling food was precisely the fate his parents wanted their son to avoid, and they didn't talk to him for months after he quit lawyering. But Huang understood instinctively that he couldn't make it work in the professional world his parents wanted him to join. "I've realized that food is one of the only places in America where we are the top dogs," he says. "Guys like David Chang or me—we can hang. There's a younger generation that grew up eating Chinese fast food. They respect our food. They may not respect anything else, but they respect our food."

Rather than strive to make himself acceptable to the world, Huang has chosen to buy his way back in, on his own terms. "What I've learned is that America is about money, and if you can make your culture commodifiable, then you're relevant," he says. "I don't believe anybody agrees with what I say or supports what I do because they truly want to love Asian people. They like my fucking pork buns, and I don't get it twisted."

.　　　.　　　.

Sometime during the hundreds of hours he spent among the mostly untouched English-language novels at the Flushing branch of the public library, Jefferson Mao discovered literature's special power of transcendence, a freedom of imagination that can send you beyond the world's hierarchies. He had written to me seeking permission to swerve off the traditional path of professional striving—to devote himself to becoming an artist—but he was unsure of what risks he was willing to take. My answer was highly ambivalent. I recognized in him something of my own youthful ambition. And I knew where that had taken me.

Unlike Mao, I was not a poor, first-generation immigrant. I finished school alienated both from Asian culture (which, in my hometown, was barely visible) and the manners and mores of my white peers. But like Mao, I wanted to be an individual. I had refused both cultures as an act of self-assertion. An education spent dutifully acquiring credentials through relentless drilling seemed to me an obscenity. So did adopting the manipulative cheeriness that seemed to secure the popularity of white Americans.

Instead, I set about contriving to live beyond both poles. I wanted what James Baldwin sought as a writer—"a power which outlasts kingdoms." Anything short of that seemed a humiliating compromise. I would become an aristocrat of the spirit, who prides himself on his incompetence in the middling tasks that are the world's business. Who does not seek after material gain. Who is his own law.

This, of course, was madness. A child of Asian immigrants born into the suburbs of New Jersey and educated at Rutgers cannot be a law unto himself. The only way to approximate this is to refuse employment because you will not be bossed around by people beneath you, and shave your expenses to the bone because you cannot afford more, and move into a decaying Victorian mansion in Jersey City so that your sense of eccentric distinction can be preserved in the midst of poverty, and cut yourself free of every form of bourgeois discipline because these are precisely the habits that will keep you chained to the mediocre fate you consider worse than death.

Throughout my twenties, I proudly turned away from one institution of American life after another (for instance, a steady job), though they had already long since turned away from me. Academe seemed another kind of death—but then again, I had a transcript marred by as many F's as A's. I had come from a culture that was the middle path incarnate. And yet for some people, there can be no middle path, only transcendence or descent into the abyss.

I was descending into the abyss.

All this was well deserved. No one had any reason to think I was anything or anyone. And yet I felt entitled to demand this recognition. I knew this was wrong and impermissible; therefore I had to double down on it. The world brings low such people. It brought me low. I haven't had health insurance in ten years. I didn't earn more than $12,000 for eight consecutive years. I went three years in the prime of my adulthood without touching a woman. I did not produce a masterpiece.

I recall one of the strangest conversations I had in the city. A woman came up to me at a party and said she had been moved by a piece of writing I had published. She confessed that prior to reading it, she had never wanted to talk to me, and had always been sure, on the basis of what she could see from across the room, that I was nobody worth talking to, that I was in fact someone to avoid.

But she had been wrong about this, she told me: It was now plain to her that I was a person with great reserves of feeling and insight. She did not ask my forgiveness for this brutal misjudgment. Instead, what she wanted to know was—why had I kept that person she had glimpsed in my essay so well hidden? She confessed something of her own hidden sorrow: She had never been beautiful and had decided, early on, that it therefore fell to her to "love the world twice as hard." Why hadn't I done that?

Here was a drunk white lady speaking what so many others over the years must have been insufficiently drunk to tell me. It was the key to many things that had, and had not, happened. I understood this encounter better after learning about LEAP, and visiting Asian Playboy's boot camp. If you are a woman who isn't beautiful, it is a social reality that you will have to work twice as hard to hold anyone's attention. You can either linger on the unfairness of this or you can get with the program. If you are an Asian person who holds himself proudly aloof, nobody will respect that, or find it intriguing, or wonder if that challenging façade hides someone worth getting to know. They will simply write you off as someone not worth the trouble of talking to.

Having glimpsed just how unacceptable the world judges my demeanor, could I too strive to make up for my shortcomings? Practice a shit-eating grin until it becomes natural? Love the world twice as hard?

I see the appeal of getting with the program. But this is not my choice. Striving to meet others' expectations may be a necessary cost of assimilation, but I am not going to do it.

Often I think my defiance is just delusional, self-glorifying bullshit that artists have always told themselves to compensate for their poverty and powerlessness. But sometimes I think it's the only thing that has preserved me intact, and that what has been preserved is not just haughty caprice but in fact the meaning of my life. So this is what I told Mao: In lieu of loving the world twice as hard, I care, in the end, about expressing my obdurate singularity at any cost. I love this hard and unyielding part of myself more than any other reward the world has to offer a newly brightened and ingratiating demeanor, and I will bear any costs associated with it.

The first step toward self-reform is to admit your deficiencies. Though my early adulthood has been a protracted education in them, I do not admit mine. I'm fine. It's the rest of you who have a problem. Fuck all y'all.

·   ·   ·

Amy Chua returned to Yale from a long, exhausting book tour in which one television interviewer had led off by noting that Internet commenters were calling her a monster. By that point, she had become practiced at the special kind of self-presentation required of a person under public siege. "I do not think that Chinese parents are superior," she declared at the annual gathering of the Asian-American Students Alliance. "I think there are many ways to be a good parent."

Much of her talk to the students, and indeed much of the conversation surrounding the book, was focused on her own parenting decisions. But just as interesting is how her parents parented her. Chua was plainly the product of a brute-force Chinese education. *Battle Hymn of the Tiger Mother* includes many lessons she was taught by her parents—lessons any LEAP student would recognize. "Be modest, be humble, be simple," her mother told her. "Never complain or make excuses," her father instructed. "If something seems unfair at school, just prove yourself by working twice as hard and being twice as good."

In the book, Chua portrays her distaste for corporate law, which she practiced before going into academe. "My entire three years at the firm, I always felt like I was playacting, ridiculous in my suit," she writes. This malaise extended even earlier, to her time as a student. "I didn't care about the rights of criminals the way others did, and I froze whenever a professor called on me. I also wasn't naturally skeptical and questioning; I just wanted to write down everything the professor said and memorize it."

At the AASA gathering at Yale, Chua made the connection between her upbringing and her adult dissatisfaction. "My parents didn't sit around talking about politics and philosophy at the dinner table," she told the students. Even after she had escaped from corporate law and made it onto a law faculty, "I was kind of lost. I just didn't feel the passion." Eventually, she made a name for herself as the author of popular books about foreign policy and became an award-winning teacher. But it's plain that she was no better prepared for legal scholarship than she had been for corporate law. "It took me a long, long time," she said. "And I went through lots and lots of rejection." She recalled her extended search for an academic post, in which she was "just not able to do a good interview, just not able to present myself well."

In other words, *Battle Hymn* provides all the material needed to refute the very cultural polemic for which it was made to stand. Chua's Chinese education had gotten her through an elite schooling, but it left her unprepared for the real world. She does not hide any of this. She had set out, she explained, to write a memoir that was "defiantly self-incriminating"—and the result was a messy jumble of conflicting impulses, part provocation, part self-critique. Western readers rode roughshod over this paradox and made of Chua a kind of Asian minstrel figure. But more than anything else, *Battle Hymn* is a very American project—one no traditional Chinese person would think to undertake. "Even if you hate the book," Chua pointed out, "the one thing it is not is meek."

"The loudest duck gets shot" is a Chinese proverb. "The nail that sticks out gets hammered down" is a Japanese one. Its Western correlative: "The squeaky wheel gets the grease." Chua had told her story and been hammered down. Yet here she was, fresh from her hammering, completely unbowed.

There is something salutary in that proud defiance. And though the debate she sparked about Asian American life has been of questionable value, we will need more people with the same kind of defiance, willing to push themselves into the spotlight and to make some noise, to beat people up, to seduce women, to make mistakes, to become entrepreneurs, to stop doggedly pursuing official paper emblems attesting to their worthiness, to stop thinking those scraps of paper will secure anyone's happiness, and to dare to be interesting.

ESPN the Magazine

FINALIST—PROFILE WRITING

In "Game of Her Life," fourteen-year-old Phiona Mutesi travels from one of the worst slums in Uganda to Siberia to compete in the 2010 Chess Olympiad–the most prestigious team chess competition in the world. Her matches are the most difficult she has ever faced, but as Tim Crothers explains, she has already beaten the odds simply by being there. Though ESPN the Magazine had often been honored for its design and photography, this was the publication's first National Magazine Award nomination in a reporting and writing category. The Queen of Katwe–Crothers's book based on "Game of Her Life"–was published in October.

Tim Crothers

Game of Her Life

She flies to Siberia in late September with nine team-mates, all in their twenties, much older than she is. When she won the match that put her on this plane she had no idea what it meant. Nobody had told her what was at stake, so she just played, like always. She had no idea that she'd qualified for the Olympiad; no idea what the Olympiad was. She had no idea that her win would send her to the city of Khanty-Mansiysk, in remote Russia; no idea where Russia was. When she learned all this, she asked just one question: "Is it cold there?"

But here she is, journeying with her countrymen twenty-seven hours across the globe. And though she has known many of them for a few years, they have no idea where she is from or where she aspires to go, because Phiona Mutesi is from a place where girls like her don't talk about that.

.   .   .

Agape church could collapse at any moment. It is a ramshackle structure that lists alarmingly to one side, held together by scrap wood, rope, a few nails, and faith. It is rickety, like everything else around it. At the church on this Saturday morning in September are thirty-seven children whose lives are equally fragile. They wander in to play a game none had heard of before they met Coach Robert, a game so foreign that there's no word for it in Luganda, their native language.

Chess.

When they walk through the door, grins crease their faces. This is home as much as any place, a refuge, the only community they know. These are their friends, their brothers and sisters of chess, and there is relative safety and comfort here. Inside Agape church it is almost possible to forget the chaos outside, in Katwe, the largest of eight slums in Kampala, Uganda, and one of the worst places on earth.

There are only seven chessboards at the church, and chess pieces are so scarce that sometimes an orphan pawn must stand in for a king. A child sits on each end of a wobbly pew, both straddling the board between their knobby knees, with captured pieces guarded in their laps. A five-year-old kid in a threadbare Denver Broncos No. 7 jersey competes against an eleven-year-old in a frayed T-shirt that reads "J'Adore Paris." Most of the kids are barefoot. Some wear flip-flops. One has on black wing tips with no laces.

It is rapid-fire street chess. When more than a few seconds elapse without a move, there is a palpable restlessness. It is remarkably quiet except for the thud of one piece slaying another and the occasional dispute over the location of a piece on a chessboard so faded that the dark spaces are barely distinguishable from the light ones. Surrender is signaled by a clattering of captured pieces on the board. A new match begins immediately without the slightest celebration.

Coach Robert Katende is here. So are Benjamin and Ivan and Brian. And up near the pulpit sits Phiona. One of two girls in the room, Phiona is juggling three matches at once and dominating them with her aggressive style, checkmating her young opponents while drawing a flower in the dirt on the floor with her toe. Phiona is fourteen, and her stone face gives no sign that the next day she will travel to Siberia to compete against the very best chess players in the world.

•   •   •

Ice? The opening ceremonies at the 2010 Chess Olympiad take place in an ice arena. Phiona has never seen ice. There are also lasers and dancers inside bubbles and people costumed as chess pieces marching around on a giant chessboard. Phiona watches it all with her hands cupping her cheeks, as if in a wonderland. She asks if this happens every night in this place, and she is told by her coach no, the arena normally serves as a home for hockey, concerts, and the circus. Phiona has never heard of those things.

She returns to the hotel, which at fifteen floors is the tallest building Phiona has ever entered. She rides the elevator with trepidation. She stares out of her room window amazed by how people on the ground look so tiny from the sixth floor. She takes a long shower, washing away the slum.

•   •   •

Phiona Mutesi is the ultimate underdog. To be African is to be an underdog in the world. To be Ugandan is to be an underdog in Africa. To be from Katwe is to be an underdog in Uganda. And finally, to be female is to be an underdog in Katwe.

She wakes at five each morning to begin a two-hour trek through Katwe to fill a jug with drinkable water, walking through lowland that is often so severely flooded by Uganda's torrential rains that many residents sleep in hammocks near their ceilings to avoid drowning. There are no sewers, and the human waste from downtown Kampala is dumped directly into the slum. There is no sanitation. Flies are everywhere. The stench is appalling.

Phiona walks past dogs, rats, and long-horned cattle, all competing with her to survive in a cramped space that grows more crowded every minute. She navigates carefully through this place where women are valued for little more than sex and child-care, where 50 percent of teen girls are mothers. It is a place where everybody is on the move but nobody ever leaves; it is said that if you are born in Katwe you die in Katwe, from disease or violence or neglect. Whenever Phiona gets scared on these journeys, she thinks of another test of survival. "Chess is a lot like my life," she says through an interpreter. "If you make smart moves you can stay away from danger, but you know any bad decision could be your last."

Phiona and her family have relocated inside Katwe six times in four years, once because all of their possessions were stolen, another time because their hut was crumbling. Their current home is a ten-foot-by-ten-foot room, its only window covered by sheet metal. The walls are brick, the roof corrugated tin held up by spindly wood beams. A curtain is drawn across the doorway when the door is open, as it always is during the sweltering daytime in this country bisected by the equator. Laundry hangs on wash lines crisscrossing the room. The walls are bare, except for etched phone numbers. There is no phone.

The contents of Phiona's home are: two water jugs, wash bin, small charcoal stove, teapot, a few plates and cups, toothbrush, tiny mirror, Bible, and two musty mattresses. The latter suffice for the five people who regularly sleep in the shack: Phiona, mother Harriet, teenage brothers Brian and Richard, and her six-year-old niece, Winnie. Pouches of curry powder, salt and tea leaves are the only hints of food.

•   •   •

Phiona enters the competition venue, an indoor tennis arena packed with hundreds of chessboards, and quickly notices that she is among the youngest of more than 1,000 players from 149 countries. She is told that this is the most accomplished collection of chess talent ever assembled, which makes her nervous. She is the second-seeded player for the Ugandan team, but she isn't playing against kids anymore; her competitors are women. She keeps thinking to herself, Do I really belong here?

Her first opponent is Dina Kagramanov, the Canadian national champion. Kagramanov, born in Baku, Azerbaijan, the hometown of former men's world champion Garry Kasparov, learned the game at age six. She is competing in her third Olympiad and, at twenty-four, has been playing elite chess longer than Phiona has been alive.

Kagramanov preys on Phiona's inexperience, setting a trap early and gaining a pawn advantage that Phiona stubbornly tries and fails to reverse. After her win, Kagramanov is shocked to learn that this is Phiona's first international match against an adult. "She's a sponge," Kagramanov says. "She picks up on whatever information you give her, and she uses it against you. Anybody can be taught moves and how to react to those moves, but to reason like she does at her age is a gift that gives her the potential for greatness."

·   ·   ·

When asked about early memories, Phiona can recall only loss. "I remember I went to my dad's village when I was about three years old to see him when he was very sick, and a week later he died of AIDS," she says. "After the funeral my family stayed in the village for a few weeks, and one morning when I woke up, my older sister, Juliet, told me she was feeling a headache. We got some herbs and gave them to her, and then she went to sleep. The following morning we found her dead in the bed. That's what I remember."

She tells also of being gravely ill when she was eight. Harriet begged her sister for money to take Phiona to the hospital, and though they were never given a diagnosis, Harriet believes her daughter had malaria. Phiona lost consciousness, doctors removed fluid from her spine, and Harriet was sure she'd have to bury another daughter. She later told Phiona, "You died for two days."

Harriet, who is often sick, is sometimes gone from the shack for days trying to make money for her family's daily meal of rice and tea. She wakes at two A.M. to walk five kilometers and buy the avocados and eggplants that she resells at a street market. Phiona, who never knows when her mother will return, is left to care for her siblings.

Phiona does not know her birthday. Nobody bothers to record such things in Katwe. There are few calendars. Fewer clocks. Most people don't know the date or the day of the week. Every day is just like the last.

For her entire life Phiona's main challenge has been to find food. One afternoon in 2005, when she was just nine but had already dropped out of school because her family couldn't afford it, she secretly followed Brian out of their shack in hopes he might lead to the first meal of the day. Brian had recently taken part in a project run by Sports Outreach Institute, a Christian mission that works to provide relief and religion through sports to the world's poorest people. Phiona watched Brian enter a dusty hallway, sit on a bench, and begin playing with some black and white objects. Phiona had never seen anything like these pieces, and she thought they were beautiful. She peeked around a corner again and again, fascinated by the game and also wondering if there might be some food there. Suddenly, she was spotted. "Young girl," said Coach Robert. "Come in. Don't be afraid."

•　　　•　　　•

She is lucky to be here. Uganda's women's team has never participated in an Olympiad before because it is expensive. But this year, according to members of the Ugandan Chess Federation, the president of FIDE, chess's governing body, is funding their trip. Phiona needs breaks like that.

On the second day of matches, she arrives early to explore. She sees Afghan women dressed in burkas, Indian women in saris, and Bolivian women in ponchos and black bowler hats. She spots a blind player and wonders how that is possible. She sees an Iraqi kneel and begin to pray toward Mecca. As she approaches her table, Phiona is asked to produce her credential to prove she is actually a competitor, perhaps because she looks so young or perhaps because with her short hair, baggy sweater, and sweatpants, she is mistaken for a boy.

Before her match begins against Elaine Lin Yu-Tong of Taiwan, Phiona slips off her sneakers. She isn't comfortable playing chess in shoes. Midway through the game, Phiona makes a tactical error, costing her two pawns. Her opponent makes a similar blunder later, but Phiona doesn't realize it until it's too late. From then on, she stares crestfallen at the board as the rest of the moves play out predictably, and she loses a match she thinks she should have won. Phiona leaves the table and bolts to the parking lot. Katende warned her never to go off on her own, but she boards a shuttle bus alone and returns to the hotel, then runs to her room and bawls into her pillow. Later that evening, Katende tries his best to comfort her, but Phiona is inconsolable. It is the only time chess has ever brought her to tears. In fact, she cannot remember the last time she cried.

.   .   .

Robert Katende was a bastard child who lived his early years with his grandmother in the village of Kiboga, outside Kampala. It wasn't until he was reunited with his mother in Kampala's Nakulabye slum, when he was four, that he learned his first name. Until then he'd been known only as Katende.

Robert's mother died in 1990, when he was eight. He then began a decade-long odyssey from aunt to aunt and from school to school. He'd started playing soccer as a small boy in Kiboga, kicking a ball made of banana leaves. He grew into a center forward of such speed and skill that whenever his guardian of the moment could not afford to send him to school, a headmaster would hear of his soccer prowess and usher him in through a back door.

When Robert was fifteen, he suffered a severe head injury crashing into a goalkeeper. He lapsed into a coma, and everyone at school assumed he was dead. Robert emerged from the coma the next morning but spent three months in the hospital, where doctors told him he would never play soccer again. They were wrong.

Nine months after his injury, despite excruciating headaches, Robert returned to the soccer field. The game provided the only money he could earn. After a club soccer match in 2003, his coach told him about a job at Sports Outreach, and Robert, a born-again Christian, found his calling. He started playing for the ministry's team and was also assigned to Katwe, where he began drawing kids from the slum with the promise of soccer and postgame porridge. After several months, he noticed some children just watching from the sidelines, and he searched for a way to engage them. He found a solution in a nearly forgotten relic, a chess set given to him by a friend back in secondary school. "I had my doubts about chess in Katwe," Katende admits. "With their education and their environment, I wondered, Can these kids really play this game?"

Katende started offering chess after soccer games, beginning with a group of six boys who came to be known as the Pioneers. Two years later, the program had twenty-five children. That's when a barefoot nine-year-old girl in a torn and muddied skirt peeked into the entryway, and Coach Robert beckoned her inside.

•   •   •

Chess. Chess. Chess. After a long day at the Olympiad, the players return to the hotel to talk about, what else, chess. If they are not talking chess, they are playing it.

Dina Kagramanov approaches Phiona in the hotel lobby and hands her two books on advanced chess. Then, with Katende interpreting, the two players break down their first-round match, Kagramanov explaining the strategy behind her own moves and asking about the decisions Phiona made instinctively.

Like each day she will spend in Siberia, Phiona is engulfed by chess, pausing only to visit the hotel restaurant where she dines three times a day at an all-you-can-eat buffet. At the first few meals Phiona makes herself sick by overeating. Even during dinner, chess moves are replayed with salt and pepper shakers.

•   •   •

"When I first saw chess, I thought, What could make all these kids so silent?" Phiona recalls. "Then I watched them play the game and get happy and excited, and I wanted a chance to be that happy."

Katende showed Phiona the pieces and explained how each was restricted by rules about how it could move. The pawns. The rooks. The bishops. The knights. The king. And finally the queen, the most powerful piece on the board. How could Phiona have imagined at the time where those thirty-two pieces and sixty-four squares would deliver her?

Phiona started walking six kilometers every day to play chess. During her early development, she played too recklessly. She often sacrificed crucial pieces in risky attempts to defeat her opponents as quickly as possible, even when playing black–which means going second and taking a defensive posture to open the match. Says Phiona, "I must have lost my first fifty matches before Coach Robert persuaded me to act more like a girl and play with calm and patience."

The first match Phiona ever won was against Joseph Asaba, a young boy who had beaten her before by utilizing a tactic called the Fool's Mate, a humiliating scheme that can produce victory in as few as four moves. One day Joseph wasn't aware that Katende had prepared Phiona with a defense against the Fool's Mate that would capture Joseph's queen. When Phiona finally checkmated Joseph, she didn't even know it until Joseph began sobbing because he had lost to a girl. While other girls in the project were afraid to play against boys, Phiona relished it. Katende eventually introduced Phiona to Ivan Mutesasira and Benjamin Mukumbya, two of the project's strongest players, who agreed to tutor her. "When I first met Phiona, I took it for granted that girls are always weak, that girls can do nothing, but I came to realize that she could play as well as a boy," Ivan says. "She plays very aggressively, like a boy. She likes to attack, and when you play against her, it feels like she's always pushing you backward until you have nowhere to move."

News eventually spread around Katwe that Katende was part of an organization run by white people, known in Uganda as *mzungu*, and Harriet began hearing disturbing rumors. "My neighbors told me that chess was a white man's game and that if I let Phiona keep going there to play, that *mzungu* would take her away," she says. "But I could not afford to feed her. What choice did I have?"

Within a year, Phiona could beat her coach, and Katende knew it was time for her and the others to face better competition outside the project. He visited local boarding schools, where children from more privileged backgrounds refused to play the slum kids because they smelled bad and seemed like they might steal from them. But Katende kept asking until ten-year-old Phiona was playing against teens in fancy blazers and knickers, beating them soundly. Then she played university players, defeating them as well.

She has learned the game strictly through trial and error, trained by a coach who has played chess recreationally off and on for years, admitting he didn't even know all of the rules until he was given *Chess for Beginners* shortly after starting the project. Phiona plays on instinct instead of relying on opening and end-game theory like more refined players. She succeeds because she possesses that precious chess gene that allows her to envision the board many moves ahead and because she focuses on the game as if her life depended on it, which in her case might be true.

Phiona first won the Uganda women's junior championship in 2007, when she was eleven. She won that title three years in a row, and it would have been four, but the Uganda Chess Federation didn't have the funds to stage it in 2010. She is still so early in her learning curve that chess experts believe her potential is staggering. "To love the game as much as she does and already be a champion at her age means her future is much bigger than any girl I've ever known," says George Zirembuzi, Uganda's national team coach, who has trained with grandmasters in Russia. "When Phiona loses, she really feels hurt, and I like that, because that characteristic will help her keep thirsting to get better."

Although Phiona is already implausibly good at something she has no business even doing, she is, like most girls and women in Uganda, uncomfortable sharing what she's thinking. Normally, nobody cares. She tries to answer any questions about herself with a shrug. When Phiona is compelled to speak, she is barely audible and usually staring at her feet. She realizes that chess makes her stand out, which makes her a target in Katwe, among the most dangerous neighborhoods in Uganda. So she is conditioned to say as little as possible. "Her personality with the outside world is still quite reserved, because she feels inferior due to her background," Katende says. "But in chess I am always reminding her that anyone can lift a piece, because it is so light. What separates you is where you choose to put it down. Chess is the one thing in Phiona's life she can control. Chess is her one chance to feel superior."

•　　　•　　　•

Chess is not a spectator sport. During matches at the Olympiad, it is not uncommon for twenty minutes to elapse without a single move. Players often leave the table for a bathroom break or to get a cup of tea or to psych out an opponent by pretending that it isn't even necessary to sit at the board to conquer it. Phiona never leaves the table. She doesn't know what it means to psych out an opponent or, fortunately for her, what it means to be psyched out.

But she is restless. These games progress too slowly for her, nothing like chess back in Uganda. She has spent two matches fidgeting and slouching in her seat, desperate for her opponents to get on with it.

Wary after Phiona's breakdown following the second match, Katende is ruing the Uganda Chess Federation's decision to place Phiona as her team's no. 2 seed, where she must face the top players from other teams rather than lower-seeded players with less experience, whom he suspects she could be defeating.

Phiona's third match is against a women's grandmaster from Egypt, Khaled Mona. Pleased by Mona's quick pace of play, Phiona gets lured into her opponent's rhythm and plays too fast, leading to fatal errors. Mona plays flawlessly and needs just twenty-four moves to win. When Phiona concedes after less than an hour, Katende looks worried, but Phiona recognizes that on this day she's been beaten by a better player. Instead of being discouraged, she is inspired. Phiona walks straight over to Katende and says, "Coach, I will be a grandmaster someday."

She looks relieved, and a bit astonished, to have spoken those words.

•   •   •

Chess had transported Phiona out of Katwe once before. In August 2009 she traveled with Benjamin and Ivan to Juba, Sudan, where the three represented Uganda in Africa's International

Children's Chess Tournament. Several other players who had qualified to join them on the national team refused to go with the slum kids.

It was Phiona's first trip out of Uganda, her first visit to an airport. "It felt like taking someone from the nineteenth century and plunging them into the present world," says Godfrey Gali, the Uganda Chess Federation's general secretary. "Everything at the airport was so strange to her; security cameras, luggage conveyors, so many white people. Then when the plane flew above the clouds, Phiona asked me, 'Mr. Gali, are we about to reach heaven?' She was totally sincere."

At their hotel in Sudan, Phiona had her own bed for the first time in her life. She had never before used a toilet that flushed. At the hotel restaurant she was handed a huge menu, a strange notion for someone who had never had a choice of what to eat at a meal before. "I could never have imagined this world I was visiting," Phiona says. "I felt like a queen."

In the tournament, the Ugandan trio, by far the youngest team in the competition, played against teams from sixteen other African nations. In her opening match, Phiona faced a Kenyan who had a reputation as the best young female player in Africa. Despite her hands trembling with each early move, Phiona built a position advantage, isolated the enemy king, then checkmated her surprised opponent. Phiona won all four matches she played. Benjamin and Ivan were undefeated as well, and the three kids from Katwe won the team championship and a trophy too big to fit into any of their tiny backpacks.

A stunned Russian chess administrator, Igor Bolotinsky, approached Phiona after the tournament and told her, "I have a son who is an international chess master, and he was not as good at your age as you are."

When the Ugandan delegation returned to Kampala, Katende met them at the airport. He tried to congratulate Phiona, but she was too busy laughing and teasing her teammates, something he had never seen her do before. For once, he realized, Phiona was just being the kid that she is.

But as Phiona, Benjamin, and Ivan were driven back into Katwe for a victory celebration, a psychological shift took place. Windows in their van were reflexively shut and backpacks pushed out of sight. Smiling faces turned solemn, the mask of the slum. The three children discussed who would keep the trophy, and it was decided that none of them could because it would surely be stolen. They were greeted with cheers and chants of "Uganda-Uganda-Uganda!"

But they were also met with some strange questions: Did you fly on the silver bird? Did you stay indoors or in the bush? Why did you come back here? "It struck me how difficult it must have been for them to go to another world and return," says Rodney Suddith, the director of Sports Outreach. "Sudan might as well be the moon to people in the slum. The three kids couldn't share their experience with the others because they just couldn't connect. It puzzled me at first, and then it made me sad, and then I wondered, Is what they have done really a good thing?"

As Phiona left the celebration headed for her home that night, someone excitedly asked her, "What is the first thing you're going to say to your mother?"

"I need to ask her," Phiona said, "'Do we have enough food for breakfast?'"

•　　　•　　　•

Who is she? Is Phiona trying to prove that she's no better than anyone else or that she's better than everyone else? Imagine that psychological tug-of-war inside the mind of the least secure creature on earth, a teenage girl, as she sits at a chessboard nearly 5,000 miles from home.

Phiona's opponent in her fourth match, an Angolan, Sonia Rosalina, keeps staring at Phiona's eyes, which Rosalina will later say are the most competitive she has faced in chess. Phiona is behind for most of the match, but refuses to surrender. She battles back and has a chance to force a draw in the end game, but at the critical moment, she plays too passively, too defensively, not like herself. After more than three hours and 144 moves, Phiona grudgingly submits, admitting that she didn't have her "courage" when she needed it most. She promises herself that she will never let that happen again.

.   .   .

No matter how far chess has taken Phiona Mutesi, a ten-foot-by-ten-foot home in Katwe remains her destination, the life of the ultimate underdog is still her routine. Although Phiona is back in school through a grant from Sports Outreach, she is just learning to read and write. Also, Phiona faces a potential hazard that could make her life even more challenging: Her father died of AIDS, and her mother worries her constant illnesses are because she is HIV-positive, but she is too afraid to be tested. Phiona has never been tested either.

Phiona says that her dream for the future is to build a house outside Katwe for her mother so that she would never have to move again. When Harriet is asked if her daughter can escape the slum, she says, "I have never thought about that." Ugandan universities are not handing out scholarships for chess, and, without benefactors stepping in again, a trip to the 2012 Olympiad in Istanbul, Turkey, is unlikely.

Katende, when pressed to describe Phiona's realistic blueprint out of Katwe, can come up only with a vision he's had about starting an academy where the children of the chess project earn money teaching the game to kids of wealthy families. He says he hopes through her chess that Phiona can begin to blaze a trail out of the slum for all of his chess kids to follow. To do that, though, Phiona must produce on a world stage like no other Ugandan, man or woman, has ever achieved.

•   •   •

September 30, 2010, in Khanty-Mansiysk is cold and dreary, like every other day at the Olympiad. Phiona hates Russian weather but loves the hotel room, the clean water, the three meals a day. She is dreading her return home in four days, when she must begin scrapping for food again.

She sits at the chessboard for her fifth match wearing a white knit hat, a black overcoat, and woolly beige boots that are several sizes too large, all gifts from various *mzungu*. Her opponent is an Ethiopian, Haregeweyn Abera, who, like Phiona, is an African teenager. For the first time in the tournament, Phiona sees someone across the table she can relate to. She sees herself. For the first time in the tournament, she is not intimidated at all.

Phiona plays black but remains patient and gradually shifts the momentum during the first twenty moves of the match until she creates an opening to attack. Suddenly she feels like she is back at Agape church, pushing and pushing and pushing Abera's pieces into retreat until there is nowhere left for Abera to move.

Abera extends her hand in defeat. Phiona tries and fails to suppress her gap-toothed grin, then rises and skips out of the hall into the frigid Siberian air. This dismissed girl from a dismissed world cocks her head back and unleashes a blissful shriek into the slate gray sky, loud enough to startle players still inside the arena.

D Magazine

WINNER—PROFILE WRITING

There's a shadow war going on, and it's raging across computer networks. One of the most fearsome antagonists in this conflict is the group known as Anonymous. In this profile of Barrett Brown, D Magazine named—and exposed—one of its animating spirits. Brown is brilliant, infuriating, dangerous, and funny, and Tim Rogers distilled his essence in this complex story from the bowels of the Internet. If you want to understand what's happening in the world of hacktivism, follow Rogers down the rabbit hole into the mind of Barrett Brown. Founded in 1974, D Magazine covers Dallas–Fort Worth, and Rogers is not only its star writer but its editor.

Tim Rogers

He Is Anonymous

T he night before Michael Isikoff came to Dallas, I got an e-mail from Barrett Brown. "Apparently Isikoff is freaked out about having another journalist here," it said. "But I'll secretly record the proceedings and provide to you."

A little context: Michael Isikoff is a former investigative reporter for *Newsweek*. Now he's a correspondent for NBC News. He flew in from Washington, D.C., in late February with a producer and a cameraman to talk to Brown about his involvement with a notorious international group of hackers called Anonymous that recently used their Low Orbit Ion Cannon to bring down the websites of MasterCard and Visa and the Swedish government, among others, because the institutions had made moves hostile to WikiLeaks and its founder, Julian Assange. It's complicated—as Isikoff would learn. But more on that in a moment.

Me, I first encountered Brown in 1998, when he was a sixteen-year-old intern at the *Met*, a now-defunct alternative weekly where I worked. Brown and I had not kept in contact, but last year he returned to Dallas from New York City, we got reacquainted, and he wrote a story for this magazine. I'd been talking with him for a few weeks about his work with Anonymous, about how they'd exposed a scheme by a government cyber-security contractor to conspire with Bank of America to ruin the careers of journalists sympathetic to WikiLeaks, about how Anonymous helped the protesters in Tunisia and other Arab countries. I wasn't about to miss out on the surreal scene of Isikoff and a television crew descending on Brown's apartment.

I had been to Brown's Uptown bachelor pad before. The 378-square-foot efficiency was dimly lit and ill-kept. Dirty dishes were piled high in the sink. A taxidermied bobcat lay on the kitchen counter. Brown is an inveterate smoker—Marlboro 100s, weed, whatever is at hand—and the place smelled like it. An overflowing ashtray sat on his work table, which stood just a few feet from his bed in the apartment's "living room." Two green plastic patio chairs faced the desk. I left with the feeling that I needed a bath.

On the morning of Isikoff's visit, though, I see that much has changed. Brown's mother, having heard that company was coming, paid to have the carpet shampooed. The kitchen is now tidy. The bobcat has been hung on a wall, replaced on the kitchen counter by a bowl of fresh fruit. A lamp casts a warm glow on Brown's work table. His twenty-four-year-old girlfriend, a graphic designer named Nikki Loehr, sits on his bed with a laptop. She borrowed a framed Peter Saul drawing worth tens of thousands of dollars from her client, Dallas art dealer Chris Byrne, to spruce up the place. Brown, of course, would have none of it. Bobcat? Yes. Fancy artwork? Television viewers might get the wrong impression. The drawing sits in his closet.

Isikoff's cameraman and producer are the first through the door. Then the man himself, suited, gray hair, short. We shake hands. It feels awkward.

Ever the congenial host, Brown introduces us. "Tim's a friend," he says to Isikoff. "He's writing a story. You guys can have a turf war if you want, but I'm on day four of withdrawals from opiates, so I don't want to get involved." Only, because he speaks in a low, rapid baritonal mumble, like he is the world's worst auctioneer, it comes out: "Timsafriendheswritingastoryyou guyscanhaveaturfwarifyouwantbutImondayfourofwithdrawal fromopiatessoIdontwanttogetinvolved."

Having mumbled the introduction, Brown steps out onto the tiny second-floor patio to smoke a cigarette, leaving me with Loehr, Isikoff, and his two-man crew. The guys from D.C. stare at me.

"What did he just say?" the producer asks.

"Barrett said that I'm a friend of his and that he's on day four of withdrawals from opiates."

Brown has used heroin at various points in his life. On the night about a year ago that he met Loehr, in fact, at the Quarter Bar on McKinney Avenue, he told her he was an ex-junkie. "Ex" is a relative prefix. To manage his addiction, Brown was prescribed Suboxone, a semisynthetic opioid that is meant to be taken orally, but he had been dissolving the film strips in water and shooting the solution to produce a more satisfying high. On the Sunday before Isikoff's visit, Brown showed me the track marks on his arm. He said he had run out of Suboxone, though, and was saving his last dose because he didn't want to suffer through withdrawals during his big television interview. Then Isikoff rescheduled from Tuesday to Thursday. Brown couldn't wait. Now he is hurting.

Isikoff and his crew seem to have trouble processing it all. Was Brown kidding about the drugs? Who is this friend again? And will he have to interpret everything Brown says? They are too befuddled to fight any "turf war." In any case, Brown returns from his smoke break and launches into a primer on Anonymous, sending the cameraman scrambling to set up his lights. The producer clips mics to Brown and Isikoff. I slip into the kitchen, where I can eat the grapes that Brown's mother bought for him while I watch the proceedings.

For the next five hours, Brown explains the concept of Anonymous (an interview session topped off with a B-roll stroll for the cameraman on the nearby Katy Trail). Several factors complicate this process. First, Brown lives under the flight path to Love Field. Southwest Airlines jets continually drown out Brown's mumblings, forcing the producer to close the patio's sliding glass door. The bright camera lights proceed to heat up the small room in no time. Exacerbating the stuffiness, Brown chain-smokes flamboyantly throughout the entire interview.

Second, Brown's computer setup makes it tough to ride shotgun. His parents gave him a large Toshiba Qosmio laptop, but Brown used it to play video games before spilling Dr Pepper on the keyboard. It is out of commission. He does his work on a Sony Vaio notebook that's so small it looks like a toy. Brown claims to have 20/16 vision, so the tiny screen doesn't bother him, but Isikoff has to squint and lean in as Brown takes him on a tour of Internet Relay Chat rooms, or IRC, where Anonymous does much of its work. (I tag along, from my iPad in the kitchen, just a few feet away. When they enter a room where Anonymous discusses its operations in Libya, I type, "Say hi to Isikoff for me." Isikoff: "Who's that?" Brown, laughing: "That's a writer I know." As they click over to another room, I pop in again: "Isikoff is clearly a government agent." So I don't help, either.)

Finally, there is the inscrutable topic itself. Anonymous is sometimes referred to in the mainstream media as a group or a collective—the *Christian Science Monitor* went with "a shadowy circle of activists"—but Anonymous, per se, doesn't exist. It has no hierarchy, no leadership. So even though Bloomberg and others have called Brown a spokesman for the group (which, again, isn't a group at all), Brown denies having any position within Anonymous.

"Anonymous is a process more than it is a thing," Brown tells Isikoff. "I can't speak on behalf of Anonymous, because there's no one who can authorize me to do that."

When he explains Anonymous to a newbie, Brown relishes the inevitable confusion and will toggle between sincerity and irony to heighten it. Until you've spent some time with him, it's hard to know what to believe. When you've gotten to know him better, it's even harder.

"You have to remember," Brown says, reclining in the green lawn chair, one arm slung over its back, a cigarette dangling between his fingers, "we're the Freemasons. Only, we've got a sense of humor. You have to wield power with a sense of humor. Otherwise you become the FBI." Here Brown is half-kidding.

Later, when Isikoff gets confused by the online lingo used by Anonymous, Brown says, "I think we've done more than Chaucer to enrich the English language. We should get a medal. Where's the medal, Michael?" Here he is entirely kidding.

I think.

•   •   •

Brown first began collaborating online with Anons in 2006, though an informal organization didn't exist at the time—much less a formal one that denies its own existence. These were just kids idling on websites such as EncyclopediaDramatica.com and the random imageboard /b/ on 4chan.org. They were interested in arcane Japanese web culture and, of course, pictures of boobs. "Everyone there was anonymous," Brown says, intending a lowercase "a." "It just started as a joke."

Brown was part of what he calls "an elite team of pranksters" that did whatever they could to make people miserable on Second Life. They developed a weapon that propagated giant Marios until certain areas of the online universe crashed. They would go into a concert and produce a loud screaming that no one could stop. They went into nightclubs for furries, people who get off by wearing animal costumes, and hassled them.

But Anonymous, with a capital "A," didn't coalesce into a recognizable phenomenon until 2008, when the Church of Scientology tried to remove an embarrassing YouTube video of a wild-eyed Tom Cruise talking about how awesome Scientology is. Anonymous claimed the move was censorship and, in response, published its own YouTube video. Over images of swiftly moving clouds, a computer-generated voice declared war on the church. That war, Project Chanology, continues to this day.

Anonymous's efforts to bring down the Church of Scientology and other enemies have evolved to include all manner of tactics, both online and off-, but the group's main weapon is the Low Orbit Ion Cannon. (For clarity's sake, I will hereinafter refer to Anonymous as a group, even though various members of the group have repeatedly stressed to me that it isn't one.) The Low Orbit Ion Cannon, or LOIC, is a piece of software. Right now, you can download it from any number of easily accessible servers and install it on your computer. Launch it, and you just joined a botnet.

A botnet is a number of computers—could be hundreds, could be tens of thousands spread across the planet—that follow the instructions of a central command. Until Anonymous came along, botnets were generally assembled by bad guys, organizations like the Russian mafia, Chinese hackers. They build botnets on the sly, installing malware on computers that turns them into zombies without their owners' knowledge. Each zombie can fire thousands of requests per second at a target website. So while you're working on that cover sheet for your TPS report, your computer is part of a joint effort to overwhelm a company's server and crash its website. That effort to crash a site is called a Distributed Denial of Service attack, or DDoS. The bad guys use DDoS attacks to extort money, but they can also use their botnets to send spam and steal people's identities. In 2009, the antivirus software firm Symantec said it had detected nearly 7 million botnets on the Internet.

Anonymous was the first group to build an operational *voluntary* botnet. By running the LOIC on your computer, you are, essentially, declaring your allegiance to Anonymous. You donate part of your computer's processing power to the cause. That cause—or, if you prefer, the target—is determined by rough consensus among Anons.

If the Church of Scientology gave Anonymous its first major target the group could agree on, then Visa and MasterCard gave Anonymous its first big kill, the trophy that made the world take notice. Last year, at the urging of Senator Joe Lieberman, who heads the Senate Committee on Homeland Security, PayPal froze WikiLeaks' account, and Amazon booted the organization off its servers. Visa and MasterCard stopped processing donations to the organization, saying in a press release that they were taking this action because WikiLeaks was engaged in illegal activity. Never mind that WikiLeaks had not even been charged with a crime. Anonymous responded with Operation Payback.

Which member of Anonymous first suggested that MasterCard should be a target of the LOIC? There's no telling. But they discussed it in an Internet Relay Chat channel that anyone could have joined—that, in fact, anyone can still join. Anonymous uses IRC because it conceals identities and because it establishes a technical barrier to entry. Though anyone *can* join the conversation, only a certain type of person *will*. There's software to download. There's lingo to learn. And so on.

Sometimes Anonymous will actually conduct an online poll to determine the target of a DDoS. It's very democratic. But the final decision about where to point the Low Orbit Ion Cannon is made by an IRC channel operator, an Anon who has the power to declare the official topic of the channel. As with the animals on Orwell's farm, all Anonymous are equal, but some are more equal than others. It's hard, obviously, to get a reliable estimate on the number of those elite Anons who are channel operators. Brown told me it could be a few dozen. When those—don't call them leaders—change the topic of an IRC channel, all the LOIC-armed computers linked to that channel will automatically fire at the target. That's when embarrassing things happen to ill-prepared companies (and governments, too).

The great thing about Anonymous' botnet is it never sleeps. With involuntary botnets, users turn off their zombie computers when they go to bed at night. The botnet army never fights at full strength. Anonymous' voluntary botnet might be small, but it packs a powerful punch.

When the Anons working on Operation Payback pointed the LOIC at MasterCard's website on December 8, 2010, it crashed in about five minutes. Visa crumbled in thirty seconds. Anonymous didn't target the servers that process credit card transactions, just the companies' websites. The key to the attack was the realization by Anonymous that Visa and MasterCard had left themselves vulnerable by locating all their servers in the same general area. Anonymous had discussed attacking Amazon, too, because it booted WikiLeaks off its servers, but Amazon houses its servers in data centers all over the globe. Take one down, and the traffic gets rerouted. Amazon stays online. Not so with Visa and MasterCard.

How many computers did it take to bring down the credit card giants? It's impossible to peg a precise number. But during the four weeks when Operation Payback was at its height, Gregg Housh says the LOIC was downloaded 60,000 times. Housh is thirty-four and lives in the Boston area, but he was born in Bedford and lived in North Texas until he was sixteen. He is intimately aware of how Anonymous works but says he doesn't participate in any of its illegal activities. In the days following the attack on MasterCard, the task of explaining all the foregoing to reporters largely fell to him. He doesn't mind speaking to the press and using his real name because, as an organizer of Project Chanology (he and a small group of collaborators posted that first Anonymous YouTube video with the clouds), his name became public in lawsuits filed by the Church of Scientology. Too, he spent three months in federal prison in his twenties for software piracy. Authorities are already well-acquainted with him.

"Everyone just knows that Gregg is willing to talk to The Man," Housh says. "A lot of news organizations, the *New York Times*, don't want to go with anonymous sources. They have policies against it." On December 10, two days after Operation Payback hit MasterCard, Housh did thirty-seven interviews. "I'll tell you, man, I work from home, so it makes it a little easier for me to do that, but it was becoming too much. And in comes the calvary, Barrett, to take some of the load. That was nice."

Housh met Brown online in February of last year, after Brown had written a story for the *Huffington Post* explaining Anonymous' actions in Australia. The government there was attempting to ban three specific forms of Internet pornography: small-breasted porn (deemed by the Australian Classification Board too similar to underage porn), female ejaculation (deemed to be a form of urination), and cartoon porn (duh). Anonymous, in response, launched Operation Titstorm, which included not only a DDoS attack that brought down the government's main website but a torrent of porn-related e-mails, faxes, and prank phone calls to government officials. In his *HuffPo* piece, Brown explained the larger context of Anonymous' actions. After referring to William Gibson's 1984 sci-fi novel, *Neuromancer*, which popularized the term "cyberspace," Brown wrote the following in an essay titled "Anonymous, Australia, and the Inevitable Fall of the Nation-State":

> Having taken a long interest in the subculture from which Anonymous is derived and the new communicative structures that make it possible, I am now certain that this phenomenon is among the most important and under-reported social developments to have occurred in decades, and that the development in question promises to threaten the institution of the nation-state and perhaps even someday replace it as the world's most fundamental and relevant method of human organization.

Bear in mind that Brown was talking about sending pictures of women with small boobs to government officials. In Australia.

"It was an interesting piece about nation-states and about their slow decline," Housh says. "I found some of what he said to be quite outlandish and some of what he said to be quite interesting. You look at a few of these that are going on right now"—meaning Tunisia, Egypt, Libya, and others—"and he might have been a little prescient."

Housh sent Brown an e-mail saying that he liked the *Huffington Post* piece and that Brown seemed to understand Anonymous better than most journalists who'd written on the topic.

Brown responded: "That's because I am Anonymous."

. . .

A week before the Michael Isikoff interview, Barrett Brown and I are sitting on the rooftop patio at the Quarter Bar. Or, rather, I am sitting. Brown is pacing like a caged animal, chain-smoking, and drinking a Cape Cod. He likes the Quarter Bar because he doesn't own a car and he can walk here from his apartment with his Sony Vaio notebook and get work done while he smokes and drinks. The staff knows him.

It's a weekday, early. McKinney Avenue is beginning to flow with shiny cars headed north. We have the patio to ourselves. Brown is wearing cowboy boots and a blue pin-striped oxford sloppily tucked into blue jeans. He wears the same outfit every day. He owns a dozen identical blue pin-striped oxford shirts. He wears only boots because he hasn't bothered to learn to tie shoelaces properly. (When Nikki Loehr told me that being Brown's girlfriend can be exhausting because she must work to keep him on track, citing as one example of Brown's ADD-powered absent-mindedness his inability to "tie his own shoes," I thought she was kidding. She wasn't.)

As Brown paces and recounts some of the highlights he's amassed in just twenty-nine years, it's tempting to brand him as a fabulist. He'll begin an anecdote with "I once had to jump out of a moving cab in Dar es Salaam." But then he mentions that he went to Preston Hollow Elementary School with George W. Bush's twin daughters. My mother taught the Bush twins at Preston Hollow. I tell him this, and he remembers my mother.

"I was the poet laureate of Preston Hollow!" he says. In third grade, he tells me, he used a phone in the principal's office to order a pizza from Domino's, which he had delivered to his classroom. He wasn't trying to make trouble. He simply didn't know there was a rule against ordering pizza. But his English teacher flipped, sent him to the principal's office, where he was held in a sort of in-school suspension during which he wrote a poem about getting in trouble. "Ask your mother about me," Brown says.

Later that night, I call my mother, who taught him art. "Do you remember a kid named Barrett Brown from Preston Hollow?"

"Barrett Brown? Oh, my God," she says, instantly recalling an elementary student she taught more than twenty years ago. "I don't remember them all. But I remember him. Yes, he was the poet laureate. I don't have it anymore, but I kept that poem for years."

Having now had several corroborative conversations like the one with my mother, I am forced to conclude that most of what Brown says is accurate—if not believable.

He grew up comfortably in Highland Park. His father, Robert Brown, hailed from East Texas and came from a family of means. "I made a lot of money when I originally came to Dallas," Robert says. "I eventually had $50 million in real estate holdings all across the state. But I got caught up like a lot of people did in the eighties. I was highly leveraged, lost pretty much everything."

Partly due to the financial strain, Brown's parents divorced when he was seven. He and his mom shared a room in his grandmother's house for a few months, until his mom could get on her feet. Karen Lancaster says her son developed a capacity for moral outrage at an early age. "He was furious when he was six and found out there was no Santa Claus," she says. "He wasn't mad about there not being a Santa. He was upset with me. He said, 'You lied to me. How could you make up such a story?'"

Lancaster says her son had severe ADD and that the classroom was torture for him. But he read voraciously on his own, diving into Ayn Rand and Hunter S. Thompson while he was still in middle school.

About that time, Brown also began investigating the possibilities of online networks. This was circa 1995, before the Internet as we know it today existed. Back then, bulletin board systems ruled, chat rooms with their own phone numbers for dial-up access with a modem. At thirteen, Brown found a BBS that changed his life. It enabled him to talk to girls. Years later, he would use the experience as grist for an essay in the *New York Press*.

"Early in our communication," Brown wrote, "Tracy informed me that I could touch her breasts if I wanted to. I conveyed in turn that this would be to my satisfaction and that I would entertain other proposals of a similar nature. Over the next months, I was able to graduate to second base, to third, and finally to dry humping."

In high school, at the Episcopal School of Dallas, Brown continued to distinguish himself. Freshman year he and a friend formed the Objectivists Club. "They began their own civil disobedience then, unbeknownst to us," Lancaster says. "Ayn Rand was an atheist, and here he was in this Episcopal school. They decided not to sing hymns in chapel. So, of course, we got calls about that."

The following year, he got into trouble for having sex with an ESD girl on a school trip to New York. The administration couldn't prove that the act had occurred, though, so he was merely given in-school suspension (he passed the time by drawing comic books about World War II). That summer, in 1998, he landed the internship at the *Met*. In a brief "Meet the Intern" feature in the front of the paper, he was pictured wearing sunglasses. The copy read: "Barrett wears sunglasses indoors. He was a sophomore last year at the Episcopal School of Dallas, but he refuses to return next year. He has earned a reputation as a phlegmy young man for loudly clearing his throat and spitting in editors' personal trash cans. He claims to have lost his virginity in New York, on Broadway. And last week he wrecked his mom's Jeep Cherokee. We asked him what he's learned here at the *Met*, and Barrett said, 'How adults really act when they think kids aren't watching.' But Barrett's a smart, hard-working kid, and he'll always have our highest recommendation."

His mother saved that clipping. She says Brown's boast about his accomplishments in New York would have gotten him expelled if he hadn't decided to forgo his junior year and instead travel with his father to Dar es Salaam, Tanzania. It was there that Brown had to jump out of a moving cab—though because of the mumbling, it's not clear why. Dar es Salaam was a dangerous place in the summer of 1998. In August, two car bombs exploded at the U.S. embassies in Nairobi, Kenya, and Dar es Salaam, killing 224 people and wounding more than 5,000 others. For many Americans, it was the first time they heard the name Osama bin Laden. Brown says he saw corpses in the street.

The trip to Tanzania was supposed to be a profitable one for Robert Brown. He's a big-game hunter, and on previous expeditions there, he'd seen vast hardwood forests that had never been harvested. He and his partners brought over $1 million worth of sawmill equipment and planned to launch an export business. But the corrupt government ruined them. With seven shipping containers loaded with equipment sitting on the docks in Dar es Salaam, Robert Brown says he simply couldn't find the right official to bribe. As the project stalled, Barrett Brown found himself with plenty of time to conduct a dual-credit correspondence course online through Texas Tech, which allowed him to graduate high school and earn college credits. When his father's money finally ran out, they returned to the States.

Brown moved back in with his mother and got a job at the Inwood Theatre, where he made popcorn, took tickets, cleaned the theater. He remembers one night when the father of the ESD girl to whom he'd lost his virginity came in and was none too pleased to see him. When he wasn't working, he was reading. Or drinking whiskey with Hockaday girls who'd come over to his house after school.

Mirna Hariz was one of those girls. After Brown eventually got into UT Austin, she wound up there, too. "We all used to hang out at his house," she says. "One day he had a test. We said, 'Barrett, I thought you had a test right now.' He said, 'I'm not going.' We said, 'You're going to have to make it up?' He said, 'No. I'm not going to school anymore.' He never mentioned it again. That was just it."

After he dropped out, Brown bounced among New York City, Austin, and Zihuatanejo, taking on a succession of writing jobs and freelance gigs. He got fired from Nerve.com, he says, for "intransigence." He wrote copy for AOL—but then he stopped. In 2007, he published a book with Jon P. Alston called *Flock of Dodos: Behind Modern Creationism, Intelligent Design, and the Easter Bunny.* Alan Derschowitz described it as being "in the great tradition of debunkers with a sense of humor, from Thomas Paine to Mark Twain."

By December 2009, Brown was living on Hariz's couch in New York City. She had become a lawyer and had moved there to work on the lawsuit filed by emergency workers who were denied long-term medical coverage for ailments caused by inhaling what was left of the World Trade Center's Twin Towers. Hariz's apartment was in the Williamsburg neighborhood of Brooklyn.

"Mirna had two rules," Brown says. "'Don't shoot up, and don't f— girls on my bed.' I broke both those rules pretty quickly."

He didn't just break the rules. Again, he bragged about it—in a fashion. For the *New York Press* he wrote an anonymous story about an encounter in Hariz's apartment with a girl who asked him to pretend to rape her on their first date. An excerpt:

> The date was going well even before it started going memorably, which was bizarre, as I gave off every warning signal as to my failures as a person, like having to share a coffee mug of vodka with the girl because I'd accidentally broken all the glasses in the apartment. At some point I actually made her look at this video game I was playing, called Dwarf Fortress, in which I pretended that I was some large number of dwarves, all living together in a fortress. Eventually she relented and we had sex, which was probably for the best.

His date wrote a companion piece, also anonymously, in which she said, "There was something appealingly wholesome about him, so all-American—he was cowboy boots, medium-rare bacon cheeseburgers, and *Monday Night Football*—that I just couldn't resist."

Not every day in Williamsburg was so debauched. Hariz remembers coming home once to find Brown playing basketball with what she calls "street toughs." "There was the one skinny white guy playing with all these huge black guys," she says. "He leads this very Kerouac-seeming life. When he goes out, it's for adventure."

But Brown wasn't going out much. By this point, he'd become deeply involved with Anonymous's efforts to support WikiLeaks, spending marathon sessions hunched over his computer.

"I would try to get him to come out with me, go to a bar, but he wouldn't," Hariz says. Instead, Brown would stay home and shoot heroin. "When he's messed up, all he does is work. It's not like he's out there, partying it up, engaging in risky behavior. He's just working—while doing drugs. I'd get up, and he'd be sitting in front of his computer, with a cigarette hanging out of his mouth. When I'd get home, he'd be sitting in the same position, working. I'd go to bed at four in the morning, wake up, and he'd still be there."

This is when Brown wrote the *Huffington Post* article about Operation Titstorm and wound up admitting to Gregg Housh that he, too, was Anonymous. But Brown didn't come out publicly until just a few months ago, after the Operation Payback DDoS attacks on Visa and MasterCard and others. Dutch authorities quickly arrested a sixteen-year-old boy in The Hague, Netherlands, identifying him only as Jeroenz0r, an IRC operator (AKA one of the Anons that determines a target for the Low Orbit Ion Cannon). Anonymous decided that it had to get its message out quickly—the message being that MasterCard, according to Anonymous, was processing payments to the Ku Klux Klan but not to WikiLeaks, which Anonymous considers not just a kindred spirit but a legitimate journalistic enterprise. In fact, Housh has said that Anonymous launches DDoS attacks in some cases with the sole aim of spurring the press to ask questions, thereby giving Anonymous a forum in which to discuss its agenda.

With Operation Payback, Anonymous had created a huge forum. Yet it had only one real spokesman to take advantage of the opportunity, poor Gregg Housh, who was, let's not forget, trying to get some actual bills-paying work done at home when the media came calling.

Enter Barrett Brown, former poet laureate of Preston Hollow.

•   •   •

The promotion to unofficial spokesman for a nonentity might seem like a swell thing for Brown, something he could write home about, tell his parents to stop worrying. There are drawbacks, though.

First, and most obvious, the nonposition comes with a non-salary. Also no health benefits nor 401(k).

Second, he's now what Anons call a namefag. The term is not intrinsically derogatory. It just means that one has publicly identified oneself as Anonymous, using the name on one's birth certificate. I've talked to Anons on IRC who are quite happy with the work Housh and Brown have done to explain Anonymous to the media and, in Brown's case, write about the group and organize legal defense for members who have been raided. One Anonymous hacker told me that Housh and Brown "are strong observers only, giving them the right to identities." But then there are those who detest namefags.

"It isn't cool at all being this person," Housh says. "About 75 percent of the people involved in things are happy someone is trying to keep the media straight. Fifteen percent don't give a shit either way and just shrug people like me off as namefags and media whores. The other 10 percent spend time every day trying to make your life hell, attacking you, telling everyone lies about you."

Housh says disgruntled Anons have handed over fake chat logs to the FBI purporting to show that he runs Anonymous. Anons have dropped dox on Brown, too, published his personal information in an effort to discredit and embarrass him.

And it's not just the lack of anonymity that riles up that 10 percent of Anonymous. Brown believes that Anonymous is a force for good, that it can and should be used to topple oppressive regimes, eradicate the necessarily corrupt nation-state. Brown has been at the vanguard of Anonymous' operations in Tunisia and other Arab nations, writing guides to street fighting and first aid that Anonymous posted on government websites it had taken control of. Much was made about how well-organized the Egyptian protestors were because they could coordinate their efforts on Facebook. Partly that's thanks to Anonymous Facebook spammers that mass-invited thousands of Egyptians into the protest groups.

This sort of work gets an Anon branded as a moralfag. I spoke online with the user who runs the Twitter account @FakeGregg-Housh. The user said the real Gregg Housh would identify her as a woman named Jennifer Emrick, but the user identified himself as Donald Wassalanya, a name that I could not find in public records. The real Housh said the user could be Emrick—or someone else. Other Anons on IRC told me Emrick was Fake Housh. In any case, Fake Housh seems to speak for that 10 percent.

"Gregg would have ya live in a world where Anon is a force for good, something that can be marketed," Fake Housh says. "We do what we do because we can, and it amuses us, not because it's just or right. Morals have their place in our society. Anonymous isn't a place for morals."

Fake Housh says that what Brown has been doing in Libya and elsewhere is "armchair protesting" that has little if any effect on the protests. "It's just a way to look good and feel good."

Finally, there is a third drawback to Brown's new, more visible role in Anonymous. He just might get arrested. Because Brown likes to brag. Just like he did with the poem at Preston Hollow and the "Meet the Intern" ditty about the eventful school trip to New York City and the *New York Press* essay about the rather flagrant violation of Mirna Hariz's second rule, Brown, now that he's a namefag, has taken to calling enemies of Anonymous and certain federal authorities (sometimes one and the same) to tell them how cool he is. Of course, that's not what he explicitly says. He says he's calling to help.

A few weeks ago, he talked to a woman in the NSA. He says he contacted her as a courtesy, to let them know that Anonymous had a copy of Stuxnet. That would be the most infamous, most complex bit of malware ever written, the world's first weaponized computer virus, which was revealed last year to have crippled much of Iran's nuclear program. Some think the Israeli government created it, possibly with help from the United States. The copy Anonymous has—meaning, also, that Brown has a

copy of Stuxnet on his harmless-looking Sony Vaio notebook—
is defanged, to an extent.

But still. Stuxnet. At the Quarter Bar.

And how, you may well wonder, did both Anonymous and
the namefag who bores his sexually adventuresome dates with
Dwarf Fortress come to own a copy of Stuxnet? First the slightly
technical explanation of Anonymous' greatest stunt yet, then
the way Stephen Colbert described it.

.   .   .

On February 4, days after authorities had raided some 40 suspected members of Anonymous in connection with Operation
Payback, Aaron Barr, the CEO of California-based cyber-security
firm and government contractor HBGary Federal, stepped up and
asked to be a target. Barr gave an interview to the *Financial Times*
in which he claimed to have identified Anonymous's leadership
using social engineering hacks—essentially trolling Facebook
and other networks. Barr told the *Financial Times* he planned to
unveil his research at an upcoming security conference.

Brown says Barr had everything wrong. He was about to release names of innocent people whom the feds would then raid.
Nonetheless, Anonymous issued a press release, partially written by Brown, conceding defeat.

Then, the very next day, they attacked. Using something
called an SQL injection, they broke into the database underlying
hbgaryfederal.com. There, Anonymous hackers found what
Brown later described in an article for the *Guardian* as a "far-
rago of embarrassments": a carelessly constructed database, systems running software with known security flaws, passwords
poorly encoded, and, worst of all, the same password used on
multiple systems.

Within hours, Anonymous had destroyed HBGary Federal
and its parent company, HBGary.

On February 24, Colbert did a lengthy segment on the hack, which by then had become international news. Here's how he played it:

"Barr threatened Anonymous by telling the *Financial Times* he had collected information on their core leaders, including many of their real names. Now, to put that in hacker terms: Anonymous is a hornet's nest. And Barr said, 'I'm going to stick my penis in that thing.'"

Colbert relayed that Anonymous took down Barr's website, stole his e-mails, deleted many gigabytes of HBGary research data, trashed Barr's Twitter account, and remotely wiped his iPad. "And he had just reached the Ham 'Em High level on Angry Birds," Colbert said, to much studio laughter. "Anonymous then published all of Barr's e-mails—including one from his wife saying, 'I will file for divorce'—and Barr's World of Warcraft name, sevrynsten. That's right. They ruined *both* his lives."

Four days after the Colbert jokes, Barr resigned his post at HBGary Federal.

Of course, Brown had called Barr an hour after the hack. He played a recording of that conversation for me. He keeps recordings like these as trophies. As the conversation grows less productive, somewhere around the ten-minute mark, Brown deadpans: "Well, you'll have a lot to talk about at the security conference." (HBGary later decided to withdraw from the conference.)

The HBGary hack would amount to nothing but lulz—laughs at someone else's expense, the only acceptable motivation for any Anon who isn't one of those moralfags—except that's how Anonymous got its copy of Stuxnet. Someone at the antivirus firm McAfee had e-mailed it to Barr. But, far more important, buried in the 70,000 HBGary e-mails (which Anonymous made available to everyone on the file-sharing service BitTorrent) was clear evidence of a far-ranging conspiracy among several powerful corporate entities to commit what could be crimes. HBGary

Federal, along with two other security firms with federal contracts, Berico Technologies and Palantir Technologies, were crafting a lucrative sales pitch to conduct a "disinformation campaign" against critics of the U.S. Chamber of Commerce. Hunton and Williams, the well-connected Washington, D.C., law and lobbying firm that was soliciting the work, also counts as a client Bank of America. The hacked e-mails show that the three security firms were working on a similar proposal to target supporters of WikiLeaks on behalf of Bank of America, which has reason to believe it might be the group's next target.

As February drew to a close and *D Magazine* went to press, about a dozen House Democrats called for an investigation into Hunton and Williams and the three security firms, saying that the hacked e-mails appear "to reveal a conspiracy to use subversive techniques to target Chamber critics," including "possible illegal actions against citizens engaged in free speech."

And so it comes to pass that the kid who first used his computer to feel a girl up, then later found he could use it to mess with furries, now finds himself using it to fight for free speech, of all things.

"Our people break laws, yes," Brown says. "When we do so, we do it as an act of civil disobedience. We do it ethically."

But everyone who's Anonymous is anonymous. So there are probably some bad people helping out. Bad people acting ethically?

"We don't do background checks on people," Brown says. "There are bad Anons, sure. They could be doing corporate evil or regular evil. But while they're with us, they're doing good."

At one point, he tells me that he's trying "to show these kids that being bad isn't awesome." He's mostly joking.

Maybe.

On the Sunday afternoon before Michael Isikoff's visit to Dallas, Barrett Brown and I are having brunch on the patio of the Old Monk, on Henderson Avenue. Or, rather, I am having brunch. Brown orders only coffee and orange juice. He is polite to the waitress, saying "please" and "thank you" each time she fills his mug. He's smoking and wearing the boots-and-blue-oxford uniform. The weather is perfect.

We come around to the topic of the future and what it holds for him. It's not something he likes to discuss. He says he doesn't like to make plans. "Hitler had plans," he says.

We talk about his prospects of earning a real living. Money hasn't held much sway over him. Having watched his father lose so much of it, he sees it as ephemeral. But he's working on a film treatment for a producer in Los Angeles. He's got another book coming out soon.

I tell him that the drugs and the constant smoking give me concern. I can't help myself. In some ways, I still see him as that phlegmy sixteen-year-old intern who could use some good advice. I tell him something Loehr told me, that if he's going to have an impact, he's going to have to connect with people, and he can't do that on heroin. Words to that effect.

"At the risk of sounding like an asshole," he says, "a lot of the rules don't apply to me. My heroin addiction is much different than everyone else's."

Then he gets serious. Sort of. "Everything I'm doing now is healthier than it was," he says. "I used to roll my own cigarettes. Now they have filters. I'm doing all this gay shit. I'm jogging on the Katy Trail. I'm dating a girl. How gay is *that*?"

The American Scholar

WINNER—COMMENTARY,
DIGITAL MEDIA

The author of the classic On
Writing Well, *William Zinsser was
in his late eighties when he began
writing a weekly column for the*
American Scholar *website. Clearly
skeptical of digital technology, he
hoped to discover whether the
personal essay "could find a place
amid the clutter and chaos of the
Internet," but he soon realized
that his writing must also "be
alive in the present moment."
Zinsser stopped writing his column
late in 2011, but his newfound
success as an old-school blogger
was soon recognized when* The
American Scholar *won a National
Magazine Award for Digital Media
for the pieces collected here.*

William Zinsser

Looking for a Model *and* The Right to Write *and* Content Management

Looking for a Model

Writing is learned by imitation; we all need models. "I'd like to write like that," we think at various moments in our journey, mentioning an author whose style we want to emulate. But our best models may be men and women writing in fields different from our own. When I wrote *On Writing Well*, in 1974, I took as my model a book that had nothing to do with writing or the English language.

My earliest models were the sportswriters of the *New York Herald Tribune*, the *New York Times*, and the baseball-obsessed *New York Sun,* an afternoon paper that I would yank out of my father's arm when he came home from work. I couldn't wait to read the latest insights of Will Wedge, who wrote three pieces every day under different bylines (my favorite was "By the Old Scout"), and of W. C. Heinz, who later achieved wide esteem as a magazine journalist and novelist. The sportswriters were my Faulkner and my Hemingway. They reared me on a style that was plain and direct but also warm. That style would last me well into my teens, when I discovered E. B. White.

White took the plain style and gave it urbanity. In his *New Yorker* essays he was a little more assured than the rest of us. He had a poet's ear for rhythm and cadence and he had perfect pitch; he knew when it was OK to drop a slang term or a colloquial phrase into an elegant sentence without defiling its elegance. I saw him as a wise elder, talking to me with common sense and humor, and I thought: "I could be a young wise elder!" I adopted that seemingly casual but hard-wrought style, and it carried me through two decades of writing for the style-proud *New York Herald Tribune* and for the best magazines of the day. I assumed I would write that way forever.

In 1970 I moved to Yale to teach nonfiction writing. During that period I did almost no writing myself, but I did a lot of thinking about how to help other people write warmly and well, and that process had nothing to do with handing down grand truths from an essayist's perch. It had to do with leading by the hand, building confidence, finding the real person inside the bundle of anxiety.

In the summer of 1974, when I was complaining to my wife that I was out of ideas, she said, "You ought to write a book about how to write." Her suggestion took me by surprise, but it felt right; I liked the thought of trying to capture my course in a book. But what kind of book? The dominant manual at that time was *The Elements of Style*, by E. B. White and William Strunk Jr., which was White's updating of the book that had most influenced *him*, written in 1919 by Strunk, his English professor at Cornell. My problem was that White was the writer who had most influenced *me*. How could I compete?

But when I analyzed White's book its terrors evaporated. I realized that it was essentially a book of pointers and admonitions: do this, don't do that. What it *didn't* teach was how to apply those principles to the various forms that nonfiction writing can take. That was what I taught in my class and it's what I would teach in my book. I wouldn't compete with *The Elements of Style*; I would complement it.

That decision gave me my pedagogical structure. It also freed me from my Svengali. I saw that I was long overdue to stop trying to write like E. B. White—and trying to *be* E. B. White, the sage essayist. Although I never met him, he and I were obviously not at all alike. White was a passive observer of events, withdrawn from the tumult, his world bounded by his office at *The New Yorker*, his apartment in mid-Manhattan, and his farm in Maine. I was a participant, a seeker of people and far places, of change and risk. Now I was also a teacher, stretched by every new student who came along. The personal voice of that teacher, not the voice of a classroom instructor, was the one I wanted narrating my book.

Such a book would require a different kind of model, written by someone whose company and turn of mind I enjoyed, whatever he or she was writing about. The book I chose was *American Popular Song: The Great Innovators, 1900–1950*, by the composer Alec Wilder. Wilder's book, which had just been published, was one I had been waiting for all my life—the bible that every collector hopes someone will write in the field of his addiction. I was an addict of the songs generically known as the Great American Songbook.

Wilder studied the sheet music of thousands of songs and selected 300 in which he felt that the composer—Jerome Kern, Harold Arlen, George Gershwin, Irving Berlin—had pushed the form into new terrain. In the book he provides the pertinent bars of music to illustrate his point or to single out a phrase that he finds original or somehow touching. But, beyond Wilder's erudition, what I loved most was his commitment to his enthusiasms, as if to say, "These are just one man's opinions—take 'em or leave 'em."

Thus I saw that I might write a book about writing that was just one man's opinions—take 'em or leave 'em. Like Wilder, I would illustrate my points with passages by my favorite nonfiction writers. Above all, I would treat the English language spaciously, not as a narrow universe of rules and regulations, talking to my readers directly ("you'll find," "don't forget") and taking them along on decisions I made during my own career as a journalist.

So it came about that I found my true style when I was in my midfifties. Until then it more probably reflected the person I wanted to be perceived as—the youthful and witty columnist and critic. But that person was never really me. Not until I became a teacher and had no agenda except to be helpful did my style become integrated with my personality and my character.

The Right to Write

Because I've long taught a course in memoir writing and have frequently written about that form, I often hear from people who want to be sure I didn't miss still another article expressing horror that so many bad memoirs keep being published. The latest object of their wrath is a recent essay in the *New York Times Book Review* by Neil Genzlinger, a staff editor.

His piece doesn't say anything new; the same article has been repeatedly written since the memoir craze erupted fifteen years ago. That was one thing that annoyed my callers. But what angered them was the writer's pious tone. Genzlinger's essay is sky-high on the smugness meter. He says, "Sorry to be so harsh" (which I doubt), "but this flood just has to be stopped. We don't have that many trees left." Literary criticism meets forestry.

In his review Genzlinger trashes three new memoirs, which, for him, typify a body of work by "people you've never heard of, writing uninterestingly about the unexceptional, apparently not realizing how commonplace their little wrinkle is or how many other people have already written about it. . . . That's what happens when immature people write memoirs. . . . Nobody wants to relive your misery." His message is: Don't even think of writing your stupid memoir.

Sorry to be so harsh, but I don't like people telling other people they shouldn't write about their life. All of us earn that right by being born; one of the deepest human impulses is to leave a record of what we did and what we thought and felt on our journey. The issue here is not whether so many bad memoirs should be written. It's whether they should be *published*—let's put the blame where it belongs—and whether, once published, they should be reviewed. The *Times* can use its space more helpfully than by allowing a critic to hyperventilate on an exhausted subject. We don't have that many trees left.

Memoirs first got a bad name in the mid-1990s. Until that time authors adhered to an agreed-upon code of modesty, drawing a veil over their most shameful acts and feelings. Then talk shows were born and shame went out the window. Overnight, no recollected event was too squalid, no family too dysfunctional, to be trotted out, for the titillation of the masses, on television and in magazines and books. Memoir became the new therapy. Everybody and his brother wallowed in their struggle with alcohol, drug addiction, recovery, abuse, illness, aging parents, troubled children, codependency, and other newly fashionable syndromes, meanwhile bashing their parents, siblings, teachers, coaches, and everyone else who ever dared to misunderstand them. It was a new literature of victimhood.

But nobody remembered those books for more than ten minutes; readers won't put up with whining. The memoirs that endure from that period are the ones that look back with love and forgiveness. Writers like Frank McCourt (*Angela's Ashes*), Mary Karr (*The Liars' Club*), Tobias Wolff (*This Boy's Life*), Pete Hamill (*A Drinking Life*), and Russell Baker (*Growing Up*) are as hard on their young selves as they are on their elders, elevating the pain of the past by arriving at a larger truth about the brokenness of families. We are not victims, they want us to know. We come from a tribe of fallible people, and we have survived to tell the story and get on with our lives.

There are many good reasons for writing your memoir that have nothing to do with being published. One is to leave your children and grandchildren a record of who you were and what heritage they were born into. Please get started on that; time tends to surprise us by running out. One of the saddest sentences I know is "I wish I had asked my mother about that."

Another reason is to paint a portrait of the town or community, now considerably changed, where you grew up. Somewhere on the shelves of every American small-town library and historical society is a makeshift volume, often written by a retired schoolteacher, that resuscitates a bygone way of life. This is a priceless gift to social historians—crucial information that isn't available anywhere else.

Writing is also a potent search mechanism, often as helpful as psychoanalysis and a lot cheaper. When you start on your memoir you'll find your subconscious mind delivering your past to you, recalling people and events you have entirely forgotten. That voyage of rediscovery is a pleasure in itself.

Finally, writing is a sanity-saving companion for people in times of grief, loss, illness, and other accidents of fate. Just getting down on paper those grim details—still another bout of surgery, still another befogged moment with a husband or wife lost to Alzheimer's—will validate your ordeal and make you feel less alone.

Most of those memoirs shouldn't be published. They are too raw and ragged, too self-absorbed and poorly written, seldom telling us anything we don't already know. But that doesn't mean you shouldn't write them. Don't worry about the trees.

Content Management

I've been reading about a new app, called The Atavist, that will provide an online home for "long-form journalism"—articles that run more than 6,000 words and explore their subject in unusual depth. Now a dying species in the shrunken universe of print, those extended magazine pieces were once a bright ornament on the American literary landscape.

The godfather of the form, Joseph Mitchell, was a huge influence on journalists of my generation. I would study his seemingly effortless *New Yorker* pieces about old-timers on the New York waterfront to figure out how such mosaic work was done. What I figured out was that only Joseph Mitchell could do it.

In the subsequent postwar era a new breed of buccaneering editors would blow Mitchell's tidy model wide open, creating a form called "the new journalism," in which writers often became actors in their own narrative and tended to mingle events that happened with events they thought might have happened.

At *Harper's*, Willie Morris ran at full length Norman Mailer's picaresque *Armies of the Night*, which featured, most conspicuously, Norman Mailer. At *Esquire*, Harold Hayes and Clay Felker turned Gay Talese and Tom Wolfe loose on vertiginous high-wire acts that are still remembered. Fifty years later, Talese's "Frank Sinatra Has a Cold" and Wolfe's "The Electric Kool-Aid Acid Test" are firmly lodged in college textbooks.

But since that golden age, with a few exceptions—notably including *The New Yorker* and *Rolling Stone*—long-form journalists have seen their market wither and have begun to look for a new home the Web. It is for those orphans that the founders of The Atavist—three young guys in Brooklyn—have developed their new site. Their purpose is to enable writers to not only publish their articles at any length but to "enhance" them with videos, photographs, audio tapes, musical selections, and other digital supplements that will "deepen the reading experience." The three guys call it a "content-management system."

Content management. Isn't that what we used to call "writing"? I've been in the content-management business all my life. I look for content that interests or amuses me and then I manage it into a narrative. It's what all writers do if they want to keep paying the bills. Dickens did it very well. So does every good crime writer: Arthur Conan Doyle, Agatha Christie, Raymond Chandler. Elmore Leonard was once asked how he keeps his novels moving so fast. He said, "I leave out the parts that people skip." That's content management.

As a teacher of writing I don't fret about the new technology. What worries me is the new terminology. In recent years I've tutored students at Columbia University's Graduate School of Journalism whose writing is disorganized almost beyond human help, but they seldom mention "writing" as what they came to the school to learn. They are here to study "new media," or "digital media," or "electronic journalism," or "videography," or some other glamorous new skill. Garbed in so much fancy labeling, they forget that journalism is just plain old content management. They return from a reporting assignment with a million notes and a million quotes and no idea what the story is *about*.

The reason, I assume—and I don't expect a Nobel Prize for this deduction—is that people now get their information mainly from random images on a screen and from random messages in their ears, and it no longer occurs to them that writing is linear and sequential; sentence B must follow sentence A. Every year student writing is a little more disheveled; I'm witnessing the slow death of logical thought. So is every English teacher in America.

"As a journalist," I tell my despairing students, "you are finally in the storytelling business." We all are. It's the oldest form of human communication, from the caveman to the crib, end-lessly riveting. Goldilocks wakes up from her nap and sees three bears at the foot of her bed. What's that all about? What happens next? We want to know and we always will.

Writers! Never forget to tell us what's up with the bears. Manage that content.

Time

Whether experimenting with Anthony Weiner–style self-portraiture, auditioning to be the next Aflac spokesduck, or memorializing Kim Kardashian's short-lived marriage, Joel Stein deploys what the National Magazine Award judges described as "his loopy wit" to deconstruct pop-cultural excess. Was Stein one of the reasons Time *was chosen as the 2012 Magazine of the Year? Citing* Time *for "captur[ing] a world in tumult with unsurpassed authority and energy," the judges also noted "the magazine's distinctive voice—a blend of exceptional reporting, powerful photography, intelligent commentary, classic design and a spark of humor." Just a spark? Readers of Stein's "Awesome Column" may feel otherwise.*

Joel Stein

Duck Tape *and* America's Next Top Weiner *and* The End of Kardaschaden-freude

Duck Tape

I don't walk like a duck or talk like a duck. But if Aflac comes calling, I will quack like a duck.

Like most people who are me, I long to be a worldwide icon. Unfortunately, my copy of *The Worldwide Icon How-to Guide* was published in 1950, when you could get famous writing a column in *Time* magazine. Now there are easier options for becoming famous—auditioning for *American Idol*, videotaping surprised cats, being a housewife who is real. But even those take some effort. Then I found out that, after a public relations disaster with its spokesduck, the multinational corporation Aflac is looking for someone to voice the duck in its commercials. I only had to quack the company's name, and America would have to endure me on an hourly basis. There's nothing more influential than representing a big corporation. I'm sure being a politician or a movie star is fulfilling, but which icon of cultural aristocracy can you picture clearly right now: Woodrow Wilson, Margaret Dumont, or Mr. Peanut?

• • •

I went to a casting office in Santa Monica, Calif., where I sat in a hallway next to Anita Gonzales, another one of the 11,200 applicants. Gonzales had a sore throat from two weeks of practicing. She also had a baseball cap with a plush duck affixed to it and a folder of photos of ducks in her yard. This seemed a little bit totally insane until associate casting director Kate Enggren gave us our orientation. She told us to create a story about a duck in our mind, not tell anyone about it, and then act that tale through quacks. I was with her on the not-tell-anyone-about-it part.

After some devious journalistic trickery to get Gonzales to reveal her story—which consisted of my asking what her story was—she said, "It's a mama duck looking for her baby ducks." I'm not a therapist, but between the photos, the hat, and the story, I was pretty sure she was hitting on me. I watched part of her audition on a monitor, and I heard all of it through two walls. She sounded exactly like a duck and also exactly like Roseanne Barr being waterboarded. I decided to go a different way. My story was about a duck that realized print was a dying medium and had to humiliate himself by making one loud human noise over and over but at least got invited to make that noise at corporate functions with cocktail shrimp at the buffet.

I walked into a room where I was being videotaped, which seemed unnecessary for Aflac's decision-making process, especially considering that up until now the duck had been performed by Gilbert Gottfried, who is in every way the opposite of Ashton Kutcher. Acting teacher James Reese told me to picture life as a duck and then say the word Aflac. Which I did, but not to Reese's satisfaction. "A little happier. A little less Brando," he told me. I get Brando a lot when I act.

Then Enggren actually told me to "have some fun with it." I did a Nixon duck talking to a Kissinger duck, which caused me, in both cases, to mispronounce Aflac in a way the FCC would fine me for. Finally, Reese had me quack as loudly as I could as I pretended to walk in a room with a buffet. Which I totally nailed. For that one moment, I wasn't just a guy pretending to be a duck. I was a guy thinking about a duck while he was pretending to be a duck. The sound guy said I was the best he'd seen all day. And it doesn't matter what the video guy thought.

• • •

I was getting excited because, while the job paid only $445.30 per ad recorded, with residuals, that could total well into the six figures annually. To negotiate my deal, I called Daniel Amos, CEO of Aflac, which is a giant company that has something to do with ducks. The commercials, it seems, aren't really that effective.

Amos hadn't watched my tape, but he said he "heard it went well." I warned him that I'm an opinion columnist who sometimes takes gutsy, poorly considered stances to get attention, since I knew Gottfried was fired for making jokes on Twitter about the Japanese earthquake, which was particularly insensitive, as 75 percent of Aflac's business is in Japan. "We'll work with you on it," promised Amos. I vowed to offend only countries too poor to buy whatever product it is he sells.

Then I asked Amos to quack for me. And it was good. It was like a duck that was so rich, he force-fed himself and then ate his own liver. It's a sound 11,200 people aspired to make. I don't think that's because the economy is bad. I think it's because all our Facebook pages, Twitter accounts, and YouTube videos make us hunger for a bigger audience, because fame hasn't been democratized in effect but only in expectation.

But what the other 11,199 people don't remember is that no one knew Gottfried was the Aflac duck until he wrote an offensive joke. Which is why I'm sticking to the job I already have. Unless they start casting for a new Aunt Jemima. I'm pretty sure I could get a lot of attention for that one.

America's Next Top Weiner

Athletes, musicians and politicians have shared theirs. Is it time for my close-up?

Unlike Anthony Weiner, I am completely familiar with all the photos ever taken of my penis. That's because there aren't any. Like any man, I would love to spend an afternoon lolling in a glade, taking pictures of my penis. But no one—not women I've dated, not a urologist, not the Museum of Modern Art—has ever said to me, "I'd love a few candids of your penis."

Other men, though, sense a greater demand. Brett Favre and Kanye West allegedly sent unrequested photos to women. So many men are doing this that *Saturday Night Live* and Funny or Die have both done sketches on professional penis-photography studios. Were men experiencing some kind of sexualized renaissance like when we wore codpieces and powdered wigs and flaunted chest hair? Is this something I'll need to teach my son Laszlo how to do? What's the right age to take photos of your penis? Because, at two, he can already use an iPhone and admire his penis.

·   ·   ·

Not wanting to fall behind the times, like when I held on to my Treo phone, I decided to consult some experts. I asked Angie Rowntree, who owns the women's erotica site Sssh.com, if I should be sending out penis pictures. She told me the users of her site would not enjoy that. She also assumed that few men took crotch shots until she asked her husband, who runs a dating site called KinkCulture.com, how many guys used their penises as their photos. Of the past eight men to sign up, three did. "It's asinine," Rowntree said. "Men haven't been able to figure out women for 2,000 years." Rowntree was definitely off the list for my penis photos.

Pete Huyck and Alex Gregory, who directed *A Good Old Fashioned Orgy*, an upcoming comedy about friends in the Hamptons who throw an intimate party, said they never considered having their lead character send a penis photo since it would have made him creepy. Even Neil Strauss, whose book *The Game* suggests wearing light-up jewelry to pick up women, said such photos are a bad idea. "It's a pathetic manifestation of the male ego," he said. "If it doesn't work out, they know in their twisted subconscious that they at least got it pretty close."

I was going to give up on the idea when sex columnist Dan Savage explained that while very few women want to see my photos, the small percentage who do are exactly the kinds of dynamic, exciting women who like travel and exotic foods. At least that's what I got out of what he said. He may have used the phrase "that sort of woman."

When I asked just such a dynamic woman if she'd like a photo of my penis, my lovely wife Cassandra said, "That's a stupid question. I've seen your penis before." The next morning, however, she saw her actor crush, Mark Ruffalo, buying coffee. I asked if she'd like to see a photo of Ruffalo's. "Sure!" she yelled. Then she thought more about it. "It would feel scary. If you met an attractive woman at a party and she sent you a picture of her boobs, wouldn't you feel like that was weirdly aggressive?" I told her it would indeed seem weirdly aggressive in a totally awesome way. "Well, imagine if you were the weaker sex. You'd think this is aggressive and threatening."

Cassandra had a point. And that point was: she is not the right kind of woman. So I asked *Playboy*'s Miss June, Mei Ling-Lam, if she wanted to see my penis. "That's a negative!" she told me in a way that seemed pretty harsh for a woman asking for $5.99 to see her vagina. "Women really don't want to see a penis. Men like to look at their penises. Freud might have gotten it wrong. Men may have the penis envy."

•   •   •

I clearly needed to increase my odds. So, like Weiner, I went to Twitter, where I wrote, "Would anyone care to see a photo of my penis?" As Savage predicted, I got a lot of nos and two "I didn't think cameras could zoom in that far"s. Jodi Mozeika, a twenty-seven-year-old bartender in New Jersey, was one of many women who politely declined, so I called her to find out why. She told me that it would ruin the experience of reading this column, which, to me, seemed a small price to pay. But Mozeika had already gotten an unrequested penis photo from a friend, and she wants no more. "Unless it was, like, Wolverine," she said. "Not Hugh Jackman as himself. He also plays Liza Minnelli's gay husband, so I don't want to see that picture. Just Wolverine."

But in between the avalanche of "eww"s and some positive responses from gay men, I got—as Savage promised—a few requests. Jen Goertler, a thirty-three-year-old married mom of two in Willoughby, Ohio, has been on the wrong side of some unrequested penis photos as well. But mine, she said, would be different, since she likes my column and has seen me on television. This is exactly why I didn't go into banking.

But when I asked Cassandra to borrow her camera, her fisheye lens, and her makeup, she told me that while she did not want my penis photos, she also didn't want Goertler to have them. It really will take us another 2,000 years to figure out women.

The End of Kardaschadenfreude

I understand the difficulties of a celebrity marriage because I'm in one: I am married to the wife of Joel Stein. I also know how hurtful it is when the public finds out private details about my marriage, which almost always happens right after I write about them. And I have a lot of empathy for Kim Kardashian, since we both appear on the E! channel, both designed our own fragrances with the same company, and both made sex tapes, although hers involved a second person.

So I feel for Kim now that she's filed for divorce from professional basketball player Kris Humphries. It's too easy to make fun of her by listing things that are longer than their seventy-two days of marriage: Sarah Jessica Parker's face, a black man's life in a horror film, the trick-or-treat line at Casey Anthony's house. I know just how easy it is because I got those jokes by typing "ThingsLongerThanKimsMarriage" into Twitter.

·   ·   ·

My own celebrity marriage has lasted nearly fifty Kardashians, but we've had enough struggles to know how quickly things can go poorly. Just twenty-six days before they split, Kim and Kris renewed their vows on *The Ellen DeGeneres Show*. Two days before, Kim was happily dancing at a New York City club's Halloween party dressed up, just like everybody else now, as a slutty version of a slut. Then, hours before she filed her divorce papers, she recorded her heartbreak on her Twitter account: "Our store #KardashianKhaos is opening tomorrow at 9am at @TheMirageLV. We are so excited!! Kardashian Khaos has arrived!"

But it's wrong to blame the couple for not keeping their marriage together longer than the trial period for their mattress. We have created a wedding culture where marriage is less important than the wedding, which is less important than the Vegas bachelorette party, which is less important than the Facebook photos of the bachelorette party. We *People* magazine readers and watchers of the *Kim's Fairytale Wedding* special on E! paid for that wedding because we are adults who are still obsessed with princesses. Even though we all know in our hearts that, as a straight man, I am saying *we* only to be nice.

Then we left Kim and Kris alone to face the daily routine of marriage, which must have seemed like drudgery after their multi-million-dollar wedding. Unlike at the wedding, in their married life they had to have dinner with people they knew. If they had stayed together much longer, they would have had to start writing thank-you notes for their wedding gifts.

My lovely wife Cassandra wanted to elope because she understood that the important part wasn't the wedding but the honeymoon. I stupidly vetoed that idea because—just like with the prom—I was brainwashed into thinking I'd regret missing out on it for the rest of my life. I also thought committing to me in front of her closest family and friends would make her too embarrassed to leave me seventy-two days later.

Kim actually divorced responsibly, before she had children or emotional attachments to her husband. And she did it with class: in her press release the day of her divorce filing, she said nice things about him, even getting his name right. "I don't think Kim should be embarrassed or shameful about getting married or getting divorced," says Stacy Morrison, an expert on weddings, divorce and celebrity, having been the editor of *Modern Bride*, the author of *Falling Apart in One Piece: One Optimist's Journey Through the Hell of Divorce*, and my editor. "What she should feel embarrassed about is the wedding. She brought back a headpiece that would be better left to history."

•   •   •

So I hope Kim ignores everyone's petty schadenfreude and, as she has throughout her career, remains completely non-schadened. I hope she realizes that we're fascinated with supershort celebrity marriages because we wonder, deep down, if they've once again found a better way to live. They skip the hard parts. Their lives are all honeymoon and no marriage. I'm able to write that sentence because, after nearly ten years of marriage, Cassandra is so over me, she no longer reads my column.

I've gotten careless with my marriage, assuming that just because things are going well on Day Seventy-one, there will be a Day Seventy-three. I'm not, to my embarrassment, even entirely sure which day we're on. But thanks to Kim's example, I'm going to be more careful and not let it turn into all partnership and no adventure. I'm going to see if Cassandra wants to hire a spray-on tanner, have some alone time to talk to a video camera, or spend all her time with her parents and siblings. I'm going to assure her that men like big butts. And if I do all that just right, I think there's a chance she'll let me take the video camera out. I'll have my own reality show in no time.

Zoetrope: All-Story

WINNER—FICTION

In this short story—described as "dazzling" by the National Magazine Award judges—an eleven-year-old boy's ride across the tall-grass prairie becomes a terrifying allegory for the struggle to survive on the American frontier. Thirty years old when "The Hox River Window" was published, Karen Russell is the author of Swamplandia!—one of the most highly praised novels of 2011—which began as a short story in Zoetrope: All Story. The magazine was founded by Francis Ford Coppola in 1997 to publish fiction that was both ambitious and entertaining. Zoetrope: All Story is an eight-time finalist for the National Magazine Award for Fiction and also won the award in 2001.

Karen Russell

The Hox River Window

"**G**o tack up, Miles!" says Mr. Johannes Zegner of the Blue Sink Zegners, pioneer of the tallgrass prairie and future owner of 160 acres of Nebraska. In most weathers, I am permitted to call him "Pa."

"See if your mother's got the Window ready. The Inspector is coming tonight. He's already on the train, can you imagine!"

A thrill moves in me; if I had a tail I would shake it. So I will have to leave within the hour, and ride quickly—because if the one-eyed Inspector really is getting off at the spur line in Beatrice, he'll hire a stagecoach and be half-way to the Hox River Settlement by one o'clock; he could be at our farm by nightfall! I think Jesus Himself would cause less of a stir stepping off that train; He'd find a tough bunch to impress in this droughty place, with no water anywhere for Him to walk on.

"Miles, listen fast," Pa continues. "Your brother is coming—"

Sure enough, Peter is galumphing toward us through the puddled glow of the winter wheat. It came in too sparse this year to make a crop, wisping out of the sod like the thin, blond hairs on Pa's hand. My father has the "settler's scar," a pink star scored into the brown leather of his palm by the handle of the moldboard plow. Peter's got one, too, a raw brand behind his knuckles that never heals—and so will I when I prove up as a man. (As yet I am the Zegner runt, with eleven years to my name and only five of those West; I cannot grow a beard any quicker than Mr. Johannes can conjure wheat, but I can *ride*.)

Pa kneels low and clasps his dirt-colored hands onto my shoulders. "Your brother is coming, but it's you I want to send to our neighbors in need. Boy, it's *you*. I trust you on a horse. I know you'll tend to that Window as if it were your own life."

"I will, sir."

"I just got word from Bud Sticksel—you got two stops. The Inspector's making two visits. The Florissants and then the Sticksels. Let's pray he keeps to that schedule, anyhow, because if he decides to go to the Sticksels first . . ."

I shiver and nod, imagining the Sticksels' stricken faces in their hole.

"The Sticksels don't have one shard of glass. You cannot fail them, Miles."

"I know, Pa."

"And once they prove up, you know what to do?"

"Yes, Pa. This time I will—"

"You take the Window back. Bundle it in burlap. Get Bud's wife to help. Then you push that Inspector's toes into stirrups— do unto others, Miles—and you bring that man to our door."

"But what if the Inspector sees me reclaiming the Window from Mr. Sticksel? He'll know how we fooled him. Won't he cancel their title?"

Pa looks at me hard, and I can hear the gears in his head clicking. "You want to be a man, don't you, Miles?"

"Yes, sir. Very much."

"So use your wits, son. Some sleight of hand. I can't think of everything."

Increasingly time matters. I can feel it speeding up in my chest, in rhythm with my pounding heart. A flock of cliff swallows lifts off the grassy bank of our house and my eyes fly with them into the gray light.

"Hey," says Peter. He comes up behind me and shovels my head under his arm—he smells sour, all vinegary sweat and bones. "What's this fuss?"

So Pa has to explain again that when the sun next rises, we'll have our autographed title. Peter's grin is as wide and handsome and full of teeth as our father's, and I smile into the mirror they make.

"Tomorrow?"

"Or even tonight."

Behind them, Ma seeps out of the dugout in her blue dress. She sees us gathered and runs down the powdery furrow like a tear—I think she would turn to water if she could.

No rain on our land since the seventh of September. That midnight we got half an inch and Pa drilled in the wheat at dawn. Most of it cooked in the ground; what came up has got only two or three leaves to a plant. Last week the stalks started turning ivory, like pieces of light. "Water," Pa growls at the blue mouth of heaven—the one mouth distant enough to ignore his fists.

He mutters that this weather will dry us all to tinder, lightning fodder, and he's spent every day since that last glorious hour of rainfall plowing firebreaks until he's too tired to stand. Ma's begun to talk to the shriveling sheaves in a crazy way, as if they were her thousand thirsty children. My brother pretends not to hear her.

"Inspection day," Pa booms at Ma's approach. "He's on the train now."

"The Inspector? Says who? Who thinks they're proving up?"

"Bud says. And we are. Daniel Florissant, Bud, the Zegners."

Pa leans in as if to kiss her, whispering; she unlatches her ear from his mouth.

"*No*! Are you crazy, Jo? The Inspector is a rumor, he's smoke! I can make you a promise: no such person is ever coming out here. How long do we have to wait before you believe that? A decade? What you want to risk—" She looks over at me and her voice gets quieter.

A silence falls over the Zegner family homestead, which Pa splits with his thundering hymn:

"You faithless woman! How can you talk like that after we have lived on this land for five years? Built our *home* here, held out through drought and hail, through locusts, Vera—"

Peter is nodding along. I have to tiptoe around the half-moon of my family to get to the sod barn. As I tack up Nore I can hear Ma worrying my father: "Oh, I am not deaf, I hear you lying to our child—'*It's verified.*'"

"Bud Sticksel is no liar," I reassure Nore's quivering rump. "Don't be scared. Ma's crazy. We'll find the Inspector."

After the defections and deaths of several settlers, the Sticksels have become our closest neighbors. Their farm is eighteen miles away. Bud used to work as a hired hand in Salmon, Ohio, says Pa. Came here the same year as our family, 1872. He's an eyeblink from being eligible to prove up and get his section title: 1. Bud's land by the lake is in grain. 2. He's put a claim shanty on the property, ten feet by twenty. 3. He has resided on his land for five years, held on through four shining seasons of drought. ("Where is God's rain?" Mrs. Sticksel murmurs to Ma.) 4. He has raised sixty acres of emerald lucerne, two beautiful daughters, and thirty evil turkeys that have heads like scratched mosquito bites. The Sticksels have met every Homestead Act requirement save one, its final strangeness, what Pa calls "the wink in the bureaucrats' wall": a glass window.

Farther south, on the new rail lines, barbed wire and crystal lamps and precut shingles fire in on the freight trains, but in the Hox River Settlement a leaded pane is as yet an unimaginable good. Almost rarer than the rain. Yet all the Hox settlers have left holes in the walls of their sod houses, squares and ovals where they intend to put their future windows. Some use waxed paper to cover these openings; the Sticksels curtained up with an oiled buffalo skin. The one time I slept at their dugout that hide flapped all night like it was trying to talk to me: *Blab blab blab.*

"I know you don't belong here," I replied—I was sympathetic, "but there isn't any glass for that empty place. There's one Window in this blue-gray ocean of tallgrass, and it's ours."

"Now, Miles," both of my parents preach at me continually, in the same tone with which they recite the wishful Bible rules, "you know the Window must benefit every settler out here. We are only its stewards." Pa long ago christened it the Hox River Window and swore it to any claimant in need. (I sometimes think my parents use me to stimulate goodness and to remind themselves of this oath, the same way I untangle my greedy thoughts by talking to the animals, Louma and Nore—because it's easy to catch oneself wanting to hoard all the prairie's violet light on the Hox panes.) He says our own walls cannot wear the Window until we prove up—it's too precious, too fragile. So we keep it hidden in the sod cave like a diamond.

Our house is a dugout in a grassy hill—I've sent three letters to my cross-eyed Cousin Bailey in Blue Sink, Pennsylvania, and in each one I fail to explain our new house to his satisfaction. Cousin Bailey uses his fingers to sum numbers; once he asked me if the winged angels in heaven eat birdseed or "man-food" like chocolate pie. The idea of a house made of sod defeats him. He writes back with questions about bedrooms and doors, closets and attics. "No, Bailey, we live in one room," I reply impatiently. "A ball of pure earth. Not enough timber for building walls on the prairie so we dug right into the sod. It's a cave, where we now live."

"A grave," says Peter, a joke I don't like one bit. It's our home, although it does look like a hiccup in the earth. The floor is sod, the roof is sod, hardened by the red Nebraska sun—if it ever rains again, water will sheet in on our heads for days. The mattress sits on a raised cage of wild plum poles. My mother covers the cookstove with her mother's pilled linen tablecloth to keep the lizards and field mice and moles and rattlesnakes and yellow spiders from falling into our supper. (Although she threatens to pull the cloth if we get cheated out of another harvest, and let every plaguey creature into our soup: "The wheat's not getting any taller, Jo, but our boys are. They need meat.")

Pa and Peter and I dug out the room. Pa used the breaking plow to sculpt the sod into six-inch slabs of what folks here call Nebraska marble. He stacked these into our walls, arranging each third layer in a cross-grain pattern with the grass side down. In summer, this room can get as hot as the held breath of the world. We dug a sod stable for the team of horses, the hogs, and Louma, our heat-demented cow. She's got the Hereford lightning up her red flanks—it looks like somebody nailed her with a bucket of scalding paint. She chews slop with a look of ancient shock, her vexed eyes staring out from a white face. In truth, her eyes look a little like Ma's.

My horse is Nore, who I've been riding since she was a two-year-old filly. She's jet black and broody and doesn't fit with my father's team. Up on her back I'm taller than any man out here, taller than a pancake stack of Peters. I saddle Nore, explain the day to her, her ears flattening at the word *Inspector*.

Behind the stalls, my father is shaking my mother like a doll.

"He's a rumor, huh? Then I'm going to shove the fellow's arms through the coat sleeves of that rumor! He's real, and so are we Zegners. By sunrise we'll own our home, if you can muster faith. Faith the size of one—damn! One seed of some kind. It moves mountains. How's that go, Vera, in the Bible? Apple? Pumpkin?"

"It's a mustard seed, Jo. Yahweh is not baking any pies." Ma's voice is shaking now, too. "Miles is eleven years old," she says slowly. "The Sticksels are a half day's ride for you . . ."

Pa catches sight of me, and I duck his gaze. I hope he shakes the looniness right out of her. I'm ready to ride.

Ma never yells at me. But lately her voice is dreadful even when it's cheerful, singing out of the well mouth of our house. Hoarse, so that it sounds as if the very sod is gargling sand. She's not sick, or no sicker than anybody else—it's the dust. I hate the strain in her voice as she tries to make a happy tune for me and my brother, when her yellowish eyes are sunk deep in her face and every long note she holds shoves her ribs through her dress. She hasn't been fat for two years.

I was the last Zegner born in Pennsylvania. The three girls were born here, and buried in a little plot under the tufting gama grass, next to the sixty acres we have in wheat. Aside from salt thistle and the big sunflowers in July, nothing grows on top of the girls. Ma won't allow it. She's of the opinion that each of her daughters would have lived had we stayed in Blue Sink. Long-nosed and blue-eyed—"like you, Miles." Tall and pin-thin, like the women in her family. That's how my sisters look to me, too. Glowing taller and taller. White legs twining moonward, like swords of wheat. They sprout after dark. Some nights the heat is suffocating and it wakes me. Through the hole in our kitchen where the Window will go I watch my mother kneeling in their field, weeding thistle. The three sisters sway behind her back. They stare at me with their hundred-year-old faces. They know they missed their chance to be girls. The middle one smiles at me, and her white teeth outshine the harrow. She gives me a little wave. I wonder if she knows I'm her brother.

When red dawn comes Ma's at the cookstove with her face to the leaping flame, and I'm afraid to ask her if I was dreaming.

I cannot tell Pa or Peter about the sisters, of course. And not Nore—she's a horse, she spooks. Lately I won't even pray on it, because what if God tells them up in heaven that I'm terrified to meet them? Sometimes I talk to the pig, who'll be butchered anyhow come Christmas Eve.

"I'll be fine, Ma."

"He'll be fine."

"Jo!"

"Do you want me to send Peter, then?" Pa says coolly.

"Oh, Jo. He *can't.* You know that." Ma chews at her lip, Louma-like.

Something is going wrong with my brother. He's not reliable. A few weeks ago, when the clouds dispersed again without releasing one drop of rain, he disappeared for three days; when he rode home his hands were wet. "Not my blood," he reassured Pa. Ma sent me on the four-mile walk to the well to haul for a bath, even though our washing day wasn't until the following Wednesday, and we boys go last—after a draw for drinking and cooking, after a draw for the garden.

Peter is sixteen, but that night he let Ma sponge the black blood off him like a child, and I almost cried like a kid myself when he splashed clean water in waves over the sides of the trough.

I am a little afraid of my brother.

"I'll go, then." Pa's whole body draws back like a viper in its gold burnoose. I close my eyes and see the shadow of his secret self throbbing along the wall of our sod barn: his head rolling to its own music and sloshing with poisons. Even in the quiet I can hear him rattling.

"Jo."

"No, sweetheart, you're right. Pete can't go, we can't spare Miles—who does that leave? I go or we forfeit our chance. We don't prove up. We don't own the land where our girls are buried."

Ma goes to get the Window.

We nightly pray for everyone in Hox to prove up, the titles from the Land Office framed on their walls. The purple and scarlet tongue of my mother's bookmark used to move around the Bible chapters with the weather, but for the past year and a half it's been stuck on Psalm 68:9. On that page, says Ma, it rains reliably.

Through the empty socket in our sod, I can see her hunched over in the richest shadows. Dust whirls around the floor in little twisters, scraping her ankles raw. She bends over the glass, and a rail of vertebrae jumps out. My mother is thirty-one years old, but the land out here paints old age onto her. All day she travels this room, sweeping a floor that is already dirt, scrubbing the dinner plates into white ovals, shaking out rugs. Ma is humming a stubborn song and won't look up from the Window on her lap. She polishes the glass by licking the end of her braid into a fine point and whisking it over the surface, like a watercolorist. Now the Window is the only clean thing in our house. It's the size of a hanging painting, with an inch border of stained glass. Two channeled lead strips run orange and jewel-blue light around it. But the inner panels are the most beautiful, I think: perfectly transparent.

Ma wraps it in some scatter rugs and penny burlap. "Good-bye, Miles," she says simply.

We fix my cargo to the horse's flank, half a dozen ropes raveling to one knot at the saddle horn. Pa hitches my leg at a painful angle, warns me not to put weight anywhere near the Window. Already I'm eager for the crystal risk of riding at a gallop. Then he gives me an envelope and kisses up to my ear like he does Ma's. "A little bribe," he says. "Tell the Inspector there's more waiting at the Zegner place."

"OK." I frown. "Is there?"

Pa thumps Nore on the rump.

When we reach the fence line a very bad thought occurs to me: "Pa! What if they don't give the Window back?" I call out. "The Sticksels—what if they try to keep it?"

"Then you'd better run fast, because those aren't our neighbors. Those are monsters, pretending to be the Sticksels. But before you run, grab the Window."

I might as well have asked him, *What if Ma leaves us? What if Peter never gets better?*

I don't look back as I glide Nore around the oak—the only tree for miles of prairie. The wind blows us forward, sends the last leaves raining around us and the October clouds flashing like horseshoes. I duck underneath the branches and touch the lowermost one for luck. When I turn to salute my father, I see that he and Ma are swaying together in the stunted wheat like a dance, his big hands tight around the spindle of her waist and her face buried in his neck, her black hair waterfalling across the caked grime on his shirt. It's only later that I realize Ma was sobbing.

.   .   .

The first family of landowners we met in Nebraska were the Henry Yotherses. Five years ago, a few weeks after our migration to the Hox River Settlement, we arrived at their July picnic "one hour shy of serendipity," as Mrs. Yothers immediately announced—too late but only just to meet the Inspector. I was a pipsqueak then, and so I remember everything: the glowering sunset and an army of Turkey Red wheat mustered by the Yotherses to support their claim, the whaleback hump of the sod house rising above the grassy sea—and Mr. Henry Yothers himself, a new king in possession of his title.

"A proven man," Pa whistled.

"Christ in heaven, love must glue you to him every fortnight," Ma joked to Mrs. Yothers—but in a hushed voice, surrounded as they were by what seemed like thousands of Yothers children. Ten thousand tiny mouths feeding on that quarter section of land, and dressed for the occasion like midget undertakers, in black trousers and bowties.

"That Inspector shook each of my children's hands," boasted Henry Yothers. "Congratulated each one of them on being 'landed gentry.' He's a curious fellow, Johannes. Lost an eye in the war. He wears a patch of dark green silk over the socket. It's no coincidence, I'm sure, that he's obsessed with the Glass Requirement."

And then we got our first look at the Hox River Window: that glorious, magical glass fusing their inner room to the outside world, gracing their home with light. Back in Blue Sink there were thousands of windows, but we only looked *through* them, never *at* them. We gasped.

Remembering this, I feel queasy all over again. Something about the big grins on everybody's faces, and all that pomp: the Inspector's checklist, the ten-dollar filing fee, the U.S. president's counterfeit autograph in an inky loop. Through the glass we watched Mrs. Yothers slide the title into its birch frame and dutifully applauded. The general mood confused me. We were going to slave and starve and wait five years to get a piece of paper so thin? Why? To prove what? Who cares what Washington, D.C., thinks?

"Congratulations!" my mother beamed at Mrs. Yothers, with a girlishness I'd never seen before, and then embarrassed us all by bursting into tears. "Oh, boys, they *proved* it to them."

"To who?"

"Who? Everybody, Miles! The people back East, who said they'd never make it a year on the frontier. The men in Washington. The Inspector will forward their papers on to the president himself. Now you come say a prayer with me—"

Back then, Ma never mentioned Pennsylvania except to say "good riddance." We'd traveled West under juicy clouds that clustered like grapes. My sisters weren't alive in her belly or dead under the thistle and sod. Our plow gleamed. Furniture from Blue Sink was still in boxes.

"Miles, if we're to make this place our home, we need it official. Same as any claimant out here. You can't understand that?"

With Pa out of earshot, I said, "No, ma'am. I really cannot."

"The Yotherses survived the grasshoppers of 1868, got hailed out twice, burned corn for fuel. They took over from the Nunemakers. Did you know that, Miles? A bunch that fled. But the Henry Yothers family prevailed—they held on to their claim. Your heart's so stingy you can't celebrate that?"

But, Ma, I wanted to say. Because I guessed that a few hours earlier, before the Inspection, the Yotherses' farm had looked no different from the proven place we'd leave—with the same children running barefoot around their cave, and in the distance the same wheat blowing. And the whole scene sliding through that Window, as real or as unreal as it had ever been.

•   •   •

What we didn't know then, as we filed our own preempt in the white beehive of the Federal Land Office: the long droughts were coming. Since that July day, over half of the Hox River homesteaders have forfeited their claims and left, dozens of families withdrawing back East. And the men and women who stayed, says Pa with teeth in his words, who sowed and abided, "we are the victors, Miles. Our roots reach deep. We Zegners were green when we came here, but now we're dust brown, the color of Hox. Proving up means you stand your ground, you win your title— 160 acres go from public to private. Clear and free, you hold it. Nobody can ever run you off. It's home."

Over the years, my father's reasoning has been whittled to its core, like everything else out here. At times he wanders around our homestead shouting at random intervals, "I know a hunger stronger than thirst!" His voice booms like thunder in my brain as we light out. Nore digs into the dry earth, happy to be running.

"Nore?" Like Pa, I whisper into the pink cone of her ear. "We'll get the Inspector, but I'll tell you a secret: I don't understand why they need that piece of paper. This place has been home for years."

•   •   •

At first it is a fine morning. Nore strikes a square trot and I goose her to a canter. Pocket gophers and kangaroo rats scramble in front of our lunging shadow; the horned larks are singing in the grasses, plumping like vain old Minister Fudd back in Blue Sink.

Soon nothing but crimson bluestem is blazing all around us. Coyotes go mousing in this meadow but today I count none. Twice I have seen eagles back here. Three miles of dead grass pass, tickling Nore's hindquarters. Whenever she sneezes I let go of the reins and grab ahold of the Window's wrought-iron frame, which feels as slender and bony as a deer's leg through the burlap case. Pa could have a million sons and none would be a better steward.

We sink into the tallgrass, happy to get swallowed and escape the midday sun. But when we emerge the sky is seamless and black, and the last yellow stitching goes dark. Something is shifting, I think. We reach a timber belt of cottonwood and Siberian elms—species not uncommon to Nebraska, yet I've never seen examples of such overpowering heights. Atmospheric salts spill through the air as birds scatter in fantastic numbers before us. The charge pucks the horse's huge nostrils, causes her devil's ears to cup around. A chill races down her bony shoulders and prickles up my neck. Between noon and one o'clock, the temperature must plummet some twenty degrees. A sound I barely recognize claps in the distance. "Oh, Nore," I mumble into her ear, sick with hope. The black sky grows blacker still.

Rain?

I dig into her soft belly too meanly, as if the moons of my spurs could burst the clouds, and maybe they can: The miracle sounds again as if the sky's been shot, and rain gushes all over us. Unstoppably, like blood from a body. I stick out my tongue to catch it. Over my scalp and Nore's coarse hair it runs and glimmers, crystal-clear and *clean*. Sheets of water hammer the tallgrass flat, and we go whooping on, Nore and I whinnying in a duet:

Rain!

Rain!

Rain!

Deeper into the storm I begin to get a picture in my mind of water flooding down the Hox glass. Rain shining the Window.

"Oh, God, I want to see that, Nore," I whisper to her. It's a scene I've imagined a thousand times through all the dry years.

I slow her to a stop and dismount. The red stump I use as Nore's hitching post is boiling with water; she stares at me, her great eyes running. I undo the knot, loosen the burlap. Rain soaks over my trembling hands; I move the scatter rugs and expose a triangle of the Hox glass. The first drop hits with a beautiful plink, and I feel like an artist. Soon this corner of the Window is jeweled with water, and I uncover the rest of the glass, floating the whole shimmery landscape through it.

I close my eyes and see my mother and father drenched outside the soddy, still dancing but joyously now; Louma in the barn rolling her twinkling eyes at real lightning; the sod crumbling from our ceiling; the house turning into a mudslide. We'll sleep outdoors and watch the wheat growing and leafing, heading out and reseeding. I angle the Window and funnel the cold rain onto my boot toes. Feelings billow and surge in me to a phenomenal height, a green joy that I wish I could share with my mother.

By now a whole river must have fallen out of heaven and into the sod, and I don't know how long I've been standing here. Then I look up and see it's not only rainfall sweeping over the prairie: a shape slips through the bluestem just ahead of us, disappears.

"Mr. Florissant?"

But the Florissant claim is still an hour from us at a gallop. And if that shape belonged to Daniel Florissant, well, he has changed considerably since the Easter picnic.

Quickly I re-bundle and rope up the Window and get astride Nore, wishing for Peter's .22 rifle or even a pocketknife as I scan the ground for flat rocks, sticks.

"Hello?"

The black figure is moving through the switchgrass. I turn Nore around and try to give chase until I realize it's not escaping through the rain at all but rather circling *us*, like a hawk or the hand of a clock.

"Mr. Florissant? Is that you?" I swallow. "Inspector . . . ?"

I wheel inside the shadow's wheeling, each of us moving against the rotation of the other like cogs, the stranger occasionally walking into sight and then vanishing again; and if he *is* the Inspector, he does not seem in any hurry to meet me. Perhaps this is part of some extra test—as if our patience requires further proof. Five years, three daughters, half an inch of rain, and no wheat crop last winter—even Cousin Bailey can sum those numbers. "Inspector!" I holler again over the thunder. Nore trembles, and I imagine that she, too, can feel the pull of this fellow's gaze, the noose he's drawing around us.

I realize that I'm shivering out of my clothes, my hands raw. Then a cold flake hits my nose. The rain is turning to snow.

Can a blizzard strike this early, in late October? Does that happen on the prairie? Immediately I regret putting the question to the sky, which seems eager to answer, suddenly very attentive to the questions of humans. "Run, Nore," I tell her. We still have to pass the Yotherses' place.

.   .   .

Only I know where the Hox River Window really came from. Pa told me by accident after a pint of beer and made me pledge my silence. It's a scary story: One December night, almost two years ago now, we believed the Inspector was coming to visit our farm. We were eighteen months short of the residency requirement, and we had no window. Frantic, Pa rode out to the Yotherses' to beg for a square of glass and found their claim abandoned.

Tack was scattered all over the barn floor. Outside, three half-starved Sauceman hogs were masticating the pale red fibers of Mrs. Yothers's dress; piles of clothing lay trampled into the sod— bouquets of children's bowties. The dugout was dark. A family of spotted black jackrabbits were licking their long feet under the table. A tarantula had closed around the bedpost like a small, gloved hand. The Window was still shining in the wall.

So Pa took it. He rode home and told Ma that he'd bartered for the Window from a man moving back to ranch West Texas.

What a whopper! I thought, and almost laughed out loud, guessing that Pa must be teasing us. Straight away I'd recognized our neighbors' glass.

I waited for Ma to dispute the story, yet she surprised me by breathing, "Oh, *thank you—*" in a little girl's voice and reaching out to the Window with dreamy eyes. Peter, too, chuckled softly and touched the glass like it was a piece of new luck, and no one ever mentioned our friends the Yotherses again. As we carried the Window down to our dugout in a Zegner parade—Ma singing and Peter's smile lighting even his eyes—those thousand kids were everywhere in my imagination, asking me why I kept quiet, asking why I was trying with all my might to forget them.

To me only, Pa confessed to coveting their title, still posted on the dirt wall—but he took the Window instead, not wanting to risk our own claim by squatting on another man's haunted land. This scared me worse than anything else: Who would leave 160 acres to which they held title? What happened to them? "What's the difference, Miles?" My father had drunk himself into a moon-squint, his eyes glowing crescents. "Dead is gone."

Now whenever he mentions "West Texas," he winks at me, and I think of my sisters under the sod, silently winking back.

"What puzzles me, Miles," he slurred at the end of the night, "is that before he left, Mr. Yothers had drilled in a new crop. At first I saw the rows behind the wheat and thought, *Ah, Henry knows how starved we are for timber, he's planted trees*—dozens of queer little trees, shaped like crosses. Just a single branch right through their middles. Saplings, sure. Only one grew about a foot and a half, and the rest were much smaller. The thin trunks were the funniest shade of milky white, my son, like no tree's wood I've ever seen; and there wasn't a leaf in that bleached grove. And who plants anything in the dead of winter, in frozen ground? On my knees I discovered that each horizontal branch was roped to its base by a hitching knot, and these white branches were knobby at the ends, almost like animal—or even human . . ."

But Pa saw my face and trailed off, and soon he began to snore, and I was left alone to fret over his riddle. Now I think we must be very near to this milky white grove, and I am grateful for the dark sky and the snowflakes on Nore's reins—because there is no time for me to dismount and wander into the rows, to prove my guess right or wrong.

Forgive us, forgive us, I think as I race Nore past the Yotherses' bleak dugout, where the empty window frame leers on, and snow swirls in lovely patterns.

We detour five miles around a carmine streambed filled with ice, where dozens of black snakes draw s-shapes like a slow, strange current, spooking Nore; and afterward I'm no longer sure of our direction. Like us, the sun is lost. The temperature continues to fall. We come upon a dam I've never seen, the Window rattling like a saber against Nore's belly.

"Oh, God, where are we, Nore?" I coax her up a low hill, and it's around then that the blizzard hits.

The wind attacks our naked skin like knives; I can nearly hear Ma's voice in it, calling me home. But I'm too brave to turn the horse around, and anyhow I wouldn't know which way to go. White octaves of snow shriek from the tallgrass to the great descending blank of the heavens. "Go, go, go," I moan into Nore's ear, wanting her to decide. A part of me is already at the Florissants', warming up by the fire, sharing a meal of drumsticks and cider and biscuits with the Inspector. Their title drying on the kitchen table. "Well, sir," I tell him, "we did have a little trouble getting here, but it was certainly worth the risk . . ." A chokecherry branch cuts my left eyelid, and the eye fills with blood. The more I rub at it the denser the red gel gets. Outside of my mind I can barely see. We go flickering through the snow, until it becomes difficult to say which colors and temperatures are inner or outer weather, where one leaves off and the other picks up. I tighten my knee's grip on the Window frame. When Nore breaks into a gallop I drop the reins and grab her neck. Snow is eating our tracks: when I look back, it's as if we no longer exist.

She shoots through the tempest like an arrow for its target, and I think, *Thank God, she must smell a barn*—but when her jaw jerks around, I see that ice coats her eyes. She's been galloping completely blind.

I am sure we're being punished—I should never have unwrapped the Window, not even for one second. Snow pummels us with its million knuckles. "Oh, my darling, oh, poor darling," I tell Nore—I don't recognize my own voice anymore; Peter would caw with laughter if he could hear my tone, my father would be sickened—"Nore, my sweet one, my love . . ." Tender words pour out of me, my Grandmother Aura's words, the kind I haven't heard since she spoke them on the cousins' rose sofa in Blue Sink, and I wish I could use them like a compass needle to lead me back.

I grab ahold of the bridle and tug Nore forward with the wind at our backs, blowing more snow in on gales. I think of trying to guide her by the reins, but the snow's banked too deep to walk. Nore's sides heave, covered in freezing lather. Her eyelashes are stiff. I can't feel my toes inside my boots.

The horse keeps going blind, and I can't stop it—the ice coating the dark circles of her purply-black eyes. She moans whenever I attempt to pry and crack them clear. The reins wriggle snakily down her back and she jumps sideways. Hatred shivers along her spine; I've got one eyelid in a pinch when she peels back her lips and tries to bite me, but misses and rears. As if in slow motion I watch the Window coming loose, thumping against her side in the snow-furred burlap; I feel myself rolling, falling out of the saddle and somehow beneath her churning hooves, reaching up as the Window slides slantwise, one point angled at my chest—

and then I'm lying in the snow with the Window in my arms, stunned, watching as Nore disappears.

Now I understand: this is a nightmare. She flies into the white heart of the storm while I pant all raggedy in the drifts with the Window hard against my chest, sucking my frozen thumb. Screaming turns out to be an agility I've taken for granted; "Nore," I try to shout, but hear nothing. For one moment more I can see her running: a black match head tearing against a wall of snow. It's a wonder the gales don't catch alight and burn.

Mr. Inspector, sir, I hope you're stuck in the weather, too. And, Mrs. Florissant, do not let us hold you up for dinner, please eat, and should you spy a man through the open socket in your wall, won't you tell him that I'm lost . . .

Suddenly I realize what I'm holding on to—did I shatter it? I'm terrified to look. (What I see instead is Louma's skeleton in dust, my fingers threading through the open sockets in her skull.) As I pry at the burlap I learn something surprising about my future, something I hadn't guessed: If the Hox glass is in pieces, I won't ever go back home. I'd rather die here than return to our dugout without it.

Oh, Father, thank you—it's intact. I push my palms down the smooth length of it twice before sealing the burlap, then roll onto my back. High above me the black sky withdraws forever into an upside-down horizon—not a blue prairie line but a cone of snows. Wind wolves go on howling. Each of my eyelids feels heavier than iron, but sleep isn't what's beckoning me; the snow is teaching me a deeper way to breathe: long spaces open up behind each inhalation, followed by a very colorful spell of coughing. There's blood on the back of my hand—I knocked loose several teeth when I fell. One is lying near my left eye in its own smeary puddle. Snow falls and falls. Tomorrow, I think, the thirsty sod will drink this storm up, guzzle the red runoff from my chin. Acres of gold wheat wave at me from the future: March, April.

Hold on to your claim, Pa hisses, and I wipe my eyes.

What am I supposed to be doing out here again? Where am I taking the glass? And wasn't there a horse? For the life of me I cannot remember the horse's name.

More than anything I want to get the Window through the storm. I crouch over the burlap like something feeding—my skin becoming one more layer of protection. Soon my clothes are soaked through. The elements seal my eyes, so that I have to keep watch over the Window blindly with my arms. I clutch at it like a raft as the prairie pitches in icy waves. Images swirl through my mind of animals freezing in their stalls, black fingers lost to doctors' saws. *Think of a Bible verse, a hymn!* What enters my head instead is my mother's humming, a weedy drone that has no tune. Hours pass, or maybe minutes or whole days; the clock of my body breaks down. The world is pitch black.

.   .   .

When I wake, water is running in spring rivers down my face; my eyelids unravel and crack open. The temperature has risen, and a sunbeam fixes an x on my hand, which burns when I flex it. The hard pillow of the Window comes into focus under my cheek. I turn my head and find I'm surrounded by leafless skeletons of trees and the sapphire ice—and a man, watching me.

I sit up. Fifty yards ahead, a willowy man takes one sideways step through the golden haze and is somehow suddenly upon me. *I'm saved!* I think—but just as quickly my cry for help dissolves. This man looks even worse off than me. His gaunt face is entirely black except for the wet cracks of his eyes and mouth and pink lesions on his cheeks, as if he has just survived some kind of explosion. At first I think the skin is charred, but then the light gives it a riverbed glow and I realize he's covered in mud—soil, sod. His shirt and trousers are stiff with the same black filth, and the dirt on his collar isn't dried at all, but oozing. A dim saucer at each knee shows he's been genuflecting in the fields. Only, what sort of man is out farming in a blizzard? Not even my father is that crazy. What would drive a person into this weather?

He shuffles toward me, removing his hat.

"Inspector?"

We shout this at the exact same moment. Then we're left to gape at one another. White frogs of breath leap from my mouth. He doesn't seem to breathe at all.

"Hello, sir," I manage, and hold out a numb hand. The feeling returns to my stiff arm, and I bite down as pain rips along the bone—the polite smile, by some miracle, still on my face. "I guess we are both mistaken, sir." ("Etiquette will take possession of you at the oddest times, won't it, Miles?" Ma murmured once, when I caught her apologizing to a cupful of grasshoppers before drowning them in kerosene.)

Well, the stranger doesn't return any of my friendliness. *I'm Miles Zegner*, I was about to offer, but I swallow it back. And I don't ask for his name, either; a queasiness stirring in my gut warns me that I might not want to know it.

I'm certain that I've never seen this man on any homestead around here—but he's dressed for the work, with his cuffs pushed to the elbows like any man in Hox; and like Pa he has the settler's scar from the moldboard plow. He's a southpaw. A sodbuster. One of us. A newcomer to the Hox River Settlement? (*No, no*, a little voice in me whispers, *not new.*) His eyes have the half-moon markings of a pronghorn antelope. He looks like he's been awake for generations.

"You did not see a horse come through here, sir?"

"No horses. No Inspectors on horseback. No bats hanging from Inspectors' noses." He giggles.

"Are you all right, sir? Are you lost, too?"

Then the man says something in a jangly tone that I can barely understand, it's so reedy and high. His voice is almost female, or animal, and the words make no sense whatsoever.

"Green me that wheel!"

"Pardon, sir?"

"Grease me that doe!"

I swallow hard.

"Sir, I am not understanding you."

He draws a rectangle in the snow-dotted air and laughs; I swear I see a nugget of earth tumble out of his mouth. His lips are plush and smeared.

"But we need to wake up now, don't we, boy? This is quite a day! It sounds like you and I are on the hunt for the same fellow. The Inspector is coming shortly, you see. Yes. I believe that he will be coming very soon."

A fine gray ash is blowing from his curly hair, which looks like it is or once might have been yellow. The wind shifts and my nose wrinkles—there's a smell, a putrescence, a mix of silage and marrow and a hideous sweetness, like the time a family of rats suffocated in our sod walls. One hand keeps fussing with his trousers, which he's belted with a double loop of rope—his rib cage is almost impossibly narrow. If he were any thinner I swear he'd disappear. My mother's voice drifts into my ear: "He's a rumor, he's smoke . . ." But his eyes are solid marbles, and his fingernails are real enough to be broken. His left hand closes on the handle of a hay knife.

"That's a beautiful knife."

He smiles at me.

"And you say you are also"—I cough—"waiting on the Inspector? You've been here for the five years, then?"

The handle of the knife is some kind of clover-toned wood. The blade looks like a long tooth.

"Oh!" The man laughs. "Even longer. Long enough to lose track of the days and seasons entirely. Suns, moons, droughts, famines—who's counting?" He laughs again. The sun is stronger now. It shifts above us but never seems to settle anywhere on him.

"Where is your quarter section?"

"You're standing on it."

"Oh." *But where are we?* "Is anyone else here? Don't you have a family?"

"I may have." He frowns and licks his black lips, as if he truly cannot remember. "Yes! I did have a family. Parents, certainly. They are buried back East. And a wife . . . yes!" He beams at me. "I *did* have one. A wife, but she wasn't worth much. Women can be so impatient, Miles. And children—I believe we had several of them."

He begins to shake his thin shoulders in the silvery *h-yuk, h-yuk, h-yuk* of a coyote. His tongue surprises me—I guess part of me thought he was a ghost, a creature like my sisters. But his tongue is as red as sunrise in his dark face. He is alive, no question. I feel relieved, then scared for fresh reasons.

"Ah, children—*that* was a wash." This time when he opens his mouth, his voice is all throat.

"You shouldn't laugh at that."

"What's the matter?" He grins, trying to rib me with his elbow. "Out here we need a sense of humor, isn't that so?"

The violence of his laughter sprays dirt into the air; I cough again and think with horror that I'm breathing a powder from his body.

"Your kids all died?"

He shrugs.

"Sons or daughters?"

"Sons and daughters, yes. Sicklings. Weak ones. None lasted."

"What happened to your wife?"

"She lost faith." He lets out a theatrical sigh. "Lost her will to prosper. Became a madwoman, if you want to know. I had to make a break with her. Had to make a fresh start"—I wince; he's talking just like Pa now—"drove her off. Or rather, plowed her under. The West is a land of infinite beginnings, isn't that right, Miles Zegner? Pick up, embark again, file a preempt, stake a new claim"—*Did I tell him my name?*—"and after many lonely seasons, I have fulfilled each of the Act's stipulations. See this?"

He's holding something out to me—half a piece of paper. I take it with a trembling hand and recognize the text of the Homestead Act. I marvel at the document's creamy white color, its ink-bleeding signature—if I didn't know better I'd swear it was the original writ. How did this dirt-streaked stranger acquire such a thing—a law that looks like it was snatched from the president's own desk?

SEC. 3. And be it further enacted, that the Register of the Land Office shall note all such applications on the tract books and plats of his office, and keep a register of all such entries, and make return thereof to the General Land Office, together with the proof upon which they have been founded . . .

The man trails a slushy finger down to the word *glass*. Every claim shanty or dugout must have a real glass window, a whimsical clause that has cost lives out here. I stare at the sod and the black ribbon of blood under his nail.

"So you see that I'm in real need here, Miles. All the other proof I have ready for this Register, the Inspector. The last thing I need is a window." He contorts his mouth into a terrible smile.

My father's instructions move my jaw, push out my breath: "Listen, sir. I have a Window. If the Inspector is coming, I can loan it to you. We can fix it so it looks like it belongs to your dugout. So you can prove up."

"You would do that? For me?"

His eyes brighten fervidly in his grimy face, but not with happiness—it's more like watching sickness take root and germinate, blazing into a wildfire fever.

I nod, thinking about Pa. For all his charity with the Hox glass, I'm the one who bears the risk of it.

Without my awareness, we have begun moving; and our march feels almost like a pleasant walk, just a normal trip to deliver the Window to a neighbor. I picture the Florissants' claim swimming toward me out of the plains. The sun casts itself like a spell across the land—as if the blizzard never happened, as if Nore was not lost. The sky out West has so many tricks to make a person forget what he's just lived through.

We enter a clearing. Shortgrass and green ash are planted in tiers as a windbreak, and I can see what must be his dugout.

There are no bones in his fingers. He is made of dust. If it ever rains again he will seep back into the earth.

Before us a wall of sod bulges and heaves—every inch of it covered with flies. Doorless and stolidly black, studded through with reddish roots, there is not one thing this heap of earth has in common with a home. The snow stops abruptly fifty yards in every direction from the structure's foundation. No grass grows on it or near it; no birds sing; the smell of death makes my nostrils burn and my eyes stream.

Dear Bailey, I write in my mind, *if you thought our sod house was difficult to understand, you'll find it impossible to imagine this one. Bailey, I might not make it out of here alive.*

"Gosh, sir," is all that squeaks out of me.

"Now, would you like to see my crops, Miles? The acres I have cultivated? They're behind the house."

"And what crops might those be, sir?"

I want his words to give me the familiar pictures. Say: *corn.* Say: *wheat, milo, hay, lucerne.* But he only smiles and replies, "Come take a look."

I let the man lead me by my elbow, and when we turn a corner I shut my eyes. I wonder if he'll pry them open—like I did Nore's.

"Quite a harvest, eh?" he's saying. "And I grew them without a drop of water."

Sometimes I dream that dark rains fall and my sisters rise out of the sod, as tall as the ten-foot wheat, shaking the midges and the dust from their tangled hair. Like rain, they thunder and moan. Their pale mouths open and they hiss. Their faces aren't like any faces I know. *Stay in the ground*, I plead. *Oh, God, please let only wheat rise up.*

Even when my eyes open, I can't stop rubbing at them—I feel like I'm still held in that dream. The scene before me is familiar and terrifying: white crosses, hundreds or maybe thousands of them, rolling outward on the prairie sea. A shovel head glints in a freshly plowed furrow, where a yellowish knob the size of an onion sticks out of the sod. And I see now why Pa was so troubled by their milky hue, because these trees aren't made of wood at all, but bone. My sisters go on hissing in my mind.

"So you see," the man says, as brightly as any Western noon, "as soon as the Inspector comes, I'll own the land—160 acres, and not one yard less."

No, you are mistaken, sir. The land owns you.

He takes my arm and guides me back toward the sod mound. "Now, if you'll just kindly help me put the window in—"

"And when do you think the Inspector is coming?" I ask in a mild voice.

The man smiles and rakes at his black eyes.

As we unpeel the snowy burlap from the Window, I find myself thinking about my home: Once, when I was nearly sleeping, a fleecy tarantula with a torso as thick as a deck of cards crawled across my mouth, and Peter laughed so hard that I started laughing, too. My father took three months to finish a table and paint it lake blue, just because he thought the color would be a relief to Ma. My mother pieced a quilt for each of her daughters in the dark. Often, at night, I wake into the perfect blankness of the dugout and watch our dreams braid together along the low ceiling. It would take lifetimes to explain to this wretched creature why our Zegner soddy is a home, even without any Inspector's stamp, while this place is a . . . tomb.

I step back and let him do the last work to widen the aperture meant to frame the Window. He grunts and scrapes at the pegs holding the shape of the breach and snows sod down all around us. He spits sootily on the glass and rubs in broad strokes with his sleeve.

"When the Inspector comes and sees my window—" he begins prattling, and a quagmire opens up in my chest, deep in its center—a terror like the suck of soft earth. And like a quagmire the terror won't release me, because the man is speaking in the voice of my own father, and of every sodbuster in the Hox River Settlement—a voice that can live for eons on dust and thimblefuls of water, that can be plowed under, hailed out, and go on whispering madly forever about *spring*, about *tomorrow*, a voice of a hope beyond the reach of reason or exhaustion (*oh, Ma, that's going to be my voice soon*)—a voice that will never let us quit the land.

"Give it back."

"It's too late for that, Miles."

"I have money," I say, remembering Pa's envelope. "Give me the glass, take the money, and I'll be on my way."

The man looks down at me, amused; he fingers a dollar bill as if it were the feather of a foreign bird, and I think that he must be even older than our country, as old as the sod itself. "What use would I have for *that*? That isn't the paper I require. And anyway, this window isn't yours. You stole it."

I reply in a daze: "You're acquainted with the Yotherses?"

"I was, in a way, but only at the end."

"I didn't steal the Window."

"No, but your father did."

"You know my father?"

"Where do you think I was coming from when I happened upon you?"

My eyes swim and land on the clover glow of his hay knife.

"When the Inspector comes and sees my window—" he's saying again, in the tone that sparkles. His back is to me, and I watch the knife bob on his hip. My legs tremble as I spread them to a wide base and get ready to lunge. In a moment, I'll have to grab his knife and stab him in the back, then reclaim the Window from the wall of his tomb and run for the Florissants' place. I can feel the nearness of these events—feel the tearing of his skin, the tug of his muscle tissue as the knife rips between his twitching shoulder blades—and I powerfully wish that I could crawl through the window of my Blue Sink bedroom, where such a feeling would be unimaginable, and drift into a dreamless sleep in my childhood bed.

As I crouch stiffly into my soles, the stranger says gently, "I thought you said you weren't a thief."

"Excuse me?" I look up—and find my image reflected in the glass.

"That's the thing with windows, isn't it, Miles?" he says. "Sometimes we see things we don't want to see."

He turns to me then, and his eyes are bottomless.

.   .   .

Mrs. Sticksel peers through the hole in her wall at a dark shape coming on a long trot through the wheat—the complex moving silhouette of a horse and rider. She breaks into a smile, relieved, and moves to stand in the doorway, the children fluttering around her. It's only then that she notices the soreness of her jaw, tense from all the anxious waiting. She waves a pale arm beneath the black night sky, beneath the still-falling snow, and thinks, *That Zegner child sure did shoot up this year*, as the rider's profile grows. The face is still a blank mask.

"Well, look who made it!" she calls. "Oh praise God, lost lamb, we've been so worried about you."

A slice of moonlight falls across the horse's flank.

"Say, isn't that the Florissants' mare? What happened to Nore?"

When the Zegner boy doesn't answer, she loosens the grip on her smile and tries a hot little laugh.

"That's you, ain't it, Miles? In this weather I can scarcely see out—"

And just as the children go rushing out to greet the rider, she has the dark feeling she should call them back.

Vanity Fair

Whether he was writing as an atheist about the legacy of the King James Bible, as an American about his adopted country's unthinking complicity with a duplicitous and corrupt Pakistani regime, or as a cancer patient about the disease that ravaged his body but not his mind, Christopher Hitchens never yielded his trademark eloquence. Though he famously professed no belief in the afterlife, his contributions to journalism, letters, and rigorous public discourse live on. His work for Vanity Fair *won the magazine National Magazine Awards for Columns and Commentary in 2007, 2011, and 2012. Christopher Hitchens died on December 15, 2011.*

Christopher Hitchens

When the King
Saved God *and*
From Abbottabad
to Worse *and*
Unspoken Truths

When the King Saved God

After she was elected the first female governor of Texas, in 1924, and got herself promptly embroiled in an argument about whether Spanish should be used in Lone Star schools, it is possible that Miriam A. "Ma" Ferguson did *not* say, "If the King's English was good enough for Jesus Christ, it's good enough for the children of Texas." I still rather hope that she did. But then, verification of quotations and sources is a tricky and sensitive thing. Abraham Lincoln lay dying in a room full of educated and literate men, in the age of the wireless telegraph, and not far from the offices of several newspapers, and we *still* do not know for sure, at the moment when his great pulse ceased to beat, whether his secretary of war, Edwin Stanton, said, "Now he belongs to the ages" or "Now he belongs to the angels."

Such questions of authenticity become even more fraught when they involve the word itself becoming flesh; the fulfillment of prophecy; the witnessing of miracles; the detection of the finger of God. Guesswork and approximation will not do: the resurrection cannot be half true or questionably attested. For the first 1,500 years of the Christian epoch, this problem of "authority," in both senses of that term, was solved by having the divine mandate wrapped up in languages that the majority of the congregation could not understand and by having it presented to them by a special caste or class who alone possessed the mystery of celestial decoding.

Four hundred years ago, just as William Shakespeare was reaching the height of his powers and showing the new scope and variety of the English language, and just as "England" itself was becoming more of a nation-state and less an offshore dependency of Europe, an extraordinary committee of clergymen and scholars completed the task of rendering the Old and New Testaments into English and claimed that the result was the "Authorized" or "King James" version. This was a fairly conservative attempt to stabilize the Crown and the kingdom, heal the breach between competing English and Scottish Christian sects, and bind the majesty of the king to his devout people. "The powers that be," it had Saint Paul saying in his Epistle to the Romans, "are ordained of God." This and other phrasings, not all of them so authoritarian and conformist, continue to echo in our language: "When I was a child, I spake as a child"; "Eat, drink, and be merry"; "From strength to strength"; "Grind the faces of the poor"; "salt of the earth"; "Our Father, which art in heaven." It's near impossible to imagine our idiom and vernacular, let alone our liturgy, without them. Not many committees in history have come up with such crystalline prose.

.   .   .

King James I, who brought the throne of Scotland along with him, was the son of Mary, Queen of Scots, and knew that his predecessor, Queen Elizabeth I, had been his mother's executioner. In Scotland, he had had to contend with extreme Puritans who were suspicious of monarchy and hated all Catholics. In England, he was faced with worldly bishops who were hostile to Puritans and jealous of their own privileges. Optimism, prosperity, and culture struck one note—Henry Hudson was setting off to the Northwest Passage, and Shakespeare's Globe Theater was drawing thoughtful crowds to see those dramas of power and legitimacy *Othello, King Lear,* and *The Tempest*—but terror and insecurity kept pace. Guy Fawkes and his fellow plotters, believed to be in league with the pope, nearly succeeded in blowing up Parliament in 1605. Much of London was stricken with visitations of the bubonic plague, which, as Bishop Lancelot Andrewes (head of the committee of translators) noted with unease, appeared to strike the godly quite as often as it smote the sinner. The need was for a tempered version of God's word that engendered compromise and a sense of protection.

Bishop Andrewes and his colleagues, a mixture of clergymen and classicists, were charged with revisiting the original Hebrew and Greek editions of the Old and New Testaments, along with the fragments of Aramaic that had found their way into the text. Understanding that their task was a patriotic and "nation-building" one (and impressed by the nascent idea of English Manifest Destiny, whereby the English people had replaced the Hebrews as God's chosen), whenever they could translate any ancient word for "people" or "tribe" as "nation," they elected to do so. The term appears 454 times in this confident form of "the King's English." Meeting in Oxford and Cambridge college libraries for the most part, they often kept their notes in Latin. Their conservative and consensual project was politically short-lived: in a few years the land was to be convulsed with civil war, and the Puritan and parliamentary forces under Oliver Cromwell would sweep the head of King Charles I from his shoulders. But the translators' legacy remains, and it is paradoxically a revolutionary one, as well as a giant step in the maturing of English literature.

Imagining the most extreme form of totalitarianism in his *Nineteen Eighty-four* dystopia, George Orwell depicted a secret class of occult power holders (the Inner Party clustered around

Big Brother) that would cement its eternal authority by recasting the entire language. In the tongue of "Newspeak," certain concepts of liberty and conscience would be literally impossible to formulate. And only within the most restricted circles of the regime would certain heretical texts, like Emmanuel Goldstein's manifesto, still be legible and available. I believe that Orwell, a strong admirer of the Protestant Reformation and the poetry of its hero John Milton, was using as his original allegory the long struggle of English dissenters to have the Bible made available in a language that the people could read.

·   ·   ·

Until the early middle years of the sixteenth century, when King Henry VIII began to quarrel with Rome about the dialectics of divorce and decapitation, a short and swift route to torture and death was the attempt to print the Bible in English. It's a long and stirring story, and its crux is the head-to-head battle between Sir Thomas More and William Tyndale (whose name in early life, I am proud to say, was William Hychyns). Their combat fully merits the term "fundamental." Infuriating More, Tyndale whenever possible was loyal to the Protestant spirit by correctly translating the word *ecclesia* to mean "the congregation" as an autonomous body, rather than "the church" as a sacrosanct institution above human law. In English churches, state-selected priests would merely incant the liturgy. Upon hearing the words "Hoc" and "corpus" (in the "For this is my body" passage), newly literate and impatient artisans in the pews would mockingly whisper, "Hocus-pocus," finding a tough slang term for the religious obfuscation at which they were beginning to chafe. The cold and righteous More, backed by his "Big Brother" the pope and leading an inner party of spies and inquisitors, watched the Channel ports for smugglers risking everything to import sheets produced by Tyndale, who was forced to do his translating and printing from exile. The rack and the rope were not stinted with dissenters, and eventually Tyndale himself was tracked down, strangled, and publicly burned. (Hilary Mantel's masterpiece historical novel, *Wolf Hall*, tells this exciting and gruesome story in such a way as to revise the shining image of "Saint" Thomas More, the "man for all seasons," almost out of existence. High time, in my view. The martyrdoms he inflicted upon others were more cruel and irrational than the one he sought and found for himself.)

Other translations into other languages, by Martin Luther himself, among others, slowly entered circulation. One of them, the so-called Geneva Bible, was a more Calvinist and Puritan English version than the book that King James commissioned and was the edition that the Pilgrim Fathers, fleeing the cultural and religious war altogether, took with them to Plymouth Rock. Thus Governor Ma Ferguson was right in one respect: America was the first and only Christian society that could take an English Bible for granted, and never had to struggle for a popular translation of "the good book." The question, rather, became that of exactly *which* English version was to be accepted as the correct one. After many false starts and unsatisfactory printings, back in England, the Anglican conclave in 1611 adopted William Tyndale's beautiful rendering almost wholesale, and out of their zeal for compromise and stability ironically made a posthumous hero out of one of the greatest literary dissidents and subversives who ever lived.

Writing about his own fascination with cadence and rhythm in *Notes of a Native Son*, James Baldwin said, "I hazard that the King James Bible, the rhetoric of the store-front church, something ironic and violent and perpetually understated in Negro speech . . . have something to do with me today; but I wouldn't stake my life on it." As a child of the black pulpit and chronicler of the Bible's huge role in the American oral tradition, Baldwin probably was "understating" at that very moment. And, as he very well knew, there had been times when biblical verses *did* involve, quite literally, the staking of one's life. This is why the nuances and details of translation were (and still are) of such huge moment. For example, in Isaiah 7:14 it is stated that, "behold, a virgin shall conceive, and bear a son, and shall call his name Immanuel." This is the scriptural warrant and prophecy for the impregnation of the Virgin Mary by the Holy Ghost. But the original Hebrew wording refers only to the pregnancy of an *almah*, or young woman. If the Hebrew language wants to identify virginity, it has other terms in which to do so. The implications are not merely textual. To translate is also to interpret or, indeed, to lay down the law. (Incidentally, the American "Revised Standard Version" of 1952 replaced the word "virgin" with "young woman." It took the fundamentalists until 1978 to restore the original misreading, in the now dominant "New International Version.")

·   ·   ·

Take an even more momentous example, cited by Adam Nicolson in his very fine book on the process, *God's Secretaries*. In the First Epistle to the Corinthians, Saint Paul reminds his readers of the fate that befell many backsliding pre-Christian Jews. He describes their dreadful punishments as having "happened unto them for ensamples," which in 1611 was a plain way of conveying the word "example" or "illustrative instance," or perhaps "lesson." However, the original Greek term was *typoi*, which by contrast may be rendered as "types" or "archetypes" and suggests that Jews were to be eternally punished for their special traits. This had been Saint Augustine's harsh reading, followed by successive Roman Catholic editions. At least one of King James's translators wanted to impose that same collective punishment on the people of Moses but was overruled. In the main existing text, the lenient word "ensamples" is given, with a marginal note in the original editions saying

that "types" may also be meant. The English spirit of compromise at its best.

Then there are seemingly small but vital matters of emphasis,
in which Tyndale did not win every round. Here is a famous
verse which one might say was central to Christian teaching:
"This is my Commandment, that you love one another, as I have
loved you. / Greater love hath no man than this, that a man lay
down his life for his friends." That's the King James version,
which has echoed in the heads of many churchgoers until their
last hour. Here is how the verse read when first translated by
Tyndale: "This is my Commandment, that you love together as I
have loved you. / Greater love than this hath no man, than that a
man bestow his life for his friends."

I do not find that the "King's English" team improved much
on the lovely simplicity of what they found. Tyndale has Jesus
groping rather appealingly to make a general precept or princi-
ple out of a common bond, whereas the bishops and scholars are
aiming to make an iron law out of love. In doing so they suggest
strenuous martyrdom ("lay down," as if Jesus had been a sacrifice to his immediate circle only). Far more human and attractive, surely, is Tyndale's warm "bestow," which suggests that a
life devoted to friendship is a noble thing in itself.

Tyndale, incidentally, was generally good on the love question. Take that same Epistle of Paul to the Corinthians, a few
chapters later. For years, I would listen to it in chapel and wonder how an insipid, neuter word like "charity" could have gained
such moral prestige. The King James version enjoins us that
"now abideth faith, hope and charity, these three; but the greatest of these is charity." Tyndale had put "love" throughout, and
even if your Greek is as poor as mine you will have to admit that
it is a greatly superior capture of the meaning of that all-impor-
tant original word *agape*. It was actually the frigid clerical bu-
reaucrat Thomas More who had made this into one of the many
disputations between himself and Tyndale, and in opting to

accept his ruling it seems as if King James's committee also hoped to damp down the risky, ardent spontaneity of unconditional love and replace it with an idea of stern duty. Does not the notion of compulsory love, in any form, have something grotesque and fanatical about it?

Most recent English translations have finally dropped More and the King and gone with Tyndale on this central question, but often at the cost of making "love" appear too husky and sentimental. Thus the "Good News Bible" for American churches, first published in 1966: "Love never gives up; and its faith, hope and patience never fail." This doesn't read at all like the outcome of a struggle to discern the essential meaning of what is perhaps our most numinous word. It more resembles a smiley-face Dale Carnegie reassurance. And, as with everything else that's designed to be instant, modern, and "accessible," it goes out of date (and out of *time*) faster than Wisconsin cheddar.

Though I am sometimes reluctant to admit it, there really *is* something "timeless" in the Tyndale/King James synthesis. For generations, it provided a common stock of references and allusions, rivaled only by Shakespeare in this respect. It resounded in the minds and memories of literate people, as well as of those who acquired it only by listening. From the stricken beach of Dunkirk in 1940, faced with a devil's choice between annihilation and surrender, a British officer sent a cable back home. It contained the three words "but if not . . ." All of those who received it were at once aware of what it signified. In the Book of Daniel, the Babylonian tyrant Nebuchadnezzar tells the three Jewish heretics Shadrach, Meshach, and Abednego that if they refuse to bow to his sacred idol they will be flung into a "burning fiery furnace." They made him an answer: "If it be so, our god whom we serve is able to deliver us from the burning fiery furnace, and he will deliver us out of thy hand, O King. / *But if not*, be it known unto thee, O King, that we will not serve thy gods, nor worship the golden image which thou hast set up."

• • •

A culture that does not possess this common store of image and allegory will be a perilously thin one. To seek restlessly to update it or make it "relevant" is to miss the point, like yearning for a hip-hop Shakespeare. "Man is born unto trouble as the sparks fly upward," says the Book of Job. Want to try to improve that for Twitter? And so bleak and spare and fatalistic—almost nonreligious—are the closing verses of Ecclesiastes that they were read at the Church of England funeral service the unbeliever George Orwell had requested in his will: "Also when they shall be afraid of that which is high, and fears shall be in the way, and the almond tree shall flourish, and the grasshopper shall be a burden, and desire shall fail: because man goeth to his long home. . . . Or ever the silver cord be loosed, or the golden bowl be broken, or the pitcher be broken at the fountain, or the wheel broken at the cistern. / Then shall the dust return to the earth as it was."

At my father's funeral I chose to read a similarly non-sermonizing part of the New Testament, this time an injunction from Saint Paul's Epistle to the Philippians: "Finally, brethren, whatsoever things are true, whatsoever things are honest, whatsoever things are just, whatsoever things are pure, whatsoever things are lovely, whatsoever things are of good report; if there be any virtue, and if there be any praise, think on these things."

• • •

As much philosophical as spiritual, with its conditional and speculative "ifs" and its closing advice—always italicized in my mind since first I heard it—to *think* and reflect on such matters: this passage was the labor of men who had wrought deeply with ideas and concepts. I now pluck down from my shelf the American Bible Society's "Contemporary English Version," which I picked up at an evangelical "Promise Keepers" rally on the Mall in Washington in 1997. Claiming to be faithful to the spirit of the King James translation, it keeps its promise in this way: "Finally, my friends, keep your minds on whatever is true, pure, right, holy, friendly and proper. Don't ever stop thinking about what is truly worthwhile and worthy of praise."

Pancake-flat: suited perhaps to a basement meeting of AA, these words could not hope to penetrate the torpid, resistant fog in the mind of a sixteen-year-old boy, as their original had done for me. There's perhaps a slightly ingratiating obeisance to gender neutrality in the substitution of "my friends" for "brethren," but to suggest that Saint Paul, of all people, was gender-neutral is to rewrite the history as well as to rinse out the prose. When the Church of England effectively dropped King James, in the 1960s, and issued what would become the "New English Bible," T. S. Eliot commented that the result was astonishing "in its combination of the vulgar, the trivial and the pedantic." (Not surprising from the author of *For Lancelot Andrewes*.) This has been true of every other stilted, patronizing, literal-minded attempt to shift the translation's emphasis from plangent poetry to utilitarian prose.

T. S. Eliot left America (and his annoyingly colorless Unitarian family) to seek the traditionalist roots of liturgical and literary tradition in England. Coming in the opposite direction across the broad Atlantic, the King James Bible slowly overhauled and overtook the Geneva version and, as the Pilgrim-type mini-theocracies of New England withered away, became one of the very few books from which almost any American could quote something. Paradoxically, this made it easy to counterfeit. When Joseph Smith began to fabricate his Book of Mormon, in the late 1820s, "translating" it from no known language, his copy of King James was never far from his side. He plagiarized 27,000 words more or less straight from the original, including several biblical stories lifted almost in their entirety, and the throat-clearing but vaguely impressive phrase "and it came to pass" is used at least

2,000 times. Such "borrowing" was a way of lending much-needed "tone" to the racket. Not long afterward, William Miller excited gigantic crowds with the news that the Second Coming of Jesus would occur in 1843. An associate followed up with an 1844 due date. These disappointed prophecies were worked out from marginal notes in Miller's copy of the King James edition, which he quarried for apocalyptic evidence. (There had always been those, from the earliest days, when it was being decided which parts of the Bible were divinely inspired and which were not, who had striven to leave out the Book of Revelation. Martin Luther himself declined to believe that it was the work of the Holy Spirit. But there Christianity still is, well and truly stuck with it.) So, of the many Christian heresies which were born in the New World and not imported from Europe, at least three—the Mormons, or Latter-day Saints; the Millerites, or Seventh-day Adventists; and their schismatic product the Jehovah's Witnesses—are indirectly mutated from a pious attempt to bring religious consensus to Jacobean England.

Not to overprize consensus, it does possess certain advantages over randomness and chaos. Since the appearance of the so-called Good News Bible, there have been no fewer than forty-eight English translations published in the United States. And the rate shows no sign of slackening. Indeed, the trend today is toward what the trade calls "niche Bibles." These include the "Couples Bible," "One Year New Testament for Busy Moms," "Extreme Teen Study Bible," "Policeman's Bible," and—somehow unavoidably—the "Celebrate Recovery Bible." (Give them credit for one thing: the biblical sales force knows how to "be fruitful and multiply.") In this cut-price spiritual cafeteria, interest groups and even individuals can have their own customized version of God's word. But there will no longer be a culture of the kind that instantly recognized what Lincoln meant when he spoke of "a house divided." The gradual eclipse of a single structure has led, not to a new clarity, but to a new Babel.

466
Christopher Hitchens

•   •   •

Those who opposed the translation of the Bible into the vernacular—rather like those Catholics who wish the Mass were still recited in Latin or those Muslims who regard it as profane to render the Koran out of Arabic—were afraid that the mystic potency of incantation and ritual would be lost, and that daylight would be let in upon magic. They also feared that if God's word became too everyday and commonplace it would become less impressive or less able to inspire awe. But the reverse turns out to have been the case, at least in this instance. The Tyndale/King James translation, even if all its copies were to be burned, would still live on in our language through its transmission by way of Shakespeare and Milton and Bunyan and Coleridge, and also by way of beloved popular idioms such as "fatted calf" and "pearls before swine." It turned out to be rather more than the sum of its ancient predecessors, as well as a repository and edifice of language that towers above its successors. Its abandonment by the Church of England establishment, which hoped to refill its churches and ended up denuding them, is yet another demonstration that religion is manmade, with inky human fingerprints all over its supposedly inspired and unalterable texts. Ma Ferguson was right in her way. She just didn't know how many Englishmen and how many Englishes, and how many Jesus stories and Jesuses, there were to choose from.

From Abbottabad to Worse

Salman Rushdie's upsettingly brilliant psycho-profile of Pakistan in his 1983 novel, *Shame*, rightly laid emphasis on the crucial part played by sexual repression in the Islamic republic. And that was *before* the Talibanization of Afghanistan, and of much of

Pakistan, too. Let me try to summarize and update the situation like this: Here is a society where rape is not a crime. It is a *punishment*. Women can be *sentenced* to be raped, by tribal and religious kangaroo courts, if even a rumor of their immodesty brings shame on their menfolk. In such an obscenely distorted context, the counterpart term to shame—which is the noble word "honor"—becomes most commonly associated with the word "killing." Moral courage consists of the willingness to butcher your own daughter.

If the most elemental of human instincts becomes warped in this bizarre manner, other morbid symptoms will disclose themselves as well. Thus, President Asif Ali Zardari cringes daily in front of the forces who openly murdered his wife, Benazir Bhutto, and who then contemptuously ordered the crime scene cleansed with fire hoses, as if to spit even on the pretense of an investigation. A man so lacking in pride—indeed lacking in manliness—will seek desperately to compensate in other ways. Swelling his puny chest even more, he promises to resist the mighty United States and to defend Pakistan's holy "sovereignty." This puffery and posing might perhaps possess a rag of credibility if he and his fellow middlemen were not avidly ingesting $3 billion worth of American subsidies every year.

There's absolutely no mystery to the "Why do they hate us?" question, at least as it arises in Pakistan. They hate us because they owe us, and are dependent upon us. The two main symbols of Pakistan's pride—its army and its nuclear program—are wholly parasitic on American indulgence and patronage. But, as I wrote for *Vanity Fair* in late 2001, in a long report from this degraded country, that army and those nukes are intended to be reserved for war against the neighboring democracy of India. Our bought-and-paid-for pretense that they have any other true purpose has led to a rancid, resentful official hypocrisy and to a state policy of revenge, large and petty, on the big, rich, dumb Americans who foot the bill. If Pakistan were a character, it would resemble the one described by Alexander Pope in his *Epistle to Dr Arbuthnot:*

> Willing to wound, and yet afraid to strike.
> Just hint a fault, and hesitate dislike:
> Alike reserved to blame, or to commend,
> A timorous foe, and a suspicious friend . . .
> So well-bred Spaniels civilly delight
> In mumbling of the game they dare not bite.

· · ·

There's an old cliché in client-state relations, about the tail wagging the dog, but have we really considered what it means when we actually are the *tail*, and the dog is our goddam lapdog? The lapdog's surreptitious revenge has consisted in the provision of kennels for attack dogs. Everybody knew that the Taliban was originally an instrument for Pakistani colonization of Afghanistan. Everybody knew that al-Qaeda forces were being sheltered in the Pakistani frontier town of Quetta, and that Khalid Sheikh Muhammed was found hiding in Rawalpindi, the headquarters of the Pakistani Army. Bernard-Henri Lévy once even produced a damning time line showing that every Pakistani "capture" of a wanted jihadist had occurred the week immediately preceding a vote in Congress on subventions to the government in Islamabad. But not even I was cynical enough to believe that Osama bin Laden himself would be given a villa in a Pakistani garrison town on Islamabad's periphery. I quote below from a letter written by my Pakistani friend Irfan Khawaja, a teacher of philosophy at Felician College, in New Jersey. He sent it to me in anguish just after bin Laden, who claimed to love death more than life, had met his presumably desired rendezvous:

I find, however, that I can't quite share in the sense of jubilation. I never believed that bin Laden was living in some hideaway "in the tribal areas." But to learn that he was living in Abbottabad, after Khalid Sheikh Muhammed was discovered in Rawalpindi, is really too much for me. I don't feel jubilation. I feel a personal, ineradicable sense of betrayal. For ten years, I've watched members of my own family taking to the streets, protesting the US military presence in northern Pakistan and the drone strikes etc. They stood there and prattled on and on about "Pakistan's sovereignty," and the supposed invasion of it by US forces.

Well, what fucking sovereignty? What fucking sovereignty were these people "protecting"? It's bad enough that the Pakistani army lacks sovereignty over the tribal area and can't control it when the country's own life depends upon it. But that bin Laden was living in the Pakistani equivalent of Annapolis, MD . . .

You will notice that Irfan is here registering genuine shame, in the sense of proper outrage and personal embarrassment, and not some vicarious parody of emotion where it is always others— usually powerless women—who are supposedly bringing the shame on you.

·   ·   ·

If the Pakistani authorities had admitted what they were doing and claimed the right to offer safe haven to al-Qaeda and the Taliban on their own soil, then the boast of "sovereignty" might at least have had some grotesque validity to it. But they were too cowardly and duplicitous for that. And they also wanted to be paid, lavishly and regularly, for pretending to fight against those very forces. Has any state ever been, in the strict sense of the term, more shameless? Over the years, I have written many pages about the sick relationship between the United States and various Third World client regimes, many of which turned out to be false friends as well as highly discreditable ones. General Pinochet, of Chile, had the unbelievable nerve to explode a car bomb in rush-hour traffic in Washington, D.C., in 1976, murdering a political rival and his American colleague. The South Vietnamese military junta made a private deal to sabotage the Paris peace talks in 1968, in order to benefit the electoral chances of Richard Nixon. Dirty money from the Shah of Iran and the Greek dictatorship made its way at different times into our electoral process. Israeli religious extremists demand American protection and then denounce us for "interference" if we demur politely about colonization of the West Bank. But our blatant manipulation by Pakistan is the most diseased and rotten thing in which the United States has ever in-volved itself. And it is also, in the grossest way, a violation of our sovereignty. Pakistan routinely—by the dispatch of barely deni-able death squads across its borders, to such locations as the Taj Hotel in Mumbai—injures the sovereignty of India as well as Af-ghanistan. But you might call that a traditional form of violation. In our case, Pakistan ingratiatingly and silkily invites young Americans to one of the vilest and most dangerous regions on earth, there to fight and die as its allies, all the while sharpening a blade for their backs. "The smiler with the knife under the cloak," as Chaucer phrased it so frigidly. (At our feet, and at our throat: Perfectly symbolic of the underhanded duality between the mer-cenary and the sycophant was the decision of the Pakistani intel-ligence services, in revenge for the Abbottabad raid, to disclose the name of the C.I.A. station chief in Islamabad.)

This is well beyond humiliation. It makes us a prisoner of the shame, and co-responsible for it. The United States was shamed when it became the Cold War armorer of the Ayub Khan dicta-torship in the 1950s and 1960s. It was shamed even more when it supported General Yahya Khan's mass murder in Bangladesh in

1971: a Muslim-on-Muslim genocide that crashingly demon-strated the utter failure of a state based on a single religion. We were then played for suckers by yet another military boss in the form of General Zia-ul-Haq, who leveraged anticommunism in Afghanistan into a free pass for the acquisition of nuclear weap-ons and the open mockery of the nonproliferation treaty. By the start of the millennium, Pakistan had become home to a Walmart of fissile material, traded as far away as Libya and North Korea by the state-subsidized nuclear entrepreneur A. Q. Khan, the country's nearest approach (which in itself tells you something) to a national hero. Among the scientists working on the project were three named sympathizers of the Taliban. And that gigan-tic betrayal, too, was uncovered only by chance.

Again to quote myself from 2001, if Pakistan were a person, he (and it would have to be a he) would have to be completely humorless, paranoid, insecure, eager to take offense, and suffer-ing from self-righteousness, self-pity, and self-hatred. That last triptych of vices is intimately connected. The self-righteousness comes from the claim to represent a religion: the very name "Pak-istan" is an acronym of Punjab, Afghanistan, Kashmir, and so forth, the resulting word in the Urdu language meaning "Land of the Pure." The self-pity derives from the sad fact that the coun-try has almost nothing else to be proud of: virtually barren of achievements and historically based on the amputation and mutilation of India in 1947 and its own self-mutilation in Ban-gladesh. The self-hatred is the consequence of being pathetically, permanently mendicant: an abject begging-bowl country that is nonetheless run by a superrich and hypercorrupt Punjabi elite. As for paranoia: This not so hypothetical Pakistani would also be a hardened anti-Semite, moaning with pleasure at the butchery of Daniel Pearl and addicted to blaming his self-inflicted woes on the all-powerful Jews.

This dreary story actually does have some bearing on the "sovereignty" issue. In the beginning, all that the Muslim League demanded from the British was "a state for Muslims." Pakistan's founder and first president, Muhammad Ali Jinnah, was a relatively secular man whose younger sister went around unveiled and whose second wife did not practice Islam at all. But there's a world of difference between a state for Muslims and a full-on Muslim state. Under the rule of General Zia there began to be imposition of Shari'a and increased persecution of non-Muslims as well as of Muslim minorities such as the Shiites, Ismailis, and Ahmadis. In recent years these theocratic tendencies have intensified with appalling speed, to the point where the state contains not one but two secret statelets within itself: the first an impenetrable enclave of covert nuclear command and control and the second a private nexus of power at the disposal of the military intelligence services and—until recently—Osama bin Laden himself. It's the sovereignty of *these* possessions that exercises General Ashfaq Kayani, head of the Pakistani Army, who five days after Abbottabad made the arrogant demand that the number of American forces in the country be reduced "to the minimum essential." He even said that any similar American action ought to warrant a "review" of the whole relationship between the two countries. How pitiful it is that a Pakistani and not an American should have been the first (and so far the only) leader to say those necessary things.

·   ·   ·

If we ever ceased to swallow our pride, so I am incessantly told in Washington, then the Pakistani oligarchy might behave even more abysmally than it already does, and the situation deteriorate even further. This stale and superficial argument ignores the awful historical fact that, each time the Pakistani leadership *did* get worse, or behave worse, it was handsomely rewarded by the United States. We have been the enablers of every stage of that wretched state's counter-evolution, to the point where it is a serious regional menace and an undisguised ally of our worst enemy, as well as the sworn enemy of some of our best allies. How could it be "worse" if we shifted our alliance and instead embraced India, our only rival in scale as a multiethnic and multireligious democracy and a nation that contains nearly as many Muslims as Pakistan? How could it be "worse" if we listened to the brave Afghans, like their former intelligence chief Amrullah Saleh, who have been telling us for years that we are fighting the war in the wrong country?

If we continue to deny or avoid this inescapable fact, then we really are dishonoring, as well as further endangering, our exemplary young volunteers. Why was the raid on Abbottabad so rightly called "daring"? Because it had to be conducted under the radar of the Pakistani Air Force, which "scrambled" its jets and would have brought the Black Hawks down if it could. That this is true is bad enough in all conscience. That we should still be submitting ourselves to lectures and admonitions from General Kayani is beyond shameful.

Unspoken Truths

I have seen the moment of my greatness flicker,
And I have seen the eternal Footman hold my coat, and snicker,
And in short, I was afraid.
> —T. S. Eliot, "The Love Song of J. Alfred Prufrock."

Like so many of life's varieties of experience, the novelty of a diagnosis of malignant cancer has a tendency to wear off. The thing begins to pall, even to become banal. One can become quite used to the specter of the eternal Footman, like some lethal old bore lurking in the hallway at the end of the evening, hoping for the chance to have a word. And I don't so much object to his holding my coat in that marked manner, as if mutely reminding me that it's time to be on my way. No, it's the *snickering* that gets me down.

On a much-too-regular basis, the disease serves me up with a teasing special of the day, or a flavor of the month. It might be random sores and ulcers, on the tongue or in the mouth. Or why not a touch of peripheral neuropathy, involving numb and chilly feet? Daily existence becomes a babyish thing, measured out not in Prufrock's coffee spoons but in tiny doses of nourishment, accompanied by heartening noises from onlookers, or solemn discussions of the operations of the digestive system, conducted with motherly strangers. On the less good days, I feel like that wooden-legged piglet belonging to a sadistically sentimental family that could bear to eat him only a chunk at a time. Except that cancer isn't so . . . considerate.

Most despond-inducing and alarming of all, so far, was the moment when my voice suddenly rose to a childish (or perhaps piglet-like) piping squeak. It then began to register all over the place, from a gruff and husky whisper to a papery, plaintive bleat. And at times it threatened, and now threatens daily, to disappear altogether. I had just returned from giving a couple of speeches in California, where with the help of morphine and adrenaline I could still successfully "project" my utterances, when I made an attempt to hail a taxi outside my home—and nothing happened. I stood, frozen, like a silly cat that had abruptly lost its meow. I used to be able to stop a New York cab at thirty paces. I could also, without the help of a microphone, reach the back row and gallery of a crowded debating hall. And it may be nothing to boast about, but people tell me that if their radio or television was on, even in the next room, they could always pick out my tones and know that I was "on," too.

Like health itself, the loss of such a thing can't be imagined until it occurs. In common with everybody else, I have played versions of the youthful "Which would you rather?" game, in which most usually it's debated whether blindness or deafness would be the most oppressive. But I don't ever recall speculating much about being struck dumb. (In the American vernacular, to say "I'd really hate to be dumb" might in any case draw another snicker.) Deprivation of the ability to speak is more like an attack of impotence or the amputation of part of the personality. To a great degree, in public and private, I "was" my voice. All the rituals and etiquette of conversation, from clearing the throat in preparation for the telling of an extremely long and taxing joke to (in younger days) trying to make my proposals more persuasive as I sank the tone by a strategic octave of shame, were innate and essential to me. I have never been able to sing, but I could once recite poetry and quote prose and was sometimes even asked to do so. And timing is everything: the exquisite moment when one can break in and cap a story or turn a line for a laugh or ridicule an opponent. I lived for moments like that. Now, if I want to enter a conversation, I have to attract attention in some other way and live with the awful fact that people are then listening "sympathetically." At least they don't have to pay attention for long: I can't keep it up and anyway can't stand to.

·   ·   ·

When you fall ill, people send you CDs. Very often, in my experience, these are by Leonard Cohen. So I have recently learned a song, entitled "If It Be Your Will." It's a tiny bit saccharine, but it's beautifully rendered and it opens like this:

> If it be your will,
> That I speak no more:
> And my voice be still,
> As it was before . . .

I find it's best not to listen to this late at night. Leonard Cohen is unimaginable without, and indissoluble from, his voice. (I now doubt that I could be bothered, or bear, to hear that song done by anybody else.) In some ways, I tell myself, I could hobble along by communicating only in writing. But this is really only because of my age. If I had been robbed of my voice earlier, I doubt that I could ever have achieved much on the page. I owe a vast debt to Simon Hoggart of *The Guardian* (son of the author of *The Uses of Literacy*), who about thirty-five years ago informed me that an article of mine was well argued but dull and advised me briskly to write "more like the way that you talk." At the time, I was near speechless at the charge of being boring and never thanked him properly, but in time I appreciated that my fear of self-indulgence and the personal pronoun was its own form of indulgence.

To my writing classes I used later to open by saying that anybody who could talk could also write. Having cheered them up with this easy-to-grasp ladder, I then replaced it with a huge and loathsome snake: "How many people in this class, would you say, can talk? I mean really talk?" That had its duly woeful effect. I told them to read every composition aloud, preferably to a trusted friend. The rules are much the same: Avoid stock expressions (like the plague, as William Safire used to say) and repetitions. Don't say that as a boy your grandmother used to read to you, unless at that stage of her life she really *was* a boy, in which case you have probably thrown away a better intro. If something is worth hearing or listening to, it's very probably worth reading. So, this above all: Find your own *voice*.

. . .

The most satisfying compliment a reader can pay is to tell me that he or she feels personally addressed. Think of your own favorite authors and see if that isn't precisely one of the things that engage you, often at first without your noticing it. A good conversation is the only human equivalent: the realizing that decent points are being made and understood, that irony is in play, and elaboration, and that a dull or obvious remark would be almost physically hurtful. This is how philosophy evolved in the symposium, before philosophy was written down. And poetry began with the voice as its only player and the ear as its only recorder. Indeed, I don't know of any really good writer who was deaf, either. How could one ever come, even with the clever signage of the good Abbé de l'Épée, to appreciate the miniscule twinges and ecstasies of nuance that the well-tuned voice imparts? Henry James and Joseph Conrad actually *dictated* their later novels—which must count as one of the greatest vocal achievements of all time, even though they might have benefited from hearing some passages read back to them—and Saul Bellow dictated much of *Humboldt's Gift*. Without our corresponding feeling for the idiolect, the stamp on the way an individual actually talks, and therefore writes, we would be deprived of a whole continent of human sympathy and of its minor-key pleasures such as mimicry and parody.

·   ·   ·

More solemnly: "All I have is a voice," wrote W. H. Auden in "September 1, 1939," his agonized attempt to comprehend, and oppose, the triumph of radical evil. "Who can reach the deaf?" he asked despairingly. "Who can speak for the dumb?" At about the same time, the German-Jewish future Nobelist Nelly Sachs found that the apparition of Hitler had caused her to become literally speechless: robbed of her very voice by the stark negation of all values. Our own everyday idiom preserves the idea, however mildly: when a devoted public servant dies, the obituaries will often say that he was "a voice" for the unheard.

From the human throat terrible banes can also emerge: bawling, droning, whining, yelling, inciting ("the windiest militant trash," as Auden phrased it in the same poem), and even snickering. It's the chance to pitch still, small voices against this torrent of babble and noise, the voices of wit and understatement, for which one yearns. All of the best recollections of wisdom and friendship, from Plato's "Apology" for Socrates to *Boswell's Life of Johnson*, resound with the spoken, unscripted moments of interplay and reason and speculation. It's in engagements like this, in competition and comparison with others, that one can hope to hit upon the elusive, magical *mot juste*. For me, to remember friendship is to recall those conversations that it seemed a sin to break off: the ones that made the sacrifice of the following day a trivial one. That was the way that Callimachus chose to remember his beloved Heraclitus (as adapted into English by William Cory):

> They told me, Heraclitus; they told me you were dead.
> They brought me bitter news to hear, and bitter tears to shed.
> I wept when I remembered how often you and I
> Had tired the sun with talking, and sent him down the sky.

Indeed, he rests his claim for his friend's immortality on the sweetness of his tones:

> Still are thy pleasant voices, thy nightingales, awake;
> For Death, he taketh all away, but them he cannot take.

Perhaps a little too much uplift in that closing line . . .

·   ·   ·

In the medical literature, the vocal "cord" is a mere "fold," a piece of gristle that strives to reach out and touch its twin, thus producing the possibility of sound effects. But I feel that there must be a deep relationship with the word "chord": the resonant vibration that can stir memory, produce music, evoke love, bring tears, move crowds to pity and mobs to passion. We may not be, as we used to boast, the only animals capable of speech. But we are the only ones who can deploy vocal communication for sheer pleasure and recreation, combining it with our two other boasts of reason and humor to produce higher syntheses. To lose this ability is to be deprived of an entire range of faculty: it is assuredly to die more than a little.

My chief consolation in this year of living dyingly has been the presence of friends. I can't eat or drink for pleasure anymore, so when they offer to come it's only for the blessed chance to talk. Some of these comrades can easily fill a hall with paying customers avid to hear them: they are talkers with whom it's a privilege just to keep up. Now at least I can do the listening for free. Can they come and see me? Yes, but only in a way. So now every day I go to a waiting room, and watch the awful news from Japan on cable TV (often closed-captioned, just to torture myself) and wait impatiently for a high dose of protons to be fired into my body at two-thirds the speed of light. What do I hope for? If not a cure, then a remission. And what do I want back? In the most beautiful apposition of two of the simplest words in our language: the freedom of speech.

National Magazine Awards 2012
Finalists and Winners

Magazine of the Year

Honors the achievement of editorial excellence both in print and on digital platforms

Esquire: David Granger, editor in chief; Peter Griffin, deputy editor; Matt Sullivan, web director, Esquire.com; David Curcurito, design director. February, May and October print issues. Esquire.com: October iPad App.

New York: Adam Moss, editor in chief; Ben Williams, editorial director, nymag.com. March 7, May 23, and September 5–12 print issues. nymag.com: "The Cut on the Runway" iPad App.

The New Yorker: David Remnick, editor; Pamela Maffei McCarthy, deputy editor. February 7, May 23, and December 19 & 26 print issues. NewYorker.com: February 7, May 23, and December 19 & 26 tablet editions.

Popular Mechanics: James B. Meigs, editor in chief; Michael Lawton, design director. July, September, and December print issues. PopularMechanics.com: Monthly iPad App.

Time [Winner]: Rick Stengel, managing editor; Catherine Sharick, managing editor, Time.com. May 20, October 17, and December 26/January 2, 2012, print issues. Time.com: Weekly iPad App.

General Excellence

General-Interest Magazines

Honors large-circulation weeklies, biweeklies, and general-interest monthlies.

Bloomberg Businessweek [Winner]: Josh Tyrangiel, editor. October 10–16, October 31–November 6 and November 14–20 issues.

GQ: Jim Nelson, editor in chief. June, September and October issues.

New York: Adam Moss, editor in chief. March 7, May 23 and September 5–12 issues.

The New Yorker: David Remnick, editor. February 14 & 21, May 23 and August 8 issues.

Vice: Rocco Castoro, editor in chief. July, November and December issues.

Women's Magazines

Honors health, fitness, and parenting publications as well as fashion, service, and lifestyle magazines

Glamour: Cynthia Leive, editor in chief. May, June and September issues.

More: Lesley Jane Seymour, editor in chief. April, October, and December 2011/ January 2012 issues.

O, The Oprah Magazine [Winner]: Oprah Winfrey, founder and editorial director; Susan Casey, editor in chief. April, May and November issues.

Real Simple: Kristin van Ogtrop, managing editor. May, September, and October issues.

W: Stefano Tonchi, editor in chief. February, September, and November issues.

Lifestyle Magazines

Honors city and regional publications as well as food, travel and shelter magazines.

Bon Appétit: Adam Rapoport, editor in chief. September, October, and November issues

Country Living: Sarah Gray Miller, editor in chief. March, September, and November issues.

Garden & Gun: Sid Evans, editor in chief. August/September and October/November issues. David DiBenedetto, editor in chief. December 2011/January 2012 issue.

House Beautiful [Winner]: Newell Turner, editor in chief. March, June, and July/ August issues.

Texas Monthly: Jake Silverstein, editor. April, October, and November issues

Active- and Special-Interest Magazines

Honors magazines serving targeted readerships.

The Fader: Matthew Schnipper, editor in chief. April/May, August/September, and October/November issues.

Field & Stream: Anthony Licata, editor in chief. February, June, and December 2011/January 2012 issues.

Inc. [Winner]: Jane Berentson, editor. February, November, and December 2011/ January 2012 issues.

Men's Health: David Zinczenko, editor in chief. June, November, and December issues.

Popular Mechanics: James B. Meigs, editor in chief. July, September, and December issues.

Thought-Leader Magazines

Honors small-circulation general-interest magazines as well as literary, scholarly, and professional publications.

The American Scholar: Robert Wilson, editor. Winter, Spring, and Summer issues.
Aperture: Melissa Harris, editor in chief. Summer, Fall, and Winter issues.
IEEE Spectrum [Winner]: Susan Hassler, editor in chief. September, October, and November issues.
The New Republic: Richard Just, editor. February 3, July 14, and November 17 issues.
Virginia Quarterly Review: Ted Genoways, editor. Spring, Summer, and Fall issues.

Design

Honors overall excellence in magazine design.

Bloomberg Businessweek: Josh Tyrangiel, editor; Richard Turley, creative director. August 15–28, October 10–16, and October 31–November 6 issues.
GQ [Winner]: Jim Nelson, editor in chief; Fred Woodward, design director. May, August, and October issues.
Interview: Fabien Baron, editorial director; Stephen Mooallem, editor in chief; Karl Templer, creative director. March, September, and October issues.
New York: Adam Moss, editor in chief; Chris Dixon, design director. May 23, August 22, and September 5–12 issues.
Wired: Chris Anderson, editor in chief; Brandon Kavulla, creative director. June, August and October issues.

Photography

Honors overall excellence in magazine photography.

GQ: Jim Nelson, editor in chief; Dora Somosi, director of photography. June, August, and November issues.
Interview: Fabien Baron, editorial director; Stephen Mooallem, editor in chief; Karl Templer, creative director. March, April, and September issues.
National Geographic: Chris Johns, editor in chief. October, November, and December issues.

Virginia Quarterly Review: Ted Genoways, editor. Winter, Summer, and Fall issues

Vogue [Winner]: Anna Wintour, editor in chief. March, October, and November issues.

News and Documentary Photography

Honors photojournalism and photography that documents news events or news-related subjects.

Harper's Magazine [Winner]: Ellen Rosenbush, editor; Stacey Clarkson, art director. "Juvenile Injustice," photographs by Richard Ross. October.

Harper's Magazine: Ellen Rosenbush, editor; Stacey Clarkson, art director. "Uncertain Exodus," photographs by Ed Ou. July.

National Geographic: Chris Johns, editor in chief. "Too Young to Wed," by Cynthia Gorney; photographs by Stephanie Sinclair. June.

The New York Times Magazine: Hugo Lindgren, editor in chief. "From Zero to 104," by Randy Kennedy; photographs by Damon Winter. September 4.

Time: Rick Stengel, managing editor. "Birds of Hope," photographs by James Nachtwey. January 17.

Feature Photography

Honors the use of original photography in a feature story, photo essay or photo portfolio.

National Geographici: Chris Johns, editor in chief. "Taming the Wild," by Evan Ratliff; photographs by Vincent J. Musi. March.

The New York Times Magazine [Winner]: Hugo Lindgren, editor in chief. "Vamps, Crooks, and Killers," photographs by Alex Prager; introduction by A.O. Scott. December 11.

Time: Rick Stengel, managing editor. "Portraits of Resilience," portfolio by Marco Grob; introduction by Nancy Gibbs. September 19.

Vogue: Anna Wintour, editor in chief. "Lady Be Good," photographs by Steven Klein. March.

W: Stefano Tonchi, editor in chief. "Planet Tilda," photographs by Tim Walker. August.

Single-Topic Issue

Honors magazines that have devoted an issue to the comprehensive examination of one subject.

Bloomberg Businessweek: Josh Tyrangiel, editor. "Steve Jobs: 1955–2011." October 10–16.

ESPN the Magazine: Chad Millman, editor in chief. "Michael Vick Defined." September 5.

Garden & Gun: Sid Evans, editor in chief. "The Southern Food Issue." October/November.

New York [Winner]: Adam Moss, editor in chief. "The Encyclopedia of 9/11." September 5–12.

Wired: Chris Anderson, editor in chief. "The Underworld Issue." February.

Magazine Section

Honors the editorial direction of a clearly branded front- or back-of-the-book department or section.

Bicycling: Peter Flax, editor in chief. "Know/How." June, September, and October.

Esquire: David Granger, editor in chief. "Man at His Best." March, June/July and December.

New York [Winner]: Adam Moss, editor in chief. "Strategist." July 11, October 10 and November 28.

Real Simple: Kristin van Ogtrop, managing editor. "Food." October, November, and December.

Wired: Chris Anderson, editor in chief. "Start." May, July, and September.

Personal Service

Honors coverage of health care, personal relationships, parenting, career planning, and personal finance.

Glamour [Winner]: Cynthia Leive, editor in chief. "The Secret That Kills Four Women a Day," by Liz Brody, editor at large. June.

Good Housekeeping: Rosemary Ellis, editor in chief. "Fractured," by Susan Ince. July.

Real Simple: Kristin van Ogtrop, managing editor. "Your Holiday-Spending Survival Guide," by Yelena Moroz, Shivani Vora, Kaija Helmetag and Brad Tuttle. November.

Redbook: Jill Herzig, editor in chief.

"Would You Get a 'Mommy Tuck'?" by Hallie Levine. April.

San Francisco: Bruce Kelley, editor in chief. "The New School of Fish," by Erik Vance. February.

Leisure Interests

Honors coverage of fashion and beauty, travel, decorating and gardening, food, fitness and active sports, cars and boats, and hobbies and crafts.

New York: Adam Moss, editor in chief. "The Urbanist's Guide To . . ." April 25.

Outdoor Life: Todd W. Smith, editor in chief. "Sniper School," by John B. Snow, shooting editor. March.

Saveur [Winner]: James Oseland, editor in chief. "Italian America," by John Mariani, Lou Di Palo, Marne Setton, Rina Oh, Greg Ferro, Jane and Michael Stern, James Oseland, Dana Bowen, Frank Castronovo and Frank Falcinelli. December.

Texas Monthly: Jake Silverstein, editor. "Home Plates," by Patricia Sharpe, Katharyn Rodemann, and June Naylor. April.

Wired: Chris Anderson, editor in chief. "The Wired Travel Optimizer." October.

Public Interest

Honors magazine journalism that illuminates issues of local or national importance.

5280 Magazine: Daniel Brogan, editor and publisher. "Direct Fail," by Natasha Gardner. December.

Harper's Magazine: Ellen Rosenbush, editor. "Tiny Little Laws," by Kathy Dobie. February.

Marie Claire: Joanna Coles, editor in chief. "The Big Business of Breast Cancer," by Lea Goldman, features director. October.

Men's Health: David Zinczenko, editor in chief. "The Signature Wound," by Bob Drury, contributing editor. November.

The New Yorker [Winner]: David Remnick, editor. "The Invisible Army," by Sarah Stillman. June 6.

Reporting

Honors reporting excellence as exemplified by one article or a series of articles.

The Atlantic: James Bennet, editor in chief. "Our Man in Kandahar," by Matthieu Aikins. November.

Los Angeles: Mary Melton, editor in chief. "What Happened to Mitrice Richardson?" by Mike Kessler. September.

The New Yorker [Winner]: David Remnick, editor. "The Apostate," by Lawrence Wright. February 14 & 21.

The New Yorker: David Remnick, editor. "Getting bin Laden," by Nicholas Schmidle. August 8.

Vanity Fair: Graydon Carter, editor. "Echoes From a Distant Battlefield," by Mark Bowden, contributing editor. December.

Feature Writing

Honors original, stylish storytelling.

Esquire [Winner]: David Granger, editor in chief. "Joplin!" by Luke Dittrich, Contributing Editor. October.

GQ: Jim Nelson, editor in chief. "The Man Who Sailed His House," by Michael Paterniti. October.

The New York Times Magazine: Hugo Lindgren, editor in chief. "You Blow My Mind. Hey, Mickey!" by John Jeremiah Sullivan, Contributing Writer. June 12.

The New Yorker: David Remnick, editor. "A Murder Foretold," by David Grann. April 4.

Rolling Stone: Jann S. Wenner, editor and publisher. Will Dana, managing editor. "Arms and the Dudes," by Guy Lawson. March 31.

Profile Writing

Honors news or feature stories about an individual or a group of closely linked individuals.

D Magazine [Winner]: Tim Rogers, editor. "He Is Anonymous," by Tim Rogers. April.

ESPN the Magazine: Gary Belsky, editor in chief. "Game of Her Life," by Tim Crothers. January 10.

Men's Journal: Will Dana, editorial director; Jason Fine, editor. "The Blind Man Who Taught Himself to See," by Michael Finkel. March.

Rolling Stone: Jann S. Wenner, editor and publisher; Will Dana, managing editor. "Santiago's Brain," by Jeff Tietz. December 8.

Sports Illustrated: Terry McDonell, editor, Time Inc. Sports Group. "Dewayne Dedmon's Leap of Faith," by Chris Ballard, Senior Writer. November 14.

Essays and Criticism

Honors long-form journalism on topics ranging from the personal to the political.

Esquire: David Granger, editor in chief. "The Loading Dock Manifesto," by John Hyduk. May.

GQ: Jim Nelson, editor in chief. "Too Much Information," by John Jeremiah Sullivan. May iPad Edition.

New York [Winner]: Adam Moss, editor in chief. "Paper Tigers," by Wesley Yang, Contributing Editor. May 16.

The New Yorker: David Remnick, editor. "The Aquarium," by Aleksandar Hemon. June 13 & 20.

Slate: David Plotz, editor in chief. "The Stutterer: How He Makes His Voice Heard," by Nathan Heller, Columnist. February 22.

Columns and Commentary

Honors political and social commentary; news analysis; and reviews and criticism.

The Atlantic: James Bennet, editor in chief. Three columns by James Parker: "Notes From the Underworld," May; "The Beast Within," June; and "The Anti-James Bond," December.

Field & Stream: Anthony Licata, editor in chief. Three columns by Bill Heavey: "Boys Should Be Boys," February; "Making the Cut," March; and "My Late Season," December 2011/January 2012.

Los Angeles: Mary Melton, editor in chief. Three reviews by Steve Erickson: "Desperate City," April; "He Still Matters," May; and "Norse Force," July.

Time: Rick Stengel, managing editor. Three columns by Joel Stein: "Duck Tape," April 25; "America's Next Top Weiner," June 20; and "The End of Kardaschadenfreude," November 14.

Vanity Fair [Winner]: Graydon Carter, editor. Three columns by Christopher Hitchens, Contributing Editor: "When the King Saved God," May; "Unspoken Truths," June; and "From Abbottobad to Worse," July.

Fiction

Honors the publication of fiction in magazines.

The Atlantic: James Bennet, editor in chief. "Scars," by Sarah Turcotte. Summer.

McSweeney's Quarterly: Dave Eggers, editor. "Ambition," by Jonathan Franzen. April.

McSweeney's Quarterly. Dave Eggers, editor. "The Northeast Kingdom," by Nathaniel Rich. August.

Virginia Quarterly Review: Ted Genoways, editor. "La Moretta," by Maggie Shipstead. Fall.

Zoetrope: All-Story [Winner]: Michael Ray, editor. "The Hox River Window," by Karen Russell. Fall.

National Magazine Awards for Digital Media 2012 Finalists And Winners

General Excellence

Honors the best magazines published on digital platforms.

The Atlantic: James Bennet, editor in chief. Bob Cohn, editorial director, Atlantic Digital.

Entertainment Weekly: Bill Gannon, managing editor, EW.com. Michael Bruno, assistant managing editor, EW.com. Chad Schlegel, assistant managing editor, EW.com.

Golf Digest: Jerry Tarde, editor in chief. Ken DeLago, creative director.

National Geographic: Chris Johns, editor in chief. Bill Marr, creative director. Melissa Wiley, e-publishing director.

New York [Winner]: Adam Moss, editor in chief. Ben Williams, editorial director, nymag.com.

Website

Honors the best magazine websites.

The Atlantic: James Bennet, editor in chief. Bob Cohn, editorial director, Atlantic Digital.

New York [Winner]: Adam Moss, editor in chief. Ben Williams, editorial director, nymag.com.

People. Larry Hackett, managing editor. Janice Morris, managing editor, *People* Digital.

Saveur: James Oseland, editor in chief. Ganda Suthivarakom, website director. Helen Rosner, senior web editor.

Slate: David Plotz, editor.

Tablet Edition

Honors magazine editions published on tablets and e-readers.

Golf Digest: Jerry Tarde, editor in chief. Craig Bestrom, editorial development director. April, November, and 2011 Hot List iPad Apps.

GQ: Jim Nelson, editor in chief. May and September iPad Apps.

National Geographic [Winner]: Chris Johns, editor in chief. Bill Marr, creative director. Melissa Wiley, e-publishing director. August, September, and November iPad Apps.

The New Yorker: David Remnick, editor. Pamela Maffei McCarthy, deputy editor. February 7, May 24, and December 19 tablet editions.

Spin. Devin Pedzwater, brand creative director. Charles Aaron, editorial director. Steve Kandell, editor in chief/magazine; SPIN Play. March, August and October iPad Apps.

Design

Honors the visual and functional excellence of magazine websites, tablet and e-reader editions and utility apps.

The Daily Beast: Tina Brown, editor in chief, *Newsweek* and *The Daily Beast*. Website.

Everyday Food: Sarah Carey, editor in chief. Kirsten Hilgendorf, senior art director. Beth Eakin, production manager. Kellee Miller, managing editor. March iPad App.

National Geographic: Chris Johns, editor in chief. Bill Marr, creative director. Melissa Wiley, e-publishing director. "7 Billion: How Your World Will Change" iPad App.

The New Yorker: David Remnick, editor. Pamela Maffei McCarthy, deputy editor. "Summer Reading Issue," June 13 & 20 iPad App.

Wired [Winner]: Chris Anderson, editor in chief. Brandon Kavulla, creative director. "The Underworld Issue," February iPad App.

Website Department

Honors the best departments, channels, or microsites.

The Atlantic: James Bennet, editor in chief. Bob Cohn, editorial director, Atlantic Digital. Alan Taylor, senior editor. "In Focus"

The Daily Beast [Winner]: Tina Brown, editor in chief, *Newsweek* and *The Daily Beast*. "Book Beast."

Discover: Corey S. Powell, editor in chief. Amos Zeeberg, managing editor, online. *Discover* Blogs.

Foreign Policy: Susan B. Glasser, editor in chief. "Middle East Channel."

Sports Illustrated: Terry McDonell, editor, Time Inc. Sports Group. Paul Fichten-baum, managing editor, SI.com. "NFL."

Utility App

Honors single-purpose apps distributed on mobile devices.

Cooking Light: Scott Mowbray, editor. Carla Frank, creative director. Ann Pittman, food editor. "Quick & Healthy Menu Maker."

Entertainment Weekly: Bill Gannon, managing editor, EW.com. Michael Bruno, assistant managing editor, EW.com. Chad Schlegel, assistant managing editor, EW.com. "viEWer."

New York: Adam Moss, editor in chief. Ben Williams, editorial director, nymag.com. "The Cut on the Runway."

Poetry: Christian Wiman, editor. Catherine Halley, director of digital programs, Poetry Foundation.

Time [Winner]: Richard Stengel, managing editor. "PopuList."

Personal Service

Honors service journalism on digital platforms/

AARP.org: Bernard Ohanian, editor in chief. Hugh Delehanty, project editor. Laurie Donnelly, video producer. "Five Weeks to a New Life," by Margery D. Rosen.

Kiplinger.com: Doug Harbrecht, new media director. "State-by-State Guide to Taxes on Retirees."

MensHealth.com: David Zinczenko, senior vice president, editor in chief. William G. Phillips, editor. "Guy Gourmet," by Adina Steiman, food and nutrition editor, and Paul Kita, associate editor.

MensHealth.com [Winner]: David Zinczenko, senior vice president, editor in chief. William G. Phillips, editor. "The Skin Cancer Center," by Adam Campbell, executive editor, and Amy Rushlow, senior editor.

Redbook: Jill Herzig, editor in chief. Mark Weinberg, vice president of programming and product strategy. "The Truth About Trying."

Reporting

Honors excellence in reporting for digital media.

The Atavist: Evan Ratliff, founder and editor. "The Instigators," by David Wolman.

IEEE Spectrum: Susan Hassler, editor in chief. Harry Goldstein, editorial director, digital. "Fukushima and the Future of Nuclear Power," by Samuel K. Moore, senior editor, news; Erico Guizzo, senior associate editor; Joshua J. Romero, associate editor; and Eliza Strickland, associate editor.

Mother Jones: Monika Bauerlein and Clara Jeffery, editors in chief. Coverage of Occupy Wall Street by Josh Harkinson, Gavin Aronsen, and James West.

Rolling Stone: Will Dana, managing editor. Eric Bates, executive editor. "The Kill Team," by Mark Boal, Contributing editor.

Wired [Winner]: Chris Anderson, editor in chief. Noah Shachtman, digital editor. "FBI Teaches Agents: 'Mainstream' Muslims Are 'Violent, Radical,'" by Spencer Ackerman, senior writer.

Commentary

Honors excellence in opinion journalism published on digital platforms.

The American Scholar [Winner]: Robert Wilson, editor. "Zinsser on Friday," by William Zinsser.

CNET: Jim Kerstetter, editor in chief. "Molly Rants," by Molly Wood.

The Daily Beast: Tina Brown, editor in chief, *Newsweek* and *The Daily Beast*. Commentary by Michelle Goldberg.

The New Yorker: David Remnick, editor. Amy Davidson, online news editor. *New Yorker* Writers on the Death of Osama bin Laden.

Rolling Stone: Will Dana, managing editor. Eric Bates, executive editor. "Taibblog," by Matt Taibbi, Contributing editor.

Multimedia

Honors the use of interactivity and multimedia in the coverage of events and subjects.

The Atavist: Jefferson Rabb, founder and creative director. "Lifted," by Evan Ratliff.

Foreign Policy [Winner]: Susan B. Glasser, editor in chief. "The Qaddafi Files: An FP Special Report."

Golf Digest: Jerry Tarde, editor in chief. Sam Weinman, web editor. Coverage of the 2011 Masters Tournament.

Popular Mechanics: James B. Meigs, editor in chief. "Touchdown," May iPad App.

Slate: David Plotz, editor. Will Oremus, staff writer. "The Presidential Horse Race."

Video

Honors the outstanding use of video by magazines published on digital platforms.

5280: Daniel Brogan, editor and publisher. "The Saddlemaker," by Jefferson Panis.

GQ: Jim Nelson, editor in chief. Three videos from the series "Tell."

The New York Times Magazine [Winner]: Hugo Lindgren, editor in chief. "My Family's Experiment in Extreme Schooling," by Julie Dressner, Shayla Harris, and Clifford J. Levy.

The New York Times Magazine: Hugo Lindgren, editor in chief. Kathy Ryan, director of photography. Three videos from the series "Touch of Evil," by Alex Prager.

Slate: David Plotz, editor. Bill Smee, executive producer, and Andy Bouve, supervising producer. David Kestenbaum and Jacob Goldstein, reporters. "Why Gold, Why Not Argon?"

All publication dates 2011 unless otherwise noted. Digital content was chiefly created in 2011 but may have been updated after submission.

National Magazine Awards 2012 Judges

Judging Chair

Larry Hackett   managing editor, *People*

Judging Leaders

Chris Anderson   editor in chief, *Wired*
John Atwood   editor, *Runner's World*
James Bennet   editor in chief, *The Atlantic*
Maile Carpenter   editor in chief, *Food Network Magazine*
Amy DuBois Barnett   editor in chief, *Ebony*
Rosemary Ellis   editor in chief, *Good Housekeeping*
David Granger   editor in chief, *Esquire*
Jill Herzig   editor in chief, *Redbook*
Mark Jannot   editor in chief, *Popular Science*; editorial director,
                          Bonnier Technology Group
Sally Lee   senior vice president, Meredith Corporation;
                          editor in chief, *Ladies' Home Journal*
Pamela Maffei McCarthy deputy editor, *The New Yorker*
Adam Moss   editor in chief, *New York*
Jim Nelson   editor in chief, *GQ*
Peggy Northrop   international editor at large, *Reader's Digest*
Kaitlin Quistgaard   editor in chief, *Yoga Journal*
Robert Safian   editor, *Fast Company*
Lesley Jane Seymour   editor in chief, *More*
Rick Stengel   managing editor, *Time*
Josh Tyrangiel   editor, *Bloomberg Businessweek*
David Willey   editor in chief, *Runner's World*; editorial director,
                          Bicycling and *Running Times*

Judges

Laurie Abraham   senior Features editor, *Elle*
Julie Vosburgh Agnone vice president, *National Geographic Kids*
David Andelman   editor in chief, *World Policy Journal*
Lisa Arbetter   deputy managing editor, *InStyle*

Philip Armour	editor in chief, *American Cowboy*
Florian Bachleda	creative director, *Fast Company*
Lisa Bain	executive editor, *Women's Health*
Richard Baker	creative director, *Parade*
Douglas S. Barasch	editor in chief, *OnEarth*
Jenny Barnett	contributing editor, *Harper's Bazaar*
Dirk Barnett	creative director, *The Newsweek Daily Beast Company*
Jennifer Barr	executive editor, *Travel + Leisure*
Melina Gerosa Bellows	executive vice president and chief creative officer, books, kids, and family, National Geographic Society
Gary Belsky	partner, Amalgamated Content
Jane Berentson	editor, *Inc.*
Amy Bernstein	editor, *Harvard Business Review*
Alex Bhattacharji	executive editor, *Details*
M. Lindsay Bierman	editor in chief, *Southern Living*
Debra Birnbaum	editor in chief, *TV Guide Magazine*
Debra Bishop	creative director, *More*
H. Emerson Blake	editor in chief, *Orion*
Janet Bodnar	editor, *Kiplinger's Personal Finance*
Michael Boodro	editor in chief, *Elle Decor*
Dana Bowen	executive editor, *Saveur*
Daniel Brogan	editor and publisher, *5280 Magazine*
Dudley M. Brooks	senior photo editor, *Ebony*
Peter Brown	editorial consultant
Laura Brown	features and special projects director, *Harper's Bazaar*
Laurie Buckle	editorial director, food, *Better Homes and Gardens*
Jess Cagle	managing editor, *Entertainment Weekly*
Dara Caponigro	editor in chief, *Veranda*
Betsy Carter	author
Andrea Chambers	director, Center for Publishing, New York University
Janet Chan	editorial consultant
Melissa Chessher	associate professor, chair, Magazine Department, S.I. Newhouse School of Public Communications, Syracuse University
David Clarke	editor, *Golf*
Ana Connery	editorial director, *Parenting*

Annemarie Conte	deputy editor, *Seventeen*
Stephen Corey	editor and director, *The Georgia Review*
Julia Cosgrove	VP, editor in chief, *Afar*
Judith Coyne	executive editor, *More*
David Curcurito	design director, *Esquire*
Will Dana	managing editor, *Rolling* Stone; editorial director, *Men's Journal*
Maxine Davidowitz	creative consultant, Maxine Davidowitz Design
James de Vries	creative director, Harvard Business Review Group
Bob Der	managing editor and publisher, *Sports Illustrated Kids*
David DiBenedetto	editor in chief, *Garden & Gun*
Mariette DiChristina	editor in chief, *Scientific American*
Lou Dilorenzo	creative director, *People StyleWatch*
Suzanne Donaldson	photo director, *Glamour*
Jonathan Dorn	vice president, AIM Outdoor Group
Simon Dumenco	media columnist, *Advertising Age*
Andrea Dunham	design director, *People*
Arem Duplessis	design director, *The New York Times Magazine*
Yolanda Edwards	executive editor, *Martha Stewart Living*
Ron Escobar	art director, *Yoga Journal*
Galina Espinoza	copresident and editorial director, *Latina*
Michael Robert Evans	associate dean for undergraduate studies, Indiana University School of Journalism
Sid Evans	group editor, Lifestyle Division, Time Inc.
Ellen Fair	managing editor, *Art + Auction* and *Modern Painters*
Michael Famighetti	managing editor, *Aperture*
Linda Fears	editor in chief, *Family Circle*
Ruth Feldman	vice president, international editorial director, Martha Stewart Living Omnimedia
John Fennell	associate professor, Meredith Chair for Service Journalism, Missouri School of Journalism
Beth Fenner	editor in chief, *Chicago*
Dan Ferrara	deputy editor, *Inc.*
Jason Fine	editor, *Men's Journal*
Steve Fine	director of photography, *Sports Illustrated*
Rose Fiorentino	creative director, *TV Guide Magazine*
Peter Flax	editor in chief, *Bicycling*
Deborah Frank	managing editor, *Departures*

Lisa Lee Freeman	editor in chief, *ShopSmart*
David Friend	editor of creative development, *Vanity Fair*
Dave Garlock	magazine sequence head, University of Texas
Chris Garrett	managing editor, *Vanity Fair*
Rip Georges	creative director, *Los Angeles Times Magazine*
Susan Glasser	editor in chief, *Foreign Policy*
Jon Gluck	deputy editor, *New York*
Lea Goldman	features director, *Marie Claire*
Susan Goodall	editorial development director, *Glamour*
Meryl Gordon	director, magazine writing, NYU Arthur L. Carter Journalism Institute
Lisa Gosselin	editorial director and editor in chief, *EatingWell*
Nancy Graham	editor and vice president, *AARP The Magazine*
Elizabeth Graves	editor in chief, *Martha Stewart Weddings*
Edward Grinnan	editor in chief and vice president, *Guideposts*
Oriol R. Gutierrez Jr.	deputy editor, *Poz*
Tish Hamilton	executive editor, *Runner's World*
James Heidenry	editor in chief, *Manhattan*
Peter Hemmel	creative director, *Prevention*
Ronald Henkoff	editor, *Bloomberg Markets*
Chris Hercik	creative director, *Sports Illustrated*
Lindy Hess	director, Columbia Publishing Course, Columbia University Graduate School of Journalism
Geraldine Hessler	design director, *Glamour*
Aaron Hicklin	editor in chief, *Out*
Hylah Hill	design director, *This Old House*
Amanda Hinnant	assistant professor, Missouri School of Journalism
Roger D. Hodge	writer andfreelance editor
Gary Hoenig	executive editor, ESPN Digital and Print Media
Regan Hofmann	editor in chief, *Poz Magazine*; editorial director, *Smart + Strong*
William W. Horne	editor, *MHQ: The Quarterly Journal of Military History*
Sarah Humphreys	executive editor, *Real Simple*
Christopher Hunt	assistant managing editor, *Sports Illustrated*
Samir A. Husni	director, Magazine Innovation Center, the University of Mississippi
Joe Hutchinson	design director, *Rolling Stone*
Adi Ignatius	editor in chief, *Harvard Business Review*
Darcy Jacobs	executive editor, *Family Circle*

Clara Jeffery	coeditor, *Mother Jones*
Sammye Johnson	Carlos Augustus de Lozano Chair in Journalism, Trinity University
Radhika Jones	executive editor, *Time*
Laurie Jones	managing editor, *Vogue*
Jim Kaminsky	media consultant
Susan Kane	editor in chief, *Success Magazine*
Janice Kaplan	media consultant
Peter Kaplan	editorial director, *Fairchild Fashion Media*
Eliot Kaplan	executive director, talent acquisition, Hearst Magazines
Susan Kaufman	editor, *People StyleWatch*
Brandon Kavulla	creative director, *Wired*
Lauren Kern	deputy editor, *The New York Times Magazine*
Christopher Keyes	editor, *Outside*
Rik Kirkland	senior managing editor, McKinsey & Company
Kimberly Kleman	editor in chief, *Consumer Reports*; deputy editorial director, Consumers Union
John Korpics	vice president and creative director, print and digital media, ESPN
Laurie Kratochvil	director of photography, Nomad Editions
Jean Kumagai	senior editor, *IEEE Spectrum*
Ellen Kunes	editor in chief, *Health*
Steven Lagerfeld	editor, *The Wilson Quarterly*
Randall Lane	editor, *Forbes*
Clifton Leaf	executive editor, *SmartMoney*
Edward Leida	design director, *Town & Country*
Jacqueline Leo	editor in chief, *The Fiscal Times*
Carolyn Ringer Leprea	associate professor and director of honors, School of Communication and the Arts, Marist College
Joe Levy	editor, *Billboard*
Anthony Licata	editorial director, Bonnier Outdoor Group; editor in chief, *Field & Stream*
Hugo Lindgren	editor in chief, *The New York Times Magazine*
Clare Lissaman	photography director, *Ladies' Home Journal*
Joe Lorio	senior editor, *Automobile Magazine*
Paul Maidment	principal and editor in chief, Bystander Media
James Marcus	deputy editor, *Harper's Magazine*
Jacqueline Marino	assistant professor, Kent State University
Paul Martinez	creative director, *Maxim*

Cathleen McGuigan	editor in chief, *Architectural Record*
Liz McMillen	editor, *The Chronicle of Higher Education*
Stephanie Mehta	global editor, *Fortune*
Mary Melton	editor in chief, *Los Angeles*
Rachel Davis Mersey	assistant professor, Medill School of Journalism, Northwestern University
Francesca Messina	senior group art director, *Architectural Record, GreenSource, Engineering News-Record,* and *Snap*
Sarah Gray Miller	editor in chief, *Country Living*
Chad Millman	editor in chief, *ESPN The Magazine*
Christian Millman	executive editor, *Taste of Home*
Marilyn Milloy	deputy editor, *AARP The Magazine*
Keija Minor	executive editor, *Brides*
Luke Mitchell	deputy editor, *Popular Science*
Peg Moline	editor in chief, *Fit Pregnancy* and *Natural Health*
Ted Moncreiff	contributing editor, *Condé Nast Traveler*
Stephen Mooallem	editor in chief, *Interview*
Peter Moore	editor, *Men's Health*
Don Morris	principal, Don Morris Design
Scott Mowbray	editor, *Cooking Light*
Courtney Murphy	creative director, *Good Housekeeping*
Cullen Murphy	editor at large, *Vanity Fair*
Christopher Napolitano	creative director, Indian Country Today Media Network
Victor Navasky	chairman, *Columbia Journalism Review*
Robert Newman	creative director, *Reader's Digest*
Catriona Ni Aolain	director of photography, *Men's Journal*
Pam O'Brien	executive editor, *Fitness*
Deb Gore Ohrn	editor in chief, Better Homes and Gardens Crafts Group
James Oseland	editor in chief, *Saveur*
Jane Shin Park	beauty and features editor, *Teen Vogue*
Barbara Paulsen	story development editor, *National Geographic*
Abe Peck	director, business to business communication, Medill School of Journalism, Northwestern University
Jodi Peckman	creative director, *Rolling Stone*
Robert Perino	creative director, *Southern Living*
Kristin Perrotta	executive editor, *Allure*

Abigail Pesta	editorial director, Women in the World, *Newsweek*
Marc Peyser	editor, *Arthur Frommer's Budget Travel*
Owen Phillips	executive editor, *The Hollywood Reporter*
Andrea Pitzer	editor, Nieman Storyboard, Nieman Foundation for Journalism
Sean Plottner	editor, *Dartmouth Alumni Magazine*
David Plotz	editor, *Slate*
Dana Points	editor in chief, *Parents* and *American Baby*
Alex Pollack	photo director, *Bon Appetit*
Kira Pollack	director of photography, *Time*
Jason Pontin	editor in chief, *MIT Technology Review*
Lynn Povich	
Corey S. Powell	editor in chief, *Discover*
Robert Priest	design director, *O, The Oprah Magazine*
Michele Promaulayko	editor in chief, *Women's Health*
Lauren Purcell	editor in chief, *Every Day With Rachael Ray*
John Rasmus	editorial director, *The Active Times*
Michael W. Robbins	editor, *Military History*
Kerry Robertson	creative director
Meredith Rollins	executive editor, *Redbook*
Catherine Romano	senior executive editor, *Glamour*
Chip Rowe	senior editor, *Playboy*
Sarah Rozen	director of photography, *Women's Health*
Margaret Russell	editor in chief, *Architectural Digest*
Kathy Ryan	director of photography, *The New York Times Magazine*
Ina Saltz	Saltz Design
Diane Salvatore	editor in chief, *Prevention*
Mary Kaye Schilling	senior articles editor, *GQ*
Cynthia H. Searight	creative director, *Self*
David Seideman	editor in chief, *Audubon*
Jake Silverstein	editor, *Texas Monthly*
Martin J. Smith	editor in chief, *Orange Coast*
Dora Somosi	director of photography, *GQ*
Nancy Soriano	publisher and director, Craft F&W Media
Alanna Stang	editor in chief, *Whole Living*
Michael Steele	editor in chief, *Us Weekly*
Lorin Stein	editor, *The Paris Review*
Jay Stowe	editor, *Cincinnati*
Doug Stumpf	executive editor, *Vanity Fair*

Suzanne Sykes	creative director, *Marie Claire*
Catherine Talese	photography editor and consultant
Rick Tetzeli	executive editor, *Fast Company*
Casey Tierney	photo director, *Real Simple*
Newell Turner	editor in chief, *House Beautiful*
Chandra Turner	executive editor, *Parents*
Antonia van der Meer	editor in chief, *Coastal Living*
Norman Vanamee	editor in chief, *Garden Design*
Mark Warren	executive editor, *Esquire*
Donovan Webster	deputy editor, *Virginia Quarterly Review*
Matt Welch	editor in chief, *Reason*
Charles Whitaker	Helen Gurley Brown Magazine Research Chair, Medill School of Journalism, Northwestern University
Constance C. R. White	editor in chief, *Essence*
Slaton White	editor, *Shot Business*
Brad Wieners	executive editor, *Bloomberg Businessweek*
Nina Willdorf	editor at large, *Arthur Frommer's Budget Travel*
Robert Wilson	editor, *The American Scholar*
Jayne Wise	senior editor, *National Geographic Traveler*
Patti Wolter	assistant professor, Medill School of Journalism, Northwestern University
Betty S. Wong	editor in chief, *Fitness*
Fred Woodward	design director, *GQ*
Daniel Zalewski	features director, *The New Yorker*
David Zinczenko	editor in chief, *Men's Health*; general manager, Rodale, Inc.
Glenn Zorpette	executive editor, *IEEE Spectrum*

The National Magazine Awards for Digital Media 2012 Judges

Judging Chair

James B. Meigs — editor in chief, *Popular Mechanics*; editorial director, Men's Enthusiast Group

Judging Leaders

Bob Cohn — editorial director, Atlantic Digital
Dana Cowin — Senior vice president, editor in chief, *Food & Wine*
Doug Crichton — director, Mobile Engagement, Meredith Corporation
Lucy Danziger — editor in chief, *Self*
Kathleen Harris — managing editor, *RealSimple.com*
Eric Schurenberg — editor, *Inc.com*
Sree Sreenivasan — dean of student affairs and professor of professional practice, the School of Journalism, Columbia University
Tanya Steel — editor in chief, *Epicurious*, *Gourmet Live*, and *Gourmet.com*
Cyndi Stivers — editor in chief, *Columbia Journalism Review*
Gael Towey — chief integration and creative director, Martha Stewart Living Omnimedia

Judges

Ian Adelman — director of Digital Design, *The New York Times*
Rosie Amodio — editor, *InStyle.com*
Jenn Andrlik
Susan Avery — digital director, *More*
Davina Baum — director of digital content, *Afar*
Rich Beattie — executive digital editor, *Travel + Leisure*
Giselle Benatar — senior director for digital, International Rescue Committee
Roger Black — Roger Black Studio
Denise Brodey

Cheryl Brown	editorial director, *Recipe.com*
Charles Butler	executive editor, *Runner's World*
Christina Caldwell	online director, *W*
Eric Capossela	design director, *Atlanta*
Michael Caruso	editor in chief, *Smithsonian*
Janice Castro	senior director, graduate education and teaching excellence, Medill School of Journalism, Northwestern University
Nick Catucci	performing arts editor, *Artinfo*
Dan Check	director of technology, the Slate Group
Roger Cohn	editor, *Yale Environment 360*
Susan Cosier	senior editor, *Audubon*
James Oliver Cury	web director, *Details.com*
Ken DeLago	creative director, *Golf Digest*
Angela Diegel	online director, *PopularMechanics.com*
Jay Ehrlich	executive online director, *Women's Health*
Blake Eskin	editor, *NewYorker.com*
Rachel Feddersen	editorial director, digital, the Parenting Group
Aileen Gallagher	assistant professor, S.I. Newhouse School of Public Communications, Syracuse University
Bill Gannon	managing editor, *EntertainmentWeekly.com*
Nick Gillespie	editor in chief, *Reason.com* and *Reason.tv*
Jane Goldman	vice president, CBS Interactive; editor in chief, *CHOW.com*
Harry Goldstein	editorial director, digital, *IEEE Spectrum*
Christie Griffin	digital director, *Fitness*
Evan Hansen	editor in chief, *Wired.com*
Douglas A. Harbrecht	director, *Kiplinger.com*
Eric Hellweg	managing director, digital strategy, and editorial director, *Harvard Business Review*
Elizabeth Meyers Hendrickson	assistant professor, University of Tennessee–Knoxville
Samantha Henig	online editor, *The New York Times Magazine*
Melinda Henneberger	*The Washington Post*
Michael Hofman	digital managing director, *Glamour*
Michael Hogan	executive entertainment editor, Huffington Post Media Group
Peter Kafka	senior editor, *All Things Digital*
Will Knight	online editor, *Technology Review*

Michael Kress	executive editor, *Parents.com*
Allison Lowery	editor, *CookingLight.com*
Eamon Lynch	executive editor, *Golf*
Bill Marr	creative director, *National Geographic*
Michael Martin	editor in chief, *Time Out New York*
Celeste McCauley	senior editor, special projects, *Guideposts*
Noah Michelson	editor, gay voices, *The Huffington Post*
Maggie Murphy	editor, *Parade*; editorial director, *Parade.com*
Alana Newhouse	editor in chief, *Tablet Magazine*
Barbara O'Dair	executive editor, *Reader's Digest*
Bernard Ohanian	vice president, content integration, AARP Publications; editor, AARP Digital
Scott Omelianuk	editor in chief, *This Old House*
Jack Otter	executive editor, *CBS MoneyWatch.com*
James Pallot	executive director, multimedia projects, *Vanity Fair*
Caroline Palmer	editor, *Vogue.com*
Chris Peacock	executive editor, *CNNMoney.com*
Bill Phillips	executive editor, *Men's Health*; editor, *MensHealth.com*
Keith Pollock	editorial director, *Elle.com*
Maura Randall	digital managing director, *Lucky*
Noah Robischon	executive editor, *Fast Company*
Jeffrey Saks	creative director, *Ladies' Home Journal*
Jeffrey Selingo	vice president and editorial director, *The Chronicle of Higher Education*
Bill Shapiro	development editor, Time Inc.
Catherine Sharick	managing editor, *Time.com*
Robin Sparkman	editor in chief, *The American Lawyer*
Dirk Standen	editor in chief, *Style.com*
Ellen Stark	editor-at-Large, *Money*
Bill Stump	
Matt Sullivan	web director, *Esquire*
Ganda Suthivarakom	digital content director, travel and epicurean group, Bonnier Corporation
Stefano Tonchi	editor in chief, *W*
Julia Turner	deputy editor, *Slate*
Liz Vaccariello	editor in chief and chief content officer, *Reader's Digest*

Permissions

Contributors

MATTHIEU AIKINS has been reporting from Afghanistan since 2008 for such publications as *The Atlantic, Harper's, The Walrus,* and *The Guardian.*

Since joining *Sports Illustrated* in September 2000, **CHRIS BALLARD** has written more than a dozen cover stories and had stories published in *Best American Sports Writing* in 2005 and 2007. His book *Hoops Nation* was named one of "Top Ten Sports Book of the Year" by *Booklist*; he is also the author of *The Butterfly Hunter* (2006) and *The Art of a Beautiful Game* (2009). Ballard has also written for the *Los Angeles Times,* the *New York Times, USA Today,* and *Men's Health.* A native Californian, Ballard graduated from Pomona College, where he played basketball and was on the track and field team. He lives with his family in Berkeley.

LIZ BRODY is an editor at large at *Glamour,* where she covers women's issues. Previously she was news and health director for *O, The Oprah Magazine* and a blogger for Yahoo! She has written for a number of other publications, including the *Los Angeles Times, InStyle, More,* and *Self.*

TIM CROTHERS is a former senior writer at *Sports Illustrated.* He is the author of *The Man Watching* and coauthor of *Hard Work,* the autobiography of UNC basketball coach Roy Williams. He lives in Chapel Hill, North Carolina, with his wife and two children.

LUKE DITTRICH began working as a journalist while living on a houseboat on the Nile. He has been a contributing editor at *Esquire* since 2007, and his stories have appeared in a variety of anthologies, including *The Best American Crime Writing, The*

Best American Science and Nature Writing, and *The Best American Travel Writing.*

BOB DRURY has been a contributing editor at *Men's Health* for eight years. A three-time National Magazine Award finalist, Drury has also been nominated for a Pulitzer Prize and is the recipient of several national journalism awards. At *Men's Health,* and for the previous five years at *GQ,* Drury has specialized in foreign reporting. He is the author, coauthor, or editor of nine nonfiction books. He is currently working on his next book, *The Heart of Everything That Is: The Untold Story of the Great Sioux Warrior-Chief Red Cloud,* to be published by Simon & Schuster in early 2013.

CHRISTOPHER HITCHENS joined *Vanity Fair* as a contributing editor in November 1992 and wrote regularly for the magazine until 2011. In recent years, Hitchens was a contributing editor to *The Atlantic,* where he wrote a monthly essay on books for nearly a dozen years, and a regular columnist at *Slate.* His books include *The Trial of Henry Kissinger* (Verso, 2001); *Letters to a Young Contrarian* (Basic, 2001); *God Is Not Great: How Religion Poisons Everything* (Twelve, 2007); *Hitch-22: A Memoir* (Twelve, 2010); *Arguably: Essays by Christopher Hitchens* (Twelve, 2011); and *Mortality* (Twelve, due out in September 2012), which includes the series of *Vanity Fair* columns for which he won the National Magazine Award for Columns and Commentary in 2011 and 2012. Christopher Hitchens died on December 15, 2011.

SUSAN INCE is a freelance journalist specializing in medicine. Trained in medical genetics, she has written health news and features for more than twenty-five years. Her articles have appeared in *Good Housekeeping, Harvard Women's Health Watch, More, Prevention, Redbook,* and many other publications. She was a Knight Science Journalism Fellow at MIT in 1990–91. Ince was a finalist for a National Magazine Award in 2000 for a *Red-book* guide, "What to Do If You Find a Lump." She lives in Kapaʻau, Hawaii.

GUY LAWSON was born in Toronto. He holds degrees from the University of Western Australia and the University of Cambridge, England. He worked briefly as an attorney on Wall Street but left the law to pursue writing. His work has appeared in many international publications, including *GQ, Harper's, The New York Review of Books, Rolling Stone*, the *New York Times, The Globe and Mail*, and *The Observer*. He is the author of *Octopus: Sam Israel, the Secret Market, and Wall Street's Wildest Con.*

TIM ROGERS is the editor of *D*, the city magazine of Dallas, where he lives with his long-suffering wife and two mostly obedient children.

KAREN RUSSELL has been featured on the following lists: *The New Yorker's* 20 Under 40, *Granta's* Best Young American Novelists. and the National Book Foundation's 5 Under 35. Her debut novel, *Swamplandia!*, was a finalist for the 2012 Pulitzer Prize.

SARAH STILLMAN is a freelance journalist and visiting scholar at NYU's Arthur L. Carter Journalism Institute, where she teaches a course on reporting the global city. Her work has appeared in *The Nation, The New Yorker, Slate*, the *Washington Post*, and the *Atlantic and New Republic* websites. She has received the Michael Kelly Award, the Overseas Press Club's Joe and Laurie Dine Award for International Human Rights Reporting, and the Hillman Prize for Magazine Journalism.

JOEL STEIN is a regular contributor to *Time* and writes the weekly "Awesome Column." Recently, he oversaw *Time's* redesign of the "Briefing" section. In addition to writing for sitcoms, Stein has made numerous appearances on VH1, E!, and Comedy Central. Before coming to *Time* in 1997, Stein worked as a writer and fact checker at *Martha Stewart Living*, as sports editor at *Time Out New York*, and as a researcher for *TV Guide*. His book *Man Made: A Stupid Quest for Masculinity* will be published in May 2012. Stein received a BA and an MA in English from Stanford University. He lives in Los Angeles. He is on Twitter @TheJoelStein.

JOHN JEREMIAH SULLIVAN, a longtime *GQ* correspondent, is now a contributing writer for the *New York Times Magazine* and the southern editor of *The Paris Review*. He also writes for *Harper's* and *The Oxford American*. His work in those publications has twice been given the National Magazine Award (in the Feature Writing and Essays categories, respectively). He has also received a Whiting Writers' Award and a Pushcart Prize. Sullivan is the author of *Blood Horses* (FSG, 2004) and *Pulphead* (FSG, 2011). He lives in Wilmington, North Carolina.

MATT TAIBBI is an author and journalist reporting on politics, media, finance, and sports for *Rolling Stone* and *Men's Journal*. He has also edited and written for *The eXile*, the *New York Press*, and *The Beast*. In 2008, Taibbi won the National Magazine Award for his columns in *Rolling Stone*. He has written several books, including *The Great Derangement: A Terrifying True Story of War, Politics, and Religion* and, most recently, the critically hailed *Griftopia*.

LAWRENCE WRIGHT has been a staff writer at *The New Yorker* since 1992. Before joining *The New Yorker*, Wright was a staff writer for *The Race Relations Reporter*, *Southern Voices*, and *Texas Monthly*. In 1980, he became a contributing editor at *Rolling Stone*. Wright's book *The Looming Tower: Al-Qaeda and the Road to 9/11* won the Pulitzer Prize in 2007. He also won the 1994 National Magazine Award for Reporting for his article "Remembering

Satan." Wright is currently finishing a book on Scientology for Knopf. He is also working on two plays: *Fallaci* is scheduled to premiere at the Berkeley Repertory Theater in March 2013; *Camp David* is being developed by the Arena Stage in Washington, D.C., which commissioned the project. Wright lives in Austin, Texas. He plays keyboards for the band WhoDo.

WESLEY YANG is a *New York* contributing editor. He won a National Magazine Award for the story included in this collection. He is currently working on a book about Asian Americans for W. W. Norton.

WILLIAM ZINSSER is the author of eighteen books, including *On Writing Well* and *Writing Places*. His online essays for *The American Scholar*, "Zinsser on Friday," received the 2012 National Magazine Award for Commentary, Digital Media. These essays have been collected in his forthcoming book, *The Writer Who Stayed*, which will be published in the fall of 2012.